THE RAF

IN THE BATTLE OF FRANCE
AND THE BATTLE OF BRITAIN

THE RAF

IN THE BATTLE OF FRANCE
AND THE BATTLE OF BRITAIN

A REAPPRAISAL OF ARMY AND AIR POLICY
1938-1940

GREG BAUGHEN

FONTHILL

Fonthill Media Language Policy

Fonthill Media publishes in the international English language market. One language edition is published worldwide. As there are minor differences in spelling and presentation, especially with regard to American English and British English, a policy is necessary to define which form of English to use. The Fonthill Policy is to use the form of English native to the author. Greg Baughen was born and educated in Britain and now lives in London; therefore British English has been adopted in this publication.

Fonthill Media Limited
Fonthill Media LLC
www.fonthill.media
office@fonthillmedia.com

First published in the United Kingdom and the United States of America 2016
Reprinted 2019

British Library Cataloguing in Publication Data:
A catalogue record for this book is available from the British Library

Copyright © Greg Baughen 2016, 2019

ISBN 978-1-78155-525-5

Typeset in 10.5pt on 13pt Minion Pro
Printed and bound in England

Acknowledgements

My thanks to the staff of the National Archives, the Hendon RAF Museum, the IWM, and the Air Historical Branch for all their help. Once again, a very special thanks to Tony Buttler, Ian White and Phil Butler for their help in finding photographs.

Contents

Introduction

On 21 May 1940, a small British force of infantry, supported by seventy-four Matilda tanks, stood poised and ready to strike the right flank of the advancing German Panzers. The German tanks were heading for the Channel, and the British, French, and Belgian armies to the north were in danger of being cut off from the bulk of the French Army further south. General Weygand, the commander of the Allied armies, had decided the only way to restore the situation was for the armies in the north to strike south and re-establish contact. A preparatory attack would be launched by the British from Arras. The force was led by Major-General Martel, who had served in the Tank Corps in the First World War and was a long-time advocate of mobile armoured warfare. This would be his chance to demonstrate what tanks could do. By striking into the enemy rear, Martel could help turn the tables on the advancing Panzers and take the first step towards rescuing the British, Belgian, and French armies.

History seemed to be repeating itself. Twenty-six years beforehand, elements of another British army, exhausted by continual retreat, had counterattacked the right flank of a previous German invasion and helped to save the day. There were no tanks in 1914, but the counterattacking British forces benefited from RFC planes scouting ahead, monitoring enemy movements and identifying where the German defences were weakest. In 1940, there were no friendly reconnaissance planes hovering above Martel's force. He did not know the strength or disposition of the enemy forces he was advancing towards; there had been no aerial reconnaissance of the area before the attack.

The attack started in the mid-afternoon. The Matilda tanks advanced, shells from German anti-tank guns bouncing harmlessly off their thick armour. For the first time in the campaign, German forces were in retreat. Alarm soon spread to the rear. Rommel reported his flank was under attack from hundreds of tanks. All seemed to be going well for Martel.

Overhead, however, German spotter planes were following Martel's advance. There were no fighters to drive them away, nor were there any fighters to beat off the dive-bombers the German observers were calling in. After advancing a couple of miles, the tanks ran into fire from anti-aircraft guns hastily thrown into the anti-tank role. The German Army had used the same tactic in the First World War. The British Army had countered by attaching observation squadrons to the Tank Corps to locate the guns, and fighter-bombers to eliminate them. In 1940, Martel had neither. The advance stalled. Uncertain he could hold the ground won, Martel felt he had little option but to fall back.

Martel's attack had disrupted German plans, but not enough to buy time for Weygand's full-scale counterattack. There would be no second chance. The German advance continued and the Allied armies encircled; soon, the only escape route would be Dunkirk.

Armies, Air Defence, or Bombers?

During the 1920s and 1930s, the prospect of another British Army enduring the horror of European battlefields was the least appealing defence option to politicians and public. Instead, successive governments had placed their trust in a much cheaper defence based on the bomber. These aircraft would deter attack or, if that failed, bomb the enemy into submission. The 1938 crisis over the Czech Sudetenland had exposed the flaws in the policy. RAF bombers were not capable of delivering the mass destruction required to be an effective deterrent, and it was not politically possible or militarily sensible to respond to German aggression on land by bombing their cities. The government felt it had little choice but to support France, their ally, on the ground. The War Office was asked to scrape together what it could. Even the Air Staff, at a loss to know what to do with their bombers, were preparing to send them off to France to support the Army. The tide seemed to be turning in favour of a British-European defence policy based on 'boots on the ground'.

Throughout the interwar years, the War Office had drawn up contingency plans for a British Expeditionary Force. Each came with an air support component, which the Air Ministry was expected to provide. For an Air Ministry convinced that the next war would be decided by long-range bombers, it all seemed rather bizarre. Enemy bombers would ensure the British Army never even made it across the Channel. Nevertheless, in the interests of inter-service goodwill, the Air Ministry went through the motions of discussing these demands. The most recent agreement had been reached in December 1935. This called for twenty-one squadrons (seven bomber, five fighter, seven army-cooperation, and two long-range reconnaissance) to accompany a first regular Army contingent of five divisions. Air Vice-Marshal Courtney, who led the Air Ministry team, later claimed he could not remember if it was seven or six bomber squadrons, deciding that it must have been six.[1] It was rather typical of the War Office's meek attitude that there were no objections.

It was easy to persuade the War Office that the bombers would be available. The RAF's short-range strategic bombers could only reach targets in Germany from bases on the continent. The Army bomber squadrons could come from this force, the so-called Advanced Air Striking Force—provided they were not needed for bombing Germany. The Air Staff was, of course, in no doubt they would be needed. To reassure the Army that they would always have some bomber support, the two long-range squadrons would be trained for a dual reconnaissance/bombing role.

To keep abreast of how these air resources might be used, the War Office had to look no further than Spain. The fascist rebels and the communist government forces were both using large numbers of planes, courtesy of Italy, Germany, and the Soviet Union. Despite all the talk of bombers revolutionising warfare, Franco's uprising became a very conventional war. Armies fought along continuous fronts that would hold for a while. One side would achieve a breakthrough and a substantial, even rapid advance might follow. Both sides used airpower to support their land forces in much the same way as the RFC and RAF had done in the First World War. Franco's attempts to take Madrid had involved bombing residential areas in the city, which added to the problems of civilians in the semi-besieged city, but morale did not crumble and the city fought on. Armies—not bombers—were determining the course of the conflict.

Reports reaching the War Office highlighted the value of air support on the battlefield. Bombers could not provide the continuous fire artillery offered, but they could be used more flexibly. They were proving particularly useful when rapid advances meant ground forces had passed beyond effective artillery range. Air attack could also be decisive in defence. In March 1937, at Guadalajara, Nationalist forces attempting to complete the encirclement of Madrid had broken through government lines, but Soviet air units had intervened directly on the battlefield to help halt the advance.[2]

Visiting British Army officers were impressed by the effectiveness of low-level close-support, both in terms of the physical damage inflicted and the effect that it had on the morale of the opposing forces.[3] They were particularly impressed by the way Nationalist commanders were able to radio for air support when they needed it.[4] For those familiar with RFC/RAF operations in the First World War and colonial air operations, there was nothing very new about any of this.[5]

The War Office were also aware that foreign observers were making similar observations. General Dentz, the Deputy Chief of the French General Staff, emphasised how the ability to bomb newly established defensive lines without waiting for supporting artillery to move into position was radically changing the pace at which battles were now fought. The French would discover first-hand how significant this was in 1940, at Sedan. Perhaps most significantly of all, the War Office noted, Dentz was claiming that operations in Spain had 'sounded the death knell' of independent air force operations.[6]

The War Office passed on what they had learnt to the Air Ministry. They explained how low-flying planes were being used to drop 2-kg anti-personnel bombs in the battlezone and wanted to know whether the RAF could do the same. They also wanted to know if any thought was being given to how fighters might be used to prevent low-level attacks on British troops.[7] The Army would need every bomber it could get, the War Office insisted; at the very least, they wanted the six agreed in December 1935 and the squadrons of the 'Advanced Air Striking Force attached to the Field Force'.

Air Vice-Marshal Douglas, Assistant Chief of the Air Staff, had to hurriedly clear up this 'misunderstanding' that the Advanced Air Striking Force would be 'attached' to the Army in any operational sense. It was part of Bomber Command, which just happened to be based on the continent because the bombers lacked the range to reach Germany from Britain. Just as soon as longer-range bombers became available, these squadrons would be withdrawn and all bombers would operate from Britain. There was, however, nothing for the War Office to worry about, Douglas insisted—if required, the bombers could support the Army just as easily from bases in Britain. Plenty of bombs suitable for low-level missions existed and new anti-personnel weapons would soon be arriving, 'You need not feel any anxiety on that score', the War Office was assured. Nevertheless, there seemed plenty the War Office might feel anxious about. The Air Ministry agreed low-level bombing was 'permissible' for turning an enemy retreat into a rout or for slowing down an enemy pursuing retreating British forces. However, the War Office was reminded, this was not a 'normal' mission for the RAF and there was no question of RAF units being on call to an Army commander.[8]

The arrival of Lieutenant-General Pownall early in 1938 as Director of Military Operations added a little more steel to War Office demands. He had no illusions about the size of the task that faced him. It would be an uphill struggle to reverse the trend of past decades, he acknowledged, but it was time 'to start the ball rolling'. The War Office had to make it clear to their Air Force counterparts that the tide was turning against independent air warfare. In Spain, China, and Abyssinia, the bombing of civilian targets had not had any effect on the course of the fighting, whereas air support on the battlefield had. This was a role the RAF was neither trained nor equipped for. France, Germany, Italy, Japan, and the USA were all developing manoeuvrable, short-range, low-flying planes armed with bombs and machine guns. Pownall wanted something similar to support the British Army. This might not necessarily require the development of new planes; high performance would not be required and it was quite possible that obsolete planes being phased out of service would have all the required qualities.[9] This desire for a slow, low-flying, Army-support capability would be a recurring theme in the years to come.

A War Office proposal to increase fighter support for the first contingent of an expeditionary force from four to twelve squadrons was dismissed by Pownall as timid. Far more fighters would be required to provide close protection for forces on the battlefield and the more general air superiority the Army would need. This was a responsibility the RAF would have to start taking a lot more seriously, he warned. Others in the War Office questioned whether the tightly controlled radar-based interceptor system Fighter Command was developing was capable of providing the fighter cover the Army needed. Much more manoeuvrable fighters would be required to deal with enemy fighters and low-level attack planes. Army fighters would have to operate over the front from temporary forward airstrips, and Fighter Command was only trained to defend fixed points from well-equipped permanent airfields.[10]

In June 1938, Pownall's directorate circulated General Staff Research Document No. 4. It was a hard-hitting document that was as critical of the War Office as it was of the Air Ministry. The War Office had not pressed the case for air support with any vigour; the RAF's high-speed interceptors would not be able to defend the Army and long-range bombers could not hit small battlefield targets. The RAF had to be ready to meet all requirements, not just those required by independent air operations. Most of all, the Army needed control. In the middle of a crucial battle, it could not rely on the whim of the Air Ministry for air support.[11]

The War Office wanted two 'support' squadrons attached to each Army corps, one for short-range bombing, the other for low-level close-support on the battlefield. Both roles might well be filled by the same plane. Indeed, the plane might be very similar to the manoeuvrable fighter that the War Office required to deal with enemy tactical bombers. The War Office was feeling its way towards (or indeed back to) the Sopwith Camel and Bristol Fighter tactical fighter-bombers of the First World War.

With the Navy's Fleet Air Arm having just gained independence from the Air Ministry, there was no reason why the Army should not expect to have a similar air arm. However, Pownall was anxious not to open old wounds and let the legitimacy of their case be lost in a revival of the debate about whether the RAF should be independent or not. Indeed, the War Office genuinely did not want to take over full responsibility for training aircrews, framing specifications, and overseeing production. However, there was a very strong case for an 'Army Command' in the RAF, equivalent to the existing Bomber, Fighter, and, most relevantly of all, Coastal Commands.

It was the clearest statement yet of what the Army actually wanted. The observation that the RAF's long-range bombers might be an unusable asset in time of war was particularly relevant following the Air Ministry's struggle to find a role for its bomber fleet during the Sudetenland crisis.[12]

The scratch force the War Office had pulled together during the 1938 crisis had consisted of just two makeshift divisions. With the crisis over, the War Office expected to start creating a proper army. The case seemed compelling. The balance of power in Europe had altered dramatically; Czechoslovakia was disintegrating and no longer a military factor. The French had lost an ally with an army of thirty-five divisions, and they could not match the German Army alone. Britain had to review her position just to make up for the loss of the Czech Army. The War Office put forward proposals to bring the four divisions of the regular Army up to strength and split the mobile armoured division into two. It was a modest proposal that was scarcely likely to satisfy France, but it was a start. However, the War Office could not even get the funding to bring the existing two makeshift divisions up to strength. The government was still giving the Air Force priority.

This priority, however, was not long-range bombers. Alarmed by the growing cost of the bomber force, early in 1938 the government had told the Air Staff to build fighters instead. This seemed the best way to protect the country from the dreaded knockout blow. The Air Staff had been and still were infuriated by this violation of the basic principles of air warfare. Domination of the enemy was achieved by having more bombers, not more fighters. The problem for the Air Staff was that RAF bombers did not seem capable of doing any dominating. During the 1938 crisis, the possibility that Bomber Command would actually have to implement its plans to bomb the Ruhr's coking and electricity plants in broad daylight had exposed how foolish the idea was. Air Chief Marshal Ludlow-Hewitt, the commander of Bomber Command, had not changed his mind. His single-engine Fairey Battles could not possibly fly around Holland or Belgium to reach the Ruhr. His twin-engine Bristol Blenheim squadrons might just about have sufficient range, if they abandoned the greater safety of the low-level approach and flew at medium altitudes. The arrival of the Hadley Page Hampden and Vickers Wellington would not make that much difference. He did not believe the former could safely penetrate any further than the Blenheim, and even the Wellington could not be expected to fly much further in daylight.[13] Air Chief Marshal Newall, the Chief of Air Staff, had been forced to concede that all existing RAF bombers could do was bomb cities near the coast and drop a few leaflets. Until the next generation of bomber (the Stirling, Manchester, and Halifax) arrived, there seemed little point in objecting too strongly to the government preference for fighters. With the Treasury holding the purse strings, there was little choice anyway.

The Air Ministry could at least take some satisfaction from the priority the government was still giving the RAF. The War Office was still very much the poor relation. Far from getting the additional air support Pownall wanted, the Army found the Air Ministry hovering like vultures over their last remaining air assets. In August 1938, four army-cooperation squadrons intended for a second BEF contingent were converted to two bomber and two fighter squadrons. All the War Office got out of it was an understanding that if the second contingent was mobilised, the fighter squadrons could be used as part of its fighter element.[14] All the remaining army-cooperation squadrons in No. 22 Group—already conveniently administered by Fighter Command—were assigned an emergency secondary fighter role.

The only consolation for the War Office was that the priority was fighters and not heavy bombers. Fighters were far more use over the battlefield—provided they were the right sort of fighter. The War Office was already concerned that the high-speed, single-seater, single-engine interceptors Fighter Command was equipped with were not what they wanted. The Army was quite right to be worried; the problem was far more serious than they imagined.

Fighter Command had been set up to defend the United Kingdom, and, as the War Office feared, its tactics and equipment were designed solely to shoot down unescorted long-range bombers. The Chain Home radar early warning system detected the bombers, and ground controllers scrambled the fighters and guided them to their targets. Pilots learned to fly in tight formation so that they could emerge from clouds as a cohesive fighting unit. There was no need for the pilots to use much initiative; they simply followed instructions, attacked the bombers, and returned to base.

If Fighter Command was going to be equipped with high-speed Hurricanes and Spitfires, the War Office would not have too much to worry about. The training, tactics, and system might not be what were required, but the fighters were not so far removed from what the Army needed over the front. However, the Air Staff was trying to move away from single-engine single-seaters to far bigger, specialist bomber destroyers. These included the twin-engine, four-cannon Whirlwind and the Defiant with its bulky turret. The heavy cannon armament was ideal for shooting down large armoured bombers and the turret fighters could fly parallel to the bomber and fire continuously at the target from the least-well-defended angle. Neither was designed to shoot down small, manoeuvrable planes. The next generation of cannon fighters were even larger—the twin-engine Gloster G.39, built to meet specification F.9/37, had a machine-gun turret and fixed cannon. The twin-engine Boulton Paul P.92, meeting F.11/37, had a four-cannon turret. These fighters were not what the Army had wanted.

All these projects were behind schedule. The Defiant was flying, but trials with a working turret had only just started. The plan was to equip one third of the fighter force with the plane, and 450 were already on order; the first deliveries were expected in the spring of 1939. Dowding was one of the few with doubts about the Defiant. It was not the turret that worried him so much as its machine-gun armament and low speed.[15] Elsewhere, there was no shortage of enthusiasm. Group Captain Stevenson (Home Operations), pointed out that the Defiant was no slower than the Hurricane; indeed, it was possibly even a little faster. In truth, this was a measure of how slow the Hurricane was rather than how fast a turret fighter might be. Stevenson was adamant that fighters like the Defiant were crucial if serious inroads were to be made in to the fleets of attacking bombers. As soon as the cannon-armed Boulton Paul F.11/37 became available, he wanted to increase the proportion of turret fighters.[16]

The suggestion that turret fighters were intrinsically faster than single-seaters horrified Air Marshal Freeman's Research and Development department. The next generation of single-seater fighters (the Hawker Tornado and Typhoon) were expected to be 60–85 mph quicker than the Gloster and Boulton Paul turret fighters. Trials with the first turret equipped Defiant seemed to prove the point. Far from achieving 315 mph, it managed just 302 mph. For a true comparison, this needed to be contrasted with the Spitfire's 360 mph rather than the Hurricane's 315 mph.

Nevertheless, Air Vice Marshal Peirse (Deputy Chief of Air Staff), Douglas and Stevenson all remained convinced the Defiant and its Boulton-Paul F.11/37 successor had a crucial role to play in home defence.[17] Douglas fretted at the constant delays afflicting the F.11/37 programme. He reminded Boulton Paul of the urgency of the project, but until the details of its revolutionary low-profile four-cannon turret could be finalised, work on building the prototype could not even begin.

For fixed-gun fighters, the Westland Whirlwind was the ministry's first choice. The twelve-machine-gun Hawker Typhoon/Tornado was the best back-up should there be problems with the Whirlwind's cannon armament.[18] The third choice was the Supermarine Spitfire; the Hawker Hurricane was a very distant fourth. Reports suggested that the latest Daimler Benz DB 601-powered version of the Do 17 was capable of 300–310 mph, nearly as fast as the Hurricane.[19] As early as February 1938, Newall had declared the Hurricane was 'fast becoming obsolescent'.[20] At the time there were actually twice as many Hurricanes on order as Spitfires. Newall was suddenly rather anxious to phase out the Hurricane as quickly as possible.

The preferred replacements, however, were a long way from being ready. The Whirlwind was supposed to fly in June 1938. As the target date passed, there was immense frustration that three years after the specification had been released, the prototype was still nowhere near ready. It seemed the plane could not reach the squadrons until the summer of 1940. Work on the back-up Tornado/Typhoon began after the Whirlwind and the first prototype was not due to fly until 1939. Hawker was dropping hints that Sydney Camm's fighter could be ordered off the drawing board. With major doubts about the Hurricane, there were advantages in replacing it on Hawker production lines as quickly as possible. The Air Ministry had not hesitated to order urgently needed bombers off the drawing board, but it was it was still very reluctant to take this risk with a fighter, especially one that was only armed with machine guns.[21] With the ongoing problems with the Napier Sabre and the Rolls Royce Vulture engines that powered the Typhoon and Tornado respectively, this was just as well. Neither version of Camm's fighter could go into production before 1940.

The Spitfire was without doubt the best fighter actually flying. In the summer of 1938, work began on a huge, purpose-built, state-of-the-art factory at Castle Bromwich in the Midlands, to build more of the fighter. Lord Nuffield of Morris Motors was put in charge. One thousand Spitfires were ordered and the factory was expected to turn out sixty per month. For the first time, there were more Spitfires on order than Hurricanes, although this did not remain the case for long.

The longer the ordering of the Typhoon/Tornado was delayed, the more Hurricanes Hawker would have to build. Newall hoped that most of these could be exported. However, it was not just the Hawker plant that would be turning out the 'fast becoming obsolescent' Hurricane. The Gloster plant, now part of the Hawker Siddeley empire, was producing the Hawker Henley light bomber.

This was loosely based on the Hurricane and used some of the same components. When the Air Staff finally decided short-range light bombers did not make good strategic bombers, the Henley contract was cut back to 200. As it used some Hurricane components, it seemed to make sense to replace it on Gloster production lines with the Hurricane. Just months after Newall had made it clear that as few Hurricanes as possible should be built, a new production line was opening. To keep Hawker and Gloster production lines going, another 1,000 Hurricanes had to be ordered. Once again, there were more Hurricanes on order than Spitfires.

It might have made more sense to turn the Gloster and even the Hawker plants over to the far superior Spitfire. With the supposedly superior Typhoon/Tornado not so far away, there was a case for sticking with the Hurricane a little longer. Nor was there any enthusiasm within the Air Ministry for asking Hawker to build its rival's Spitfire, but it was not just the sensibilities of aircraft manufacturers that was influencing decisions; the cost of the Spitfire, the ministry claimed, had rocketed to nearly twice that of the Hurricane.[22] The Air Ministry was also genuinely fed up with the constant problems they had been having with Supermarine. Sub-contractors were complaining about the inaccurate drawings they were getting and inspectors described the situation at the Supermarine works as 'pitiful', with seventy-eight complete fuselages but only three sets of wings.[23] In contrast, praise was heaped on Camm and Hawker, a firm that knew how to do things properly.[24]

Although the Spitfire was clearly the best fighter available, the Air Ministry seemed determined to play down the plane's superiority. Air Ministry documents of the time frequently quote the Spitfire's top speed as below 350 mph, although in trials, speeds of 360 mph had been achieved. In their letter to the Treasury asking for the financial backing to confirm the increased Hurricane orders, Freeman seemed to find all sorts of reasons for preferring the Hurricane. Supermarine had let the Air Ministry down 'over and over again'. The Spitfire had not even been fully cleared for operations, which was a rather harsh way of describing the relatively minor teething problems No. 19 Squadron were having with the first production models. Freeman assured the Treasury that every possible scheme for improving fighter production had been considered and insisted the Hurricane was 'the very best machine [they had] at the present time and available to go into production forthwith'.[25] This was simply not the case.

The Treasury did not question the choice of fighter—they were just happy that the Air Ministry was ordering fighters and not bombers. The request for the 1,000 Hurricanes received their instant blessing, along with the hope that this indicated a genuine shift in Air Ministry thinking. It was a massive order for a plane that was 'fast approaching obsolescence' and might not be faster than the latest German bombers. Gloster even set up an entirely new Hurricane production line, running in parallel to the ex-Henley line. It was intended to be just a temporary increase in Hurricane output. In June 1939, it was still hoped that production would be phased out by September 1940.[26] Nevertheless, for the immediate future, the Hurricane had priority over the Spitfire.

The autumn 1938 Scheme M required the fighter force to increase to fifty squadrons by March 1941. Light-bomber squadrons converting to the fighter role would enable forty of these to be available by April 1939.[27] Two hundred pupil pilots were switched from bomber to fighter training. Another 1,850 fighters were ordered immediately, with a similar number to follow later. As the Blenheim IV replaced the Blenheim I in the bomber squadrons, the latter would be converted to the fighter role by adding a battery of four machine guns. The RAE were working 'night and day' to develop a suitable pack.[28]

Scheme M was not all bad news for the bomber advocates. Target front-line strength would remain at around 1,300 bombers, but they would all now be heavy. It was another setback for the Army; they had already lost the light bomber, and now the medium bomber was to be abolished as well. The larger and heavier bombers became, the less useful they were for tactical air support. The only consolation was that the RAF had a rather flexible definition of a 'heavy bomber'. Even in 1942, many of these 'heavies' would be still be Wellingtons and Hampdens—planes that had been designed as medium day bombers and were broadly similar to the German He 111 and the later models of the Do 17.

There would be no acceleration of the production of exiting bombers; only enough would be ordered to keep factories ticking over until the Stirlings, Halifaxes, and Manchesters were ready.[29] By March 1939, Bomber Command strength had contracted from the sixty-eight squadrons it possessed in the spring of 1938 to fifty-seven squadrons.[30] Even some of these were to play their part in the defence. Five Blenheim bomber squadrons were to be issued with four-gun conversion kits to allow them to operate as fighters if required. The two long-range army-cooperation squadrons would also get the fighter version of the Blenheim instead of the bomber-reconnaissance version. With seven other army-cooperation squadrons receiving some fighter training, in an emergency, fifty fighter squadrons of sorts would be in place by September 1939.[31]

The orders placed for Hurricanes and Spitfires were seen very much as the swansong for the traditional single-engine, single-seater. As long as the fixed-gun fighter carried more guns than the turret fighter, there was still a place for planes like the Hurricane and Spitfire. However, there were doubts that the wings of single-engine planes could ever absorb the recoil of cannon, especially if the Air Staff insisted fighters had to carry at least four. There were also doubts that it would be possible to aim fixed guns at the speeds future fighters would fly. Even planes like the twin-engine Whirlwind might not be effective, leaving the turret fighter as the only option. If cannon turrets turned out to be impossible, turrets with twelve machine guns would have to be used instead. The fighter of the future would be large—possibly very large.

In November 1938, Group Captain Saundby (Operational Requirements) was so anxious to move to cannon-armed turret fighters that he suggested Boulton Paul should be given the go-ahead for production of their P.92 F.11/37 proposal, even though no prototype was possible before March 1940.[32] Another suggestion was that Wellingtons or Hampdens could be used as interim turret fighters, just as the Demon fighter had been adapted from the Hart bomber.[33] The Air Staff was conjuring up an extraordinary fighter force.

Trials in 1938 confirmed how little damage machine guns could inflict on modern aircraft structures protected by even a little armour.[34] Douglas declared the machine gun obsolete and became even more anxious to get the Whirlwind into service.[35] Westland promised deliveries could begin in nine months if the Air Ministry was willing take a risk and order it before the prototype flew. However, even the lure of its four-cannon armament could not persuade the Air Ministry to take a chance with a fighter. The Whirlwind prototype finally took to the air in October 1938. At the end of December, it was rushed to Martlesham Heath for official trials. The fighter was declared satisfactory and the first contract for 200 machines was confirmed in January 1939. With a top speed of around 360 mph and its fearsome armament, it looked a formidable bomber destroyer, but none could reach the squadrons until 1940.[36]

Out of the blue, Bristol came up with an alternative. The company was developing the Beaufort, a torpedo bomber version of the Blenheim. In October 1938, a few days after the prototype's first flight, Bristol suggested a long-range fighter version. The ministry was not interested in long-range fighters, but it was interested in a fighter that could carry four cannon. Bristol redrafted their proposal and claimed that with the latest 1,600-hp Hercules VI engines, their Beaufort fighter—soon to be abbreviated to Beaufighter—would be as fast as the Westland Whirlwind. It would also have one major advantage. At this time, only drum-fed cannon (with a very limited firing time) were available. The Bristol proposal was large enough and powerful enough to accommodate a second crew member, who would reload the cannon in flight. The Beaufort had been ordered off the drawing board, so the preparations for production were well-advanced. Bristol claimed that the Beauforts coming off the assembly lines could easily be modified to become Beaufighters; if ordered immediately, the first could be delivered as early as September 1939.[37]

The Beaufighter was a very different plane to the Whirlwind. The Westland plane was designed as a fighter and was about as compact and as manoeuvrable as a twin-engine design could be. The Beaufighter was a converted torpedo bomber. It was twice as heavy as the Whirlwind and had twice the wing area. The plane was actually 50 per cent heavier than the makeshift Blenheim IF fighter. In February 1939, the Air Ministry, unperturbed by the aircraft's large size, ordered 300 as an 'interim replacement for the Whirlwind'.[38]

By March, both Bristol and Westland were being warned that orders for their twin-engine fighters might be doubled. A second production line was being considered for the Whirlwind, and planned Spitfire output at Castle Bromwich was halved to 120 fighters per month to enable sixty Whirlwinds (and twenty Halifax bombers) to be built.[39] The Air Staff also wanted a third cannon-armed twin-engine plane, the Gloster G.39, in the production programme.[40] With its turret removed and flown as a single-seater, it could carry five fixed 20-mm cannon. The prototype flew in April 1939, displaying outstanding handling characteristics and achieving a top speed of 360 mph.[41]

All that was saving Dowding from an influx of unwanted twin-engine fighters were the engine problems that were afflicting all three planes. The Whirlwind's Peregrine, the Beaufighter's Hercules and the Gloster F.9/37's Taurus had all run into problems. The Gloster fighter was ruled out completely when, in July 1939, the prototype was severely damaged in a landing accident as it arrived at Martlesham Heath for official trials. For their Beaufighter, Bristol was forced to use the less powerful Hercules III in the first production version. This was expected to reduce top speed to 336 mph. The Beaufort adaptation Bristol was promising also proved problematic; by the time the company had finished modifying the Beaufort, there was not much left of the original torpedo bomber, and there was therefore no question of adapting existing Beauforts as they came off the production line. It was effectively a new plane. The prototype Beaufighter flew in July 1939 and none could not possibly be delivered before the end of 1939. With production of the Whirlwind held up by problems with its Peregrine engine, there was very little prospect of getting any cannon-armed fighters into service until well into 1940.

Meanwhile, plans were being laid for larger and even more heavily armed fighters. Twenty-mm cannon were not enough—the Air Ministry and Dowding wanted to move to 40-mm cannon as soon as possible. With these weapons, a bomber could knock out another bomber with just a single shot.[42] The Air Staff had been considering a new heavy-calibre cannon since 1936, but they had not got very far with specifying what they wanted. The Sudetenland crisis focused minds and a specification was hastily released. In future, fighter designers would have to bear in mind the possibility of replacing 20-mm with 40-mm cannon. Vickers were already working on a 40-mm weapon and hoped to have a prototype ready by the end of 1938.[43] In the spring of 1939, specifications were being prepared for a 400-mph 'local defence fighter' (F.6/39) to replace the Whirlwind/Beaufighter generation. Proposed armament was four 20-mm or two 40-mm cannon. A 400 mph turret fighter (F.26/39) was also required, and this too would eventually be armed with 40-mm cannon. The 40-mm-cannon version would be a three-seater, with a third crew member to reload the cannon.[44] Vickers were also working on their own two-seater (the Vickers 414) with a moveable 40-mm cannon in the nose. The Air Ministry wrote F.22/39 around this proposal.[45] The RAF was going back to the aerial dreadnoughts that had been envisaged at the beginning of the First World War.

After the 40-mm cannon would come the air-to-air missile. The Air Staff and Dowding saw no reason why the unguided ground-to-air anti-aircraft missiles the War Office was developing could not be fired from fighters, and so designers were asked to bear this possibility in mind as well.[46] Slow-firing 40-mm cannon and unguided missiles could only be successful against large planes flying in straight lines; they could not possibly be used against fighters or the manoeuvrable ground attack and tactical-reconnaissance planes the Army wanted dealt with. Even four 20-mm cannon (the equivalent to the weight of fire produced by twenty-five machine guns) was excessive for the type of planes the RAF was likely to meet. German and French fighters carried one cannon, or a maximum of two. Heavier armament meant larger, less manoeuvrable fighters. The fighters designers were asked to develop could only be used for intercepting bombers, but this was all the Air Staff wanted.

To make sure these bomber destroyers found their targets, the RAF had radar. The brilliance of the early warning system and its value for defending British airspace are beyond doubt. It was a unique, even bizarre, system, which involved huge towers suspending aerial arrays hundreds of feet in the air, capable of detecting aircraft at medium altitudes over 100 miles away. Low altitude was a problem, but by good fortune it was discovered that equipment designed for ranging coastal artillery on naval targets also happened to be good at spotting low-flying aircraft. The lower wavelength meant the aerials were just about small enough to rotate, making it more straightforward to estimate bearing. Nevertheless, it was a cumbersome arrangement. Separate transmitters and receivers had to be rotated in unison, using man (or, more often than not, woman) pedal power. It all added to the Heath Robinson aspect of the system, but it worked. By 1939, Chain Home (CH) and Chain Home Low (CHL) stations covered most of the coast from the Shetlands to Portsmouth.

Standard directing finding techniques tracked the course of the intercepting fighters. It took fourteen seconds to get a fix. With each formation transmitting every sixty seconds, four formations could just about be tracked simultaneously. The initial aim of getting the fighters to within 1 mile of the target proved far too optimistic. Four miles was about the best possible, but this was ample for the pilots to make visual contact in daylight. By night, it was not nearly close enough. Successfully stopping a daylight offensive would count for nothing if the bombers returned to obliterate cities under cover of darkness. Even the original aim of getting an interceptor to just 1 mile of the target was not good enough. Edward 'Taffy' Bowen, one of the original RDF research team, was already working on an AI (Airborne Interception) radar system that could close the gap between what the ground-based stations could do and what the naked eye could see. Bowen was told that meant getting fighters to within 1,000 feet of the target.

Having got the equipment down to the size a plane could carry, Bowen had been side-tracked into investigating the far easier task of locating the position of ships. In the wake of the Sudetenland crisis, Bowen received very clear instructions to get back to the air defence problem. As it turned out, the techniques he had developed also worked for aircraft. To detect ships, Bowen arranged a receiver on each side of the aeroplane, and with the fuselage providing a barrier, all the pilot had to do was adjust his course until the signals received by both were equal. The plane would then be flying straight towards the ship. The same principle could be used to give the vertical bearing of an enemy plane. A balanced signal from couple of additional receivers above and below the wing, feeding a second cathode ray tube, told the pilot when the plane was climbing towards the target.

This was not quite what the Air Ministry had wanted. Bowen was supposed to be developing a system for single-seater fighters. Expecting the pilot to stare into two separate cathode ray tubes was scarcely ideal. There were also inherent limitations with the 1.5-metre wavelength the system used. The transmissions could not be sharply focused, so the signals were emitted in all directions. At 15,000 feet, the tiny reflection from a plane 3 miles ahead would be blotted out by the much larger reflection from the ground 3 miles below. Indeed, because ground is uneven, ever-weakening reflections would be picked up from ahead of the plane. This produced the so-called 'Christmas tree' effect on the cathode ray tube. Any plane further away than the height the plane was flying was lost in the ground reflection. At 15,000 feet, the maximum range possible was 3 miles.

Minimum range was also a problem. Once the interceptor got too close to the target, the beginning of the reflected pulse arrived back before the end of the pulse had left. The maximum range possible (the point at which the intercepting plane picked up the intruder) and the minimum range (the point at which contact was lost) were the two crucial performance parameters.

Despite these problems, Bowen was suddenly very confident that he had a workable system. In November 1938, he claimed his equipment could get a fighter within the required 1,000 feet of a target. The equipment was still too bulky for a single-seater fighter and it needed a specialist operator, but if a larger plane like the Fairey Battle or the Blenheim was used, Bowen believed there was no reason why the system could not be deployed operationally as it was.[47] Dowding was more than

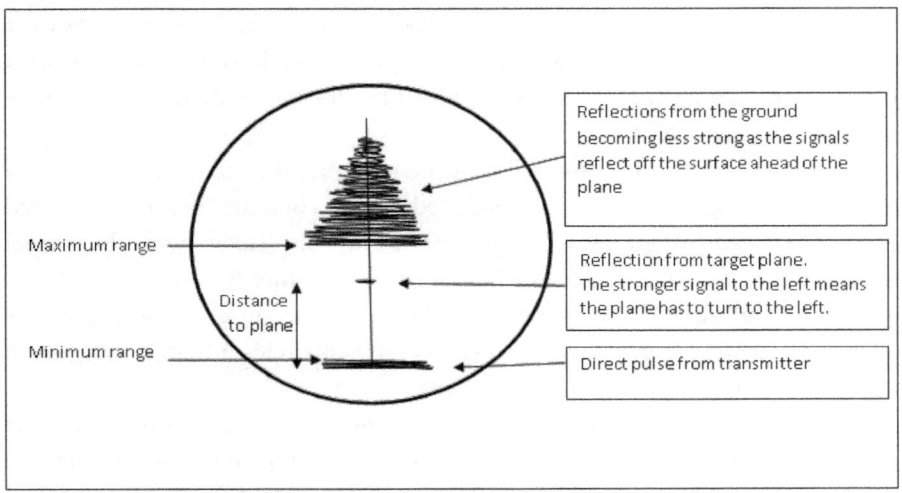

The Christmas Tree.

happy to use twin-engine fighters if it would speed up development. Coincidentally, it had been decided that Blenheim I bomber should be converted into fighters so that there was no shortage of suitable planes. It also provided a useful way of using the Beaufighters that had been hoisted upon Dowding.

At this stage, neither Albert Rowe—in charge of the AMRE (Air Ministry Research Establishment)—nor Dowding were particularly optimistic about AI. It was so far down Dowding's list of priorities that it was only after returning from a visit to Rowe in Dundee that Dowding remembered he had forgotten to ask how AI was coming along. Rowe was relieved that he had forgotten; there was no progress to report. He assured Dowding that of all the applications of radar, AI was the least promising. Bowen, however, would soon force Rowe to change his mind.

Bowen was now so confident that he wrote directly to Dowding, telling him that the problem of using radar to intercept night bombers had been solved in principle. He invited the Commander-in-Chief to come and have a look.[48] On 14 June, Rowe came down to check if there was anything worth showing to Dowding; what he found there was a revelation. Bowen's equipment had no problems tracking a Harrow bomber. The trial was taking place in daylight, but when the bomber disappeared into clouds, Bowen was able to tell the pilot where it was. Rowe could scarcely contain his excitement. On returning to Dundee, the normally punctilious Rowe ignored official channels and rushed off a personal letter to Dowding, informing him of what he had just witnessed.[49]

The following month, Dowding visited Bawdsey to see for himself how far the scientists had got. He was assured the system could take a fighter to 900 feet of the target on a regular basis; on occasion, it had even continued working as close as 220 feet. Dowding was given a full demonstration. With Bowen and Dowding squeezed into the cockpit of a Fairey Battle—a black sheet covering them so they could see the cathode ray tube display—Bowen guided the pilot of the Battle towards the target plane. At the point of closest approach, with the cathode ray tube showing the bomber 1,500 feet away, Dowding told the pilot to hold his position. The black cloth was whisked away and he saw the target bomber immediately above them, apparently dangerously close.

An astonished Dowding insisted that the equipment needed recalibrating.[50] Bowen was well-aware that even experienced airmen consistently underestimated distances between aircraft. He knew the cathode ray tube was showing the correct distance, but he accepted the criticism gracefully. Whether Bowen genuinely did not want to contradict the notoriously gruff Commander-in-Chief or whether he preferred to let Dowding believe AI could get the fighter closer than it really could was probably not clear even in Bowen's mind.

Indeed, the scientists did emanate quite a bit of misleading information about the capabilities of AI. Everyone was quite rightly anxious to emphasise that the range limit imposed by ground reflections was an inherent weakness of the system. However, so much was being made of this that the impression was gaining ground that this was the only factor limiting range. Rowe suggested that if the interception took place over the sea, reflections from ahead would not reflect back to the plane. There would just be a brief blind spot when the enemy plane was the same distance away as the sea below. Beyond that, range would only be limited by power, and a range of 10 miles was very possible. This was all very misleading; the theoretical ability to identify targets up to 10 miles away was irrelevant when the range of the equipment being trialled was at best 2 miles. Above 10,000 feet, the power of the equipment was the limiting factor, not the ground reflections. As for a well-defined 'dead zone', even Dowding pointed out that the sea is not that flat.[51]

Nevertheless, Dowding was impressed. Rowe began to worry that expectations had been raised too high. He assured Dowding that he really had got no nearer than 1,500 feet during the Bowen demonstration, but Dowding was not going to let his newly found enthusiasm be dampened.[52] With the conviction of the converted, he was convinced radar was the only way forward; he did not want any more effort wasted on developing AI for single-seaters. The pilot's night vision would inevitably be impaired by staring at a cathode tube display. The focus should be equipping the Blenheim and Beaufighter with the existing equipment. Interestingly, Dowding preferred the Blenheim because it had a turret and could attack from below. He argued that a fighter with fixed weapons—forced to attack from directly behind the bomber, where there would be less reflecting surface—would be more likely to lose radar contact. Dowding was already eyeing up the Defiant as another possible night fighter.[53]

At this time, all fighter squadrons were supposed to operate by day and night. Dowding issued instructions that in future, one of the three squadrons in each sector would be equipped with twin-engine fighters specifically for night-fighting duties.[54] After all the problems in the early 1930s involving the attempts to combine a day and night fighting capability in the same plane, the single-seater Spitfire and Hurricane fighters that had eventually emerged would now only be used by day.[55]

The Bawdsey team were indeed guilty of overselling the AI system's capabilities. With the equipment available, the claimed 220-foot minimum range could only have been a fluke. The scientists at Bawdsey had also become experts at getting the best out of the temperamental and tricky equipment. How less patient and less motivated service personnel would manage remained to be seen.

Even Bowen was surprised by the speed with which they were now expected to move. Two Blenheim 1s arrived for trials in July, and at the beginning of August, with the situation in Europe rapidly deteriorating, instructions arrived to equip thirty Blenheims with AI by the end of the month. A first batch of six was to go to No. 25 Squadron as soon as possible for operational trials. The scientists who had developed the system were the only people who knew enough about the equipment to install it and get it working. Further development was effectively suspended as the scientists became aircraft fitters.

There was an air of frenzy about the programme. All the material arrived in bits and pieces rather than installable units and had to be pieced together. The transmitters that had been ordered turned out to be the wrong model and proved almost useless. By good fortune, Pye had come up with a more advanced receiver, which compensated. Getting the receivers to work on the slab-sided Blenheim, rather than the streamlined fuselage of the Fairey Battle, caused more delays.[56] Despite the problems, the first fully converted machine, with the RDF operator conveniently positioned next to the pilot, was delivered to No. 25 Squadron on 30 August. Dowding immediately objected to operator in the nose. All the glowing valves and cathode ray tubes would be clearly visible to the bomber being pursued, so the operator and his equipment was hastily moved to the rear fuselage. This at least had the advantage of making the screen easier to see. The disadvantage was that the operators' instructions to the pilot would now have to be given through the aircraft intercom. Nevertheless, London had its first AI-equipped night fighter.

By night and day, the country's air defences were as good as they could be. Britain's air defence system was way ahead of anything developed anywhere else in the world. If future wars were to be decided by long-range bombing, no country was better prepared defensively than Britain.

This was reassuring for the government, but the Air Staff saw the emphasis on defence as unfortunate, even dangerous. Fighters did not win wars—only bombers could do that. The existing bombers might have their problems, but the bombing strategy was sound. Everything would be resolved when the new Manchesters, Halifaxes, and Stirlings arrived.

In the summer of 1938, none of these planes had even flown, but it was still believed they would equip ten RAF squadrons as early as April 1940.[57] The Treasury was not happy with the cost; the latest estimates suggested the new heavy bombers would be nearly twice as expensive as originally expected.[58] Nevertheless, the Air Staff always had the cheap Armstrong Whitworth Albemarle to fall back on. Made from steel tubing and plywood, the plane could be constructed by unskilled labour outside the aircraft industry.[59] With a cruising speed of just 250 mph and a limited lifting capability, it was a very poor second best, and yet it joined the Halifax, Manchester, and Stirling as the future equipment of Bomber Command.

The Air Ministry fought hard to curb the government preference for more fighters. It was claimed that there was a limit to the number of fighters the RAF could use. Any more than the proposed fifty fighter squadrons would result in too much congestion for the fighters to operate effectively.[60] Wherever they could, the Air Ministry slipped more bombers into the production programme. With plans to phase out Hurricane production by September 1940, it was argued that there was little point in setting up a second Gloster production line to build the fighter. The ministry managed to get this line turned over to the Albemarle, with deliveries beginning in June 1940.[61] Westland was expected to set up a production line for the Halifax in parallel to their Whirlwind production line. The Air Ministry even managed to get planned fighter production at Castle Bromwich cut back to allow twenty Halifaxes to be built per month.[62]

Before production of any of these bombers could get the final go-ahead, the prototypes had to be tested. The Short Stirling was the first to fly. It was a disastrous first flight; the undercarriage collapsed on landing and the prototype was destroyed. A second would not be ready until December 1939. The Manchester took to the air in July 1939, but immediately there were serious problems. The wings had to be extended and a third tail plane added to improve control. Even more worryingly, its Vulture engines were unreliable and not generating the expected power. First deliveries were put back until well into 1940. The Halifax would not fly until after the outbreak of war, the Albemarle not until 1940.

To make matters worse, the Wellington, which had been considered a fairly good substitute for these bombers, was also not living up to expectations. In the summer of 1938, trials took place with the completely redesigned first production prototype. These revealed that the introduction of turrets reduced the plane's performance considerably. The turrets were not particularly effective either; the ventral dustbin turret was so poor that there were doubts aircrews would even attempt to use it in combat.[63] The Vickers nose and tail turrets were unreliable and, with the gunner stationary (just the guns moved), they were difficult to use. Subsequent production batches were to have Frazer Nash turrets, but these were even heavier and the plane was only safe to fly with 500 lbs of ballast in the nose. Bomb load at a range of 2,000 miles was slashed from 1,400 lbs to just 650 lbs. The Vickers bomber had seriously dipped in Air Ministry estimations.

Armour was another additional weight all bombers might have to carry. Trials had shown that even a small amount of protection greatly improved the chances of a bomber surviving. Douglas was appalled by the prospect of aircrews having to go into battle in unarmoured planes and wanted all front-line planes modified by the end of 1938.[64] By September 1939 arrangements for armouring the Battle, Blenheim, Hampden, and Wellington had been approved.[65] Self-sealing tanks—almost forgotten since they had been introduced at the end of the First World War—were also back on the agenda. Trials were encouraging, but it was another additional weight.[66] The reduced range and bomb load meant there was a reluctance to fit armour or self-sealing tanks; it seemed reasonable to wait and see if they were needed.

Defensive armament for the new heavy bombers also had to be rethought. With fighter speed already well beyond the 300-mph mark, the idea that the Halifax and Manchester would be so fast they would not need to protect their flanks now looked absurd. Both these bombers would have to have turrets amidships, ideally dorsal and ventral, which would slow them down even more. To complicate the issue, the much-vaunted tail turret, which designers had gone to so much trouble to incorporate into their designs, was beginning to look like a mistake. The field of fire it offered was second to none, but even on exercises, the psychological strain on the gunner of being so isolated was clear. It would be much worse during long missions over enemy territory. When Ludlow-Hewitt was told it would be impossible give his tail gunner any armour protection, he insisted tail turrets should be abandoned on all future bombers.[67]

The Air Staff had, in fact, already been forced to do this for purely technical reasons. If future fighters carried cannon, bombers would have to carry them too, but cannon turrets were too heavy to go in the tail. Future bombers would have to rely on dorsal and ventral turrets. These would be the new low-profile turret designed for the Boulton Paul F.11/37 fighter. The B.19/38 'Ideal Bomber' specification was supposed to produce the first cannon-armed bombers, but this had been shelved and 'Mark 2' versions of the Halifax, Stirling and Manchester, ordered instead. These would have no tail turret and four-cannon dorsal and ventral turrets instead.[68] Whether blending these wide-diameter turrets into relatively narrow fuselages was possible remained questionable. The redesign required would be so radical they would effectively be new planes.[69] It would not even be attempted on the more basic Albemarle.

Even as the Manchester, Halifax, and Stirling prototypes were taking to the air, there were already major doubts about their speed and defensive capabilities. Ludlow-Hewitt did not think they could even attack a relatively close target like the Ruhr, and even the Air Ministry's normally upbeat Plans department agreed.[70] The aircraft were beginning to look so inadequate, the B.19/38 'Ideal Bomber' specification was revisited. To deal with the fighter of the future, this new aircraft would have to be armed with 40-mm cannon. These would be too inaccurate at close quarters, so to deal with fighters that broke through the outer defences, there would be a second line of defence with 20-mm cannon. Five thousand pounds of armour would provide the last line of defence. A preposterous 65,000-lb aerial dreadnought was emerging. To keep the project alive, bomb load was cut back to 9,000 lbs, armour to 1,200 lbs, and cruising speed to 280 mph. Armament was limited to 20-mm cannon and a weight limit of 50,000 lbs imposed. The specification was released in this form in early 1939 as B.1/39.[71] However, there was very little manufacturers could do with it. The new low-drag ventral and dorsal cannon turrets, so central to the entire design, were still being developed. Nine companies tended proposals, but since these produced little more than what was expected from the 'Mark 2' versions of the Stirling, Manchester, and Halifax, there seemed little point in pursuing the project. The development of half-scale models continued as research projects, but the B.1/39 'Ideal Bomber' got no further than its B.19/38 predecessor.[72]

There did not seem to be any viable alternative approach. High-flying bombers might evade the defences. Vickers were given the go-ahead for a version of the Wellington with a pressurised cabin that would enable the bomber to fly at 35,000 feet. Rather optimistically, it was hoped this would be beyond any fighter in the 'near future'. These test models were to be fully operational so that if they were successful, more could be quickly converted for squadron trials. With work on pressurised cabins at a very early stage, it was very long-term solution.[73]

High speed was another option. Ludlow-Hewitt was campaigning for a much smaller, more flexible 'speed bomber' that could perform high-level harassing, low-level attack, and dive bombing missions. Unbeknown to Ludlow-Hewitt, in March 1938 Douglas and Newall had agreed that a specification should be drawn up in case such a type was needed.[74] The whole idea was thoroughly demolished by Peirse's Operations department. Saundby, quite reasonably, argued that even if it was possible to develop a bomber faster than any fighter, it would only take the emergence of an even faster fighter to turn an invulnerable bomber into a very vulnerable one overnight. A bomber with a range of 1,000 miles might be capable of 360 mph, but Ludlow-Hewitt was reminded such a bomber would be pitted against fighters with a top speed of around 400 mph. Much was made of the 463 mph world record recently achieved by a specially boosted Bf 109.

This was all very true, but Ludlow-Hewitt protested that he did not want an unarmed bomber, just one that was not bristling with turrets. Peirse assured Ludlow-Hewitt that his speed bomber could only have a 20 mph advantage over the Halifax. The proposed 'Ideal Bomber' would be just as capable of low-level attack, dive-bombing, and high-level harassing. The 'Ideal Bomber' was not only the most efficient bomber for long-range operations, 'it was the only possible type'.[75] 'Try as we may' Peirse solemnly informed Ludlow-Hewitt, 'Saundby and I cannot make any sort of case for your bomber.' Further discussion was pointless.[76] The problem was that development of the 'Ideal Bomber' seemed equally pointless. It was difficult to see where bomber development was supposed to go next.

In fact, the Air Staff was setting itself an impossible task. There was no bomber that could defend itself—it needed a fighter escort. Over the years, the Air Staff had resolutely dismissed the escort option as a technical impossibility, but reports from Spain kept reminding the Air Staff that both sides were using single-seater fighters on a regular basis to protect their bombers. 'A confession of weakness and a waste of effort on our part even to contemplate' was one early Air Ministry assessment.[77] Douglas later suggested that escorts were only being used in Spain because both sides had so few bombers that they had to be treated as precious assets.[78] Why Bomber Command planes should be any less precious was not clear.

Escorts were becoming more practicable simply because higher cruising speeds meant fighters could travel much further for a given endurance. Even the low-endurance Spitfire had a reasonable range, and there was scope for extending it. In the spring of 1938, Stevenson (Home Operations) was looking into ways of extending the ferry range of the Hurricane and Spitfire. As he did so, he wondered if the extra fuel would enable these fighters to be used operationally in an escort role. He thought that they would be particularly useful for tackling the German fighters that were expected to lie in wait for RAF bombers as they flew round a neutral Holland. There seemed no reason why the Spitfire and Hurricane could not fly 750 miles.[79]

The opposition to this idea was fierce. Saundby insisted that as soon as a single-seater headed for home, it would inevitably be exposed to attack from the rear. The only solution was for the escorts to have the endurance to stay over the target until the defending interceptors ran out of fuel. Saundby suggested that meant a two-hour patrol capability at maximum range.[80] This was so outrageously unreasonable, it seemed Saundby was trying to make sure the concept got no further. Others, including

Dowding, insisted that the single-seater escort would always be drawn away from the bombers it was supposed to protect.[81] This might be true, but any interceptor occupied by an escort was one less fighter for the bombers to deal with. The Air Ministry, however, was adamant. Trying to use a fixed-gun fighter to protect bombers was just 'throwing good money after bad'.[82] Ludlow-Hewitt did not agree. 'Experience in China demonstrates that fighter escort is absolutely essential,' he insisted, but he too felt the plane had to be something like the German Bf 110 two-seater, with rear defence.[83] He had to admit that even this would not be able to escort bombers across the North Sea, but it might be useful for bombers operating from the continent.

The general view was that if there was to be an escort, it would have to be a turreted fighter. These could maintain formation with the bombers. If caught on their own, they would be able to protect themselves when the time came to retreat. This line of argument inevitably led the Air Ministry back to an escort that would essentially be the same as the bomber it was escorting. It was just necessary to fit some bombers with more guns and fly them without bombs. No special plane was required.[84]

There was perhaps a reluctance to mention the biggest problem with the single-seater escort. Limiting targets to the range of a single-seater would be a major restriction on what could be bombed. Cost was another unmentioned issue. Strategic bombers were expensive enough; a fleet of escort fighters would make the strategy even more so. The Air Ministry had to hope formations of bombers—even ones armed only with machine-guns—would have the firepower to deal with interceptors. Accepting the need for fighter escorts was tantamount to accepting that a long-range strategic air offensive was not a practicable proposition.

Doubts about the prospects of the next generation of long-range bombers only served to underline how inadequate existing equipment was. In the wake of the Sudetenland crisis, Newall seemed to have accepted that a daylight strike on the Ruhr was impossible. Ludlow-Hewitt also managed to persuade the Chief of Air Staff that his bomber crews needed to be broken in more gently. Missions of a shorter range needed to be attempted before something as ambitious as an attack on the Ruhr. However, as the memory of the 1938 crisis faded, so did the need for caution. Within months of the Munich Agreement, a daring low-level daylight strike on the Ruhr around a neutral Belgium and Netherlands was once more back on the agenda.

In Plans, Group Captain Slessor revived a scheme that had existed before the Sudetenland crisis for an all-out daylight attack on the electricity generating stations and coking plants in the Ruhr. Newall gave the plan his backing and told Ludlow-Hewitt he had changed his mind about breaking crews in gently. Only the Ruhr was worth attacking, and it was crucial to achieve surprise with a maximum-strength first strike.[85] The only reassurance Newall could offer Ludlow-Hewitt was that if losses proved too heavy, the policy would be reviewed. A startled Ludlow-Hewitt insisted that his force should be conserved until better equipment was available. He asked if Newall was really willing to send Blenheims 150 miles into enemy airspace by day; the answer was a very brief and unequivocal 'yes'.[86] It was not just

Blenheims he was willing to risk; the Fairey Battle would also have to play its part. Some of the targets were small, so many of the Battles, Hampdens, and Blenheims would have to attack at low level. Only the less manoeuvrable Wellingtons would be used exclusively from higher altitudes.[87]

Ludlow-Hewitt was horrified. He doubted his aircrews were sufficiently experienced; without high-quality, low-level photo-reconnaissance of the routes they were expected to take, he worried that they would be unable even to find their targets. Sending Blenheims to the Ruhr was bad enough, but expecting Battles to penetrate 150 miles in skies dominated by German fighters could only lead to losses out of all proportion to the results achieved.[88]

Ludlow-Hewitt got little sympathy from Slessor. Britain was now cooperating more closely with France, so a tricky North Sea crossing was no longer required— the bombers could refuel in France and attack the Ruhr from the south. To reach the Ruhr from France would admittedly involve the Battle flying beyond its agreed 100-mile limit, but Bomber Command was too reliant on them to drop them from the plan. Whatever their shortcomings, both the Blenheim and the Battle would have to play their full part. 'Only the experience of war can say if losses will be high,' Slessor ventured, insisting the potential gains were well worth the risk.[89]

Ludlow-Hewitt doubted even the Hampdens were up to the task. The Wellington was not much better. No. 3 Group, converting to Wellingtons, was complaining about the turrets, the lack of armour protection for the gunners, and its vulnerability to beam attacks.[90] The first Wellington Ia (with the more efficient power-operated Nash and Frasier turrets, but no ventral turret) reached the squadrons in September 1939. With no defence to beam attacks, there were serious doubts about how suitable this version was for day operations.[91] If even the Wellingtons could not operate by day, Bomber Command had a serious problem. All the evidence from night bombing trials suggested that hitting a target was impossible. The Whitley and Harrow night bombers were only included in the Ruhr bombing plan because they had to be used for something; they were not expected to hit anything useful.

It was just clutching at straws to believe all would come good when the Manchester, Halifax, and Stirling arrived. The Hampden and Wellington were as good as any bomber in the world—no more could be done with mid-1930s technology. They might not have been capable of unescorted daylight missions deep into enemy airspace, but no bombers in the world were any more capable. It was wishful thinking to propose that a future generation of long-range bombers would be any better at coping with the defences they would meet. The need for massive armour and all-round defensive fire with 20-mm or even 40-mm cannon underlined just how vulnerable bombers would always be. Since it was easier to develop fighters, interceptors powered by the next generation of engines were likely to reach the squadrons before the equivalent bombers. The unescorted long-range daylight bomber would always be vulnerable, and bombers might have to be used against targets much closer to the front line. Tactical bombing was perhaps the only option.

The Army Gets the Call

Early in 1939, the government took the first tentative steps towards creating a new British Expeditionary Force. In February, funds were released for a second armoured division. The two infantry divisions assembled during the Sudetenland crisis would be brought up to full strength. The remaining two regular divisions were to be capable of deployment within two months of the outbreak of war, with the first four territorial divisions in a position to follow four months later. The move towards a strategy based on ground forces was gaining momentum.

In March, the War Office made a rather tentative approach to the Air Ministry for the air resources these increased land forces would need. The Army wanted an extra five army-cooperation squadrons. Since a second contingent was now going to be mobilised, the agreement the previous August to convert four army-cooperation squadrons into two bomber and two air defence/Field Force fighter squadrons was no longer considered binding. The War Office wanted these to revert to army-cooperation squadrons, but they asked if they could still have the two extra fighter squadrons the Air Ministry had half-promised them as part of the deal.

It was no more than a hint of what was to come. There was no mention of bomber support. In a covering letter, it was suggested that the time had arrived to reconsider the role of the bomber in the context of Army operations. The Air Ministry was reminded that at the December 1935 meeting, the Air Ministry's own team, led by Courtney, had agreed that bombing was an essential part of Field Force operations. This was news to Slessor. He was astonished that anybody representing the Air Ministry could ever have agreed to such an unsound principle.[1]

On 15 March, German forces occupied the remainder of Czechoslovakia. Chamberlain was enraged by this blatant disregard for the promises made at Munich. It was the end of appeasement. With Germany demanding a land corridor to East Prussia and the return of the predominantly German-speaking port of Danzig, it looked like Poland would be Hitler's next target. It was time to make a stand. Britain, with France, entered into a military alliance with Poland. It was morally laudable, but nonetheless a militarily bizarre decision. In 1938, Britain had found herself being drawn—against her will—into a hopeless commitment to guarantee the security of a nation on the other side of Europe. In a fit of pique, Chamberlain now chose to make a similar commitment to an even more distant eastern European country. The Chiefs of Staff once again found themselves confronted with the problems of supporting a country that neither Britain nor France were connected to territorially.

Chamberlain still needed convincing that this political commitment had to be backed by an expansion of the Army. Duff Cooper, the ex-Secretary of State for War, now at the Admiralty, pointed out how absurd it would be for Britain to have 3 million able-bodied men out of uniform while France was fighting for her life.[2] Chamberlin accepted the French Army alone could not be expected to take on the German Army. Even more worryingly, without support on the ground, the French might choose to come to an understanding with Hitler's Germany, leaving Britain completely isolated.

Chamberlain introduced conscription in April, and plans were laid for a thirty-two-division British Expeditionary Force. The infrastructure should exist so that twenty-two infantry divisions, three armoured divisions, six motorised divisions, and one cavalry division could be formed within eleven months of the outbreak of war. It was a dramatic reversal of policy that required a phenomenal expansion of the Army. It was not so much a judgement on the relative merits of ground forces and strategic bombing as a political decision to stiffen the resolve of the French. Nevertheless, Britain was finally preparing for the sort of war it would soon find itself fighting.

There was still no official change in air policy. Bomber Command was still to develop the strike capability required by Scheme M, and the government still believed it was a war-winning weapon. However, the expansion of the Army had serious implications for Bomber Command's plans. Even with no Army, the Air Ministry had struggled to create an effective force with the available budget. The War Office would now expect a greater share of the defence budget and there would be more pressure on the Air Ministry to devote more of its air resources to Army air support.

The Air Staff would accept its new responsibility with an air of resignation. In the months ahead, the Air Ministry would genuinely try to meet its new obligations, but by this time air strategy was so far off-track that even the most conciliatory of attitudes did not approach what was required.

In terms of equipment, the RAF was not as unprepared for a tactical role as it might have been. Although the Air Staff had spent twenty years developing its strategic bombing role, it had not developed the heavy bombers it required. Four-engine bombers were on the way, but planes like the Blenheim and Wellington were no more unsuited for tactical air support than the Do 17 and He 111 the Luftwaffe was using in Spain. In the Hawker Henley, which was just beginning to come off the production lines, the RAF even had an equivalent to the Ju 87 Stuka. Perhaps most significantly of all, Air Staff plans to use their bombers strategically were in trouble. The case for using the RAF tactically was far stronger and posed far fewer problems than the Army imagined.

It was with some trepidation that the War Office prepared to inform the Air Ministry that not only were the figures agreed in 1935 inadequate for the existing regular and territorial units, but a far larger force would be required for the thirty-two divisions the government now wanted. On 29 April, the War Office very tentatively informed the Air Ministry that new requirements were being worked out and warned that they would be substantial.[3] It seemed sensible to break the news gently.

By this time, the Air Ministry was already under pressure from Britain's new military partner to give details of the tactical air support future Allied Armies in France could expect. To reassure the French, the government instructed the Air Ministry to open staff talks to discuss how the RAF would support the French Army. The first meeting was held at the end of March 1939, with Slessor leading the RAF team. Slessor was as ardent a believer in strategic bombing as anyone, but these encounters with the French would cause some reflection.

Slessor had a reputation for flirting with tactical airpower. In 1936, he had devoted an entire book, *Airpower and Armies*, to the question of Army air support in a major war. Despite the encouraging title, there was little in it to reassure the War Office. There would only be a real need to cooperate with the Army in the opening stages of a war, as British forces secured the air bases in Belgium the RAF required. Once these were secured and the German invasion was held, the role of the Army would become defensive and secondary. The war would be won by air attack on the vital centres of the enemy, not by pointless assaults on the German Army.[4] Even the air support provided in the initial stages would only be indirect. Aircraft would attack lines of communication behind the front line rather than forces at the front. 'The aeroplane is not a battlefield weapon', Slessor's book proclaimed.[5] If they had read it, the French officers Slessor was meeting would not have been particularly encouraged.

Slessor was at least sympathetic to the idea that air power had an important tactical role to play in the opening stages of a war. It was indeed the initial German offensive that worried the French. The German Army would almost certainly come through southern Holland and Belgium in order to outflank the French Maginot line; to slow down such an offensive, the French suggested three categories of target for RAF bombers. Firstly, German Air Force airfields and aircraft factories would be targeted to relieve the level of air attack on the Allied armies; secondly, lines of communication leading to the front; and, finally, advancing enemy columns.

French fears about a German offensive made a deep impression on Slessor. He recognised the RAF had to play its part. Newall was also sympathetic. Bomber Command had a series of Western Air (WA) plans to deal with different contingencies. The French were told Bomber Command could best help by attacking targets outlined in WA1 (German airfields and aircraft industry), WA4 (German Army lines of communication), and WA5 (the Ruhr). The French had asked for the first two—the third, they had not. There was no Bomber Command plan for attacking enemy columns. Ludlow-Hewitt was not enthusiastic about attacking the heavily defended Ruhr and many of the aircraft factories required the deep penetration he feared his bombers were not capable of. German Army lines of communication were far closer and easier targets to attack; these seemed the best option purely on the grounds of what was operationally feasible.

Pressure was also coming from the War Office to make sure the RAF had planes that could attack targets like troop columns. Douglas agreed that Army support 'must be considered' and pointed out that while the Battle and Blenheim were reasonably suitable for tactical air support, the larger bombers that would be replacing them would not be so suitable. Ludlow-Hewitt's more versatile 'speed bomber' might be the sort of plane that would be required.[6]

There was, however, also plenty of opposition to straying from the strategic-bombing path. Many saw Newall's more flexible attitude as a lack of steadfastness and a failure to take a firm grip of the situation. His critics included Marshal of the RAF Hugh Trenchard, the former Chief of Air Staff and, in the view of many, the father of the Royal Air Force. Former Chiefs of Air Staff Salmond and Ellington had already disappointed Trenchard; with Newall, it seemed that yet another of his protégés was not living up to expectations.[7]

Air Vice-Marshal Tedder, the Director General of Research and Development who, later in his career, would be credited with advancing the cause of Army air support, produced his own careful analysis of the close-support requirement. In his typically conciliatorily style, he suggested the use of low-level attack bombers in Spain had 'raised a question mark' over the issue. However, he then went on to repeat the usual arguments about the particular circumstances in Spain not being normal. Anti-aircraft defences were weak, bombers had to compensate for a shortage of artillery, and losses providing low-level support had been heavy. He rounded off his argument by suggesting that even when close air support was a success, one had to consider whether even better results could have been achieved if those air resources had been used strategically.[8] There was no way of ever defeating that sort of thinking.

In February 1939, the Committee of Imperial Defence Joint Intelligence Committee attempted to provide a balanced summary of the lessons of the fighting in Spain. The value of air support on the battlefield attracted particular attention. The report was sprinkled with Air Ministry-inspired scepticism. It argued that in Spain, air power had to be used tactically rather than strategically because it was a civil war and there was therefore a natural desire not to inflict damage on one's own country.[9] It seemed a reasonable argument, but given the savagery of the conflict, it is difficult to believe this was often a consideration.

The report emphasised how initially the forces on both sides in Spain were relatively weak, which meant that aircraft had to be used to substitute for the tanks and artillery that neither side had. However, the report also noted that even when the two sides were much better equipped, aircraft continued to be used in and around the battlefield and continued to be effective. One of the great assets of airpower, the report observed, was the speed with which it could be switched to any sector of the front and the surprise this could achieve.[10] This was no more than the RFC had discovered in the First World War.

The report described how aircraft had been used in defence to blunt an offensive and used offensively to disorganise forces in retreat. Low-flying planes had successfully strafed and bombed troops in the front line as well as targets such as artillery in the rear. Strafing and small bombs dropped by fighters from low level had been more effective than larger bombs dropped by bombers from higher altitudes. These attacks often continued under cover of darkness. Tactical bombing had been possible even on moonless nights. Attacking communication targets further to the rear had brought mixed results. Anti-aircraft defences had often deterred the bombers in Spain, and Japanese attempts to cut railway communications in China had been singularly unsuccessful.[11] The lesson seemed to be that the closer to the front line aircraft were used, the greater the effect they had on the course of the battle. To make the most of air power, specially designed aircraft, specialist training, and control procedures to direct the planes to their targets were all needed. The lessons learned in the First World War were slowly re-emerging.

The report noted how slow, 140-mph Soviet Polikarpov R-5 two-seater biplanes and faster German, Italian, and Russian single-seater fighters armed with bombs had been used for low-level ground attack. The Polikarpov I-16 monoplane had apparently been less successful than biplanes due to its high speed. Slower planes were able to attack targets more accurately, and even very slow planes like the R-5 could be used if targets were close to the front line. Escorts for all bombers and fighter-bombers were standard, with sometimes twice as many escorts as attacking planes. The fighters would often be stacked up in tiers above the attacking formations, each layer of fighters providing cover for the fighters below.[12]

It was difficult for the Air Ministry input into the report to make much impression on the overwhelming case being made for battlefield tactical air support. It was argued that the terrain in Spain was often mountainous, which made the movement of artillery difficult. Both sides had therefore been forced to use aircraft in the ground-attack role as a substitute (a little more than a year later, the Wehrmacht would give another demonstration of this in the French Ardennes). Low-flying aircraft were so much more vulnerable than tanks or artillery that they were not an economic way of supporting an Army. It would certainly not be a good idea to rely on air support because if air superiority was lost, air support would not be possible. It seemed a rather desperate objection, surely no more than a reason for ensuring air superiority was not lost. In exceptional circumstances air support on the battlefield might prove invaluable, but that was as far as the Air Ministry would allow the report to go. Tactical bombing was proving important in Spain, but, the argument went, it would not be so crucial in a war somewhere else in Europe.

Slessor was determined not to allow the Air Force to get involved in air support on the battlefield, but he was willing to provide much closer indirect support by attacking targets leading to the battlefield. These could include troop columns. Indeed, he suggested that Bomber Command should be ready to commit its entire front-line strength to supporting a French Army advance or covering a retreat.

Slessor asked Ludlow-Hewitt to work out the best way of attacking columns advancing along roads. Trials on Salisbury Plain showed that the single-engine Fairey Battle was manoeuvrable enough for low-level attack, and even the twin-engine Blenheim could be used if individual machines flew low along routes the enemy was known to be using until they ran into an enemy column. The trials also demonstrated that contrary to reports from Spain, high-speed monoplane fighters could be used for ground strafing.[13]

Ludlow-Hewitt had no objection to his squadrons being used in this way. He was anxious to avoid using any of his bombers to penetrate deep inside enemy airspace. He wanted to move as much of his command as possible to France so his squadrons were closer to targets in Germany and better-placed to support Allied armies. Nos 1 and 2 Groups were already committed, although only until their Battles and Blenheims had been replaced with heavy-bombers. Ludlow-Hewitt now wanted this to be a permanent move, with No. 3 Group Wellingtons and No. 5 Group Hampdens joining them. This would leave just the Whitleys of No. 4 Group to operate from the United Kingdom.[14] Slessor felt bombers based in Britain had more options open to them, but he agreed that Nos 1 and 2 Groups should stay in France, with Army support being one of their roles. In addition, one of the three remaining bomber groups in the United Kingdom should be fully mobile so that it could move to the continent if required.

Meanwhile, Douglas was looking into the sort of plane that might be needed for low-level air support. Although he agreed that the close air support tactics used in Spain were interesting, he only wanted aircraft used this way if there was a dire emergency. He used the March 1918 German offensive as an example of such a crisis.[15] There was, he believed, a strong case for Bomber Command having a suitable plane just in case it was needed. Douglas suggested a small, very fast, manoeuvrable, armoured two-seater with fixed forward-firing machine guns for strafing and a 1,000-lb bomb load. This did not seem so dissimilar to the 'speed bomber' Ludlow-Hewitt had been pushing for. The same plane ought to be able to combine the tactical flexibility Ludlow-Hewitt wanted for his strategic air offensive with an Army support capability. It would definitely not be the sort of ultra-short-range machine capable of 'going over the top with the infantry and bombing targets in the battlezone'.[16] Nevertheless, the Air Ministry was moving towards the sort of plane the Army wanted.

In June 1939, the Air Ministry began preparing specification B.11/39 to fill this role. It would only have a range of 500 miles. Although it was supposed to be small and fast, it would still be handicapped by the seemingly obligatory four-gun power-operated dorsal turret.[17] Only in 'special, infrequent' circumstances would it be used to attack battlefield targets; its main function would be 'holding the ring', attacking targets outside the range of normal artillery.[18] It was hoped that existing planes could be adapted. A 350-mph Vulture-powered Fairey Battle was one proposal.[19] This would have produced a plane with the same size and power as the

Soviet Ilyushin Il-2 Sturmovik, which, coincidentally, was just about to enter trials. Another was a bomber version of the Beaufighter. This would bring the design full circle, back to its Blenheim bomber origins.

Tactical bombing was now very much on the Air Ministry agenda. Even Peirse was warming to the new RAF role, going so far as to propose a specialist tactical bomber force should be created.[20] Slessor was not willing to go this far; he felt it was just a question of ensuring the bomber force was sufficiently flexible to respond to tactical and strategic demands. No specialisation was required. A target was a target—it made no difference if it was a tank or a tank factory. The Air Ministry always took personal affront at any suggestion that their pilots needed special training to hit naval or military targets.

However, if aircraft were used in emergencies to hit targets close to the front line, close Army/air coordination would be vital. It was the communication systems used in Spain that had so impressed the British Army observers. It seemed commanders could radio for air support whenever they needed it. The idea was not new. Towards the end of the First World War, the British Army had used planes hovering over the front to identify targets and radio instructions to specialist ground-attack squadrons on standby. The Army and Air Force continued to develop these techniques in various interwar colonial conflicts. Portable radios were becoming available by the 1930s, which allowed commanders in the front line to call in support. During the 1936 Arab revolt in Palestine, ground forces could call up air support *via* a radio link and have an aircraft engaging the enemy forces within thirty minutes. Personnel with flying experience (and therefore a greater awareness of what planes could and could not do) were often attached to the ground forces to assist.[21] The support provided was very close; targets were often only hundreds of yards ahead of friendly forces. To improve response time, in India Slessor developed what later became known as the 'cab rank' system. Aircraft patrolling close to the front could respond to any request for support within minutes, and planes on standby would replace them when they had used all their ammunition or were low on fuel. Many of these ideas were later used by the 2nd Tactical Air Force.[22]

These were sophisticated procedures, but the Air Force was convinced that the techniques developed for use against 'primitive races' were not relevant to a 'modern' European war. Even in a colonial context, Slessor only saw his 'cab rank' system as a way of sustaining a flawed policy. He could not see why Army columns had to be sent out in the first place—a straightforward punitive bombing mission would have had much the same effect and at far less cost. In July 1938, Air Commodore Arthur Harris took over in Palestine and spent 'a busy year teaching the British Army the advantages and the rebels the effectiveness of airpower'.[23] However, the lesson was not the value of coordinated close air support; Harris's idea of air support was 'a bomb in each village that speaks out of turn'.[24] Using airpower independently (and rather bluntly) was a policy that was transferrable to a 'modern' war, but it seems the more sophisticated application of on-call battlefield air support was not.

In the colonies, the RAF and Army worked together well on an operational level. There were no strategic bomber or interceptor forces to muddle the issues, and the troops had access to any available RAF aircraft. In Britain, the only RAF planes the Army had 'on call' were the small proportion of Jack-of-all-trades army-cooperation planes. This high-performance aircraft was intended to carry out just about any mission the Army might expect, from short-range observation and medium-range reconnaissance to ground attack and dive-bombing. Yet the plane still had to be capable of landing on small improvised landing strips close to Army command posts. This was asking a lot.[25]

Both services had good reason to want such a versatile machine. The War Office knew it was the only plane they could count on, so the more it could do, the better. From the Air Ministry's point of view, the more it could do, the less reason the Army would have to call on other RAF squadrons. Westland's young designer, Teddy Petter, had done his best, and the result was the Lysander. It was a high-wing monoplane that could land and take off in a remarkably short space and nearly met its minimum 245-mph speed requirement. The problem was that when the requirement was framed in 1934, 245 mph was not far short of the speeds expected from the next generation of fighter. No plane suffered more than the Lysander from the revolution in fighter performance that took place in the mid-1930s. The plane entered service at around the same time as the Spitfire; instead of being nearly as fast, it was over 100 mph slower.

This was not immediately seen as a problem. The Spitfire was a specialist short-range air defence interceptor for protecting targets in the rear, while the Lysander operated over the front line, where there would be no high-speed interceptors. Even if there were, there was a theory that it was not the Lysander that would have a problem with speed of the interceptor—it was the interceptor that would have a problem dealing with the manoeuvrable Lysander. The aircrews who had to fly the plane were not convinced. They asked for advice on how they were supposed to survive in the face of modern interceptors.[26] The best solution trials could come up with was that the Lysander should fly as slowly as possible and hopefully the fighter pilot would lose control of his plane.[27] It was asking a lot of aircrews to place their trust in such a tactic.

The Air Ministry solution to the problem was more power. The Lysander's successor was to be a low-wing monoplane with a retractable undercarriage. The plane would be armoured and have self-sealing tanks and a power-operated turret. It would carry 500 lbs of bombs and still be capable of operating from a field. With a Hercules engine, 253 mph might be possible, and if the landing and take-off requirements were relaxed substantially, the plane might manage 282 mph. A massive Vulture engine might push speed up to 300 mph. By the spring of 1939, fixed forward-firing and turret armament had both been increased to four machine guns. The plane was becoming a dinosaur—and it was still not going to be fast enough. The specialist army-cooperation type was losing its way.[28]

The very idea of a 'specialist' Jack-of-all-trades was a contradiction. There was nothing wrong with a slow-flying plane that could operate from within the Army's ranks, land in a field next to Army HQ, and observe the enemy front line. There was not much wrong with a slow-flying plane that could attack front-line positions. Expecting the same plane to penetrate up to 100 miles inside enemy airspace or fly at 28,000 feet was expecting too much.[29]

In Spain, neither side seemed to be using these so-called specialist army-cooperation planes—high-performance bombers were used for long-range reconnaissance and fighters for the short-range tactical reconnaissance. It was easy to argue that these planes had to be used because more suitable equipment was not available,[30] but since the Air Ministry could not work out what that more suitable equipment might be, what appeared to be makeshift solutions might in fact be the answer—or at least part of the answer.

Expecting a single plane to perform so many different roles was the crux of the problem. The War Office was already moving away from this approach by suggesting a specialist short-range machine should take over the ground-attack capability. Observation was another role where specialisation might pay dividends. To direct artillery fire, a plane did not have to be capable of flying to 28,000 feet—a few thousand feet was ample. The Army Royal Artillery Flying Club was already experimenting with privately owned low-performance sports planes. The Air Ministry agreed to official trials, although they could not see why anyone would want to use a plane in the combat zone with the same performance as a First World War B.E.2. The ministry insisted that Audax and Lysanders were used—the very type of plane the artillery officers were trying to get away from. This rather underlined the growing gulf between the two services. An expensive, high-performance plane with a supercharged engine was not needed just to peep over the front line. The War Office pressed on with the light aircraft approach, using two-seaters produced by Taylorcraft Aviation, but with no control over aircraft development or purchasing, it was difficult to see how the idea could make much progress.

For fighters too, the Army was totally reliant on what the Air Ministry considered suitable. Of the specialist bomber interceptors available, the Spitfire and Hurricane were closest to the S.E.5a and Sopwith Camel of the First World War. There seemed to be no reason to believe single-seaters were not still best, but the Air Ministry managed to think of some. It seemed the passing of time had distorted memories; it was not the success of the single-seater that everyone remembered, but rather its vulnerability to attack from the rear, along with a rather exaggerated idea of what the two-seater Bristol Fighter had achieved. In the early '30s, it was decided that the two-seater Hawker Demon was the best fighter for protecting the Army. This would be replaced by the Defiant and eventually the twin-engine cannon-armed Boulton Paul F.11/37 turret fighter.

It was a strange turn of events. The turret fighter had been developed because the fixed-gun, single-seater tactical fighter of the First World War was not considered suitable for defending cities; now the plane designed to bring down unescorted bombers in the rear was being touted as an offensive 'air superiority fighter' that would be capable of dealing with enemy fighters inside enemy airspace.[31] Dowding could not understand why a Field Force fighter needed defensive armament and predicted they would end up being used in the same 'bloody and wasteful' way as the F.E.2s on the Somme in 1916. Still, Dowding did not feel it was his problem, and if it meant the Defiants would go abroad instead of Fighter Command, then so much the better.[32] The fact that the obdurate and idiosyncratic Dowding did not think the Defiant would work as a tactical fighter merely served to reinforce the Air Staff in its belief that it would. The only way the Field Force might be denied the Defiant was, according to Peirse, if the fighter proved to be far too valuable an asset for home defence to be wasted abroad.[33]

With deliveries of the first Defiants still some way off, the Army would need something better than the 186-mph Demon biplane. As an interim measure, the makeshift Blenheim fighter would be used.[34] It was another extraordinary decision. Little was expected of the fighter version of the Blenheim bomber, although, as Air Commodore Park, the future commander of No. 11 Group Fighter Command, pointed out, it had to be an improvement on the Demon.[35] No. 64 Squadron, perhaps expecting worse, were actually pleasantly surprised by how manoeuvrable the plane was. A well-trained flight ought to be able to intercept bombers. However, if engaged in a dogfight with enemy fighters, the odds would be 'most unfavourable'.[36] Other units were far less generous. The plane lacked the speed, rate of climb, manoeuvrability, and firepower to be effective even as a bomber interceptor. The plane was not even a very stable gun platform. Tracer bullets might have to be used just to give the pilot some idea of where his fire was going.[37] This then was the fighter assigned the task of taking on the German Messerschmitts over the battlefield. The four fighter squadrons that were supposed to accompany the BEF would be the first to reequip with the Blenheim. Early in 1939, only one of these was fully mobile and capable of accompanying the Army to France. If war broke out, the British Army would be defended by one squadron of Blenheims.

What the French would have made of this one can only imagine. With Franco on the brink of victory in Spain, France now had to protect her Spanish as well as German and Italian frontiers. They made it clear to Slessor that they did not have enough fighters to provide cover for British forces as well. How many fighters the British could or should send to France now became a major issue. The Air Ministry wanted to send as few as possible and could always rely on a nervous government giving home defence priority; however, confronted with French fears about the outcome of a potentially crucial confrontation with a German Army, Slessor seemed to appreciate the problem:

> We might be faced in the initial stage of such a war with the spectacle of five or six hundred good short-range fighters sitting in England unable to contribute

at all to the issue of the struggle in the Low Countries, a struggle on which the subsequent fate of England might depend.[38]

He went on to describe how the quite 'natural and proper obsession' with the aerial knockout blow had led to all effort being focused on types of fighter and a static air defence system needed to protect Britain at the expense of the ability to resist the potentially equally decisive knockout blow on land the French Army might have to deal with. This was indeed radical thinking from the Air Ministry in 1939. He suggested eight fighter squadrons should be ready to move to France. His colleagues in the Air Staff were not so enthusiastic, but it was agreed that the first four squadrons should go immediately and Slessor drew up plans for getting these over to France on the first day of war.

However, they were not going to be attached to the Army, as the War Office had been promised. Slessor argued that if the French had their backs to the wall defending the Maginot Line and the British sector was quiet, it would be ridiculous for British fighters to be wasting their time patrolling the British front and not assisting their French allies.[39] The Army had no quarrel with this. During the First World War, both the French and British had moved squadrons to support their ally when required. The War Office insistence on operational control was inspired by a fear of losing fighter squadrons to home defence, not the French.

It was not just a question of control. Slessor did not want to use the fighters to protect front-line troops. Bombers were not a battlefield weapon and the Germans could not be expected to make the mistake of using theirs this way. It was well behind the front that the German bombers would cause problems, and this was where fighters would be needed.

Slessor, now warming to the task, began questioning the whole static nature of the Royal Air Force. The force was essentially 'immobile outside [their] tactical range'. Britain had a lot to learn from foreign air forces in this respect, he admitted. He envisaged an Anglo-French defensive line stretching from Scapa Flow to Tunisia, with mobile squadrons capable of responding to any concentration of enemy airpower. Slessor suggested that initially ten RAF fighter squadrons (eventually rising to twenty) should be fully mobile to provide this strategic flexibility.[40] However, it was strategic mobility within a rigid air defence system; effectively, Slessor wanted to extend the Fighter Command sector system through France to North Africa.

The problem was that French fighters were not deployed in the linear way Fighter Command was organised. French fighter squadrons were either attached to armies or stationed around key cities and communication centres. The British and French systems did not mesh.[41] The solution, as far as the Air Staff was concerned, was to convert the French to the British way of thinking. Plans were drawn up to deploy the first four squadrons in two sectors between the French coast and Lille.[42] The new sectors would even have their own early warning radar, a more basic 7.5-metre system that just about worked over land. It was very basic, with a limited range (30–45 miles) and no height-finding capability.

Not all agreed that the flexibility Slessor wanted was possible. Dowding had always scoffed at the idea of holding up an attack on London while reinforcements flew down from Scotland.[43] Peirse argued that it was no longer like the First World War, when fighter squadrons operated from any open field. Modern fighter squadrons needed large aerodromes, well-organised facilities, and sophisticated communication equipment. They could not be moved 'hither and thither'.[44] Herein lay the problem. If fighter squadrons were going to be used tactically, they had to start learning how to operate from basic, improvised airstrips again. Slessor had identified the problem with the RAF preoccupation with home defence, but he still could not envisage fighters operating outside Fighter Command's sophisticated integrated air defence system.

To Dowding, Slessor's ideas just looked like a way of justifying the transfer of squadrons out of the United Kingdom. Much to Dowding's frustration, it was agreed that six squadrons (in addition to the four Field Force squadrons) would be available for operations in France by early 1940. These were squadrons Dowding felt he could not afford to lose. In the spring of 1939, Fighter Command's main line of defence was extended to Edinburgh. It also had to protect Belfast and the Fleet in Scapa Flow. Dowding wanted fifty-three squadrons to meet these new commitments, but in the summer of 1939 he only had thirty-nine, and many of these were in the process of forming. He insisted that if war broke out, no squadrons should go to France until the basic defence requirements of the United Kingdom had been met. He certainly believed this was the agreed policy, but he was soon to discover otherwise.[45]

Dowding cannot be criticised for this single-minded determination to maximise the number of fighter squadrons available for home defence. He had been given the task of defending the country, and this was precisely what he intended to do. The likes of Slessor were beginning to see there might be more to the next war than defending British cities and bombing German ones, but with the politicians terrified by the catastrophic consequences of air attacks, the priority attached to Home Defence had a momentum that was going to make changing tack very difficult—especially with Dowding in charge. His qualities were doggedness in seeing a task through, not flexibility in changing circumstances.

Dowding was supposed to retire in June 1939. Courtney, the officer Slessor had castigated for being so accommodating to the Army in the December 1935 discussions with the War Office, was due to take his place. When Courtney was seriously injured in a plane crash, the Air Staff extended Dowding's tenure at Fighter Command to June 1940. At a time of rapid expansion within the Command and a worsening political situation, continuity seemed important. Perhaps more significantly, for all his cantankerousness—indeed, because of it—Dowding could be relied on to give home defence priority.

While Slessor was making these proposals, the Air Ministry was having second thoughts about whether the Bristol Blenheim was the right fighter to send to France. Park was determined that Spitfire or Hurricane squadrons should not go instead. He warned that his single-seater fighter squadrons were not trained or equipped for the fighter-*versus*-fighter role.[46] Park was clearly aware that different tactics were required. The fact that a year later he would still be offering the same excuse would suggest that as far as Park was concerned, it was a reason for them not going to France rather than a deficiency that needed to be put right.

Park argued his interceptors were too fast and not manoeuvrable enough to deal with opposing fighters and slow, low-flying army-cooperation planes. The Gloster Gladiator was a far more suitable plane. It is tempting to conclude Park just wanted to keep the best fighters for home defence, but there was an element of truth in his argument. The lighter, more compact biplane was far more manoeuvrable than a monoplane, and this quality was required for fighter-*versus*-fighter combat. Even so, yanking fighter speeds back to 250 mph to get it was a little extreme. Plans to send all the Gladiators to the Middle East seemed to put an end to Park's idea. This left the Spitfire and Hurricane. Since the latest plan was to use fighters in France as interceptors in the rear, there was no reason not to send them.

Peirse now had the delicate task of informing Dowding that he would be losing single-seater fighters rather than Blenheims. Peirse explained that there had been a change of policy, with high-speed interceptors now required rather than tactical fighters; rather than belonging to the Army, these squadrons would be an extension of his Fighter Command. Indeed, they would provide Britain with some defence from the south. Blenheims could not perform the interceptor role, so Hurricanes or Spitfires would have to go instead, but as soon as Defiants became available, these would replace the single-seaters.[47] It was a carefully constructed argument that seemed to suggest the Blenheim would have been satisfactory if a tactical fighter had been required.

Dowding stoically accepted the loss of these squadrons, but he refused to allow them to be equipped with the Spitfire; for him, this was non-negotiable. The Hurricane might be too slow to catch the latest Ju 88 bomber, and he needed his fastest fighter—the needs of home defence had to come first. The decision meant that Britain's best fighter would only have to deal with unescorted bombers over Britain, while the inferior Hurricane, nearer the front line, would inevitably have to cope with the Bf 109.

Dowding saw the loss as permanent, believing that the Hurricane would never be replaced by the Defiant. The turret fighter would inevitably be considered just as unsuitable as the Demon and Blenheim.[48] Ironically, it was a report written by Dowding for the Air Fighting Committee that made sure this was what happened. He agreed with Slessor that the fighters in France should be interceptors defending fixed points in the rear. Using fighters inside enemy airspace would be as pointless as Trenchard's costly First World War offensive patrols. Being closer to the front, these interceptors would be more likely to encounter enemy fighters. Manoeuvrability for fighter-*versus*-fighter combat would therefore be more important. Nevertheless, the role was still essentially bomber interception.

No. 22 (Army Cooperation) Group did not agree. Field Force fighters had to do far more than just protect the rear; they also had to establish air superiority over the battlezone, especially low down, where enemy ground-attack and tactical-reconnaissance planes were operating. The debate that followed again emphasised the need for slower, more manoeuvrable fighters. Ludlow-Hewitt suggested even slower Gauntlets, as well as Gladiators, might be the best available options. Only Group Captain Orlebar (famous for leading the RAF's winning Schneider Trophy team) saw no problem using the Spitfire tactically. He had no doubts that the plane had ample manoeuvrability to deal with anything it might come across over the battlefield. Ludlow-Hewitt wanted escorts for his bombers and Dowding agreed that unescorted bombers would 'obviously' stand no chance. However, if escorts were required, they would be bombers with more guns, not single-seaters. The consensus view was that the principal role for the fighter would be defending targets in the rear and that required high-speed single-seaters.[49]

The tactics the fighters would use would be no different to those designed to deal with unescorted bombers over the United Kingdom. Fighters would fly in tight formation and be guided to their target by ground-based radar. As enemy fighters were more likely to be encountered in France, seat armour might be introduced to provide some protection from the rear; turret fighters might also provide some protection. However, no thought was given to the tactics single-seater fighter pilots might have to use to deal with enemy fighters.

It was all rather typical of the reactive approach the Air Staff was adopting. Bombers might intervene on the battlefield if there was an emergency, and fighters would respond to threats in the rear, but neither would impose themselves proactively on the battle. Neither would even be present in the battlezone. Air Ministry policy was effectively conceding air superiority over the front.

The Air Staff believed they were doing their best to accommodate the needs of the Field Force the government had rather suddenly decided to create. Bombers would be allocated tactical targets, specialised short-range bombers would be developed, and more fighters were being made available sooner for employment in France. They genuinely believed that in the name of inter-service cooperation, they had gone that extra mile to meet the needs of the Army. They were totally unprepared for the demands the War Office was about to make.

In June, the War Office finally plucked up the courage to let the Air Ministry know what they really needed. The War Office carefully outlined the history of Army requests for air support, including the December 1935 meeting in which the Air Ministry appeared to have agreed that tactical bombing was important and the Army should control it. Since then, the War Office emphasised, events had demonstrated that tactical air power was even more important than previously supposed. All the major powers were now organising close-support squadrons for their ground forces. These would not just attack targets beyond the range of artillery; they would also tackle targets on the battlefield that artillery could not engage as effectively or, if the situation on the ground was changing rapidly, could not engage at all. Fighter protection over the battlefield would be crucial to prevent the enemy benefitting from similar support.[50]

The War Office estimated that the full Field Force of thirty-two divisions would require thirty-nine army-cooperation squadrons, six long-range reconnaissance squadrons, twenty-four support bomber squadrons, and four communication squadrons. The number of fighter squadrons was left to be decided after discussions with the Air Ministry. With Pownall already making it clear that twelve squadrons for just the first contingent of four divisions was not enough, it is tempting to conclude the War Office did not dare put a figure on their requirements for thirty-two divisions.[51]

It would be some time before the Army was ready to field thirty-two divisions. If war was to break out on 1 September—an ironic, arbitrary date—Army requirements would be a more modest nine support squadrons, six fighter squadrons, two communication squadrons, eighteen army-cooperation squadrons, and four long-range reconnaissance squadrons within six months. All these would be under Army control—there was no question of the fighter squadrons operating in the rear as an extension of Fighter Command.[52]

The War Office document went out of its way not to antagonise the Air Ministry. The aim was to provide adequate air support for ground units, not to open old controversies. The War Office made it clear that it accepted the existence of an independent Royal Air Force, and the Army was more than happy to leave the training of aircrews and development of the required aircraft in the hands of the Air Ministry. However, it did expect that units intended to operate with ground forces should be directly commanded by the Army. To this end, No. 22 (Army Cooperation) Group (still an annex of Fighter Command) should be expanded to a new 'Army Command' to parallel Bomber, Fighter, and Coastal Commands.[53]

The War Office requirements were greeted with a mixture of shock and disbelief. Slessor, who had recently demonstrated much sympathy for the Army cause, simply could not believe what he was reading. The War Office proposals, he believed:

> … were based on a misconception of the strategic employment of the main striking force and an obsolete conception of the employment of airpower in conjunction with land force, which tends to show they have learnt little or nothing from the lessons of the war in 1914–18 and recent campaigns in Spain and China.[54]

Slessor accused the War Office of drawing 'false lessons' from the fighting in Spain and China. Using aircraft to attack targets on the battlefield was just 'using expensive and highly trained aircrews as a propellant for artillery shells', Slessor colourfully suggested. He dismissed the idea that air support might be used instead of artillery to help maintain the momentum of an offensive. Only in exceptional circumstances could the bomber be used on the battlefield. As for the number of squadrons required, with fighter squadrons, which Slessor assumed to be only fourteen, the War Office was talking about some ninety squadrons with 1,280 planes. This was a huge force to create and then maintain, especially with the heavy losses that even the War Office seemed resigned to. The more limited air resources the War Office expected if war should break out on 1 September were, in Slessor's view, equally unrealistic.[55]

By the standards of the First World War, the War Office requirements were not at all extravagant, being broadly in line with the 2,700 aircraft the Air Ministry had deemed necessary in 1918 to support the sixty divisions the British were then fielding in France. In 1918, the Air Ministry had also been hoping to create a force of around 2,000 machines for home defence and strategic bombing. This was not dissimilar to the aims of the recently approved Scheme M. In 1918, with a generous wartime budget, it had been impossible to find the resources to build such a large strategic air force and continue to meet the needs of the Army. It was not going to be any easier two decades later. Slessor's dismay stemmed more from the impossibility of the task than the unreasonableness of the request.

The Air Ministry argued that if the available air resources were not divided up, the Army could expect far greater support than even the War Office was asking for. If the Luftwaffe was going to be used as a yardstick, the Army really needed nearer fifty close-support bomber squadrons, not twenty-four. By throwing in the entire resources of Bomber Command, the Army would get them. With fighters too, Slessor's twenty-strong mobile fighter force was the way to meet home defence and Army requirements. Operational flexibility and centralised control were the keys to providing adequate bomber and fighter support; all the Army had to do was trust the RAF to provide air support when it was required. However, the problem was that the Army did not trust the Air Force.

The Air Ministry quite rightly pointed out aircraft were not like artillery. They were much more mobile and could always be moved rapidly to wherever they were required. There was no need to attach them to particular Army units. It was a popular Air Ministry argument, but attaching squadrons to Army units did not necessarily restrict mobility. In the First World War, most RFC/RAF squadrons had been attached to armies or Army corps, but this did not prevent them being moved to entirely different sectors of the front if the situation required it. The Army was well-aware of the flexibility of air power. In the March 1918 German offensive, it had exploited this mobility brilliantly, but to do this required control.[56] If you were not in control, mobility was a problem. As Pownall put it: 'It's this mobility of aircraft again—so infernally mobile that they'll never be where they are wanted—they'll have flown away!'[57] It was one thing for the Army to decide where the squadrons should be deployed, but it was quite another to have such matters decided by another service with a different outlook on how, when, and indeed if air support should be provided.

Although the tactical requirements of the Army were not unreasonable in terms of overall size, the proposed composition was very different to the 1918 force. The fourteen fighter squadrons Slessor was assuming was far smaller than the fighter force required in 1918. The number of army-cooperation squadrons, on the other hand, was relatively high. In the interwar years, the Army based its army-cooperation requirement on one squadron per division. During the First World War, it had been one squadron per corps (two or three divisions). The French and German armies still worked on a squadron-per-corps basis. There was scope for adjustment, but the final figure was going to be broadly the number the War Office was putting forward.

The Air Ministry tried to give the War Office the squadrons the Army wanted without the control. It offered to meet the War Office demand for twenty-four close-support squadrons with the ten Battle and seven Blenheim squadrons of Nos 1 and 2 Groups. The Air Ministry assumed the War Office was planning on twelve planes per squadron, so seventeen squadrons at sixteen planes per squadron was almost enough. However, they would remain firmly under RAF control. They would be dual-purpose, with aircrews trained to carry out both tactical and strategic missions. Since the Air Ministry had always argued this was already the case for all Bomber Command squadrons, the Army was not really getting anything new. Peirse was, however, able to assure the Army that a new specification (B.11/39) was being prepared for a specialist short-range bomber as an eventual successor to the Battle and Blenheim. Ironically, it was the type Peirse had so fiercely opposed.[58]

Newall skirted around what sort of targets the Army could expect these bomber squadrons to engage, how far behind the front-line bombers would normally operate, and exactly what circumstances would justify their involvement. The War Office tried to get their requirements formally discussed at Chiefs of Staff meetings, but twice Newall managed to get the item removed from the agenda.[59] Instead, these issues were deferred to various committees for further discussion. While the Air Ministry dragged its heels, time was running out.

The Lessons of War

Less than a year after the Munich agreement, Britain once again stood on the brink of war. German troops were again massing threateningly, this time along the Polish frontier. With Chamberlain determined not to be humiliated a second time, war seemed inevitable. The nightmare scenario of massive aerial assaults on British cities and huge loss of civilian life seemed about to become a reality. Thirty-nine Fighter Command squadrons stood ready to repel the assault. Ten had Spitfires, sixteen Hurricanes, seven Blenheims, four Gladiators, and two were making do with Hinds and Gauntlets.[1]

Whether the Germans knew about Fighter Command's radar system was not known, but 300-foot towers along the coast were difficult to hide. In fact, Germany's own radar programme was far more advanced than anyone in Britain imagined. The Germans were indeed curious about what the British might be up to, although what 300-foot towers had to do with radar was not obvious. In the summer of 1939, their Graf Zeppelin LZ-130 was sent along the British coast to investigate. Radio operators on board listened out for the tell-tale signs of the probing beams that would indicate radar systems were in operation. There was nothing apart from some mysterious and rather annoying background interference. They returned home and reported Britain had no radar. In fact, the interference they had been picking up was the British Home Chain system. The Zeppelin had been tracked all the way down the British coastline, the British operators suppressing a desire to radio them and tell them the positions they were reporting back to Germany were wrong. The British radar system had demonstrated one rather unexpected advantage—it was too crude to be recognised as an early warning system.[2]

On the evening of 31 August 1939, the BBC announced that the evacuation of threatened cities would begin the following day. Normal train services were suspended and major roads out of cities were turned into one-way dual carriageways. In the next four days, an armada of busses, coaches, and trains evacuated 1.5 million mothers, children, and babies to safety. Over 5,000 prisoners were freed from jails in threatened areas, while 140,000 patients were sent home from hospital to make way for the flood of casualties. London expected to take the brunt of the assault. Over 20,000 civil servants joined the women and children fleeing the capital, and plans existed for the government to follow should London become uninhabitable. Fifty-six thousand beds awaited the first wave of casualties.[3]

On 1 September 1939, German troops crossed the Polish frontier and Chamberlain issued his final ultimatum. Unless the British Government received assurances that German forces would be withdrawn from Poland within the following two days, Britain and Germany would be at war. At 11.15 a.m. on 3 September, Chamberlain grimly confirmed that no such assurances had been received. There was little surprise when, a few minutes later, air raid sirens started wailing throughout the capital. Traffic ground to a halt, cars were abandoned in the middle of the street, and civilians scurried to the nearest air raid shelter. Streets emptied and a deathly hush fell over the city. It was a false alarm; the sirens had been triggered by a French plane making its way to Croydon Airport.

An hour before Chamberlain declared war, Roosevelt appealed to all belligerents to refrain from unrestricted bombing. With almost indecent haste, the British Government agreed, as long as the German Air Force also confined operations to military targets. The country held its collective breath. There was no response from Germany, but over the next few days the truce seemed to hold—in the west, at least. Bombs were already raining down on Polish cities, and there remained the suspicion that it was only Germany's preoccupation with their campaign in Poland that might be delaying a full-scale assault on Britain.

For some it was a missed opportunity rather than a lucky respite. Slessor argued that with German forces fully occupied in Poland, this was precisely the time to unleash Bomber Command on the Ruhr. He admitted that the RAF was outnumbered in terms of bombers and there would be great risks involved in such an audacious daylight strike, but he also stated:

> Victory does not always go to the big battalions. At present we have the initiative. If we seize it now we may gain important results; if we lose it by waiting we shall probably lose far more than we gain.[4]

Enough bombs had fallen on Polish cities to make a British counter-strike perfectly legitimate. Fortunately for Bomber Command, Slessor's appeal fell on deaf ears.

Meanwhile, Dowding was getting a breathing space he had not expected. He was still well short of the fifty-three squadrons he felt he needed to defend the country. When the Air Staff instructed the four Field Force Hurricane squadrons to France, a furious Dowding immediately countermanded the order. He claimed that he had no choice if he was to keep a promise he had made to the British people; in a pre-war broadcast, he had assured the public that adequate air defences existed. He had only done this on the understanding that no fighter squadrons would go to France until the defences of the United Kingdom were secure. He had been tricked into misleading the people, he claimed. The Air Staff were able to produce countless memos where Dowding was clearly conceding that he knew he would lose these squadrons. Nevertheless, he had a point when he claimed that every promise in the interwar years to support the Army had come with the caveat that this would only be possible if the situation on the Home Front allowed it. Inconveniently for Dowding, no attack on London came. He was overruled, and the four Hurricane squadrons arrived in France a week behind schedule.

History seemed to be repeating itself. In 1914, the government and population had been anxiously awaiting the arrival of the Zeppelins. None came. In 1939, no bombers came. The response to the threats could not have been more different. At the outbreak of the First World War, RFC commanders wanted to send the entire air force to support the Army. They were furious when the government told them to hold back a small proportion to defend London. In 1939 there was controversy over whether a small proportion of the fighter force should support the Army in France. Dowding lost this particular battle, but air defence of the homeland still had priority and Dowding was determined to keep it that way. The stage was now set for a titanic struggle in which, for Dowding, the problem was not Luftwaffe bombers, but the requirements of the Allied armies in France.

Dowding despondently talked of the fighter 'tap' having been turned on. Every Hurricane that went to France was putting the future of the country at risk. Air Vice-Marshal Welsh, in charge of supply, was just as perturbed. On 14 September, he contacted Freeman, in charge of development and production: 'I expect you are disturbed as everyone by the Hurricane position'. He explained that although production was exceeding expectations, existing output was only just meeting 'wastage', and this before any major operations had taken place.[5] In fact, no Hurricane squadron had yet encountered an enemy plane and the only 'wastage' was the Hurricanes being sent to France. The idea was gaining ground that 'wastage' meant a plane shot down by the enemy or one sent to defend the Army in France.

Welsh suggested future squadrons going to France could be equipped with Gladiators. 'The Gladiator will come into its own in this war for fighter offence because of its manoeuvrability', he insisted. He described how popular the Gladiator had been with Chinese pilots and insisted the fighting in Spain had confirmed the value of the biplane. He suggested 'as a first step' that 300 should be prepared for combat in case they were needed.[6] As Welsh suggested, the next two fighter squadrons to go to France would indeed be equipped with the biplane.

Meanwhile, Germany had completed her victory in Poland. There was still no assault on London; indeed, Hitler signalled his intention to join the truce on indiscriminate bombing, which conveniently meant any civilian casualties in Poland did not count. Days turned to weeks and weeks to months, and still no bombs fell on British cites. On the sidelines, Trenchard chided the Air Ministry and government for not taking advantage, first when the Germans were fully occupied in Poland and then when the long winter nights would have provided bombers with opportunities to strike deep into the heart of Germany.[7]

Both sides, however, carefully avoided any bombing that might involve civilian casualties. Bomber Command crews set off for German cities with no more than propaganda leaflets to drop. The first bomb did not fall on British soil until 13 November; it fell on the Shetlands and the only victim was a rabbit. The prophets of doom had been proven wrong once again. Even the fierce fighting in Poland provided no evidence that the Germans had tried to bring about victory by intimidation of the civilian population. Warsaw had been bombed several times, especially severely towards the end of the campaign, as the remaining elements of the Polish Army gathered in the city for a final stand. However, the German victory was not the result of a knockout blow against the civilian population. The War Office may not have fully understood the way the Germans were using their armoured forces, but the Polish campaign very clearly confirmed their belief that it was 'armies supported by air forces which [would] decide the war'.[8]

The first squadrons to move to France were the ten Fairey Battle squadrons of No. 1 Group, now renamed the Advanced Air Striking Force. This force was commanded Air Vice-Marshal Playfair. It had always been planned to base this element of the strategic bomber force in France because of the limited range of the Battle. It was now supposed to have a rather ill-defined dual tactical/strategic role, but it remained under Bomber Command control. Requests to use it to support ground forces had to be made to Ludlow-Hewitt. The second element of the RAF force in France was the Air Component, which incorporated squadrons from No. 22 (Army Cooperation) Group and the four fighter squadrons the Army had been promised. It was led by Air Vice-Marshal Blount, whose sole task was to support Lord Gort's British Expeditionary Force. By October, in addition to the Hurricane squadrons, Blount had two Blenheim I reconnaissance/bomber squadrons at BEF HQ and, for each of the first two corps, two Lysander and one night reconnaissance Blenheim IV squadron.[9] The two Blenheim I squadrons were the only bombers under direct Army control. Air Marshal Barratt was given the task of coordinating RAF operations with the French.

The Air Component was based with the British divisions on the Belgian frontier. These were ready to move forward into Belgium as soon as the German Army invaded. The AASF was based further south, on airfields near Reims. Early in October, two of the Hurricane squadrons were transferred to the AASF, to provide their airfields with some protection. This left just two fighter squadrons to cover the four British divisions. General Vuillemin, the French Air Force commander, pointed out that the RAF was sending substantial numbers of bombers and reconnaissance planes, but not the means to protect their airfields or escort them on missions. This burden would fall on his overstretched fighter force. With the French expecting a German offensive in mid-October, he insisted that the RAF get more fighters to France.

Vuillemin was promised that two Gladiator squadrons would arrive within a month. This, he was assured, was a fighter that was particularly suited to tactical duties because of its manoeuvrability.[10] The French, who at the time were desperately trying to replace their last biplane fighters with modern monoplanes, must have been intrigued by this British line of reasoning. The Air Ministry could probably not disentangle in their own minds the belief that the Gladiator was the best fighter for the job and the desire not to send anything more modern.

Newall was trying to strike a balance between Army needs and home defence. He assured Dowding he would do everything possible to resist government pressure to send more fighters to France but he also warned Dowding: 'We must face facts, one of which is that we could possibly lose the war in France, just as well as in England.'[11] If the Army was fighting with its backs to the wall, the RAF had to help. To try and provide the required flexibility, Fighter Wing Servicing Units were formed. These were skeleton formations based in France, each capable of handling two squadrons, which would enable squadrons to fly over and begin operations immediately.

As tension mounted over a possible German autumn offensive, Dowding was instructed to prepare for the dispatch of another two Hurricane squadrons to France, in addition to the Gladiators. Squadrons in France were also to have the facilities to deal with an extra flight attached to each squadron.[12] Newall even suggested that Spitfires, flying from Britain and refuelling in northern France, might operate as far inland as the Meuse/Albert Canal.[13]

In November, with the French still expecting an imminent German attack, the two Gladiator squadrons joined the Air Component. Dowding furiously complained that fighter commitments to France and the extension of the fighter defences to the north of Britain had 'drawn all the blood to the extremities and left the heart of the country exposed'.[14] It was dramatic talk, but one of those 'extremities' was Britain's Army. Dowding stubbornly resisted any attempts to transfer more of his squadrons permanently to France. He would not even let his home-based squadrons be rotated through France to enable the pilots to gain some combat experience.[15] Spitfire squadrons were especially precious; to make sure they did not operate anywhere near the Meuse/Albert Canal, they were forbidden to cross the continental coastline in any circumstances.

The French were quite right to suspect an autumn offensive; it was only bad weather that was delaying the operation. When a plane carrying German invasion plans fell into Belgian hands, all offensive action was postponed until the following spring, and France and Britain got time to mobilise and organise their defences. For Britain, this meant creating an Army. For the French, it was a chance to modernise their air force. Their Morane Saulnier M.S.406 and American Curtiss Hawk fighters were superior to the Jumo-powered Bf 109, but markedly slower than the latest Daimler Benz-powered Bf 109E. French bomber equipment was so obsolete that most of the squadrons had to be pulled back to the rear until more modern aircraft arrived. Better bombers and fighters were beginning to come off French production lines. Modern planes, including the Douglas DB7 (Boston) and Martin 167 (Maryland) light bombers, were also arriving from the United States, but the French Air Force still needed time to complete its re-equipment, just as Britain needed time to create an army.

For the War Office, the Germany Army's crushing victory in Poland was conclusive proof that armies and air forces working together would decide the outcome of the war. General Ismay, Chamberlain's top military advisor, spoke of the 'smashing success' of the 'German Army-cum-Air Force' and thought the British should 'take a leaf out of their book'. Perhaps it was time to try and reopen the Army-air-support issue with Newall, he suggested.[16] Leslie Hore-Belisha, the Secretary of State for War, warned Chamberlain how unsatisfactory the current situation was. The German Air Force was largely trained for army support, whereas the RAF was not; it was 'dangerous to talk glibly about switching it from England to France at will'. Only by allocating a proportion of the Air Force to the Army could the necessary air support be guaranteed.[17]

Chamberlain seemed rather frustrated that this was an issue that needed to be raised at ministerial level. He asked Chatfield, the Minister for the Coordination of Defence, to sort it out. Chatfield was equally annoyed that such controversies should emerge at this late hour and felt it really was something the Chiefs of Staff ought to be able to sort out between themselves.[18] Given that having a European Expeditionary Force was not on the agenda until months before the outbreak of war, it was perhaps not so surprising. As a former First Sea Lord, Chatfield should have been more aware than most of the Air Ministry's traditional reluctance to cooperate with either Army or Navy.

The Air Ministry found itself very much on the defensive. Even their own intelligence reports agreed that in Poland the German Air Force had been used to support the German Army, not to deliver a knockout blow. It was also clear that they had done this very successfully. All sorts of planes from heavy bombers to fighters seemed to have been used in low-level attacks on Polish forces. As long as the Polish fighter force was still active, these operations had been covered by substantial fighter escorts. Attacks on communication centres had caused civilian casualties, but the intended targets were communications rather than people.

This indirect support was more in line with Air Staff thinking, and this was what the Air Ministry tried to focus attention on. Poland had collapsed because bombing in the rear had caused commanders to lose control, and to prove this was the Luftwaffe's aim, Air Ministry staff trawled through German General Staff manuals to find evidence that this was official policy. As for the low-level attacks on Polish troops, these would have suffered heavy casualties if they had been tried against an 'organised air defence system'.[19]

The Air Staff were determined to make radar the cornerstone of the tactical fighter force. The British lectured their ally on the inadequacies of their air defence reporting system. They explained their plans to incorporate French fighters into a continuous air defence system stretching from the Orkneys to Tunisia. The French were as worried by long-range bombing as the British, and they were very happy to use radar to strengthen rear defence. It was agreed that forty RDF stations would be deployed along a line stretching from the Channel coast to Switzerland. However, the French had no intention of relying on controlled interception to win air superiority over the battlefield. As No. 22 Group had tried to explain, fighters had to be used far more flexibly. Even in the interception role, enemy bombers could hit a front-line target and retreat long before scrambled fighters could reach them. The British hoped the French would eventually see the error of their ways and set about extending the Fighter Command system. By the spring of 1940, six radar sites were operating, covering the North East of France as far south as Le Cateau.[20]

While the Air Ministry chose to focus on what happened to the rear of the Polish Army, War Office reports passed on to the Air Ministry emphasised how close air support had supported the German Army on the battlefield by helping to break through Polish defences and disrupt counterattacks. German reconnaissance planes identified the targets. Dive-bombers, low-level fighters, and even medium bombers engaged the targets. The 'fighters' probably included the small number of Henschel HS 123 single-seater ground-attack biplanes the Luftwaffe had used. These had made an enormous impression on the Poles. As in Spain, low-level strafing and bombing had caused more problems than the heavier bomb loads dropped from higher altitudes.[21]

The Air Ministry took all these observations in their stride. In the 'special' conditions prevailing in Poland, 'where complete air superiority was obtained, close support was, as we anticipated, very effective'.[22] The obvious corollary of this was to make sure that the enemy did not have air superiority over the British and French Armies by providing adequate fighter cover—or, indeed, to go one step further and exploit that superiority to provide Allied forces with maximum close air support. However, the Air Staff had no intention of developing the argument that far.

The Air Staff stubbornly insisted that events in Poland had done no more than reinforce the lesson already learned in the First World War, China, and Spain; in all these examples, close air support had been a misuse of airpower. The Air Staff struggled to think of any examples in the First World War where British air support on the battlefield had been effective. There was, however, no shortage of examples where opportunities had been missed to use air power correctly to isolate the battlefield and prevent reinforcements arriving.

When Air Staff talked about air support on the battlefield not being 'effective', they really meant 'decisive'. There were countless examples where it had been effective, but there were no examples where it had been decisive on its own. The opportunities to isolate the battlefield had not been missed—it had been attempted many times—but it simply had not been possible to do. The truth was that air power was not capable of achieving decisive results in the rear or on the battlefield. However, it could achieve useful results, and the closer to the front line the Air Force was operating, the more useful they were.

For the Air Staff, however, being useful was not enough. It did not want the Air Force to be 'ancillary' or 'auxiliary'; the all-conquering bomber was worthy of a more decisive role. Air forces should be wining wars on their own, ideally by bombing the enemy country. If airpower had to be used tactically, it should at least have the opportunity to win a battle on its own. Attacking communications deep in the rear gave the Air Force a semi-independent role with an opportunity to claim a clear-cut, decisive influence on the outcome of a battle. The Air Force did not want to be just another Army tool. The battlefield was not the place for an air force. The Air Staff confidently concluded that the concentration of fighters and anti-aircraft guns on the Western Front would make close air support impossible for both sides.[23] Unfortunately for the Allies, this would prove to be only half-true; the Luftwaffe would make sure it was possible for one side.

The success the Luftwaffe had achieved in Poland required an adjustment in Air Staff theory. AASF Operational Instruction No. 3 conceded that bomber aircraft had proved extremely valuable 'in support' (underlined in the original document) of an advancing army, but it had not yet proven it could be used in defence *against* an advancing army.[24] Arguably, this was only because the Wehrmacht had not yet been forced to retreat. It was a convenient argument given that neither the French nor British armies were planning to advance at this stage of the war.

This conclusion ignored the fact that one of the most successful interventions on the battlefield by the RFC in the First World War helped halt the German advance in March 1918. This had always been viewed by the Air Ministry as a special case, a dire emergency that justified risking direct intervention. Turning an enemy retreat into a rout, as had happened with the Turkish and Austrian armies at the end of the First World War, was another special case.[25] In fact, in the closing stages of the First World War, close air support on the battlefield was a standard Air Force contribution in all defensive and offensive actions.[26] Two decades later, it seemed the British Army could only expect direct support on the battlefield if it had already won the battle or was about to lose it.

The War Office expected much more. Gen. Hugh Massy, the Deputy Chief of the Imperial General Staff, insisted that close cooperation between Allied ground and air forces on the Western Front would be essential if a German offensive was to be defeated. Britain had some catching up to do; the Germans had unified control of air and land forces, whereas the British did not. The British Army had to have its own support squadrons specifically designed for low-level bombing and strafing.

As the Air Ministry did not want to do anything about it, the War Office decided they would take matters into their own hands. They would design their own specialist Army support plane and get Army personnel to fly them. In September, the War Office laid out its plans for a massive tactical strike force. Each division would have three close-support squadrons, each with eighteen planes, which meant over 500 close-support planes for the first ten divisions. It was assumed losses would be heavy. Advancing infantry could expect 50 per cent losses in an assault, so it seemed reasonable to assume similarly heavy losses among the air units supporting them. Substantial reserves would therefore be required. Once full mobilisation was complete, the British Army would require a fleet of over 10,000 machines for its fifty-five divisions.[27] A call went out for any soldiers with any flying experience to volunteer for what was now being referred to as 'our Air Arm'. Hore-Belisha asked Newall to arrange for their training.

The aircraft they were to fly was to be similar to the Soviet Polikarpov R-5 and German Henschel HS 123 biplanes used in Spain and Poland. The aircraft would be slow (just 160 mph), but very manoeuvrable, unsophisticated, and cheap to mass-produce. John Moore-Brabazon, an early aviation pioneer, ex-RFC officer, and now a Conservative MP, came up with some designs. One was a simple single-seater pusher, which he believed could be built at the rate of 500 per month. The second was a 200-mph low-powered twin-engine plane, similar in concept to the early versions of the Henschel HS 129 the Germans were testing at the time. He claimed this could be in production by the end of 1940. To save time, Sir Edmund Ironside, the recently appointed Chief of the Imperial General Staff, suggested that suitable aircraft could be ordered from abroad.[28]

The concept caused enormous excitement within the War Office. Like the German close-support planes in Poland, they would be guided to their targets by army-cooperation aircraft hovering above the battlefield. The plane was expected to make as big an impression on the enemy as the tank had in the First World War. This time, the War Office would not make the mistake of deploying their new weapon prematurely, as they had with the tank; the new tactical bomber force would be created in secret and not deployed until it was capable of making a decisive contribution. The expectation that the appearance of this huge fleet of close-support bombers would come as a great shock to the enemy was perhaps rather optimistic given that the idea was based on the widespread use of similar tactics by the Luftwaffe.

It seemed like an absurd, even naïve suggestion, but once again the Army was feeling its way towards a low-flying, slow-moving close-support aircraft that would have plenty of time to line up its target. The Army did not need a plane capable of flying huge distances at enormous altitudes and high speeds; their close-support bomber would operate from within the ranks of the Army and would literally accompany the troops into battle. The concept was essentially extremely sophisticated; the high loss rates might have belonged to the First World War, but the ability to fly low and slow over the battlefield belonged to a future era of attack helicopters.

As far as the Air Ministry was concerned, it was all total madness. Moore-Brabazon's proposals were underpowered, would require an enormous take off run, would be difficult to control, and would be easily shot down. The resources did not exist to build them, nor to train the crews to fly them; it was far better for the Army to rely on the existing RAF bomber force.[29] The Air Ministry had every reason to be worried by the production problems, having already been forced to cut back planned aircraft production from 3,000 per month to 2,550 per month in order to free up resources for the expanding Army. The more production capacity that went into building army support planes, the less there would be for strategic bombers.

On 8 November 1939, the War Cabinet ruled that it was 'essential that the whole of the Air Striking Force should be available for whatever the strategic situation might demand'. The Air Ministry was told to reassure the War Office that the Army would get the RAF's full support if it needed it and that a proportion of suitable machines would be earmarked specifically for Army support. Chatfield was given the task of hammering out an agreement between the Air Ministry and the War Office. Given that Chatfield had led the crusade to free the Fleet Air Arm from Air Ministry control, the Army might have expected some sympathy for a similar independent, Army-controlled air arm. Chatfield, however, ruled out any possibility of an 'Army Air Force'. The AASF would be detached from Bomber Command and combined with the Air Component to form the British Air Forces in France (BAFF). On 15 January, Barratt took command. Chatfield described this 'command' as analogous to Coastal Command, although the key word, 'command', was significantly missing in its title.[30] It was only as permanent as the existence of British forces in France. In January 1940, this seemed permanent enough.

The Army seemed to have the control they wanted. The AASF could be reassigned to Bomber Command for strategic air operations, but only if the cabinet approved. No. 2 Group remained part of Bomber Command, but the understanding was that this Group would also be available to BAFF for tactical operations. In total, the BEF would have around 250 bombers. As far as equipment was concerned, the cheap, low-performance ground-attack plane the War Office wanted could not possibly become available before 1941. In any case, the Air Ministry insisted it would be inferior to existing medium bombers.[31]

Nevertheless, the War Cabinet had specifically committed the Air Ministry to the design and manufacture of a specialist Army support bomber.[32] Three days later— wasting no time—the Air Staff informed the Army General Staff that the Blenheim was the specialist Army support bomber it wanted.[33] This was scarcely the case. It was a very large plane to be operating low over the battlefield; trials had already demonstrated that even the Blenheim I did not have sufficient manoeuvrability at low level to pick out and hit specific targets. The heavier, longer-range Blenheim IV was even less manoeuvrable. There was also no need for the Army to have a plane with a range of nearly 1,500 miles. The Hawker Henley, which was still in production, was much closer to what the Army wanted.

However, the Henley only had a range of 500 miles, and range was important for the Air Ministry. It only needed cabinet approval to get the BAFF bombers back into the strategic fold and the Air Staff wanted to make sure its future equipment would be suitable. Newall remained convinced that bombing would win the war, and his priority was still to get the get the strategic air offensive going as quickly as possible. An invasion of Belgium and the Netherlands would not be the signal to start bombing German Army lines of communication, but rather an opportunity for RAF bombers to take the direct route to the Ruhr before the Germans could push their air defences further west. The Air Staff still hoped No. 2 Group Blenheims and even AASF Battles would take part.

If the RAF was to take advantage of this brief window of opportunity at the beginning of a German offensive, the Air Staff had to have authorisation from the British and French governments in advance. Opposition was fierce. General Gamelin, the overall Allied commander, was appalled by the idea, believing that the beginning of a potentially decisive battle was the worst possible time to divert bombers to an attack on German industry. Even if the attacks were successful, they could not possibly have any effect on the battle in progress. The Air Ministry disagreed, arguing that the Germans would be forced to pull back fighter and anti-aircraft defences to defend the Ruhr, making it easier to attack German columns. Anyway, the Ruhr was so close to the front line that the general disruption bombing would cause would be bound to delay the German advance.[34]

British Army commanders were quick to back Gamelin. Pownall, now Gort's chief of staff at BEF HQ, did not think delaying the offensive against the Ruhr by a week would make any difference to such a long-term offensive. On the other hand, 'a week or so's air attack on invading Germans might well be disastrous to their whole campaign on land'.[35] There was no immediate decision from the politicians, but if the RAF could not bomb the Ruhr, the Air Staff did not want to waste their 'heavies' bombing communication targets. All the British and French Generals could squeeze out of the Air Ministry was a promise to use two Whitley squadrons to bomb communications in Germany west of the Rhine. The rest of the force would be waiting for permission to bomb the Ruhr.

The War Office was assured that 'if the land operations assume decisive importance', Bomber Command would intervene. The problem was determining at which point a battle assumed sufficient importance. If Bomber Command only intervened when the enemy had gained the upper hand and the Allies were facing defeat, it might already be too late. The Army wanted bomber intervention as early as possible to prevent a crisis arising. Ludlow-Hewitt did not believe he could afford to divert any more bombers from the Ruhr offensive, having already lost the Battles and probably the Blenheims. Without the Blenheims, Ludlow-Hewitt feared the attack would fail. The Air Ministry assured Ludlow-Hewitt it would do its best to make sure they were available, but it warned him that it might be difficult to fend off Army appeals for help if ground operations were underway.[36] Supporting the Army was seen as an onerous task that was getting in the way of Air Staff plans.

Operations on the Western Front soon made the idea of using the Battle against the Ruhr—even in a 25-mile dash across the Dutch border—seem rather fanciful. The Battle squadrons in France were soon flying 'high altitude' photo-reconnaissance missions. As these penetrated further into enemy airspace, the risks of interception grew. Escorts were not provided; it was assumed that by flying in flights of three to six planes, the Battles would be able to beat off any attack.[37] The term 'high altitude' was rather misleading. The Battle could not fly very high and formation flying required the planes to fly well below their ceiling. Playfair, the commander of the AASF, was sufficiently concerned to fly the missions when he knew French fighters were in the vicinity.[38] On 20 September, however, no fighters were around to prevent two out of a formation of three being shot down. The French duly agreed to provide much closer fighter escorts.

These would not last very long. On 28 September, a meeting was held with French Air Force officials to discuss French requests for more British fighters. Vuillemin, the commander of the French Air Force, used the need to escort British reconnaissance planes as an example of the ever-increasing demands on his limited fighter strength. Air Vice-Marshal Evill, Barratt's Senior Air Staff Officer, rather curtly explained that RAF bombers and reconnaissance planes had no need of French escorts. What Playfair (or indeed the French) made of this is not clear, but the French Air Force commander can hardly be blamed for ordering these apparently unwanted escorts to cease.[39] Two days later, five unescorted Battles were intercepted by Bf 109s and four were shot down. The fifth was chased back to its base, where it crash-landed. That was the end of unescorted formations of reconnaissance planes. It was not just the Battles that were vulnerable. The day before, two Blenheims flying separate long-range reconnaissance missions were also shot down. No-one believed the short-range Lysanders would do any better when their turn came. A new approach to reconnaissance was required.

Flying Officer Maurice Longbottom and Wing Commander Bob Cotton were already investigating alternatives. Both had been members of a pre-war clandestine photo-reconnaissance flight that had conducted surveillance missions over Germany. They were now set the task of evading detection in normal combat operations. A highly polished and lightened Blenheim failed to achieve the required performance, so Cotton's team tried the same approach with a Spitfire. A couple of wing cameras replaced the guns, and with even the smallest crevice smoothed over, the plane was 15 mph faster than the standard fighter version. Cotton was soon investigating ways of making the aircraft fly a little further. When a heavier metal airscrew replaced the early wooden model, a 75-lb lead weight had to be inserted in the rear fuselage to balance the plane. This happened to be about the weight of an empty 29-gallon fuel tank, so Cotton replaced the ballast with a tank. When the tank was full, the plane was a little more difficult to handle, but as soon as the fuel was used up, handling was normal. This version was able to photograph the German naval base at Wilhelmshaven. The cavities in the leading edge of the Spitfire's wing, where the fighter's original evaporative cooling system had been, was another convenient place for more fuel. Eventually, with additional wing tanks, the plane would be capable of flying as far as Berlin.[40]

In November 1939, a special survey flight arrived in France to reconnoitre targets for Bomber Command. The unit included a single photo-reconnaissance Spitfire.

Although intended for strategic reconnaissance, Barratt was soon using the aircraft to gather information on German front-line defences. The results were so impressive that Barratt asked for more, and No. 212 Squadron, with eight photo-reconnaissance Spitfires, was attached to Barrett's headquarters.[41] Cloud or mist often made it impossible to achieve usable results, and even when skies were clear, the appearance of condensation trails often made the position of the plane so obvious that sorties had to be abandoned. There was, however, no reason why the Spitfire could not use its speed to evade interception at lower altitudes, especially over shorter distances. As the fighting in Spain had demonstrated, single-seater fighters made very good reconnaissance planes.

The problem was that Spitfires were very precious commodities. Dowding wanted every machine he could lay his hands on, and Cotton could not get enough for the high-altitude strategic reconnaissance role the Air Staff considered important. Getting any for tactical reconnaissance was even more difficult. The RAF would have to continue relying on Blenheims and Lysanders; the only hope was that the Air Staff would change its mind about fighter escorts.

Meanwhile, the specialist army support plane Peirse had promised the War Office would replace the Battle and Blenheim was providing more evidence of the Air Staff's determination to prioritise strategic bombing. Specification B.11/39 was supposed to produce a dual-purpose low/medium-level bomber for tactical and short-range strategic missions. The cabinet instruction to make sure the RAF had planes suitable for Army support seems to have jolted the Air Ministry into dropping the medium-level bombing capability. When Slessor heard about this, he was furious. The decision was, he claimed, the result of the 'misconception that the bomber will be used primarily against targets on the battlefield'.[42] Its medium-altitude bombing capability was hastily restored.

Neither of the proposed adaptations of existing planes—the Vulture-powered Battle and the Beaubomber—looked like they could contribute much to a long-range bombing offensive. No one wanted another single-engine long-range bomber. Freeman thought the Beaubomber was a waste of everybody's time and only went to see a mock-up because he felt he ought to go through the motions of showing some interest.[43] Something with more long-range potential was required. The project was re-launched as B.7/40.[44] It required an even larger machine with power-operated dorsal and ventral turrets. It was not likely to produce a nimble attack bomber.[45]

The Blenheim was the interim solution the Air Ministry had promised the War Office. Specification B.6/40 listed the modifications required to turn the Blenheim IV medium bomber into low-level ground-attack plane. The Blenheim V would have Mercury engines optimised to give high output at low-level. It would be armoured, carry a 1,000-lb bomb load, and have a range of just 450 miles. However, the armour was to be removable so that it could carry more bombs and fuel and operate as a conventional medium bomber. For the low-level role, it would fly as a two-seater with a solid nose and fixed forward-firing guns for strafing.

For longer-range missions, the plane was to carry a crew of three or four, with the solid nose replaced by a glazed bomb-aiming position.[46]

It was not a quick fix. The new exchangeable nose was a major redesign, and the plane would have to be re-stressed to make sure it could manoeuvre at low altitude. With the plane now expected to stay in service until 1943, it was felt that several refinements that had previously not been worth bothering with should now be introduced. It was virtually a new plane. There was no lack of urgency— extra draughtsmen were brought in from the Rootes car firm to help out,[47] but a first prototype of what had now become the Bisley[48] was not expected until the autumn of 1940.

There was no immediate prospect of a replacement for the Blenheim or Battle. The Blenheim was the better long-range bomber and it began replacing AASF Battles, but after two squadrons had converted, it was realised that not enough were being built to enable both No. 2 Group and the AASF to operate the plane. There might be enough Blenheims by the autumn of 1940,[49] but with the Air Staff prioritising heavy bomber production, even this was far from certain. With the Fairey Battle being phased out of production, there might be nothing for the AASF. The Air Staff admitted that it might struggle to keep its promise to maintain a force of 250 tactical bombers for Army support.[50]

In December 1939, 300 American Douglas DB7s were ordered to help ease the problem. Rather than using the DB7a version Douglas were supplying to the French, the Air Ministry preferred to wait for the heavier and longer-range but slower and less manoeuvrable DB7b. This version would not be available until 1941, but the Air Staff considered it worth the wait because it would be more capable of contributing to the strategic air offensive. It was not clear exactly what would happen between September 1940, when the RAF would start running out of Battles, and the following spring, when the American DB7b Bostons began to arrive. The Hampden and even the Albemarle—both far larger than the Blenheim—were suggested as alternatives. The squadrons might have to carry on until the spring of 1941 with whatever Battles remained.[51]

The decision to soldier on with the Battle through the decisive 1940 summer campaigning season made getting the best out of the bomber an urgent issue. History has decided that the Fairey Battle was no better suited to short-range tactical bombing than its original role of long-range strategic bombing. It was slow and large, but it was no slower than the German Ju 87 Stuka and not much larger than the Russian Il-2 Sturmovik ground-attack plane. It was reasonably manoeuvrable and offered a smaller target to ground fire than other twin-engine bombers available to the RAF. However, to survive low-level operations it either had to be escorted at medium altitude (like the Ju 87) or armoured (like the Il-2). Preferably it needed both.

Fighter escorts were not RAF policy, so it seemed the only alternative was to use the Battle at low-level. Mock attacks on BEF columns immediately suggested losses to anti-aircraft fire might be heavy.[52] Air Chief Marshal Brooke-Popham, one of the RFC's first squadron commanders and a leading figure in the development of the RFC and RAF, thought something should be done about it. Some basic armour had already been fitted to the Battle, mainly to protect the crew from fighter attack. Brooke-Popham suggested more armour and self-sealing tanks should be added. The initial response from Fairey was not encouraging. The plane was already at the limits of what it could safely carry. However, in its new short-range tactical role it did not have to carry its full fuel load, and removing the fuselage tank saved 300 lbs. This would enable the plane to carry an extra gun, firing rearwards through the floor of the plane, and an extra 200 lbs of armour. This appears to have been approved, and ninety sets of armour were apparently dispatched to France.[53] More weight could have been saved by dispensing with the navigator and autopilot, both scarcely necessary for short-range missions. However, the Air Staff were determined to keep open the option of using the Battle to attack the Ruhr. It seems the ventral gun was fitted, but not the extra armour.[54] The autopilot and the third crew member were also retained.[55]

Interestingly, for some of the exercises, the Battles flew with Hurricane escorts. It was an early indication that the RAF in France was beginning to adapt now that it was freed from the control of Bomber and Fighter Commands and had the French Air Force as an alternative model. There were problems escorting low-flying bombers; a close escort puts the fighters at a serious height disadvantage, while a more indirect escort at altitude might not provide much protection. Ideally, both are required. In Spain, bombers had been covered by tiers of fighters. The two Hurricane squadrons attached to the AASF had their primary role switched from airfield defence to escort, but defending ten squadrons required more than two fighter squadrons. In Spain, there had often been twice as many fighter escorts as bombers. The Air Component had the same problem; even Park was warning Dowding that the Lysander army-cooperation squadrons could not hope to operate successfully without a fighter escort.[56] The Blenheims also needed escorts, yet there were only four fighter squadrons to defend nine Blenheim and Lysander squadrons.

With the French pleading for more fighters, the British had every reason to feel guilty about Slessor's 'five or six hundred good short-range fighters sitting in England unable to contribute'. The number of RAF fighters in the United Kingdom was not going unnoticed across the Channel. The French pointed out to the British Government that the Allied fighter force in France faced a far stronger threat than RAF squadrons in Britain. Just to equalise the odds required the transfer of an additional 180 fighters from Britain to France. The British Ambassador in Paris reinforced the message. The French needed as much support as Britain could provide, and, rather pointedly, suggested that the question of air reinforcements to France should not be left in the hands of Air Force commanders. Chatfield was not impressed and told Chamberlain to take no notice.[57]

The French had been promised another couple of fighter squadrons if the Germans launched an autumn offensive, but just listing what these eight squadrons would be expected to do underlined how inadequate the number was. The two Gladiator squadrons were to protect the BEF, two Hurricane squadrons would escort the reconnaissance Blenheims and Lysanders, two more would defend BEF communications in the rear, and two would 'assist' the AASF.[58] It was easy to dismiss the inadequate number of fighters as a French problem, but the French were not asking for British fighters to defend their cities; it was not altruism that was required. It was in Britain's interest to make sure the French could resist a German attack—Britain could not afford to lose France. Yet there were not even enough British fighters in France to defend RAF planes.

Dowding did not see this as his problem. His Fighter Command was not a resource for the benefit of the Allied cause; it existed solely to defend Britain. The German bomber was the danger, not the German Army.

4

The Bomber Reigns Supreme

For the Air Staff, it was not just the number of fighters going to France that was a problem. They were equally unhappy that so many fighters were being built. Daylight bombing would win the war, not air defences. The Battles and their hand-held guns might have been unable to fight their way through enemy defences, but surely the better-armed twin-engined bombers and their power-operated turrets would do better.

Targets with any civilians nearby were still off-limits for Bomber Command, but there were plenty of warships to bomb in the Wilhelmshaven area. Initially, flak, rather than fighters, appeared to be the main problem. On the afternoon of 4 September, ten Blenheims bombed German warships from low altitude. Four were lost to flak and a fifth to a fighter. Even this had been damaged by flak first. Fighters also shot down two out of fourteen Wellingtons, but Bomber Command preferred to believe that these too had been the victims of flak.[1]

These were already unsustainable loss rates, but the Air Staff seemed to take some comfort from the fact that anti-aircraft fire seemed to be the main problem. Their theories about bombers defending themselves had not been disproved. On 29 September, a formation of five Hampdens set off to bomb more German warships. They were intercepted by Bf 109s and all five were shot down. The disappearance of an entire formation meant that there were few clues as to what had happened. A German broadcast rather obligingly revealed that the formation had been the victims of German fighters, but it was easy to believe that this was mischievous misinformation. In truth, it was scarcely any consolation that it might be flak rather than fighters that was causing the problem. The horrendous losses being suffered by bomber formations that were not even crossing the German coast seemed to have already proved that a daylight strategic air offensive against targets inside Germany was impossible.

Poor weather in October and November prevented any major operations, but on 3 December twenty-four Wellingtons set off to attack more German naval targets. Some of the Wellingtons now had the far more efficient power-operated Frazer Nash tail and nose turrets. The formation was picked up by the rapidly expanding

German radar system and intercepted by Bf 109s and Bf 110s. Crews reported that in the face of concentrated defensive fire, German pilots appeared reluctant to press home their attack. No bombers were lost to fighters or flak and one fighter was claimed destroyed. This was much more encouraging. The Luftwaffe did indeed lose one fighter and they were impressed by the defensive firepower of the Wellington.

On 14 December, more Wellingtons attacked German warships of Wilhelmshaven from low-level. They were engaged over the target by anti-aircraft fire and Bf 109s of II/JG 7. This time, the German fighters claimed seven Wellingtons; in fact, five were shot down over the target and a sixth crashed in England. Crews were again convinced the losses had been inflicted by flak, but no claims were made by German anti-aircraft units.[2]

Four days later, another twenty-two Wellingtons attacked shipping in the same area. This time they flew at 10,000 feet to avoid the anti-aircraft guns. However, this also made it easier for German radar to pick up the formation. Cannon-armed Bf 110s and Bf 109s rose to intercept and were able to attack the British bombers from beyond the range of their machine-gun defensive fire. The Messerschmitts also had ample performance to attack the undefended flanks of the bomber formation. Even so, attacking from the rear was easier, and, for accuracy, many pilots approached within machine-gun range. The German pilots noted that the Wellington burned easily. Many were seen fleeing the battlezone with petrol pouring from their punctured, unprotected fuel tanks. Eleven were shot down over the target, one crashed in the North Sea, and six more crashed in England. Eighteen out of twenty-two had been lost. Britain's best bomber had been blown out of the skies.[3]

RAF commanders were stunned. This time there could be no doubt that fighters were responsible. The belief that the defensive fire from tight formations would enable the bomber to fight their way through lay in tatters. The Air Ministry desperately sought explanations; perhaps the bombers had been particularly unlucky and had met a crack German unit? Some blamed the losses on ill-discipline among the crews. In what was described as 'criminal' conduct, aircrews were unfairly and shamefully accused of endangering their comrades by failing to maintain the correct defensive formation.[4]

Many had anticipated problems, but not even the pessimistic Ludlow-Hewitt had feared anything on this scale. These were not missions skirting around Belgium and the Netherlands, heading for the Ruhr—the bombers were not even crossing the German coastline. It was a catastrophe for the entire British bombing strategy.

At least the concerns that many had been expressing for some time, and the earlier losses, meant steps were already being taken to make RAF bombers less vulnerable. The plans for armouring planes—forgotten once memories of the Sudetenland crisis had passed—were hastily revived. By October, all production Battles, Blenheims, and Hampdens were being delivered with some armour fitted, and those already in service were being retrospectively armoured. In November, it had been agreed that all combat planes had to be equipped with self-sealing tanks wherever possible.[5] Where it was not (as with the Wellington's integral wing tanks), they would get some armour protection. The first Wellingtons with armoured wing tanks became available early in 1940.[6] The loss of two Wellingtons out of a formation of three on one of their first missions was not encouraging.

There were ways of improving the defensive armament of the bombers. Fitting ventral guns in the case of the Blenheim[7] and beam guns in the Wellington and Hampden, or reinstating the ventral turret in the case of the Wellington, would eliminate some of the blind spots. Twin machine guns could replace single guns. The decision to double the Hampden's dorsal and ventral armament was taken early in October, and an interim arrangement, with a limited traverse, was introduced immediately, while a proper mounting was developed. The heavy losses had also forced Ludlow-Hewitt to change his mind about tail turrets. He now wanted these retained in future designs, with heavy, 0.5-inch calibre machine guns if cannon were not possible.[8]

Cannon seemed the only sure way of ensuring the bombers would not be outgunned by interceptors. Manufacturers were preparing mock-ups of the 'Mark 2' Stirling, Halifax, and Manchester with the low-profile dorsal and ventral cannon turrets, but doubts remained about whether these designs could accommodate the new turrets.[9] All these bombers would also have to carry extra armour and self-sealing tanks. Bomb load and range were bound to be reduced. Even if it was possible to introduce all the changes, the new versions were not going to be available for some time.

There were already enough problems to resolve with the initial production versions of these bombers. The Stirling had crashed, the Manchester's Vulture engines were unreliable, and the top speeds of the Manchester and Halifax were no better than those of the Hampden and Blenheim. The armament of the Manchester had been increased with a machine-gun dorsal turret and the Halifax with a ventral turret, but even these were stretching the designs to the limit. The 700-lb turrets meant 700 lbs less fuel or bombs.[10] The next generation of heavy bombers were looking inadequate before they even entered service.

There was no hint of any of these problems when discussing the future prospects of the bomber force with the government. In January 1940, Peirse assured the cabinet that the Halifax/Stirling/Manchester generation of bombers flew too high and too fast and were too well-armed for the German air defences to cope with. With these planes, Bomber Command would be able to strike targets deep inside Germany by day at will. When it was suggested that the Luftwaffe might come up with some new type of fighter that could deal with these bombers, Peirse agreed that they might try, but they would never have one ready in time.[11] In fact, even before these bombers entered production, the German Air Force already had fighters in service with ample performance and firepower, and the Air Staff knew it. Peirse was misleading the government.

To complete the tale of woe, in March 1940, the one bomber type Peirse had avoided mentioning to the cabinet—the cheap, better-than-nothing Albemarle—finally struggled into the air. It only just about managed to get off the runway. The experimental steel tube/wood composite structure was far heavier than expected, and performance could not even match the Wellington. Even so, production went ahead.[12]

In desperation, the Air Staff turned to the shelved cannon-armed B.1/39 bombers. Handley Page and Bristol were both told to abandon work on their half-scale models and move straight to full-scale prototypes. However, there had been no dramatic technological breakthrough that made the specification any more realistic than when it had been abandoned just a few months before. The unpalatable truth was that the combination of defensive firepower, speed, range, and bomb load the Air Staff needed was simply not possible.

A new approach was needed. On 16 November, even before the catastrophic Wellington mission, Douglas had seen enough to become convinced that the high-speed bomber should at least be looked into.[13] High-speed versions of the Manchester, the Beaubomber, and even the existing Beaufighter and Beaufort were all considered,[14] but none of these offered anything like the required speed to outrun even the current generation of fighters.

De Havilland's proposal for an all-wooden design (at this stage still with a tail turret) was another option.[15] Freeman now ruled that the plane should carry no defensive armament whatsoever.[16] De Havilland claimed that by using the same Merlin as the Spitfire, they could produce an unarmed plane that was 20 mph quicker. They believed they could keep ahead of the opposition with constant upgrades as new, more powerful engines emerged. Each upgrade might bring six to nine months of superiority.[17] This scarcely seemed to be the basis for a sustained bomber offensive.

In March 1940, the Merlin-powered prototype of what would become the Mosquito was ordered and a contract placed for fifty, but there was not much confidence that this was the solution. The initial batch was to be built primarily for reconnaissance, with conversion to the bomber role only an option.[18] It seemed no existing bomber could deliver a sustained offensive by day, and there was little prospect of developing one that could.[19]

There was still the option of a fighter-escort, which would indeed eventually prove to be the solution. Ludlow-Hewitt had always wanted escorts. Before the war, Stevenson had suggested long-range versions of the Spitfire and Hurricane; after war had broken out, there was pressure from several different sources to produce long-range fighters. Dudley Pound, the First Sea Lord, wanted bombers approaching the country intercepted as far east as possible to protect the North Sea. Air Marshal Joubert de la Ferté at Coastal Command also began enquiring about the possibility of the Spitfire and Hurricane supporting his squadrons on the far side of the North Sea.[20]

For Dowding, it was all too reminiscent of 1916 and the distant offensive patrols flown beyond the Somme battlefields. Fighter patrols over the Western Approaches, where there would be no enemy fighters, were one thing, but operating on the other side of the North Sea, close to enemy airfields, was asking for trouble. Dowding wanted nothing to do with such half-baked ideas. Fighter Command's responsibilities extended as far as his early warning radar—anything beyond that was Coastal Command's responsibility.[21]

Nevertheless, there was enough interest in long-range fighters for the Air Staff to prepare a paper outlining what was possible. Four roles were listed: the protection of sea routes, fighter support for Naval operations, the interception of bombers heading for the United Kingdom, and fighter support in the Wilhelmshaven region and 'elsewhere in Germany'. The report stated:

> ...offensive operations against land targets in Germany, against objectives in Heligoland Bight, German naval bases or the Baltic would be facilitated by offensive fighter action in these areas.[22]

This would require a fighter capable of patrolling 450 miles from its base for one hour—a stiff requirement. A fighter with such a performance would not only be capable of operating over the Heligoland Bight; from bases in France, it could also patrol over Berlin for an hour.

Douglas was not optimistic,[23] but the work done on the long-range photo-reconnaissance Spitfire had shown that a lot of fuel could be packed into the single-seater.[24] These, of course, did not have to engage in high-speed combat, but much of the extra fuel would be burnt off just crossing the North Sea. Using the same additional internal tanks as the reconnaissance version and a couple of drop tanks, the range of the Spitfire could be increased to 1,000 miles with only a 5 mph loss of speed.[25] Douglas converted this into an ability to patrol for twenty minutes 350 miles from base. This brought the Ruhr within range of bases in the UK.

There were plenty of objections; the navigational problems would be too complex for the lone pilots and the long flights would be a severe test of morale. However, these problems had not stopped the development of the long-range reconnaissance Spitfire, where the pilot really was on his own. Supermarine warned that any attempt to introduce integral wing tanks on the production line would slow down deliveries. Douglas insisted the idea of a single-seater escort fighter was a myth anyway. The long-range Spitfire would be far inferior to the Bf 110. The twin-engine Bristol Beaufighter seemed a better bet,[26] or even larger three-seaters with turrets.[27]

Douglas agreed to allow development of the long-range Spitfire to continue, but not for the escort role. He saw it as a useful long-range interceptor that could operate over Holland and Belgium from bases in Britain. He ordered 100 sets of the rear fuselage tank and a further fifty sets of wing tanks for the longer-range version. Further orders would follow if these proved successful.[28] In France, air commanders were beginning to appreciate escorts were needed but the Air Staff and commanders in Britain continued to insist escorts were a misuse of fighter resources. It was not a question of range; single-seaters were simply inherently unsuited for the role.

There were no options left for daylight strategic bombing. Ludlow-Hewitt was now convinced that even if Bomber Command could fly across the Lowlands to the Ruhr, the proposed daylight strike on the Ruhr was an absurd proposition. A low-level approach would run into barrage balloon cables and heavy anti-aircraft fire. At higher altitudes, there was no way of avoiding enemy fighters and bombers would probably not be able to hit their targets. He warned the Air Staff that up to 50 per cent of the force might be lost. He did not believe the 170–180 bombers that would probably be available would achieve the degree of destruction that justified such losses. The consequences for Bomber Command would be catastrophic. The future commanders that would lead the more capable Stirlings, Halifaxes, and Manchesters into battle would be lost. An alternative way of using the bomber force had to be found until these better bombers arrived.[29] It seems that Ludlow-Hewitt still believed the Manchester, Halifax, and Stirling would solve all the problems.

Ludlow-Hewitt's dire predictions should have put paid to the Ruhr plan. The Air Staff, however, was not yet persuaded. There were already suspicions about Ludlow-Hewitt's commitment to the cause. The commander's warnings were ignored. In February, the Air Staff decided to approve the plan; however, as the losses might be heavy, it would only go ahead if the German Army was threatening to breakthrough on the Western Front. It was an extraordinary suggestion. Even if the expected devastation could be inflicted on the Ruhr, it is not clear why this would help stop a German advance.

If there was no critical crisis at the front, a way of sustaining an air offensive at a reduced cost had to be found.[30] Avoiding the heavily defended Ruhr might help. A new target was chosen—oil. This became Plan WA6 in Bomber Command's Western Air Plans. There seemed to be plenty of evidence that Germany was very short of this commodity. Germany had no natural supply and had invested huge sums in developing a rather uneconomic way of turning coal into oil. Here was a target that the British and French Army commanders might find more attractive; tanks and aircraft needed petrol, and if German production could be cut dramatically, the effects might be felt at the front quite quickly.[31] Oil refineries were relatively small targets, but at least they ought to be highly combustible. They were also spread throughout Germany and potentially less well-defended than the Ruhr.

Oil might be an easier target to sell to the generals, but there was no reason to suppose it would be any easier to attack. Many of the oil plants were in the Ruhr anyway, and those that were not would require a much deeper penetration into enemy airspace. However, the Whitleys of No. 5 Group had, perhaps, shown the way forward. Since the outbreak of war, these planes had been flying nightly missions deep inside German territory, dropping leaflets on German cities. The total ineffectiveness of German night defences came as almost as great a surprise as their effectiveness by day. Squadrons suffered very few losses to enemy action and, despite the often-atrocious weather, claimed to have found their targets with relative ease. They also reported seeing many inviting targets that deserved more than a bundle of leaflets. Here was a way to get the bomber offensive back on track; Bomber Command would use the cover of darkness to deliver precision attacks.

As early as January, Ludlow-Hewitt had been suggesting that until improved bombers arrived, a closer look should be taken at night bombing, 'a possibility little attention [had] so far been paid to'. This was not quite true; sufficient attention had been paid to it during the interwar years to establish that it was virtually impossible to hit anything by night. The fact that bomber crews had stumbled across inviting targets by chance was scarcely a guarantee that they would find a specified target on a specific night. It was certainly no guarantee they could hit it. Air Commodore Coningham, the commander of the Whitley Group, doubted his crews were dropping the leaflets on their assigned targets. Even Ludlow-Hewitt was realistic enough to suggest the scientists would need to come up with some way of making bombing by night easier.[32]

Desperation, however, drove the fantasy. Claims that night bombing could be just as accurate as day bombing were put forward as serious, sober judgments. Coningham came up with a clever system whereby bombers aimed at a prominent geographical feature a known distance from the target, with the bombsight offset appropriately. In trials, with no defences to worry about, bombs still missed their target by between 1,200 yards and 5,280 yards. In true Trenchardian style, the evidence was not allowed to get in the way of the theory. Nobody even considered investigating whether the available navigational equipment would enable bomber crews to get close enough to their target to start looking for it.[33] By deluding themselves into believing that the problems of bombing accurately by night had mysteriously and suddenly disappeared, the Air Staff had, at a stroke, solved the problem.

The early months of 1940 saw more effort put into preparing the force for nocturnal bombing than improving its chances of surviving by day. From January 1940, Wellingtons and Hampdens joined the Whitley on their leaflet-dropping missions.[34] The Blenheims of No. 2 Group and the Battles of the AASF also spent considerable time on night-flying training. Despite their tactical role, the Battles were being prepared for a nocturnal mine-laying operation along the Rhine, and the Ruhr was back as a potential target.[35]

Meanwhile, Bomber Command was trying out its new nocturnal precision-bombing strategy. On 19 March, as retaliation for a German raid on Scapa Flow, forty-seven Whitleys and Hampdens bombed the German seaplane base on the island of Sylt. It was a clear night with a quarter moon. Forty-one planes claimed to have found the base. No crews reported any difficulty hitting the target, and only one plane was lost; the raid was declared a major success, and confirmation soon arrived from various quarters. A friend of the air attaché in Denmark knew three workers who had been on the island at the time. After some 'liberal refreshment … to loosen the tongue', they revealed the damage had been severe. Other reports from visitors to Germany spoke of 150 dead and injured and a German nation shaken by the severity of the attack. Douglas thought it 'was probably the heaviest air attack on a single objective ever delivered'.[36]

However, photos brought back by Blenheims on 21 and 27 March failed to show any obvious damage. The crews reported an air base operating as normal.[37] It seemed possible that the delay had given the Germans enough time to repair or at least conceal the damage, but the final report on the raid was not entirely convinced. There was certainly no evidence to confirm precision bombing was possible by night. The report concluded that against easily identifiable targets on coasts or rivers and in good visibility, only about 50 per cent of experienced crews would even find the target. Very few inexperienced crews flying in less favourable circumstances were likely to be successful. It was an ominous assessment, but it was not allowed to dampen enthusiasm for precision nocturnal bombing.

In April 1940, Air Marshal Portal replaced Ludlow-Hewitt at Bomber Command. Ludlow-Hewitt's realism and reluctance to waste the lives of his aircrews in inadequate equipment was seen by many as defeatism, and many believed that it was time to replace him with someone who was less aware of the problems. Portal did not suffer from any of the doubts that afflicted his predecessor. In the First World War, he had been a fearless Army corps pilot who had thought nothing of weighing down his notoriously temperamental R.E.8 reconnaissance plane with bombs and setting off in darkness to find the enemy.[38] He perhaps found it difficult to appreciate the problems lesser pilots might face.

In the early '30s, while commanding British forces in Aden, Portal had demonstrated his ruthlessness by using his planes to bomb any tribes that stepped out of line. Portal was convinced an equally forthright application of the long-range strategic bombing force in a European conflict would bring equally decisive results. He was far less impressed than Ludlow-Hewitt about the value of tactical bombing. He believed using Blenheims and Battles to support the Army was a total waste of time—losses were bound to be heavy, and the sacrifice of the crews would serve no purpose. The practice would just divert effort away from the crucial offensive against German industry.

Portal was soon confidently predicting that even existing bombers could find and hit oil plants by night and do 'immense damage'.[39] This was the sort of talk the bomber advocates wanted to hear. Trenchard, convinced the war would have been won by now if RAF bombers had been allowed to bomb Germany, purred with delight as yet another of his protégés got the chance to show what the bomber could do.[40] The talk was confident, but strength of personality was not going to make it any easier for his bomber crews to find and hit their targets.

One unfortunate consequence of this confidence in nocturnal bombing was that it made Britain feel even more vulnerable. Nobody doubted that the German Air

Force had far more bombers and could inflict far more damage on Britain than Bomber Command could on Germany. Both Peirse and Douglas were genuinely nervous about taking the initiative in strategic bombing for fear of provoking a crippling counterblow by the Luftwaffe. There was now more reason than ever to close the gap and ensure the RAF could give as good as it got by building bombers rather than fighters.

This was not Dowding's priority. He had always insisted that until the home defence force had the required minimum fifty-three squadrons, priority had to go to expanding the fighter force. Having been pushed into a defensive stance by German superiority, the Air Staff was determined not to be pushed even further onto the defensive by Dowding. Soon after the outbreak of war, it was agreed that Dowding needed his fifty-three squadrons, and their formation was approved. However, resources had to be shared appropriately. Since the bomber force would be the main RAF contribution to victory, it should have priority.[41]

Dowding had at least got his squadrons. He was not going to give Newall the chance to change his mind; on the basis that once a squadron was formed, it was unlikely to be disbanded, he immediately set about creating (in embryonic form at least) the balance of eighteen squadrons with whatever was to hand. Maintenance units were combed for any half-serviceable combat planes. Commanders were transferred from other squadrons. Pilots were rushed from training units. Initially, none of these squadrons was anything like operational. Some could do no better than a handful of Battle bombers as token front-line equipment. Nevertheless, by the end of 1939, all fifty-three squadrons existed in some form or other. Many of them were equipped with the makeshift Blenheim IF, but this was not a problem for Dowding. He wanted a third of his fighter force to be equipped planes that could carry airborne radar and operate by night. Indeed, the more confidence there was in Bomber Command's ability to hit German targets under cover of darkness, the more AI-equipped night fighters were needed to defend Britain.[42]

It was far from certain how long the remaining two-thirds of the fighter force would continue to receive single-seaters. The immediate future of the Spitfire and Hurricane seemed secure—on the outbreak of war, orders for both were increased, with production switching to more powerful variants as quickly as possible. The massive new, state-of-the-art factory at Castle Bromwich would build the Spitfire II, powered by the Merlin XII with an upgraded supercharger. After that would come the vastly more powerful 1,400-hp Merlin XX, with a two-speed supercharger that maximised engine output at two different altitudes. This would power the Spitfire III and Hurricane II.[43]

This was as far as the Air Ministry wanted to take the Spitfire and Hurricane. The Air Ministry was anxious to move onto cannon-armed fighters (or at least the twelve-machine-gun Typhoon/Tornado) as quickly as possible. An additional 850 Hurricanes and 550 Spitfires were ordered, but these contracts were dwarfed by the orders for 1,500 Tornados (first delivery May 1940) and nearly 3,000

Beaufighters (first delivery January 1940). By January 1941, even Supermarine would be building Beaufighters instead of Spitfires. By January 1942, there would be no less than five Beaufighter production lines.[44]

No more Whirlwinds were ordered, partly because Westland had to concentrate on building Lysanders for the expanding Army,[45] but also because the Air Staff preferred the much larger Beaufighter. Dowding was not so enthusiastic about the cumbersome twin-engine fighter that was being hoisted upon him. The aircraft was ideal for carrying AI radar, but he was going to get far more than were required by the proposed number of night fighter squadrons. For the Air Staff, the Beaufighter was the future for day and night air defence.

Until the Beaufighter arrived, the Hurricane would be Fighter Command's principal fighter. It was extraordinary that more than a year after the fighter had been described as 'approaching obsolescence', the Air Ministry should be ordering more additional Hurricanes than Spitfires. By July 1940, the aircraft industry would be turning out 150 Hurricanes per month compared to just seventy-five Spitfires. Only in the spring of 1941 would Spitfire production overtake Hurricane output, by which time, it was hoped, both would be reaching the end of their operational careers.

There was reasonable confidence these fighters could deal with the bomber menace by day, but night defence was causing far more concern. This was the battle many thought would decide the war, and victory or defeat might depend on how well Bowen's Airborne Interception radar worked. In the winter of 1939–40, no one knew how long the bomber truce would hold. Bowen's team were left in no doubt that they were involved in a desperate race against time in which no less than the survival of the country was at stake.

With their east coast Bawdsey research centre considered too vulnerable, Bowen's team were shunted first to Perth, in Scotland, and then St Athan, in south Wales. There they had to set up their laboratories in a huge unheated hangar. Often open to the elements, the scientists were reduced to working in overcoats and gloves.[46] A visit from the King gave some idea of the importance attached to their work; the appalling conditions they were working under did not. As fast as the sets could be built, Blenheims were equipped with AI and rushed to No. 25 Squadron. The AI Mark I sets the scientists were fitting had scarcely been properly tested—never mind trialled—but front-line squadrons were now expected to use them.

They soon discovered how inadequate it was. This first version of AI had a range of less than 2 miles (9,000 feet). This would have been fine if ground radar could get the plane to within the promised 1 mile, as Bowen had been assuming. In practice, the figure was 4 miles at best. There was a gap between what ground radar could do and what airborne radar needed. If by good fortune the target was acquired, the problems were far from over. On the ground, with demonstration equipment, it all looked very straightforward—the target plane showed up as a clear kink on the 'trunk' of the Christmas tree. When the AI operators got into the air, they found the reality was quite different. The neat lines were quivering with interference and the distinctive kink of the aircraft echo was barely visible. The equipment often broke down, and when it did work, it was capricious to say the least. There were all sorts of puzzling anomalies. Aircraft that appeared to be in front were actually sometimes behind, and echoes suggesting the aircraft was on one side of the intercepting plane came from a target that was on the other side. Huge patience and constant tuning was required to coax any information out of the system.

Disillusion soon set in. Dowding ignored advice that it was probably counterproductive to expect squadrons to use equipment that clearly did not work. He insisted the training of No. 25 Squadron continue so that at least aircrews became more 'AI minded'. Indeed, a second squadron, No. 600, began getting the AI radar. Both squadrons were set the task of intercepting German planes dropping magnetic mines from 500 feet; unsurprisingly, not a single enemy plane was intercepted.[47] The fact that this failure came as a complete surprise to Fighter Command underlined how little the weaknesses of the system were understood. There was a huge gap between what Fighter Command believed it had and what the available equipment could do.[48] Many of the problems could only come to light by trial and error, and deploying AI operationally was arguably the quickest way of identifying the problems. However, exposing service personnel to a system that was so far short of anything remotely useful could only promote a deep distrust of the whole idea.

More reliable equipment was supposed to be on the way. The version of AI that No. 25 Squadron had to work with had always been considered an emergency effort, and only thirty sets were built. The fully engineered production version was expected to eliminate the most serious technical bugs. Better transmitters and receivers were also now available, and it was anticipated that these would improve performance. Three hundred AI Mark II sets were ordered in October for delivery by December, and four more Blenheim IF squadrons joined Nos 25 and 600 Squadrons. The new version was supposed to be capable of detecting a Heinkel-sized bomber at 3.5–4 miles and taking the fighter to within 300–500 feet of the target.[49] This just about made the handover from ground radar to AI possible, provided, of course, that the plane was more than 3.5–4 miles above the ground and not lost in the ground reflection.[50] In practice, the equipment rarely managed the performance it was credited with. Try as they might, the technicians could not get minimum range below 1,200 feet; on one test, maximum range was a mere 3,000 feet. Nor was it known why the equipment kept showing the target plane on the wrong side. The equipment was as useless as AI Mark I. An anxious Kingsley-Wood, the Secretary of State for Air, demanded regular updates on progress; a desperate Bowen worked through the Christmas holidays, trying to get to the bottom of the problems, but was forced to concede defeat. Plans to equip 300 Blenheims with the AI Mark II had to be abandoned. A handful were delivered for training purposes only.[51]

With the possibility of the bomber truce coming to an end at any moment, the pressure was intense, the frustration enormous, and tempers were becoming frayed.

Bowen thought he had solved the problem of the equipment showing the target on the wrong side by moving the aerials from the fuselage to the far side of the engines. He was furious when he discovered Rowe was allowing deliveries to go ahead with the old layout. Rowe was equally forthright in his response.[52] As it turned out, the new layout did not solve the problem anyway.

More sharp words were exchanged on how close the night fighter needed to get to see the enemy bomber. Bowen had been told to aim for 1,000 feet, but Rowe had been sent results of some more recent night visibility trials that suggested the fighter might have to get as close as 300 feet.[53] According to Rowe, Dowding told him that he would happily accept a maximum range of just 0.25 miles if he could get minimum range down to 100 feet. Rowe was left in no doubt about the seriousness of the problem; reducing minimum range might be the difference between winning and losing the war.[54] Bowen did not see minimum range as the biggest problem, and given the many problems he faced, he had a point. Since Bowen did not seem to want to do anything about it, Rowe got his AMRE team in Dundee and private companies working on the problem. More heated exchanges ensued when Bowen discovered that he was being bypassed.[55]

This frenzied endeavour was producing few dividends. For AI Mark III, Rowe's AMRE team installed a second transmitter to cancel out the fading end of each pulse. The shorter, more clearly defined pulse ought to reduce minimum range. An improved receiver and a more powerful transmitter were supposed to make possible the 3.5-mile range the abandoned Mark II should have achieved.[56] Despite these efforts, it was still impossible to detect a bomber closer than 1,000 feet. One hundred AI Mark III-equipped Blenheims were ordered in May 1940, more in hope than expectation.[57]

Doubts were growing that airborne radar could ever be the solution. Stevenson persuaded Douglas (Deputy Chief of the Air Staff) to set up a 'high powered committee … bending all its efforts to a solution of the urgent night fighting problem'.[58] In March, the 'Night Fighting Committee' sat for the first time. All the usual suspects (infrared, sound detection, 'stray radiation'—trials had detected it at a range of ten yards!) got an airing. Wing Commander William Helmore suggested mounting a searchlight in the nose of an AI-equipped fighter to solve the minimum range problem. Accompanying single-seaters would actually engage the enemy plane. Professor Frederick Lindemann, a close friend of Winston Churchill, wanted mines dropped on parachutes on the predicted path of a bomber. After attending one meeting, Saundby complained it was just like the old Tizard committee, with the same old ideas being discussed 'over and over again'.[59]

Airborne radar still seemed the best bet, but Tizard feared a practicable system could still take up to two years to develop.[60] One constructive decision made was to form an experimental flight to test night interception techniques, rather than using operational squadrons as testing grounds. On 10 April 1940, the FIU ('Fighter Interceptor Unit') was established at Tangmere.

No useable system had yet emerged, but the scientific breakthroughs kept coming. Bowen knew that many of the problems with AI would disappear if sufficient power at lower wavelengths could be achieved. A 30-cm wavelength would enable the signal to be focused ahead, which would eliminate ground reflections.[61] Getting it down to 15 cm would mean the focusing dish would fit in the nose of an aeroplane, but this seemed impossible—commercial companies were reluctant to try for anything less than 50 cm.[62] Then, in February 1940, two scientists at Birmingham University, John Randal and Harry Boot, stumbled across a way of producing as much power as the 1.5-metre system at just 10 cm. Centimetric radar was born. It meant greater precision and the end of the problems with ground reflections—so long as it could be turned into a useable system.

Dramatic progress was also being made with systems single-seater fighters could use. EMI developed a display where information on the horizontal and vertical elevation was fed into a single cathode ray tube with a spot representing the position of the enemy relative to the intercepting plane.[63] Range was displayed on a second tube. The radar operator had merely to highlight the chosen echo on the range indicator and the information on that target would appear automatically on the first screen. The pilot manoeuvred his plane until the dot was in the middle of the screen and the target would be straight ahead. This became AI Mark V. With the next version, AI Mark VI, the selection of the target would be automatic. Range was indicated by a horizontal bar that passed through the dot. The closer the bomber, the wider the line became. As the interceptor approached the intruder, the dot on the screen sprouted what looked like wings, which got bigger as the interceptor closed in on its target. The pilot would see in his cathode ray tube an electronic version of what he might expect to see in his gun sight.[64]

It was dazzling technology, but it was not producing a useable system. Even worse, it was not tackling the greatest danger facing the Allies. The bomber was not the most serious threat; it was the German blitzkrieg tank/air combination, which had defeated Poland so rapidly, that Britain should have been more worried about. As was the case with all radar research, the national resources invested were not huge and the development would have been justified whatever the country's overall defence priorities had been. However, while the government obsessed over the country's vulnerability to air attack, the failure to form even one of the three proposed armoured divisions attracted no concern, nor even comment. The tunnel-vision focus on defending the country from air attack was fatally weakening the country's ability to win the war, or indeed to avoid defeat. The crucial battles were going to be fought on the ground, not in the air over British cities.

While Dowding feared a future battle over British cities might be lost, RAF fighters in France were already losing a far more crucial battle. By April 1940, two Fighter Wing Servicing Units were in France, ready to accept four more fighter squadrons. As soon as Germany launched its offensive, the number of fighter squadrons in France would increase to ten.[65] It was still far too few to meet even RAF escort requirements;

with so few fighters, direct close escort was impossible. The only tactic that made any sense was to sweep clear of enemy fighters the area where RAF bombers and reconnaissance planes were operating. This at least seemed a plausible strategy, although with so few fighters, there was no real reason to believe it could succeed.[66]

With escort now on the BAFF agenda, fighter-*versus*-fighter combat had become one of the Hurricane's primary roles. Still, there was no rethink on the bomber-interception tactics pilots had been trained to use. Fighters still flew in tight 'vic' formations, which meant pilots were paying too much attention to the plane next to them and not enough to possible enemy fighters on their tail. With most RAF squadrons based far from the German frontier, there were few opportunities to find out how unsuitable these formations were. Hurricanes did not encounter German fighters until 22 December, when three Hurricanes of No. 73 Squadron, flying their normal 'vic' formation, were surprised by Bf 109Es of III/JG 53. Two were immediately shot down.[67] The advantages of the looser formations their German opponents were using were not appreciated. German fighters seemed to be jinking around all over the place, and these untidy-looking formations seemed to reflect ill-discipline and lower standards of training. It all looked very unprofessional compared to the inch-perfect, air-display RAF formations.

The first reaction to the German hit-and-run tactics was to get some protection—both pilots in the 22 December engagement had been killed instantly by bullets through the head. The decision to provide seat armour for fighters in France had been taken before the war and the first batch of thirty-two sets were sent to France in November, but they were then apparently forgotten.[68] It was only after this first encounter with German fighters that they were suddenly remembered. No. 1 Squadron, not waiting for officially approved armour, improvised its own by acquiring some armour plate from a crashed Battle.[69]

In the spring, the two AASF fighter squadrons were moved closer to the front. On 29 March, No. 1 Squadron had its first encounter with Bf 109s, claiming one without loss,[70] but on 23 April another flight of six Hurricanes from No. 73 Squadron were jumped by Bf 109Es, losing two of their number. Both pilots survived, which demonstrated the value of the armour, but the ease with which the Hurricane formations were being surprised by attacks from the rear was worrying. The British experimented with one or two pilots weaving to the rear of and higher than the main formation, watching out for enemy fighters. This was not a solution, just a way of enabling the pilots to focus all their attention on maintaining formation; the pilots needed to be looking out for the enemy, not where the fighter next to them was. Often, the two 'tail-end Charlies' would be the first to be picked off by the high-flying Messerschmitts.

At least the pilots of Nos 1 and 73 Squadrons were getting some experience of fighter-*versus*-fighter combat. The Air Component fighter squadrons stationed with the BEF behind the Belgian frontier had no chance of gaining any experience. No. 87 Squadron moved up to the front in May and shot down a Bf 110 on 9 May, but that was about it.

It should have been clear from the few combats that had taken place that the Hurricane was inferior to the German Bf 109E, especially in terms of speed. It seems these early encounters were enough to suggest that the theory that the even slower Gladiator was the ideal tactical fighter should not be put to the test. In April, the two Gladiator squadrons began converting to the Hurricane. Yet the advocates of the Gladiator had a point; in terms of manoeuvrability and responsiveness, the Gladiator was far superior to the Spitfire and Hurricane. At high speed, both the Spitfire and Hurricane were virtually impossible to manoeuvre. This was not too much of a problem for a bomber interceptor, but it was a problem for fighter-*versus*-fighter combat. Both the War Office and the Air Staff had been quite right to believe that high-speed interceptors were not ideal for tactical fighter operations, but the Gladiator was far too slow to be the solution.

In 1938, the French had given the Air Ministry an early clue that all might not be well with British fighter design. France was one of many countries showing an interest in the Spitfire. There were no immediate plans to release any for export, but as a gesture of friendship, the French were allowed to test an example.[71] Much to the Air Ministry's surprise, instead of pleas for immediate deliveries, the French decided they did not want it. They were impressed by its speed and very anxious to get hold of its Merlin engine, but the plane itself lacked the handling characteristics the French expected from a fighter. In this respect, it was markedly inferior to their own M.S.406 and the imported Curtiss Hawk.[72] This was confirmed by an RAF pilot who had flown a Hawk. He reported the American fighter was exceptionally easy to fly; it was more manoeuvrable than the Spitfire or Hurricane and there was no sign of any vibration, flutter, or snaking even when diving at 400 mph. At high speed, the pilot of a Hawk still had crisp, light, and effective control.[73]

A somewhat perplexed Air Ministry borrowed a French Curtiss Hawk to find out if it really was as good as it appeared. The American fighter was compared to the Spitfire and, interestingly, the sole prototype of Folland's Gloster F.5/34. This was effectively the monoplane development of the Gladiator, built to meet the same requirement as the Spitfire and Hurricane. It had first flown in 1936 and was as fast as the Hurricane, yet it retained the exceptional handling characteristics of its Gladiator predecessor.[74]

The trials confirmed that the Curtiss Hawk fully deserved its reputation. It was so easy to fly, the report concluded, that 'anyone who could fly a Hart could be sent off in one of these'. It responded well at low speeds and could outmanoeuvre the Hurricane and Spitfire, especially at high speed. It had an impressive rate of roll, which enabled the fighter to change directions quickly; this was not important for a bomber interceptor, but crucial in fighter-*versus*-fighter combat. The Curtiss fighter also offered the pilot a far better all-round view—again, not important when trying to shoot down a bomber in front, but, as Hurricane pilots were discovering, extremely valuable when enemy fighters were around. The fighter's only drawback was its relatively low top speed.

The Gloster F.5/34 was also flown against the Curtiss Hawk. It possessed many of the Hawk's qualities; it did not quite match the manoeuvrability of the American fighter, but it was just as easy to fly at high speed. It was also faster.[75] Indeed, with the same top speed as the Hurricane, the Gloster plane was the better fighter all round. Both the Hawk and the Gloster F.5/34 were much closer than the Hurricane to the agile fighter the War Office felt was needed over the battlefield.

The full significance of these findings was not appreciated, partly because trials with a captured Bf 109E revealed the German fighter was also a handful to fly at high speed. Nevertheless, the German fighter's other advantages should have made it clear it completely outclassed the Hurricane. As so often happens in comparative trials, it seems the advantages of the less familiar enemy type were underestimated. The trials demonstrated that the Bf 109E was 30–40 mph faster in level flight, quicker in the climb, and far superior at altitude. The Hurricane was considered more manoeuvrable, although this just referred to its ability to turn more tightly. This was expected to be decisive once the Bf 109Es were engaged in combat. In practice, a German pilot was more likely to use his fighter's higher rate of roll, rate of climb, or diving speed to evade a chasing Hurricane. Even the Hurricane's superior turning circle was more theoretical than real. The gentle stall of the Bf 109 meant that German pilots could push their fighter to the limit with more confidence. Rather remarkably, despite the Hurricane's obvious limitations, the report concluded that even with odds of two to one against, the Hurricane ought to come out on top.[76]

Despite the optimism of the report, it was clear something had to be done to improve the performances of the Hurricane. Acceleration had never been an issue for intercepting bombers, but in combat, with opposing fighters, it was priceless. Hurricanes and Spitfires used fixed-pitch two-blade wooden airscrews, which were light, but the blades were set at an angle, which was neither ideal for taking off nor high speed. Following the first clashes with the Bf 109, Hurricanes were hurriedly converted to two-pitch, three-blade metal propellers. They helped, but the Hurricane was still far too slow to compete with the Bf 109.

The only solution was more power to drag the bulky Hurricane airframe though the air quicker, and the 1,400-hp Merlin XX provided it. Both Supermarine and Hawker were already adapting their fighters to take the new engine. Supermarine decided the extra power deserved a complete overhaul of their design. Camm, with his Typhoon/Tornado in the pipeline, made the minimum changes to his Hurricane II. Even so, the Spitfire III was flying in March, achieving 400 mph.[77] The Hurricane II would not fly until June, managing just 342 mph. Even with the extra power, it was still slower than the Spitfire I.

At least the Hurricane was a traditional single-engine, single-seater; 60 per cent of the fighters on order were turreted or twin-engine. The good news for Dowding and the Army was that they were all behind schedule. Another 250 Defiants had been ordered on the outbreak of war, taking total orders to 850.[78] The first, however, did not reach the squadrons until December, and only fifty-six had been delivered by May 1940. Only two squadrons had the plane, and the pilots were struggling to get more than 300 mph out of the fighter. Even so, outside Dowding's HQ, the fighter was still generating enormous excitement. Only delays with production were holding up plans to equip a third of the fighter force with the plane.

Deliveries of the Beaufighter were supposed to begin in January 1940. It was only in December 1939 that Peirse discovered that it was not simply a Beaufort with bomb gear replaced by cannon—it had become an entirely new plane, and the ambitious production estimates were hopelessly inaccurate.[79] The Hercules VI engines the original 360-mph speed forecasts was based on were still not available and the prototypes tested at Martlesham Heath in early 1940 had a top speed of just 335 mph at best. One version managed only 309 mph. Performance at altitude was even more disappointing.

The twin-engine Westland Whirlwind was also behind schedule. The first started trickling off the production line early in 1940, but the problems with the troublesome Peregrine engines had still not been fully resolved. At low altitudes, the plane was as fast as the Spitfire, but performance at high altitude was not much better than the Beaufighter's. The first did not reach a squadron until the summer of 1940, and the plane was so troublesome the squadron remained non-operational. Rather fortuitously, nearly all Dowding's day fighter squadron were still equipped with Hurricanes and Spitfires.

Dowding may not have wanted twin-engine fighters for day fighting, but he wanted their cannon armament. The limited combat experience Fighter Command gained during the Phoney War seemed to confirm that the self-sealing tanks and armour German bombers were using made cannon essential.[80] Supermarine and Hawker were confident that the more powerful Merlin XX versions of the Spitfire and Hurricane would be able to carry four cannon. To get something into service sooner, Hawker and Supermarine were asked to mount a single cannon in each wing of the current versions of the Hurricane and Spitfire. Trials with the cannon-armed Spitfire seemed to be satisfactory, and thirty were ordered for operational trials with No. 19 Squadron.[81] Hawker sent a two-cannon Hurricane I to No. 151 Squadron for trials.

The Air Staff were still insisting two cannon were not enough. Camm was asked to investigate replacing the twelve machine guns on his Typhoon/Tornado with four cannon.[82] Peirse felt even four might not be enough.[83] In fact, four was already excessive; two delivered ample weight of fire to destroy anything Fighter Command was likely to encounter in the foreseeable future. More than two was an unnecessary burden that reduced manoeuvrability, whereas being limited to only two was actually an advantage.

Dowding was more than happy to rely on cannon-armed single-engine fighters for day interception, but this left the problem of what to do with all the Beaufighters that had been ordered. Some were needed for AI night fighting, but there were far too many on order for this. Plans to replace the Spitfire with the Beaufighter on Supermarine production lines were dropped. Coastal Command were asked if they might be able to use the plane—they still needed a long-range fighter and a low-level strike plane, and the Beaufighter seemed ideal.[84] The plane was morphing back to its torpedo bomber Beaufort origins. It was still planned to use the more manoeuvrable twin-engine Whirlwind by day, but there was no question of stepping up production. Plans to build the fighter at the Castle Bromwich plant were dropped. The idea of making the day fighter force predominantly twin-engine had been ditched.

Meanwhile, Dowding and the Air Staff were moving the fighter requirement goalposts. Dowding had said that once he had his fifty-three squadrons, it would be time to pay more attention to Army fighter requirements. However, by the spring of 1940, he was insisting the threat had grown and he now wanted sixty squadrons by 1 September 1940 and eighty by 1 April 1941. On the face of it, it was more bad news for the Army, although at least Dowding was pushing for more fighters. For the Air Ministry, it was a 'staggering, possibly impossible' demand.[85] Such a force was not beyond British industrial resources, it was just a question of priorities. Five Spitfires required the same man hours to build as a single Stirling heavy bomber.[86] Dowding's eighty squadrons were only impossible if Britain wanted a heavy bomber force as well. With current fighter production rates, losses expected to rise during the summer, and the need to reequip squadrons in the Middle East, there were doubts that it would be possible to maintain even the existing fifty-three squadrons.[87] The dire shortage made Dowding even more determined not to fritter away precious fighters over the front in France.

Nevertheless, there was still an uneasy feeling within the Air Ministry—not to say a sense of embarrassment—that Britain was holding on to far too many fighters for home defence. While Dowding felt he needed eighty squadrons, even thirty-two BEF divisions were supposed to make do with just twenty. Slessor pointed out that on a strictly pro-rata basis, the existing ten divisions of the BEF were entitled to an extra couple of squadrons. Given the scale of the imbalance, two squadrons was perhaps mere tinkering, but Peirse did not want to make even this small concession. The situation on the home front was far graver than in France, he insisted. Fighter reinforcements could always be flown over the Channel if required.[88]

Throwing units into an ongoing battle piecemeal was not a formula for success, as the Air Ministry would soon find out. Arguably, it would be easier to have the squadrons in France and have them transfer back to their bases in Britain if the Western Front was quiet and London was being bombed. The squadrons were well-trained in a home-defence role, but they needed experience in tactical air combat. Dowding could never contemplate such a move. There was a genuine, widespread belief that an aerial attack on London would be so sudden and so devastating that by the time the fighters flew back to Britain it would be too late. Nothing so immediately catastrophic could possibly happen on the Western Front—or so everyone believed.

Meanwhile, German forces were finally on the move—although not in the direction anyone expected.

Norwegian Warning

Days after Chamberlain had claimed that Hitler had 'missed the bus' by not attacking sooner, the German Army struck. Of course, Chamberlain was not talking about offensives on land—he was referring to the much feared knockout aerial blow. He still expected Germany to launch such an assault 'without scruple and without mercy', but he assured his audience that Britain could now respond 'with interest'.[1] The German invasion of Denmark and Norway on 9 April was not a blow that would worry Chamberlain too much. Indeed, the German move into Norway was a blessing in disguise; Hitler had saved the Prime Minister from the embarrassment of being branded the aggressor against the very same nation.

The issue at stake was the Swedish iron ore being shipped to Germany *via* Narvik. For some time, Britain and France had been preparing to cut off the supply by occupying Narvik; initially, the plan was to do this on the pretext of assisting Finland in her war against the Soviet Union. When Finland agreed peace terms, it was decided to mine Norwegian waters instead. If German forces intervened, the forces that would have occupied Narvik would be used to occupy Narvik, Trondheim, Stavanger, and Bergen. The minelayers were actually on their way when the Germans launched their attack. British intentions meant the forces required to respond to the German invasion were ready and waiting.

Unfortunately, they were not particularly well-equipped, with little in the way of artillery or any other heavy weapons. There were no plans for an air element to accompany the landings, just some vague suggestions for a fighter and army-cooperation squadron to join the Narvik force once it was established.[2] Nor was any Naval air support planned. The only aircraft carrier in home waters, HMS *Furious*, was conducting anti-submarine patrols with a couple of Swordfish squadrons on board. For air support, the Allied forces would rely on anything the RAF and Fleet Air Arm could muster from very distant airfields in Britain. It was not a well-thought-out intervention.

Before the Royal Navy minelayers even reached Norwegian waters, all the ports the Allies had lined up for occupation were in German hands, along with the Norwegian capital, Oslo, and the whole of Denmark. British and German bombers

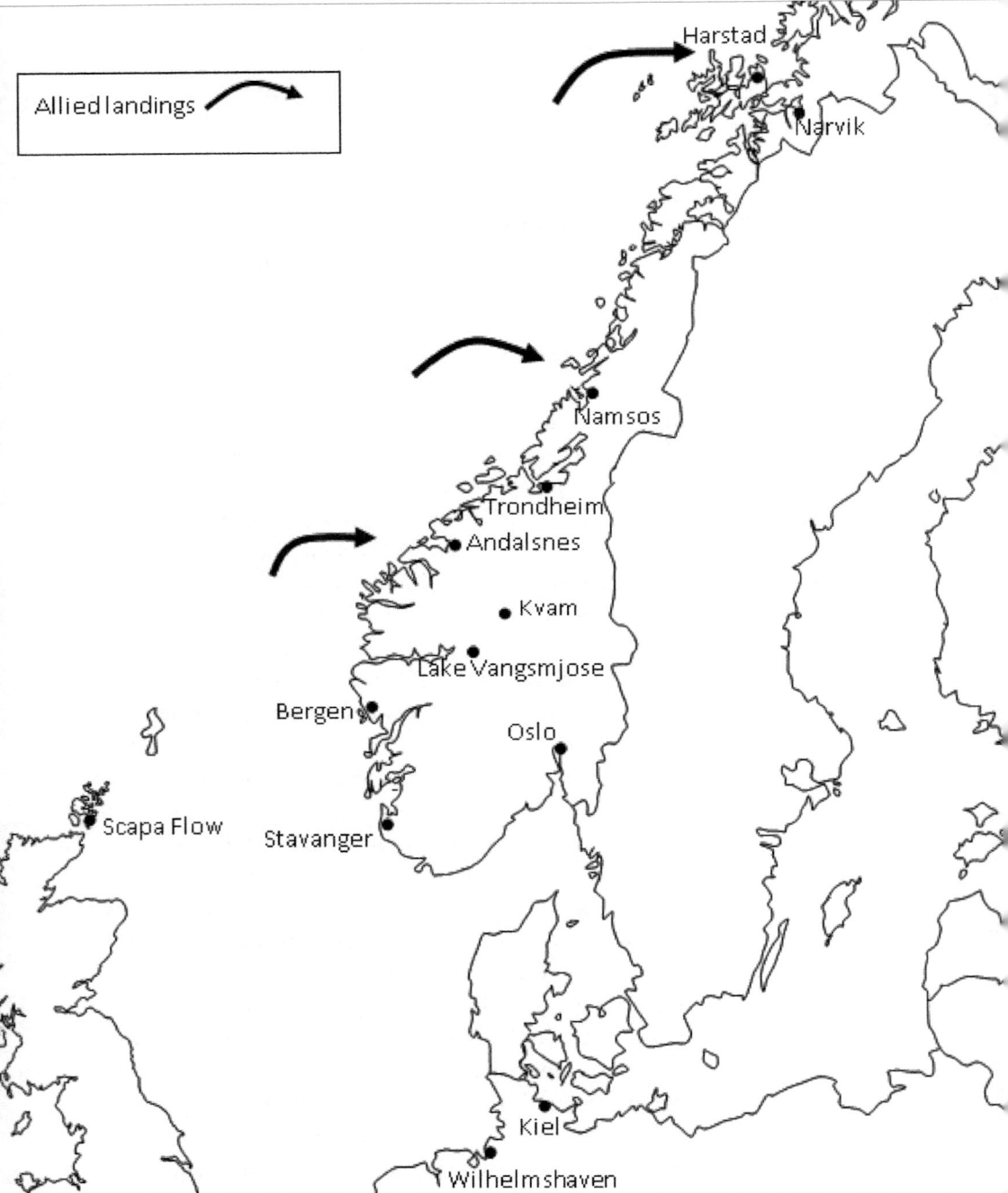

Norway in April 1940.

were soon in action. The early skirmishes in the air saw both sides using their bombers well beyond any possible fighter support, and both were soon suffering losses. The main Royal Navy base at Scapa Flow was well defended by four single-seater fighter squadrons (three RAF Hurricane squadrons and a Fleet Air Arm Sea Gladiator squadron). On 8 April, four out of twenty-four He 111s attacking the base were shot down.[3] The Luftwaffe attacked again two days later, with thirty-eight He 111s and Ju 88s. Another five bombers failed to return.[4]

On 12 April it was Bomber Command's turn to suffer. Eighty-three Blenheims, Hampdens, and Wellingtons bombed German shipping in the Stavanger area. Self-sealing tanks and the increased armour protection ensured that there was no repeat of the December massacre, but three out of thirty-six Wellingtons and six out of twenty-four Hampdens were shot down.[5] Both types were still vulnerable to beam attacks. The ventral turrets fitted to the Wellington proved almost impossible to use, and the interim twin dorsal and ventral guns on the Hampden could not turn far enough to deal with beam attacks. Bf 110s flew parallel to the Hampdens and the German rear gunners were able to fire at the bombers unopposed. One by one, the helpless Hampdens fell. The Luftwaffe was proving the thinking behind the Boulton Paul Defiant was perfectly valid.[6]

The German fighters did not escape unscathed. German pilots would invariably approach to within machine-gun range. Their cannon armament was not making the machine gun as obsolete as some had feared. The Hampdens were unable to do anything about the Bf 110s, but five Bf 109s were shot down.[7] British bombers were not defenceless, nor had ways of improving defensive firepower been exhausted. Better dorsal and ventral gun mountings for the Hampden were supposed to be on the way, and beam guns had been successfully trialled on the Wellington.

No matter how much defensive firepower was improved, both sides were learning that unescorted bombers were vulnerable. The Luftwaffe, however, would persevere. German bombers would get better defensive armament, more armour, and, most importantly of all, would have escorts whenever possible. For Bomber Command, it was the last straw. These early efforts in the Norwegian campaign would be the last major daylight operations by the Hampden and Wellington; in future, these two day bombers would be used almost exclusively by night.

Rather conveniently, the Hampden and Wellington were always grouped together with the Whitley as 'heavies'. In terms of their bomb load and range, this was reasonable, but it was also misleading. The Whitley was a heavy bomber designed principally for night operations; it did not have the performance to operate by day. The Hampden and Wellington were medium bombers designed for day operation, with a broadly similar level of performance to German day bombers. Grouping them with the Whitley helped to cement the decision to use them only by night.

This decision had serious implications for future RAF Army support operations. The Air Staff was not distinguishing between short-range tactical and long-range strategic operations. The fact that shorter-range missions could be escorted was irrelevant—the Air Staff did not believe in escorts. If the Wellingtons and Hampdens were ever used to support the Army, it would only be by night.

While the RAF bombers withdrew from the contest, German bombers continued to strike British Naval units and Norwegian ground forces at will. With the sole Norwegian Air Force fighter squadron eliminated on the first day of operations, there was no opposition in the air. The Royal Navy relied on anti-aircraft guns for defence, which were formidable, but the German bombers soon sank a destroyer and damaged several other ships. Fifteen Fleet Air Arm Skua dive-bombers, operating from Britain, sank a light cruiser moored in Bergen harbour. Both sides were discovering warships were vulnerable to air attack, but whereas German anti-shipping operations were the norm, the Fleet Air Arm attack was an exception.

With captured bases in Norway, the Luftwaffe was well-placed to dominate the region. Restricted to bases in Britain, the RAF and Fleet Air Arm were operating at a great disadvantage, but this need not have been the case. Britain could now rely on the full cooperation of the Norwegian authorities to provide them with airfields, but ever since the first plans were made to support the Finns, neither the Army, Navy, nor RAF had attached sufficient importance to the role air power might play.

For the German commanders, air support had been an integral part of their planning. The German armed forces were acting as one, but on the Allied side, the three services all had their own agenda. As far as the Air Ministry was concerned, the whole campaign was another diversion from their main strategic bombing role. It did not want to get involved. For the Admiralty, it was a crucial battle; if the German Navy could use Norwegian ports, it would make it far easier for German warships to break out into the Atlantic. The Army did not really want effort to be diverted from the Western Front but found itself committed to amphibious operations to recapture Narvik and Trondheim. There were still no plans for RAF squadrons to accompany the Allied forces, but at least the Admiralty was now taking the need for air support more seriously; the aircraft carriers *Ark Royal* and *Glorious*, both in the Mediterranean, were ordered to join *Furious* in Home Waters.

Unfortunately, the Fleet Air Arm was not much better prepared for supporting ground forces than the RAF. British carrier planes were designed primarily for operations in mid-ocean, far from any enemy air bases. No attempt had been made to make them competitive with land-based planes. The standard torpedo bomber was the 138-mph biplane Swordfish. The Admiralty did not believe in single-seater fighters because there had to be a navigator to help the pilot find his way back to the carrier. The two-seater 225-mph Skua doubled as a fighter and dive-bomber. The Navy had some single-seater Gladiators, but it had only accepted these reluctantly, because their next two-seater, the 280-mph Fairey Fulmar, was not available yet. In 1940, the Royal Navy had some of the most modern aircraft carriers in the world, but the aircraft that were operating from them were, by contemporary American and Japanese standards, hopelessly inadequate.

Furious was soon operating off the Norwegian coast. On 11 April it launched an unsuccessful torpedo strike with its Swordfish on German warships in the Trondheim Fjord. German bombers struck back with more success, sinking one of the destroyers protecting the carrier. *Furious* carried no fighters, so the force had to retreat northwards, out of range of the Luftwaffe. The carrier was subsequently used to support the Allied forces landed near Narvik.[8]

Further south, Portal, determined not to waste too many of his precious bombers, was scaling down bomber operations. Airfields in the south of Norway were bombed, and occasional sorties were carried out as far north as Trondheim. On the night of 16–17 April, the Vaernes Airfield was bombed by five Whitleys. In the area there were frozen lakes that the Germans were suspected of using as airfields, and these were also attacked. However, it was a half-hearted effort. Following the attack on 12 April, Bomber Command rarely flew more than a dozen sorties per day; Portal insisted that he had to hold his bombers back so that they could be thrown against the expected German offensive in the Lowlands.[9]

Meanwhile, plans were going ahead to land British and French troops in Norway. By this time both the War Office and Admiralty were becoming very nervous about how the Luftwaffe might interfere with the operation. The losses the Royal Navy had already suffered were enough to persuade the Navy that a direct assault on Trondheim was far too risky.[10] Instead, troops would be landed 100 miles north and south of Trondheim, at the Norwegian-controlled ports of Namsos and Andalsnes.

When British forces set sail on 12 April, *Ark Royal* and *Glorious* were still on their way from the Mediterranean. Between the 14th and 18th, 20,000 troops were landed at Namsos and Andalsnes. Further north, more troops landed at Harstad, near Narvik. As none of these were opposed landings, there was no reason why airstrips could not be organised fairly quickly for RAF planes to move into, even if it was only a few Lysanders. This was where the plane's famed ability to operate from the smallest open space might prove very useful. There was also the option of using the airstrips being used by the remnants of the Norwegian Air Force. It was not the way the RAF thought. The assault on Trondheim required an advance over 100 miles across tricky terrain, but it would have to be carried out without any close air support, fighter cover, or even a single reconnaissance plane. Until the carriers arrived, the only air support would come from what the RAF could provide from bases in Britain, 450 miles away.

With no air cover whatsoever, disembarkation had to take place under cover of darkness. Troops were immediately dispersed in the hope of avoiding detection. There were even instructions not to open fire on any planes for fear of attracting the Luftwaffe's attention. Despite these precautions, the German reconnaissance planes soon spotted the landings and the bombing began. With no effective air defences, the bombers could fly as low as they liked and take aim at leisure. Namsos was particularly heavily hit. The wooden wharves and limited storage facilities of the small port were soon destroyed. The troops pushing inland were also heavily bombed; even large He 111 bombers were able to fly low and bomb and strafe troops.

Any movement by day became hazardous. These were not the circumstances in which Army commanders could deploy their forces with any freedom. German forces, on the other hand, were able to move with the confidence that came from knowing that they need not fear any threat from the air.

This was the British Army's first taste of intensive air bombardment. Despite the concerns the War Office had expressed before the landings took place, it still managed to come as a shock to troops and commanders alike. Resignation turned into resentment and concerns became demands. After days of endless bombardment and disruption, the two Army commanders, Lt-Gen. De Wiart in the north and Brigadier Morgan in the south, warned the War Office that unless the scale of enemy attacks could be reduced, their forces could achieve nothing. More troops were on their way to Andalsnes, but before they left Britain, their commander, General Paget, insisted these pleas for more air protection must be acted on. On 24 April, De Wiat received assurances that aircraft carriers with fighters would soon be arriving, with vaguer promises of RAF fighters to follow.[11] It was perhaps ironic that the Army would be relying on the Fleet Air Arm, the Naval equivalent of the air arm the Army felt it should always have had.

A reluctant Air Staff was forced into making a more solid commitment. One squadron would be assigned the task of defending Trondheim and the forces pushing inland. The War Office was told the Gladiator was the best plane for the task. Slow, more manoeuvrable biplanes made better tactical fighters, the Air Staff was still insisting. There was more justification in the claim that they would be easier to fly off aircraft carriers and operate from small, improvised airstrips. There never seemed to be a shortage of reasons for using Gladiators. A second squadron was already preparing to join them, but it would have to be equipped with Hurricanes—the RAF was running out of Gladiators. No effort was made to find out where RAF planes might operate from until 17 April. The airstrip the Norwegian Air Force was using at Lake Vangsmosa was the initial choice of the liaison officer in Norway, but Lake Lesjeskogen, nearer Andalsnes, was eventually chosen.[12]

On 20 April, nearly two weeks after the German invasion, No. 263 Squadron moved north to board *Glorious*. This set sail on the 22nd, along with the *Ark Royal*. As well as the RAF Gladiators, the aircraft carriers had on board twenty-one Swordfish, eighteen Sea Gladiators, and thirty Skuas and Rocs (the Fleet Air Arm's 220-mph equivalent to the Defiant). They arrived off the Norwegian coast on 23 April, and on the 26th the RAF Gladiator squadron was flown off the carrier. The carriers then withdrew to a safer distance from the coast. Only the Skuas would have the range to cover the ground forces.[13]

For No. 263 Squadron, operating in Norway would prove to be a torrid experience. The Luftwaffe identified the lake they were operating from almost immediately, and for two days they mounted continuous attacks. The situation was particularly traumatic for the ground crews, whom the RAF tended to see as noncombatant technicians. They were totally unprepared for the harsh realities of war. As soon as the bombing began, most of them disappeared into the surrounding woods and were reluctant to return.[14]

The Gladiators managed forty-nine sorties, most of which were flown in defence of their own airfield. Some sorties were flown over the front around Kvam, where British and Norwegian forces were trying to hold up the German advance on Trondheim from the south.[15] In the absence of any other air support, they also flew the odd reconnaissance and even an artillery observation mission. Thirty-nine interceptions were made and six aircraft claimed.[16] The squadron had at least diverted a proportion of German air effort away from the Allied ground forces, but any relief was short-lived. Within two days, most of the Gladiators had been destroyed.

For the Air Ministry, it just demonstrated the futility of sending the fighters in the first place. In reality, the futility was relying on just one ill-prepared squadron equipped with obsolete fighters and not providing adequate anti-aircraft protection for the base. Blenheims of No. 254 Squadron, operating from Britain, tried to provide some sort of fighter presence and managed the odd success, but small flights of two or three planes operating at extreme range could not hope to achieve much.[17]

Paget could not see why he should not get the sort of air support German forces were getting. Large bombers like the He 111 were bombing and strafing his troops from low altitudes and he expected RAF 'heavies' to be used in the same way. Enemy artillery in the Kvam area and supply lines leading to that front were suggested targets. The request was greeted with little enthusiasm. Paget was told these targets were out of range, which was not true for the heavy bombers Paget was suggesting the RAF use.[18] Bomber Command was, however, instructed to step up its raids on German air bases in the south of Norway. Thirty-four sorties were flown against airfields on the night of 23–24 April and another eighteen on the night of the 25th–26th. It was scarcely an all-out assault.

The carriers did their best. Skuas were responsible for the destruction of three He 111s on the 24th, the first serious losses the German Air Force had suffered attacking targets in central Norway. The next day, Swordfish destroyed seven Ju 87Rs on the ground at Vaernes. Skuas attacked targets of opportunity in areas requested by the Army.[19] On the 26th, Skuas shot down two more He 111s, and another five the following day. These efforts made a difference; Army commanders reported that when German raids were opposed, the bombing was more scattered and the damage reduced.[20] If the Fleet Air Arm had been equipped with modern single-seater fighters, much more might have been achieved.

The efforts of No. 263 Squadron and the Fleet Air Arm were not enough. On the night of 27–28 April, the Allied forces in central Norway were ordered to pull out. This was frustrating for Paget; his troops were holding their position, and with artillery and air support, there was no reason why they could not continue to do so. Since there was no intention of supplying either, withdrawal was the only sensible option.

Ark Royal and *Glorious* did their best to cover the withdrawal.[21] The RAF stepped up its efforts, flying sixty-two sorties against various airfields in the south of the country. On the 30th, Blenheims attacked by day and Wellingtons at dusk, followed by Whitleys and Hampdens under cover of darkness. Four out of thirteen Wellingtons were shot down, but the Luftwaffe lost a Bf 109D and three Bf 110s in the process. Again, RAF bombers were proving they were not entirely defenceless. Over three days, Bomber Command flew 120 sorties and lost nine planes. The airfield at Stavanger was temporarily put out of action. Ten Ju 52 transports were destroyed and another twenty-seven damaged at Oslo's Fornebu Airfield.[22]

As Allied forces pulled out of central Norway, the focus switched to operations around Narvik. On 21 May, No. 263 Squadron, fully re-equipped with Gladiators, was flown off *Furious*, followed a few days later by the Hurricanes of No. 46 Squadron from *Glorious*. No. 263 Squadron was much better prepared this time, and both squadrons operated more successfully. Naval Skuas and Swordfish provided the only British bomber support, backed up by a handful of rather old Norwegian Air Force Fokker C.V biplane reconnaissance-bombers and He 115 floatplanes, which, ironically, had been bought from Germany. Even 135-mph Fleet Air Arm Walrus amphibians were used to attack ground targets.[23] On 28 May, Narvik was recaptured, and the Allied forces were poised to finish off the Germans driven out of the port; however, by this time, events further south had made this a hollow and irrelevant victory.

At the time, it seemed the entire Scandinavian venture had been doomed from the very start—a hopeless undertaking in the face of overwhelming German superiority. In fact, at sea, the Royal Navy possessed hugely superior forces. Even on land, the Allied troops outnumbered the German forces. Only in the air were the Allies outnumbered. It was not that the RAF did not have the aircraft, it was just that they were not willing to use them. The strength of German air support was determined by what was necessary for the task, whereas RAF involvement was based on the minimum the Air Ministry could get away with. The Luftwaffe was set up to support the Army; the RAF was not. Within hours of invading, the Luftwaffe had squadrons operating from captured airfields. In early May, the Luftwaffe still had around thirty Luftwaffe squadrons operating from Norwegian soil. Even with the full cooperation of Norwegian authorities, the RAF never managed more than two squadrons. There was a determination not to let the Air Force get too involved in the land campaign; until this attitude changed, British military successes were likely to be few and far between.

The War Office was very aware what the absence of air support meant. The Luftwaffe had disrupted supply lines and demoralised front line troops. It was one thing to observe such events in a distant land, but it was quite another when British soldiers were on the receiving end. Yet there was none of the anger that would surface just weeks later. Too much had gone wrong on the Army side of the operation for the War Office to be too critical. The War Office often complained that going to war without air support was like entering a battle with no artillery or tanks. In Norway, the British Army had to do without all three.

Portal was totally unmoved by the part German air power had played in the defeat. Instead of learning what appropriately trained and equipped air forces could achieve in support of ground forces, the perverse idea was gaining ground that the German Air Force was demonstrating how air power should not be used. Portal used events in Norway to support his own belief that the tactical deployment of his bomber forces was a misuse of resources. The relatively poor results achieved and the heavy losses suffered proved his point. Once Bomber Command could deal with enemy strength at source, results would be quite different. Portal and the Air Staff could not wait to demonstrate to the world how air power should be used.

In France, Barratt was much more willing to support the Army. He set up his HQ at Chauny, alongside the French Air Force commander in the North East, General d'Astier de La Vigerie. A Central Air Bureau assessed requests for air support, and Barratt would decide whether the targets could best be engaged by his AASF squadrons or No. 2 Group. Immediate decisions could be made about using the AASF, but the No. 2 Group Blenheims were not under his direct control; approval from Portal had to be sought first. Instruction would then be passed onto No. 2 Group and then down to the squadrons.[24] Bombers then had up to 250 miles to fly to reach their targets. The response was bound to be delayed.

Barratt could do nothing about his complicated lines of communication with No. 2 Group, but he tried to make sure his squadrons in France could respond quickly. He organised radio-equipped mobile teams with forward troops so that he would always know what was going on at the front.[25] There was also a system, instigated by the French, whereby reconnaissance planes that had spotted a particularly attractive target would fly straight to a bomber base. This would allow a briefing to take place while authorisation for the attack was sought. One AASF wing was always on standby for such operations.[26]

All this was anathema to Portal. However, in a rather bizarre sequence of events, long before Portal took over, Bomber Command had also set up a system to speed response time. Rather unpromisingly, it all began with an Air Staff decision that if the Netherlands was invaded, it would be a complete waste of time and resources providing the Dutch with any air support. If the Dutch asked for RAF support, they should be told it was not possible; if they wanted to know why, it was because no arrangements had been set up with the Dutch High Command, so it would be impossible to know where any appropriate targets were. If the Dutch suggested RAF planes could perhaps identify targets, they should be told that Bomber Command had no reconnaissance planes.[27]

However, for political reasons, it was decided that token air support should be offered, although just enough to show the world that Britain was not abandoning an ally. To achieve this, the tail of the German columns advancing into Holland could be bombed. Ostensibly, this was to make sure no Dutch units were bombed by mistake.

In reality, the idea was to make sure the bombing was taking place as far inside Germany as possible. Indeed, rather conveniently, it might even be decided that the tail of the advance was in the Ruhr.

Even Slessor thought this was going slightly too far. Perhaps not fully appreciating the deviousness of the policy, Slessor suggested that this 'token' support should have a least some value. Attacking the lead columns rather than the tail would cause far more delay, and the latter might be difficult to identify. It would also probably mean a deeper penetration and heavier losses. To ensure friendly forces were not hit by mistake, Slessor suggested that there should be a direct telephone line from the British Embassy in The Hague to the Air Ministry. The Dutch High Command could then pass on, *via* the air attaché, how far the Germans had advanced.[28] The telephone line was duly installed.

Portal, however, had his own ideas about how the Dutch should be supported. He came up with a new variant of WA4, the category of plans that detailed how Bomber Command would support Allied armies by bombing German Army communications. Portal's variant, WA4(c), appropriately planned to 'cause the maximum dislocation on the lines of communication of German advance through the Lowlands'. Targets included troop concentrations and marshalling yards.

However, these targets were mere camouflage for the true aim. The two Whitley squadrons already promised would cover the troop-concentration aspect of the plan by attacking communications west of the Rhine. The attack on marshalling yards within the Ruhr would be 'confined to harassing action', whereas 'the principal weight of attack should be directed against the oil plants'. The designation of the plan was misleading to say the least; it was no more than the WA6 oil plan dressed up as a WA4 communications plan. Nevertheless, the plan was sold to the French and the War Office as a way of disrupting a German advance. The oil refineries were tucked away as an example of the sort of target 'vital to the German war effort' that might also be attacked because they were 'in the area immediately behind the German advance'.[29]

Gamelin was not happy about any bombing far from the frontline, especially if it was likely to involve civilian casualties. With the entire French bomber fleet still converting to modern equipment, and no means of retaliating, the French had good reason to be cautious.[30] The likes of Peirse (now Vice-Chief of Air Staff) and Douglas had expressed exactly the same concerns. Others, including elements in the War Office, liked to see French caution as feebleness. It was a prejudice the Air Ministry was able to exploit to get War Office backing for their WA4(c) plan. For Gamelin, the weakness of the French bomber fleet was just another very good reason for not wasting bombs on the Ruhr—there were far more useful targets to attack. Since the Air Staff thought bombing German industry was the only way to fight the war, from their perspective, it looked as if Gamelin was trying to prevent Bomber Command from taking any part in the war. Chamberlain, who at this stage was not fully aware of the strategic oil aspect of the plan, was persuaded to get the

French government to overrule Gamelin's objections. The French agreed to leave the decision to implement WA4(c) in the hands of the British Government.[31]

To the dismay of the Air Staff, however, the War Office was also now beginning to see no point in attacking targets so far east. Following their experiences in Norway, there was a real fear that German bombing would prevent the BEF reaching its positions in Belgium in time to establish a solid defensive line. To even up the odds, the Army wanted the entire front-line strength of Bomber Command to be used to slow down the German advance. Bombing marshalling yards, oil reserves, and 'other important installations' east of the Rhine would not bring any immediate benefits.[32] The RAF had to focus on targets west of the Rhine.

The Air Ministry claimed, rather dubiously, that the relevant region west of the Rhine—some 5,000 square miles of German territory—was not big enough for more than the promised two Whitley squadrons to operate in. If the rest of the force was not used east of the Rhine, it could not be used at all.[33] On 5 May, with evidence growing that the German offensive was just days away, the War Office made another effort to shift Bomber Command focus westwards. The Army was now sure the Germans had moved their main supply dumps west of the Rhine, and that any bombing to the east of the river would now be a complete waste of time. The War Office reminded the Air Ministry that in Norway, the German Air Force had been able to bomb bottlenecks from relatively high altitudes with demoralising effect, and the Army was now expecting the same from the RAF. Indeed, turning Air Ministry logic on its head, if there really were so few targets west of the Rhine worth attacking, then it should be possible to hit them very heavily and continuously.[34]

It was now becoming clearer to the government and War Office what Plan WA 4(c) was really about; the 'other important installations' meant the German oil industry. The War Office insisted that an offensive against oil targets was a long-term policy that could not possibly affect the outcome of the forthcoming battle. The full weight of Bomber Command had to be focused on the short-term policy of stopping the German offensive, which, if successful, might finish the war very quickly. It accepted that the 'heavies' might not be suitable for attacks on enemy columns, but general destruction in built-up areas in Germany or the Low Countries would disrupt lines of communication.[35]

Chamberlain also doubted bombing oil refineries would help the Allied armies and probably only provoke retaliation. Newall assured the government that attacking targets in the Ruhr was the only way all the 'heavies' could be used. Indeed, even with the marshalling yards in the Ruhr, there were insufficient targets. Oil refineries or other targets would have to be attacked if Bomber Command was to make full use of its resources.[36] Chamberlain was not persuaded. The government only gave Portal the go-ahead for attacks on troop columns and marshalling yards west of the Rhine.[37]

The day before the German offensive, Portal warned Newall that using bombers against advancing enemy columns, based on information that was necessarily out of date, was 'fundamentally unsound'. Such operations would result in 50 per cent losses and were 'likely to have disastrous consequences on the future of the war in the air'. The Air Staff stuck to their line that only in a desperate emergency (such as March 1918) could a chance be taken and the 'heavies' risked against purely 'military objectives'.[38] The War Office was left hoping that the Air Staff would stick to this commitment. Such a desperate emergency was now only days away.

Ironically, while the French High Command and War Office fretted about what might happen in France and Belgium, the apparent ease with which Germany had occupied Norway raised fears that Hitler might attempt to invade Britain. Just days before the Germans launched their offensive in the west, Stevenson, the Director of Home Operations, was claiming that the level of control the Luftwaffe had established in the skies over Norway could quite easily allow an invasion fleet to cross the North Sea.[39] If Belgium and the Netherlands were occupied, Ju 87 dive-bombers would be able to support an invasion and Bf 109s could provide protection. The possibility of single-seater fighters operating over England led to the sudden decision to fit home-based fighters with the seat armour that fighters in France were getting.[40]

With the BEF in France, there was very little in the United Kingdom that could oppose an enemy landing. Stevenson suggested that civilians could be used to form militia units, a recommendation that would lead to the formation of the 'Home Guard'.[41] The RAF also had to be prepared to play its part. Bomber Command had more important things to do than worry about invasions. The Command was to be relieved of this 'distraction' by giving training schools the task of repelling an assault. Tiger Moths, Hawker Harts, and other obsolescent planes would be used as short-range dive-bombers, leaving Bomber Command free 'for its true role'.[42] The anti-invasion 'Banquet Scheme' was born. Suddenly, there was an air of urgency about developing a ground-attack capability; bomb racks were quickly improvised to enable trainers to carry 20-lb bombs.

The best way of reducing the risk of an invasion was to deny the Germans bases in the Lowlands. The suspicion was growing that the next German move would be against the Netherlands, not Belgium, with the aim of establishing a launching pad for an air assault on Britain or even an invasion. The three Chiefs of Staff agreed that it was 'therefore vital to use all [their] forces to dispute the occupation of Holland'.[43] Coincidentally, Gamelin had also decided that the Netherlands should be saved; the country provided a good base from which a future offensive into Germany might be launched. Indeed, both British and French governments believed that a German attack on the Netherlands would be enough to trigger the advance of the Allied armies into Belgium, whether the Belgians agreed or not. This would include the French 7th Army, which would advance into the southern Netherlands to link up with the Dutch Army.

Suddenly Britain was very keen to do everything it could to help the Dutch. It was assumed the Wehrmacht would use the same tactics that had been so successful in

Norway, with transport planes flying troops in to airfields captured by paratroopers. Spitfires and Hurricanes ought to have ample range to protect airfields in western Holland, and Blenheims might be risked over airfields further east. Advice was passed on to the Dutch on how to defend their airfields against airborne landings, along with assurances that the RAF would be able to help protect their airfields, provided the British were told soon enough.[44] With Slessor's direct telephone line from the British Embassy to the Air Ministry, the means existed to do this. It was help the Dutch Army would soon need; German forces were already massing on the Dutch frontier.

Unfortunately for the Dutch, defending their airfields from paratroopers and bombing advancing German forces was not going to be the principal way of helping. The Air Staff believed their WA4(c) plan was a much better method; the RAF would support the Dutch Army by unleashing the 'heavies' on the Ruhr. Slessor saw no alternative. Opening the aerial war was a grave decision, he admitted, and German retaliation was certain. It would almost certainly come by night, and Britain still had no way of fending off such an attack. However, any attempt by Germany to occupy the Netherlands would be such a decisive threat to Britain, Slessor claimed, that 'we should not shrink from using everything we have got' to cause 'the utmost dislocation and delay' in the enemy's rear. The RAF would do this by bombing German oil plants. Efforts would have to be made to prepare the British people for the retribution that would surely follow—but the only alternative to bombing the Ruhr, Slessor insisted, was to do nothing.[45]

It was typical Slessor. One moment he could see the pitfalls of Air Staff strategy with stunning clarity, but the next he was totally beguiled by the strategic bombing dream. The British Army would have to play its part, he continued, by advancing into Belgium and forcing the Luftwaffe to waste their bombers in support of the German Army. By offering themselves as a target, British soldiers would be making an important contribution to winning the aerial bomber exchange.[46]

This was the mind-set with which the Air Ministry entered the battle that might decide the fate of Europe.

The Dutch Abandoned

The withdrawal from Central Norway was enough to bring down Chamberlain's government. Winston Churchill took over on 10 May—the day Germany invaded Belgium, Holland, and Luxembourg. The most crucial battle of the war so far was underway. Losing Norway was a setback that would make winning the war more difficult, but a major defeat in France would be far more serious.

On paper, the opposing sides were evenly matched. The German Army had 136 divisions, including ten armoured divisions with 2,400 tanks. The French, with some ninety-four divisions, provided the bulk of the land forces opposing the Germans. The Belgians had mobilised twenty-two divisions and the Dutch ten. Britain added another ten. The British divisions were all very well-equipped, especially in terms of motorised transport—unlike in the Belgian, Dutch, French, and German armies, there was not a horse to be seen. They were, however, all infantry divisions. Britain's first armoured division was still forming. The only British armoured unit in France was the 1st Tank Brigade, with around 100 slow Matilda infantry support tanks. The French had over 3,000 tanks. Half of these were concentrated in six armoured divisions (three light and three heavy), while the remainder were with infantry support battalions.[1]

The Allied forces lacked combat experience and they were facing battle-hardened troops, experienced commanders, and outstanding generals. The first serious fighting was bound to be a severe test for everyone on the Allied side, from the humblest private to the generals at the top. In these circumstances, initial setbacks were perhaps inevitable—a retreat an acceptable price to pay for the experience gained.

In the air, on the north-east front, the French had seventeen fighter groups, each with two squadrons, totalling around 500 planes. Eight groups had the M.S.406, five the Bloch MB-152, and four the American Curtiss Hawk. There were another eight groups in the south, which were either available to deploy further north or were reequipping with more modern planes. The fighters available were broadly equivalent to the Hurricane—slower than the British fighter, but more agile. With one or two cannon, the French-designed fighters were also better-armed. The French were well-aware that they did not yet have an engine that was the equal of the British Merlin or German DB 601. Their fighters could not match the 354 mph of the Bf 109E, but they were closing the gap with the Dewoitine D.520 (330 mph) and Arsenal VG-33 (347 mph). The first units with the former were about to become operational, and the latter was just beginning to roll off the production lines.[2]

The first squadrons with a new generation of French bombers and American Douglas DB7 and Martin 167 imports were also about to become operational. The only bombers immediately available on 10 May were two squadrons with the rather old-fashioned looking but efficient four-engine Farman 222 heavy bomber and four squadrons of obsolete Amiot 143s. The French also had around 150 reconnaissance and nearly 400 army-cooperation planes distributed amongst its armies.[3]

The Dutch and Belgian Air Forces added another 300 combat planes to the Allied cause. The Dutch Air Force relied almost entirely on designs produced by Anthony Fokker, including the manoeuvrable Fokker D.21 single-seater (three squadrons), the twin-engined eight-gun Fokker G.1 (two squadrons), a squadron of Fokker T.V bombers, and less-modern Fokker C.V and C.X biplane reconnaissance bombers. There was also a squadron of American Douglas 8A-3N attack bombers, which the Dutch were planning to use as fighters.[4] The Belgians mustered six fighter squadrons (one Hurricane, one Gladiator, two Fiat CR.42s, and two Fairey Fox VIs), one bomber (Fairey Battle), and nine reconnaissance/army-cooperation (Fairey Fox and Renard R.31) squadrons.

With the RAF possessing around 1,900 planes, once all the French squadrons were available, the combined Allied air forces would not be far short of matching the 4,500 planes the Luftwaffe possessed. The war was on a knife edge. With modern planes arriving and production increasing, the French Air Force was a rising force. Britain was in the process of creating a powerful army, and Belgium and the Netherlands provided valuable manpower resources. If the four Allies could weather the initial storm, victory might not be too distant a prospect. With 900 fighters and 650 bombers, the RAF was capable of making a substantial contribution to ensuring the German offensive did not succeed.

This was not how the Air Staff saw it. Preoccupied with visions of wars decided by long-range bombing, they could not see the danger. They ignored warnings that unless the Allies threw everything into the initial battle, they might suffer a major defeat. Instead, they were convinced the land battle could not be decisive. It was the battle of the bombers that would decide the war. Eighteen of the twenty Wellington, Hampden, and Whitley squadrons were being held back for the attack on the Ruhr, which was where the real battle would begin. Even the two Whitley squadrons assigned the task of attacking German Army communications were, as Portal put it, merely a way to 'forward our plans towards the destruction of the German war industry'.[5] The targets the Whitleys bombed were to be as close to the Ruhr as possible.

Of the forty-three fighter squadrons in the UK, four would fly to France as soon as the German offensive began. Of the rest, four (two Hurricane and two Blenheim) were to patrol the English Channel, providing flank protection for the French 7th Army.[6] Two more were earmarked for Norway, leaving thirty-three—including all nineteen Spitfire squadrons. The Royal Air Force was not going to over-commit to a battle that could not be decisive.

On 10 May, German forces started moving forward on a 300-mile front from the north of the Netherlands to Luxembourg. The advance was spearheaded by ten Panzer divisions. One was heading for Rotterdam, four for Gembloux and Dinant in Belgium, and five for Montherme and Sedan in France. In the early hours of the 10th, a first wave of 500 German bombers set off in small formations to attack seventy-two French, Dutch, and Belgian airfields. Around 100 Allied combat planes were destroyed.[7] The Dutch suffered the most heavily. The airfields were as far west as possible to try maximise warning time, but the German Air Force simply flew out into the North Sea and attacked from the west. Warning was virtually zero. Twenty-eight aircraft were destroyed on the ground; one Fokker G.1 squadron was wiped out.[8]

The Belgian Air Force also suffered heavily in these first attacks. Most of the sole Hurricane squadron and one of the Fiat CR.42 squadrons was destroyed. The RAF

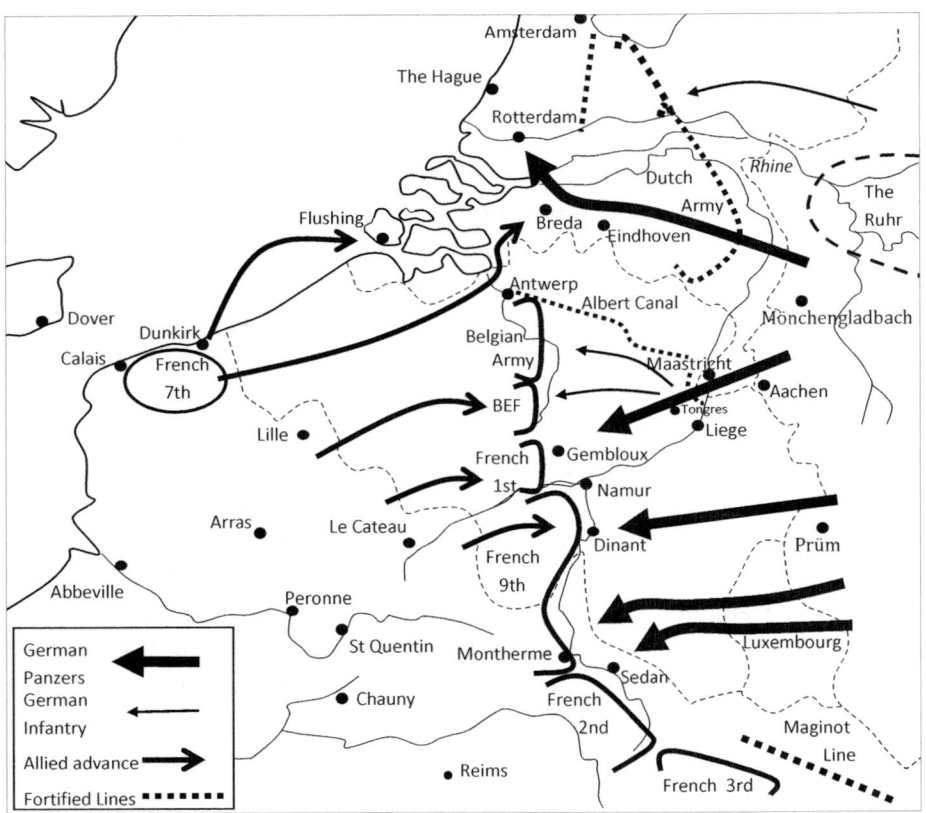

France on 10 May 1940.

and French Air Force emerged relatively unscathed. One French MS 406 squadron and, much later in the day, one AASF Blenheim bomber squadron lost virtually all their planes. The second wave of German bomber attacks found the defences largely intact. Around 500 bombers, again mostly flying in small formations, struck around 150 communication targets, many deep in the Allied rear, beyond escort range.[9]

No. 615 Squadron was still converting from Gladiators to Hurricanes and not available, but from dawn on the 10th the other five RAF fighter squadrons were fully engaged. They found themselves dealing largely with the unescorted bomber formations they were trained to deal with. Around 200 sorties were flown and the pilots claimed forty-two victories.[10] Fifteen Hurricanes were lost or crash-landed; six pilots were wounded, but none killed.[11]

The Dutch response was ferocious and effective. Even the Fokker T.V medium bombers took off to engage the waves of bombers and Ju 52 transports. It was a desperately difficult situation. Fighters scrambled as bombs fell around them and pilots found themselves having to deal with powerful fighter escorts. Twenty Dutch fighters were shot down to add to the twenty-one already lost on the ground. However, despite the losses—and the odds against them—the survivors were soon flying their second mission of the day. During nearly 100 fighter sorties, twelve bombers, seven transports, and eight Bf 109Es were claimed, matching the success rate of the RAF squadrons.[12] By contrast, most of the Belgian fighter squadrons spent the day moving from one airfield to another, trying to avoid the catastrophic losses their Dutch neighbours were suffering. This might have made sense if what was happening were the first tentative moves in a long, drawn-out struggle, but as the Dutch appreciated, events were moving fast. The Belgians did not escape heavy losses either. During the day, around forty of their combat planes were destroyed on the ground, including twenty-three fighters.[13]

French fighter squadrons were not operating in quite such difficult circumstances as their Dutch and Belgian allies, but encounters with escorts were not rare. The thirty-eight French fighter squadrons engaged managed around 360 sorties, claiming forty-four planes.[14] In total, the Allies flew around 800 sorties on this opening day, compared to the 2,000 flown by the German fighter force.[15] German losses closely matched Allied claims, with 120 combat planes lost or written off.[16] Of these, around 100 were bombers, representing 7 per cent of the available force. Many more returned damaged with dead and wounded aircrew aboard. It was a loss rate that the Luftwaffe could not afford to suffer too often. The next day, medium bomber sorties dropped from around 1,500 to 1,000.

Luftwaffe bomber losses were heavy, but RAF losses were catastrophic. At 10.30 a.m., Barratt arrived at the joint RAF/French Air Force headquarters in Chauny. He discussed with d'Astier reports from French reconnaissance of German columns moving through Luxembourg, and at 12.20 p.m. he ordered his bombers into action. Thirty-two Battles from seven squadrons were sent off, flying at low-level in flights of between two and four aircraft. Fighter support was provided for the first 'wave' of eight, but it consisted of just five Hurricanes from No. 1 Squadron and three from No. 73 Squadron. These were supposed to patrol over the city of Luxembourg and clear the area of enemy fighters. The number of fighters was ludicrously small for the task, and the two formations were not even working together. Given the rather vague nature of their 'escort' orders, it is not surprising that the three Hurricanes of No. 73 Squadron should turn their attention to some apparently unescorted German bombers they came across. In fact, there was an escort. The Hurricanes were bounced before they reached the bombers and at least one was shot down. By chance, No. 1 Squadron Hurricanes saw the difficulty their comrades were in but were flying too low to offer any help.[17] If the two formations had been working together as a team, one providing cover at altitude, the interception might have been more successful.

Meanwhile, the Battles were heading for their targets at treetop height. The low-level approach helped avoid enemy fighters, but the hail of light flak that greeted them over their targets proved just as deadly. A flight of two from No. 12 Squadron attacked from 30 feet. As the two Battles manoeuvred into position to fly down the road, one of them was shot down before it got close enough to drop its bombs. The second, piloted by Flt-Lt Simpson, strafed the enemy column with the single forward-firing machine gun as he dropped his bombs. It must have been frustrating for the pilot to attack with such boldness and have only a single machine gun to take on the targets ahead of him. Simpson was convinced he could not miss his target from such an altitude, but neither could the German defensive fire. He was immediately hit and forced to crash-land in a nearby field.[18] Of the thirty-two Battles sent out during the course of the afternoon, thirteen suffered a similar fate.

It was a disastrous operational debut for the Battle as a tactical bomber. British plans for tactical air support were in tatters. Flying high, the Battles were vulnerable to fighters; flying low, they were equally vulnerable to ground fire. The columns the Battles attacked were not even high-value targets the Germans might feel a particular need to defend. They were just random columns.

It was the first of many such expensive raids that would seal the Fairey Battle's reputation as one of the worst planes ever to enter service with the RAF. A plane designed to carry enough fuel to fly 1,000 miles was never going to be ideal for short-range, low-level tactical bombing. The proposed extra armour might have helped; the promised self-sealing tanks had also not yet arrived. Perhaps even more significant was the inexperience of the aircrews, who were using these low-level tactics in action for the first time. Determined not to waste their bombs, pilots were perhaps taking too long to line up the target. Some of the attacks seemed to have taken place in the sort of flat terrain where the enemy was very visible, but equally the anti-aircraft defences had plenty of warning of the approaching bombers. With experience, pilots would come to learn that successful ground attack in any aeroplane relies on using the surrounding terrain as much as possible and delivering the attack quickly, sacrificing precision for the chance to fight another day. The AASF really needed to have found out about the problems in a non-critical situation, during the 'Phoney War', as Bomber Command had—not at the start of a crucial battle. With more experience, and with the extra protection Brooke-Popham had proposed, the Fairey Battle could have been a lot more effective.

Initially, the forces the Battles were attacking did not appear to be the most serious threat. The terrain in the Ardennes did not seem particularly suitable for the movement of substantial motorised forces, and they had some way to go before they even reached the main French line of defence along the Meuse. The Panzers thrusting through the plains of southern Belgium and westwards towards Rotterdam seemed far more dangerous.

As soon as the German forces invaded Belgium, the BEF headed for the Dyle. Further south, the French 9th Army took up position on the Meuse at Dinant. The French 1st Army, with two of France's precious armoured divisions, rushed to fill the gap between the two rivers. Another French armoured division (1st Light Armoured) raced through northern Belgium to link up with French forces landing at Flushing. The combined force was then supposed to push north and secure a link with the Dutch. While the British and French moved into position, the brunt of the initial German assault would be met by the Belgian Army, along the Albert Canal, and Dutch forces, defending Fortress Holland.

The Dutch were relying on the natural obstacles provided by the Zuiderzee in the north and the numerous waterways at the mouth of the Maas in the south. In the west, the main defensive position was the Grebbe Line running along the Geld Valley. Behind that was a fallback position running from just east of Amsterdam to the east of Rotterdam. Both lines took maximum advantage of low-lying land that could be flooded. South of the Maas, the Peel marshes were only lightly held. The Dutch had chosen the shortest and easiest lines to defend. The disadvantage was that their main southern defences ran parallel to the Belgian northern Albert Canal defences, leaving a corridor between for the Germans to advance through.

The German High Command hoped to eliminate Holland on the very first day by landing troops inside 'Fortress Holland'. Airborne troops were to capture three airfields (Ypenburg, Ockenburg and Valkenburg) around The Hague, from where they would push into the city and capture the Dutch Royal family. If this failed, paratroopers dropped on the Moerdijk, Dordrecht, and the Willemsbrug bridges and Waalhaven Airfield would clear a path for the 9th Panzer Division racing through southern Holland.

The German forces that landed in and around The Hague were soon in trouble. Many of the Ju 52 transports were either shot down, destroyed by obstacles erected on the airfields, or simply found the Dutch airfields were unable to support their weight. The damaged and wrecked planes that littered the airstrips prevented the follow-up waves from landing. Many had to force land on any nearby flat land they could find. The surviving German troops were soon fighting for their lives.

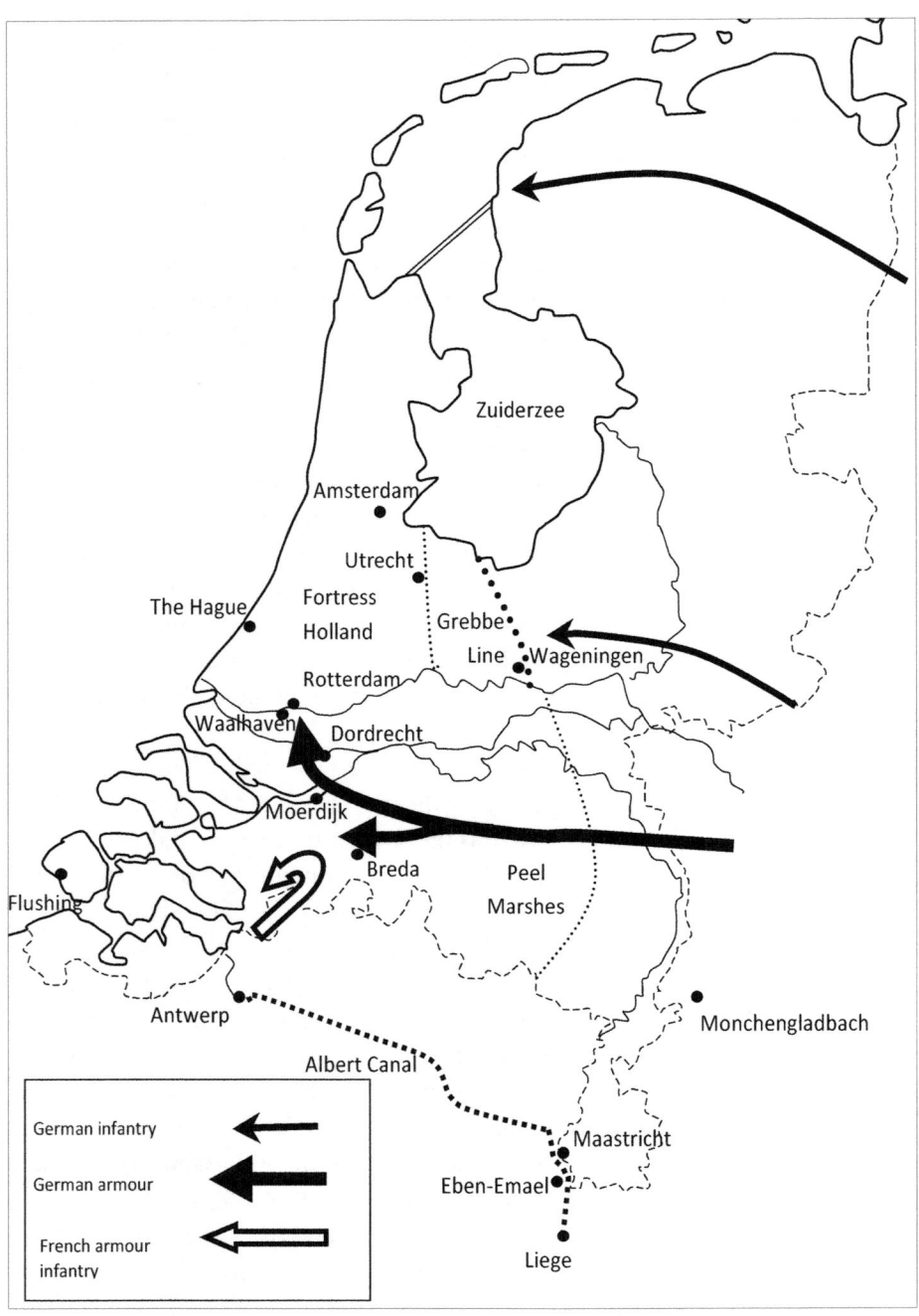

The Netherlands in May 1940.

Forty ground-attack sorties flown by Dutch fighters and light bombers supported the Dutch counterattacks.[19] Further east, Dutch forces withdrew in fairly good order to the Grebbe Line. In the south, Panzers and the Ju 87 dive-bombers of Fliegerkorps VIII, the Luftwaffe's short-range close-support force, had little difficulty blasting their way through the weakly held Peel Marsh defences.

As soon as the attack was underway, the air attaché informed the Dutch Army commander about the RAF plans to bomb advancing German columns, provided their location could be established. At 7.30 a.m., the Dutch told the air attaché that the German forces landing at Waalhaven were the most serious threat and asked for the airfield to be bombed. The message was passed on to London. When no attack came, the air attaché was bombarded with calls emphasising how critical the situation was becoming and demanding to know what was holding up the RAF.[20]

The message certainly got through to Newall. Armed with the information provided by the air attaché, Newall told the morning cabinet meeting that the Dutch had matters in hand around The Hague, but Waalhaven was a problem and six fighter Blenheims were being sent to strafe the airfield. Newall explained that he had decided not to use bombers because of the risk of civilian casualties. In fact, Dutch aircraft were already bombing their own airfields. The six Blenheims were in fact the only Air Ministry attempt to implement the fighter support the Air Ministry had promised. Their primary mission was to shoot down enemy aircraft and only strafe the airfield if none were encountered.[21]

By midday, requests were coming from Barratt in France for Bomber Command to intervene in the Netherlands. The missions subsequently flown appear to have been based on information gathered by reconnaissance planes rather than as a response to requests from The Hague. Twenty-four Blenheims attacked German forces in The Hague region, where, as Newall had explained to the cabinet, the Dutch felt they were in reasonable control.[22] Twelve of the planes bombed Ypenberg Airfield after it had been recaptured by the Dutch. Early in the afternoon, nine Blenheims bombed Waalhaven. This was the only RAF bombing attack on the airfield that day, and even this appears to have been a response to Barratt's demand for some action rather than the Dutch pleas *via* the air attaché. Three of the thirty-one Blenheim bombers were lost—ironically, two of them shot down as they attacked the recaptured Ypenburg Airfield. The Blenheim fighters operating over Waalhaven did not fare so well. The original plans for protecting Dutch airfields had proposed using Spitfires or Hurricanes where possible—using Blenheims would be risky. So it proved. Five of the six Blenheims were shot down by Bf 110s.

The next planned Bomber Command support for the Dutch was to be the attack on the Ruhr. The Air Ministry was expecting the government to give the go-ahead for the operation that night.[23] The desperate appeals to do something about the growing strength of the German forces holding Waalhaven seemed to be falling on deaf ears.

By the end of the day, Dutch counterattacks had recaptured all the occupied airfields except for Waalhaven. Fortunately for the Dutch, the British Government did not authorise the Ruhr operation. A frustrated Portal ordered the Wellingtons of No. 3 Group to attack Waalhaven instead. The Dutch lit a bonfire to guide the bombers in, and thirty-six Wellingtons kept up a steady bombardment throughout the night. Flying at little more than 2,000 feet, the Wellingtons dropped 58 tons of bombs on the beleaguered German forces. The Dutch were delighted, and at 5 a.m. they requested a halt to the bombardment so that they could launch their next counterattack. Less appreciated or indeed even noticed were the nine sorties flown by the two Whitley squadrons against bridges just over the Dutch border, in German territory.[24]

On the morning of the 11th, the Dutch attempt to retake the airfield failed. The RAF was asked to resume their bombardment while the few remaining serviceable Dutch planes focused their efforts on the German troops still holding both ends of the nearby Willemsbrug bridge. The aim at this stage was not to destroy any of the captured bridges. The Dutch wanted them intact so that the advancing French could use them to reinforce Fortress Holland. In the morning, and again in the afternoon, the two surviving Fokker T.V bombers, flying low and escorted by Fokker D.21s, scattered 50-kg bombs on the German troops around the bridge. The RAF attacks on the airfield, however, did not materialise; indeed, the air attaché was informed that there would be no more attacks. No reason was given. At around midday, an embarrassed air attaché told the Air Ministry the Dutch were 'seriously upset' by the decision and were pleading for it to be reconsidered. A succession of Dutch Army officers turned up at the embassy to emphasise the huge importance of eliminating the besieged German forces holding Waalhaven. The Dutch ambassador in London was told to try and speak to Churchill in person.[25]

On the 11th, Fighter Command was more active over southern Holland. Crowds cheered as Hurricanes patrolled The Hague.[26] However, a patrol by twelve Hurricanes of No. 56 Squadron in The Hague-Rotterdam area ended in disaster when the formation was surprised by Bf 109s and five were shot down. The next day, two out of a flight of three Blenheims were lost. A flight of three Spitfires was caught by Bf 109s, losing one of their number.[27]

For many of the British-based pilots, this was their first experience of combat. The circumstances could not have been more demanding. They were not trained in fighter-*versus*-fighter combat, and they were confronted by confident, experienced Luftwaffe fighter pilots. They were operating in small numbers—often lone flights of six, sometimes just sections of three—so they were invariably outnumbered. Operating in these circumstances, so far from their home bases, was not the ideal way to gain combat experience.

Something had to be done about the way British fighters were being taken by surprise and picked off by the high-flying German Messerschmitts. Instead of changing the tight vic formations that were largely responsible for the problem, Defiants were assigned the task of covering the rear. It was a chance to test the theory that the turret fighter could be used to establish air superiority in skies dominated by the enemy. The composite Defiant/Spitfire formation had its first real test on the 13th. The formation was engaging Ju 87 dive-bombers west of Rotterdam when it was bounced by the German escort. The German pilots might well have mistaken the Defiants for defenceless single-seaters and been surprised by the defensive fire that greeted them, but their surprise was short-lived; five of the clumsy Defiants and a Spitfire were shot down for the loss of just one Messerschmitt. It seemed fairly conclusive proof that Dowding had been right—using the Defiant offensively could be no more successful than Trenchard's offensive F.E.2 patrols of the First World War. However, the advocates of the turret fighter were still not convinced. The Defiants had claimed four Ju 87s before the German fighters intervened, and this was enough to ensure the experiment continued—once the battered Defiant squadron had recovered.

On the ground, the situation in the south of the Netherlands was already becoming critical. On the 11th, forward elements of the French 7th Army approaching Breda were brushed aside by the 9th Panzer and its supporting Ju 87 dive bombers. The French instinctively sought sanctuary in a safe defensive line and lost all interest in helping recapture the Moerdijk Bridge. General Winkelman, the Dutch Army commander, now realised that there was little likelihood of any help from the French; the only hope was to try and destroy the captured bridges to the south of the city and hang on in Fortress Holland. The Grebbe Line was just about holding. The main Dutch concern was still the German forces clinging on to their foothold inside Fortress Holland, around the Willemsbrug Bridge and nearby Waalhaven. The air attaché in The Hague was still furiously relaying Dutch appeals for air support to the Air Ministry, but getting no response. In desperation, the Dutch asked the military attaché at the embassy to pass on a message *via* the War Office, begging 'most earnestly' that Waalhaven be bombed.[28] The only response came from the Navy; while Portal's bombers waited for permission to bomb the Ruhr, at dusk on the 12th, six Coastal Command Beauforts and nine Fleet Air Arm Swordfish attacked the airfield.[29] By this time, the 9th Panzer Division had reached the German paratroopers holding the Willemsbrug Bridge.

The Dutch did the best with their own dwindling air resources. After flying most of its ground-attack missions on the 10th without fighter escort, for the remainder of the campaign the Dutch Air Force provided their low-level bombers with close escorts. This put the fighters at a tactical disadvantage, but it did mean they could actually help the bombers if they encountered enemy fighters. If no enemy fighters were around, they were in a good position to join in the attack. Anthony Fokker had lost none of his flair for designing fighters; the Fokker D.21, with its fixed undercarriage, might have lacked the speed of more modern fighters, but its superb handling and agility gave the Dutch pilots a fighting chance. With an escort, the hedgehopping Fokker C.V and C.X biplanes managed to deliver their attacks without incurring the crippling losses suffered by the Battle squadrons.

On the third day of the invasion, the Dutch Air Force was engaged all along the front. Operating from emergency airstrips away from their main airfields, ground-attack missions were flown against German forces threatening the defences that secured the northern end of the dyke at the mouth of the Zuiderzee. Retreating remnants from The Hague landings, trying to fight their way south to Rotterdam, were also targeted. Waalhaven was bombed. Troop columns and artillery positions around the Wageningen sector of the Grebbe Line, where the Dutch defences were under particular pressure, were also attacked. The numbers were tiny—the largest operation was just seven Fokker C.Xs with six Fokker D.21s escorting. The smallest was a lone Fokker T.V with a single D.21 escort.[30] The attacks may not have been devastatingly effective, but they were at least in the areas the Dutch Army needed them. Just the sight of their own planes roaring in at low level raised the spirits of the Dutch troops.

By the evening of the 12th, German troops had achieved a shallow penetration of the Dutch defences in the Wageningen sector, forcing the Dutch back to their last line of defence. The Grebbe Line was in danger of collapsing. The Dutch Defence Minister personally asked for the RAF to bomb the Moerdijk Bridge (to halt the advance from the south) and the roads leading to Wageningen (to slow down the German advance from the east). He was told the bridge was far too solid to be destroyed by air attack, which was true, and that attacks on roads could only bring temporary relief. This was also true, but that was what was all the Dutch wanted.[31] No. 2 Group in East Anglia could not help, but, rather bizarrely, the Dutch request was passed on to Barratt in France to see if his Battle squadrons south of Reims could lend any support.[32]

Dutch frustration was growing. The Air Ministry had refused Dutch pleas to base RAF squadrons in the Netherlands. Could they at least use Dutch airstrips to refuel, as French aircraft were doing? The Air Ministry came up with all sorts of reasons why this was impossible: Dutch fuel hoses were the wrong size; British planes needed different fuel.[33] In truth, if the Air Staff and Dowding were reluctant to send fighters to France to support the British Army, they were hardly likely to send them to the Netherlands to support the Dutch Army. The Dutch were told that there were always more crucial battles elsewhere and the RAF was needed there. This was true, but it was not true that the RAF was fully engaged in these crucial battles. Most of the Wellington, Hampden, and Whitley squadrons were just sitting on their airfields, waiting for the offensive against the Ruhr to start. Two-thirds of RAF fighter squadrons were waiting for the German bombers to come.

Dutch pleas now became ultimatums. The Dutch Foreign Minister spelt it out—first to members of the Air Staff, and then to Ismay, Churchill's military advisor. Either the British provided air support or the Dutch government would have to consider surrendering.[34] No assurances were forthcoming, and the Dutch government and Royal Family prepared to leave the country. Winkelman was given full authority to cease fighting if he judged the military situation had become hopeless.

Far from stepping up its efforts, Fighter Command was reducing the scale of its operations. Too many fighters had already been lost. Cover was provided for the evacuation of British citizens from Ostend and the Dutch Royal Family and government from The Hague, but there was nothing in the key battlezone. Early on the morning of the 13th, the last Fokker T.V, escorted by two Fokker G.1s, set off for the Moerdijk Bridge with 300-kg bombs. The damage these large bombs could inflict on the huge structure was never put to the test; only one hit the bridge, and it failed to explode.

On the Grebbe Line, a Dutch counterattack on the morning of the 13th on the Wageningen sector was defeated by heavy German artillery and Luftwaffe air support. A withdrawal to the final 'Fortress Holland' line became the only option. With the Luftwaffe dominating the skies, this was not possible until the sun had set. It would be a desperately difficult day for the Dutch Army. Low cloud provided some respite from German air strikes, and despite the weather, the Dutch Air Force was still flying and provided as much support as possible. Around twenty Fokker D.21s, C.Xs, and G.1s strafed and bombed German artillery positions and troops in the Wageningen area. Yet another plea to the British Embassy revealed the staff had joined the exodus to Britain. Despite the problems, during the following night the Dutch forces successfully withdrew along the entire front to their last line of defence.

On the morning of the 14th, the situation looked relatively stable. The Dutch forces were well-established in Rotterdam; the German forces holding the northern end of the bridge could not be dislodged, but Dutch guns were preventing any movement across the waterway. In the east of the country, the Germans were only slowly following up the Dutch withdrawal from the Grebbe Line. Hitler, frustrated by the slow progress, ordered an intensification of effort on all fronts. An assault on Rotterdam would be preceded by the bombing of the Dutch Army positions on the north bank. The target area would stretch as far as the city centre. The Dutch were warned an air attack was on the way and given one last chance to surrender.

Winkelman was not convinced there was any immediate need to surrender. The Dutch were certainly in no hurry to come to a decision—there was no reason to fear this particular German bomber threat more than previous bombing. The German Air Force had been bombing the country for four days. A second deadline was approaching and the negotiations were still in progress. Ninety He 111s of KG/54 were already heading for Rotterdam. The German commander tried to delay the attack, but only half the force saw the warning red Very lights. Fifty-four Heinkel bombers dropped 97 tons of bombs on the designated target area. There was no anti-aircraft defence, and the last serviceable Dutch fighters, five Fokker D.21s and five G.1s, were further north, providing cover for the troops still pulling back from the Grebbe Line. The Heinkels were able to drop their bombs with precision from 2,000 feet.

Unopposed bombing from low level can be particularly destructive. Even so, nobody anticipated what was about to happen. The bombs were high-explosive rather than incendiary, but the target area contained warehouses full of inflammable produce. These were among the first buildings to be hit, and flames soon engulfed the wooden houses of the historic city centre. One square mile of the city was devastated; 800 people lost their lives. Winkelman was severely shaken by the scale of the destruction. The German commanders on the spot were just as stunned. The German propaganda machine was quick to exploit the situation. If the Dutch did not surrender, a similar fate would befall Utrecht, which was also now in the front line. Winkelman ordered all Dutch forces on the mainland to lay down their arms.

At the time, the death toll in Rotterdam was put as high as 30,000. It seemed the prophets of doom had been right; bombing alone could bring a country to its knees. Whether the same decision would have been made if the bombing had occurred on 10 May, with Allies apparently coming to Holland's aid, is open to question. By the time the attack was launched on the 14th, the Dutch government had in principle already taken the decision to surrender. Nevertheless, for the Air Staff it was conclusive proof of how destructive and decisive bombers could be and a reminder of why Britain had to keep fighters back to defend British cities.

Lack of British support was not the only reason for the Dutch defeat, nor even the main one. The French reluctance and inability to engage the Panzers in mobile warfare around Breda was at least as significant. Nevertheless, the Dutch might have reasonably expected more support from a major military power like Britain. Given the importance attached to preventing the Netherlands from falling into German hands, Britain might have been expected to provide it. Not even the fear of invasion or heavier bombing raids on London, or the advantage of having friendly territory on the approach to the Ruhr, could induce the Air Staff to use the RAF as Dutch Army commanders wanted.

Another useful ally had been lost to the Allied cause. It was one thing to allow Poland, a valiant ally on the other side of Europe, to be overwhelmed by a powerful neighbour, or indeed Norway, a nation many hundreds of miles from our shores. It was quite another matter to allow a similar fate to befall an equally valiant ally just the other side of the North Sea. Britain could not afford to lose allies so easily.

Sedan:
A Lesson in Army Air Support

Further south, Britain's most important ally was also in trouble. Since 10 May, French reconnaissance planes had been monitoring the powerful armoured forces moving through the Luxembourg Ardennes towards the French defences on the Meuse, and more were moving across southern Belgium towards Gembloux. Initially, the latter seemed the greater threat; there was no natural obstacle to aid the defence in the 30-mile gap between the BEF on the Dyle and the French forces on the Meuse. The well-equipped French 1st Army had the task of plugging this gap. The 2nd and 3rd Light Armoured divisions pushed as far east as possible to buy time for the French infantry to dig in.

Before the German forces could even think about breaking through the 'Gembloux Gap', they had to cross the River Mass, which ran through the Dutch town of Maastricht. Just a couple of miles beyond that, in Belgium, there was another major obstacle—the Albert Canal. The Maastricht crossing was not important to Dutch defences, but the local troops did their duty and destroyed the bridges over the Maas before the Germans could seize them. German forces had more success just over the frontier, in Belgium. Troops in gliders landed near the three bridges over the Albert Canal and the fort at Eben-Emael, which was supposed to cover them. Belgian engineers blew one of the bridges, but those at Vroenhoven and Veldwezelt were captured intact and Eben-Emael was quickly neutralised.

With the Maastricht bridges blown, the Belgians had the best part of a day before any major reinforcements could reach the lightly armed German airborne troops holding the Albert Canal bridges. The German forces, however, had the firepower of the Stuka dive-bombers to help them fend of the Belgian counterattacks. The Belgian troops had no air support or fighter cover; apart from escorting the odd reconnaissance mission, Belgian fighters stayed on the ground. The Fairey Fox was as capable of carrying bombs as the Fokker C.V and C.X, but these and the Belgian Battles did not intervene. The blown bridges at Maastricht caused a huge bottleneck as German columns waited for the engineers to construct the pontoons. It was one of those rare occasions where there was no alternative route. The backed-up columns made an attractive target for the eleven unemployed Hampden and Whitley squadrons, not to mention the two Whitley squadrons attempting to hit less vital communication targets further north.

Sifting through the reports coming from the front, it was not German bottlenecks the Air Staff was looking for, but rather any evidence that the Luftwaffe was bombing civilians. The cabinet meetings that day spent much time discussing whether there was justification for unleashing Bomber Command on the Ruhr, but they reached no final decision.[1] Apart from Wellington and Whitley attacks on Waalhaven and communication targets west of the Ruhr, no other missions were flown on the night of 10–11 May. This is not to say that the French effort was more intensive—only two of the six night bomber squadrons flew. Twelve aircraft made some rather ineffectual attacks on German airfields.[2]

Five reconnaissance Blenheims, flying singly and unescorted, were dispatched during the course of 11 May to find out what was happening in the Maastricht/ Albert Canal region. Three were lost and the two that made it back were badly damaged. They confirmed the Belgian frontier defences had been breached and armoured forces were heading for Gembloux.[3] These missions also confirmed that using unescorted Blenheims for reconnaissance was not an efficient way of acquiring information; even the Belgians were escorting their reconnaissance planes. Only the photo-reconnaissance Spitfires could operate unescorted, but No. 212 Squadron had so few planes that it rarely managed to fly more than two sorties a day.[4] The most important role of any air force has always been and probably always will be reconnaissance. A few more reconnaissance Spitfires would have been a very good investment.

Early on the morning of the 11th, Belgian Air Force Battles attempted to destroy the two intact bridges over the Albert Canal. The Gladiator escort was intercepted before it met up with the bombers, and only one of the eight Battles returned. No bombs had hit the bridges, and the 50-kg bombs they were carrying would not have made much impression anyway.[5] The Belgians appealed to their British and French Allies to try.

In fact, Maastricht was the more rewarding target. The bridges high over the Albert Canal could not be easily replaced, but nor could they be easily destroyed. The pontoons the Germans had thrown across the Maas were far more vulnerable and any damage to the town itself would block roads. No. 2 Group Blenheims attacked the pontoon bridges in Maastricht (eleven sorties) and enemy columns pushing towards Tongres (twelve sorties). Twelve French LeO 451s, the first of the new French bombers, also bombed Maastricht. The French bombers had a close escort of M.S.406 fighters, while the Blenheims had to rely on Hurricanes operating in the general area, but it would seem the air defences were not that strong on the 11th. Two Blenheims were lost—one to fighters and one to flak.

Instead of continuing the attack during the night, Bomber Command stuck rigidly to its pre-offensive plane to bomb communication targets west of the Rhine in Germany. Nineteen Hampdens and eighteen Whitleys bombed Mönchengladbach. It was the first time Bomber Command had attacked a German city. Four civilians were killed.[6] How the Germans were supposed to distinguish between this and attacks on German industry east of the Rhine is not clear; nor would it have been clear to the Germans why Mönchengladbach was chosen as the crucial tactical target that merited Bomber Command's only effort that night. Lines of communication from the city led into southern Holland and to Maastricht, but it was too far from either front line to be crucial. All the French could put into the air was five ancient Amiot 143s, but at least they were in a more relevant area, bombing Maastricht and targets around Aachen.[7]

The fifty bombing sorties flown in the Maastricht area on the 11th were dwarfed by the number of bomber and dive-bomber sorties flown by the Luftwaffe. Nevertheless, they made sufficient impression for German Army commanders to demand better air cover. In response, on 12 May German fighter squadrons maintained a permanent watch, operating from airfields just a few minutes' flying time from Maastricht. Operating without a close escort was now going to be very dangerous. To make matters worse, while the Luftwaffe was stepping up its efforts in the Maastricht area, Air Component Hurricanes had to divide their resources between Maastricht and the Belgian forces falling back on Antwerp. The bombers paid the price. Nine AASF Blenheims were intercepted just after attacking German troop columns and seven were shot down. Five Battles from No. 12 Squadron attempted to destroy the Vroenhoven and Veldwezelt bridges. Two squadrons of Blenheims bombing Maastricht from medium altitude were supposed to distract the defenders, but they arrived too late and the bridges were not destroyed. Ten of the twenty-four Blenheims were lost to fighters and flak, and all five Battles were also shot down.

An irate German officer scolded one of the shaken survivors:

You British are mad. We capture the bridge early Friday morning. You give us all Friday and Saturday to get our flak guns up in circles all round the bridge, and then on Sunday, when all is ready, you come along with three aircraft and try and blow the thing up![8]

It was a fair point. If they had struck quickly, before the defences were ready, the chances of surviving were much greater.

Other attacks on troop column heading for Tongres brought the total number of No. 2 Group sorties to forty-five for the loss of eleven Blenheims. This was an unsustainable loss rate. Fighter escorts helped the French medium bombers avoid heavy losses, but no escort could prevent eight of eighteen hedge-hopping Breguet 693 ground-attack bombers from being shot down by flak.[9] Like the Battle aircrews, the French were flying their first mission, and they were equally taken aback by the lethality of the light anti-aircraft defences. The Breguet 693 was smaller and much faster than the Battle, but the French aircrews were no more experienced than their RAF counterparts.

Three more RAF Hurricane squadrons flew to France on the evening of the 10th, and the promised tenth squadron arrived on the 12th. Even so, the number of RAF fighters available was still inadequate for all the tasks they were required to carry out. RAF fighters were not being used as bomber interceptors deep in the rear, as Slessor and Dowding had anticipated; they were inevitably drawn to where the fighting on the ground was taking place, and the further east they went, the more frequent were encounters with Bf 109Es. Galland describes how he almost felt sorry for what he thought was a formation of Belgian Hurricanes he came across; it was actually an RAF squadron, probably No. 87. The German ace shot down two with an ease that he found embarrassing.[10] The Battle and Blenheim raid on the Albert Canal/Maastricht bridges was supposed to be covered by three fighter squadrons, but they were committed piecemeal and engaged by German fighters over a wide area. Only the eight Hurricanes of No. 1 Squadron were in the Maastricht area, and only three of them returned intact, although all the pilots eventually made it back. Thirteen French-based Hurricanes were lost on the 12th, marking the first serious pilot losses—four killed and two wounded.

The 100-odd bomber sorties flown by the Allied air forces on 11 and 12 May in the Maastricht region caused delays, especially to the 4th Panzer. This could only help the French racing to meet them,[11] but it was only partial compensation for the far more powerful blows that were delaying the French. These were spearheaded by the 300 Stuka dive-bombers of Fliegerkorps VIII. This mobile close-support unit had helped smash a way through the Dutch Peel Marshes defences, had beaten off the Belgian counterattacks around Eben-Emael, had forced the French tanks advancing on Breda to retreat, and was now supporting the drive on Gembloux. The idea that German Army commanders could radio for help whenever they needed it was perhaps an exaggeration, but the Germans were very good at concentrating their air resources where they were needed.

The French 2nd and 3rd Light Armoured divisions first clashed with the 3rd and 4th Panzer Divisions on 12 May. From the 13th to the 15th, a fierce tank battle raged east of Gembloux. The French suffered heavily at the hands of their more experienced opponents, but the German Panzers failed to break through.[12] In a hard-fought and close battle, by imposing some delays, the Allied day bombers could claim to have made a small but useful contribution. Perhaps significantly, for most of the battle the French tanks were spared the full attention of the German Stukas. On the 13th, most of Fliegerkorps VIII moved south. The French thought they were dealing with the most serious threat; in fact, the heaviest German blow was to fall on the Meuse.

Since the first day of the offensive, the French had been following the progress of the Panzers heading through Luxembourg and southern Belgium towards the Meuse. On the 11th, two flights of four AASF Battles were involved in a rather ambitious attempt to bomb roads around Prüm, in Germany. Only one returned. The survivors reported that the three other planes in their flight had been shot down by flak before reaching the target. In view of the heavy losses to ground fire, Barratt suggested that the Battles should be used from a higher altitude. Playfair argued that the highest altitude for accurate bombing would still be within range of light flak, and flying as low as possible was still the best option. This seemed to be borne out in further raids on the 12th, when a first wave of three attacking from 20 feet suffered no losses, a second wave of six attacking from 100 feet lost two, and a third wave of six attacking from 1,000 feet lost four.[13] There had been eight months of phoney war and a campaign in Norway to try out different tactics. The middle of a crucial battle was an unfortunate time to be debating solutions.

As far as the Air Staff was concerned, the losses proved they had been right all along. Portal had predicted 50 per cent losses and that was what was happening. In fact, the losses in tactical operations had been no more disastrous that those suffered in the Wilhelmshaven raids. The Air Staff's response, however, was very different. The heavy Hampdens and Wellington losses had not been allowed to throw into doubt the validity of strategic bombing; they had just hardened Air Staff resolve to find ways around the problem. The heavy losses in tactical operations were gratefully accepted as proof that Army air support did not work.

The only problem was that the Luftwaffe was proving the contrary. The Air Staff were left sticking gamely to their argument that direct air support for ground forces only worked for armies going forward; only armies that were advancing knew what needed to be attacked, whereas armies that were retreating would always be less sure. The Air Staff liked to conjure up the image of bombers desperately scouring the countryside, looking for a particular enemy column the Army wanted bombed. In fact, in such a large-scale offensive, the bombers had no problems finding suitable targets. Their losses to anti-aircraft fire were a testament to that. Two of the raids on 12 May were actually witnessed by Guderian, the commander of the German tank forces heading for Sedan.[14] The bombers were in the right areas.

The problem was the losses they were suffering. In critical situations, the AASF was supposed to fly repeat missions every two hours. If his had been possible, even the relatively small AASF could have had a major impact on the German columns winding their way through the Ardennes. This was what the German commanders had most feared. As it was, repeat missions were out of the question. Indeed, there were doubts about continuing to use the Battle at all in the low-level attack role. Much to their relief, the Germans were able to complete their three-day approach march to the main French defensive position along the Meuse relatively unscathed.

On Newall's orders, Barratt instructed Playfair not to fly any missions on the 13th—the Battles had to be conserved for the decisive phase of the battle.[15] Given the losses so far suffered, the decision was understandable. Unfortunately, the 13th was to be the decisive day of the entire campaign. This was far from obvious to the French that morning; the Germans had reached the Meuse, but all the bridges had been blown and French artillery dominated the battlefield. The French expected a pause of a few days while the Germans brought their artillery up to support a crossing of the river, and the situation seemed far more critical elsewhere. The tank battle at Gembloux was about to begin, and the French 7th Army was in difficulty around Breda, in the Netherlands. The only mission flown by the AASF on the 13th was an attempt to slow down the German advance by blocking roads in Breda.[16] While Battles were flying all the way from Reims to support the French Army in the Netherlands, the real danger was much closer to hand.

Events on the Meuse were moving far faster than the French had anticipated. The German forces had no intention of waiting for artillery to move up. Instead, the Luftwaffe gave a classic demonstration of how airpower could substitute for artillery. Throughout the 13th, the French positions at Sedan, in the front line and artillery to the rear, were subjected to waves of medium bombers and dive-bombers. Under the cover of this continuous air bombardment, German infantry established bridgeheads on the west bank of the Meuse. So fierce was the aerial bombardment that some French troops holding the front line panicked and fled.[17] There could be no doubt now about the impact tactical bombing could have on the battlefield. It was, however, still only German infantry on the west bank. The Panzers would have to wait until the German engineers could get their pontoon bridges across the river.

Further north, at Dinant, the German forces had nothing like the same air support. Nevertheless, at Houx, just north of Dinant, Rommel managed to get a small party of infantry across the Meuse and establish the first tiny, precarious bridgehead on the west bank. The German troops were spotted by a French reconnaissance plane. The pilot appreciated the significance of the discovery and knew what to do; following the guidelines established before the offensive for dealing with important fleeting targets, he headed for the base of No. 12 Battle Squadron. On 13 May, there could be no more important a target of opportunity than German forces on the west bank of the Meuse. Playfair wanted to strike, but Barratt, anxious to avoid unnecessary losses, denied permission.[18] Perhaps a single strike by a squadron of Battles would not have been enough to defeat Rommel's first attempt to cross the Meuse, but the Allies would never find out. By the evening, the bridgehead was large enough to allow work to begin on a pontoon bridge.

The French planned to retrieve the situation at Sedan by a counterattack by two tank battalions. These slow-moving infantry support tanks were quite capable of dealing with lightly armed infantry. If bridges enabled German Panzers to cross the river, the odds would swing heavily against the French. The counterattack was supposed to be launched at dawn on the 14th, but it had to be put back because of the confusion caused by retreating troops.[19] The French desperately needed a little more time.

At 10 p.m. on 13 May, General Billotte, the commander of all Allied armies on the North-Eastern front, instructed D'Astier and Barratt to take immediate action against the bridges the Germans were building. He wanted the attacks to begin that night if possible. D'Astier immediately switched his four night bomber squadrons from the Maastricht region to the Ardennes and prepared to launch every available bomber against the bridges the following day. Barratt was more cautious. He committed himself to just one small raid at dawn.[20]

The Meuse crossings were a much easier target for the Allied air forces than the Maastricht/Albert Canal bridges. The German fighter pilots would now be operating much further from their bases. The bridges were only temporary pontoons and they were only a short distance from Allied airfields. As Billotte appreciated, the attacks had to be launched quickly, not just because of the urgency of the situation, but to deny the Germans time to organise their air defences. On the morning of the 14th, the Germans were still desperately trying to extract flak units from the miles of columns queuing back from the Meuse.

As promised, early on the 14th, six Battles attacked the Sedan crossing points. All made it back to their base, although one wounded pilot had to force-land. Encouraged by this relative success, another flight of four was dispatched. They reported light flak, but all four returned.[21] At 9 a.m., eight French Breguet 693s attacked armoured units spotted by the Battle crews, losing one plane. At this point, no Panzers had yet crossed the Meuse and the anti-aircraft defences were still relatively disorganised. A more substantial effort might have brought a greater reward at less cost than the British bombers were about to suffer.

Soon after these raids, the French launched their counterattack. Almost simultaneously, the 1st Panzer Division started crossing the Meuse. The French tanks advanced until they ran into the German Panzers, at which point they were quickly scattered. The situation at Sedan had suddenly become extremely critical.[22]

French hopes of restoring the situation rested with General Flavigny's XXI Corps, a substantial force with motorised troops, light tanks, and one of the three French heavy armoured divisions. This was moving north towards the Sedan bridgehead, with instructions to strike as soon as possible. To buy time for these reinforcements to move into position, all bombing effort was to be focused on Sedan. Barratt was persuaded to join the French in one all-out effort. At around midday, he instructed the AASF to launch every available Battle and Blenheim against the Sedan bridges that afternoon.[23]

The French would attack first, followed by the AASF bombers. Both forces would rearm, return, and attack again. Blenheims from No. 2 Group would round off the assault. The first AASF attack would consist of three waves, with two escorted by Hurricanes and the third by French fighters. Hurricanes and French fighters would escort No. 2 Group Blenheims in the final attack. Five Hurricane squadrons would be involved; it was the first time Hurricanes had been switched from Belgium to the French front. They were joined by around fifteen now somewhat under-strength French fighter squadrons. Two of them, however, were equipped with the new Dewoitine D.520.

The RAF escorts were again indirect. At least three of the Hurricane squadrons were distracted by formations of Ju 87 dive-bombers. These were very worthy targets and the Hurricanes inflicted heavy losses, but this was little consolation to the AASF bomber crews they were supposed to be protecting. The Bf 109Es of JG 53 alone claimed thirteen Battles.[24] Arguably, the Dutch tactics of providing a close escort, with the fighters joining in the attack if possible, would have been more successful.

It seems the French 'escorts' were not the standard close escort they were providing for their own bombers. At least some of the French fighters were actually escorting a French reconnaissance plane. The Bloch 152 that were supposed to be escorting the Blenheims of No. 2 Group were covering Flavigny's forces moving up from the south.[25] It seems the RAF was happy to accept French fighters operating in the area on other duties as an escort.

By the time the first French bombers appeared, German fighter and flak defences were ready. This first wave consisted of just twenty-one bombers, thirteen of which were Amiot 143s—obsolete, ungainly medium bombers that previously the French had only dared use by night. They did at least get a substantial escort; twelve M.S.406s flew with the bombers, while Bloch 152s and Dewoitine D.520s provided cover at a higher altitude.[26] The French fighters fought valiantly to protect their vulnerable charges and were reasonably successful. Two Amiots were shot down by Bf 110s and another two were lost to flak, while one of the eight LeO 451s was also shot down. It could have been a lot worse.

For the AASF bombers that followed, it was a lot worse. Forty of the seventy-one Battles and Blenheims were lost to fighters and flak. So many of the returning French and British bombers were damaged that the repeat attacks had to be abandoned. Twenty-eight Blenheims of No. 2 Group attacked in the evening; only five Hurricanes could be mustered for the RAF element of the escort, and even these got side-tracked by German observation planes. Again, these were very worthy targets, but shooting down reconnaissance planes was not the role of the fighters on this occasion. Given their rather vague instructions, the pilots can scarcely be criticised for attacking any enemy aircraft they came across, but another six bombers were lost.

The dive-bombers and observation planes shot down by the Hurricanes did not help the bombers, but these successes did underline how many very vulnerable German planes there were in the battlezone. It was not surprising that Pownall was fuming at the 'the thirty-four squadrons at home where there is no attack'.[27] There would have been plenty of targets for them in France. Even the fighters that were available were affecting German operations. On 15 May, Guderian's XIX Corps reported its aerial reconnaissance was 'severely impeded' by Allied fighters and it was no longer possible for squadrons 'to carry out vigorous, extensive reconnaissance, as, owing to casualties, more than half of their aircraft are not now available'.[28] It was fortunate for the Luftwaffe that so many RAF fighter squadrons were still in Britain.

During the course of the 14th, twenty-eight French-based Hurricanes were shot down. Nearly all these were victims of Bf 109s and 110s. Nineteen pilots were killed or wounded.[29] The Hurricane was effective enough against German bomber and reconnaissance planes, but it was losing the battle with the Messerschmitts. Total Battle losses since the start of the offensive had risen to seventy—over half of the force. The AASF was withdrawn from daylight operations once again.

The French did their best to maintain the pressure on the Sedan bridgehead. During the night of 14–15 May, huge four-engine long-range Farman 222 bombers were ordered to join the tactical night offensive, but the two groups only had six serviceable machines. The four Amiot 143 bomber groups, after flying the previous night and in the daylight attack, were in action again on the night of 13–14 May; in the circumstances, the tired crews did well to manage sixteen sorties. Still the 'heavies' of Bomber Command remained idle. After the thirty-seven sorties flown on the night of the 11–12 May, the Air Ministry instructed Bomber Command to conserve its strength as cabinet permission for the bombing of the Ruhr was believed to be imminent. On 12–13 May, just twelve sorties were flown by the 250-strong force, and these were mainly near the Dutch/German border. On the 13th–14th, another twelve operated rather vaguely in the Eindhoven-Aachen-Maastricht region.

Bomber Command stepped up its efforts on the night of 14–15 May, but not over the Meuse. The French assured Barratt that the heroism of RAF crews had saved the day by allowing time for a French counterattack to restore the situation. Perhaps the French were slightly too enthusiastic with their appreciation; they convinced Barratt that the danger had passed. The French Air Force continued to focus on the Meuse crossings, but Barratt suggested that Bomber Command should concentrate on Breda and Maastricht. Always anxious to bomb something inside Germany, Portal added Aachen and Mönchengladbach. Twelve Hampdens attacked targets in and around Breda in support of the retreating French 7th Army, and eighteen Wellingtons bombed Aachen and Maastricht in support of the 1st Army. Twelve Whitleys revisited Mönchengladbach in support of no one in particular.[30]

The Allied bombing at Sedan might well have helped restore the situation—if Flavigny had actually launched his counterattack. The 150 bomber sorties the Allies had flown against the Meuse bridgehead on the 14th had caused delays. Guderian's XIX Corps reported: 'Throughout the day all three divisions have had to endure constant air attack—especially at the crossing and bridging points. Our fighter cover is inadequate.'[31] These delays could have been significant. While the attacks were taking place, Guderian had decided to push his 1st and 2nd Panzer divisions as far west as possible, despite their rather precarious base. The 10th Panzer division was supposed to cover the left flank. This began crossing the Meuse on the morning of the 14th, but the air attacks meant it was not fully deployed on the west bank until the 15th. Had Flavigny's corps attacked on the evening of the 14th, as had been the original intention, he might well have sliced between the Panzers pushing west and the delayed 10th Panzer. Unfortunately, the French could not really decide if Flavigny should attack the bridgehead or secure the left flank of the Maginot Line.[32] Flavigny went on to the defence and the opportunity was missed.

The situation on the ground now went from bad to worse. The French forces at Dinant tried to pull back to the frontier positions they had held on 10 May, but under incessant air attack, the retreat turned into a rout. The two remaining French armoured divisions in the rear were taken by surprise by the advancing Panzers and scattered. By the morning of the 16th, the Germans had achieved a complete breakthrough along a 60-mile front. No substantial Allied units stood between the Panzers and Paris—or the English Channel.

The situation was remarkably similar to March 1918, when the Germans had also broken through on a 60-mile front. It was the scenario that the Air Ministry and Air Staff had so frequently mentioned as the only circumstances justifying the use of the 'heavies' in support of the Army. It had worked in 1918, when the intervention of the RFC and French Air Force had bought the Allies sufficient time to bring reserves into position. This, however, was not 1918. The Germans were now exploiting their breakthrough with fast-moving armoured and motorised forces. The Allied air forces in 1918 had been battle-hardened formations, but in 1940 they were still inexperienced. In 1918, the RFC had not suffered horrendous losses. The British and French had excellent SE5a, Camel and Spad fighters. In 1940, however, it was the German Air Force that had the best fighter operating over the battlefield. Perhaps most significantly of all, in 1918, most of the RFC was in France; in 1940, most of the RAF was in Britain.

Still, the battle was far from lost. Indeed, in the period following the breakthrough, the German forces were probably at their most vulnerable, both to counterattacks on their weakly held flanks and air attack on their lengthening supply lines. The Bf 109 had a very limited range, and the Meuse was already some way from German airfields. The Panzer forces were now racing even further west. Bf 109 squadrons began moving westwards, but the number that could be maintained so far forward was limited, and protection against Allied bomber attack could not be so effective. The French were doing their best to bring up air reinforcements to take advantage; bomber squadrons in the process of converting to modern equipment were rushed to the front. Those that were not ready were told to use their old equipment by night. French naval bombers were ordered to operate against the advancing German forces.

However, the largest single untapped bomber resource available to the Allies was the 250 Whitleys, Wellingtons, and Hampdens of Bomber Command. It seemed it was time for the Air Staff to deliver on its promise to intervene if a crisis arose.

The Gloves Are Off:
The RAF Strikes Back

The Air Staff were eager for the RAF to play its part in the struggle, but they wanted to do it their way. Since the Germans had launched their offensive, Newall had been trying to get the government to authorise Plan WA4(c)—a plan with the nominal aim of disrupting German Army communications, but which was actually an attack on the German oil industry. This was the way to win the war, and the sooner the RAF could get started, the better. From afar, Trenchard would no doubt have approved of such subterfuge. In a note to Portal just days before the German offensive, the 'father of the Royal Air Force' commiserated with Portal for his inability to use his bombers as he wanted. If he had, 'it would probably have ended the war by now'.[1] Portal may not have been totally convinced by such a bold claim, but he agreed with the sentiment.

The cabinet meeting on the morning of 10 May discussed at length whether the Ruhr should be bombed. Newall was able to report that bombs had fallen on The Hague, but he did not mention the urgent requests to bomb Waalhaven that accompanied this information. Newall wanted the offensive to start that night. The cabinet agreed there was sufficient justification to let Bomber Command loose on the Ruhr, but a final decision was delayed until the afternoon cabinet meeting.[2]

At this second meeting, Newall assured the cabinet that even at this late point in the day, he could launch an attack that night with forty bombers and maintain that level of attack for as long as necessary. He stated that he believed 'the psychological effect of an immediate blow at the enemy's most vulnerable spot would be very great throughout the world', which gives some idea of the fantasy world the Air Staff and government had entered. No-one questioned whether forty bombers looking for their targets in darkness would be capable of producing consequences that would reverberate around the world.

However, there was growing opposition to the plan. Ironside objected on the grounds that there might soon be requests for Bomber Command to support Allied armies. If the force was used against strategic targets and then had to switch to tactical targets, it might fail to achieve much against either. As Newall listened, he knew the Dutch were already pleading for just such support. The cabinet decided it was better to wait a little longer. The launching of the offensive was postponed until the situation on the ground became clearer.[3]

The issue was not discussed on the 11th, but the Air Staff were still very confident the go-ahead would be given very soon. Portal was instructed to do 'the absolute minimum', which meant using just the two Whitley squadrons. Even these would still only attack targets inside Germany. It was much better practice than bombing Waalhaven or Maastricht. At an evening cabinet meeting on the 12th, Newall emphasised the importance of getting the offensive going before the Germans completed the occupation of the Netherlands and were able to deepen the Ruhr air defences. Newall suspected that the offensive through Belgium was merely a diversion, and that the main German aim was probably to capture airfields in the Netherlands so they could bomb Britain.[4] Newall seemed very concerned about an advance his own Air Force was doing so little to slow down.

The cabinet was persuaded. Even Ironside felt that using Bomber Command to bomb the Ruhr had to be better than the force just sitting there, doing nothing. It was agreed in principle that the offensive should begin on the night of 14–15 May, although a final decision was delayed until the following day because two cabinet members, Atlee and Greenwood, were not present.[5] A frustrated Portal informed his group commanders they would have to hold back a little longer.[6]

This delay was almost decisive. The cabinet was beginning to have second thoughts; Chamberlain did not believe that the main German aim was just the occupation of airfields on the Channel coast, and if a major offensive was developing, it would not be sensible to invite air attacks on the UK at a time when it might be necessary to reinforce the fighter force in France. Sinclair (Churchill's new Secretary of State for Air) and Newall were both horrified that anyone was considering sending more fighters to France. Fighter Command had just thirty-nine of the minimum sixty squadrons required to defend Britain. With home defences so weak, sending more squadrons to France would be a big risk, Newall insisted. To many in the cabinet, however, it seemed that launching an attack on the Ruhr and potentially provoking a retaliation was just as great a risk.[7]

Under-Secretary of State for War Anthony Eden and Ironside reminded the cabinet that an offensive on the Ruhr could not have an immediate effect on the course of the land battle. Chamberlain and Atlee agreed. All effort, they argued, should be concentrated on striking at the German Army's lines of communications, 'on which we could not direct too great a scale of attack'. Churchill, however, still mesmerised by the apocalyptic power of the bomber, remained adamant that Bomber Command should not be 'frittered away' in an Army support role. Nor should the Army expect more fighters. These had to defend the UK. Churchill, however, was clearly not that sure. He suggested that the Ruhr offensive should be delayed for a further three or four days. Newall objected; the moon was just entering the right phase for nocturnal missions, and a three or four-day delay would waste a valuable opportunity. Mussolini was becoming restless, and the destruction his bombers would wreak could deter Italy from entering the war. Nevertheless, the decision stood.[8]

At this point, neither Ironside nor Churchill were convinced that a major land battle was developing. Germany had 'only' committed her 'specialised troops' at Sedan, and these mechanised forces would soon be forced to retreat. They believed the bulk of the German Army was still being held back.[9] This conversation was taking place as the German Panzers were smashing through the French defences on the Meuse. Even before the scale of the problem in France was appreciated, Churchill had doubts about launching the Ruhr offensive.

Newall was alarmed by the increasing clamour for more fighters for France. Thirty-two Hurricanes and pilots had been sent just that day as reinforcements. He insisted that Dowding should put his views to the cabinet before any more crossed the Channel. Dowding maintained that his fighter force was effectively down to thirty-six squadrons; his problem was that these squadrons were doing very little while a desperate struggle was taking place on the other side of the Channel. Not a single bomb had yet fallen on London or any other city. Slessor's prediction that 500 or 600 fighters might be left sitting idle on British airfields while the fate of Britain was being decided in France now had a very prophetic ring about it.

Dowding could see the unanswerable logic of moving fighters that were not being used to where they were desperately needed. However, things would look very different if the Germans could be goaded into bombing Britain. On the 14th, he wrote to the Peirse (copied to Portal), urging that the offensive against German industrial oil targets should be launched as quickly as possible. He rather optimistically claimed that the oil shortages that would result from such an attack would force the Germans to reduce the scale of their air and mechanised operations in France. More significantly, these attacks would draw reprisals from the Luftwaffe on British targets, enabling Fighter Command to enter the battle. 'I want Fighter Command to pull its weight in this battle, but over Britain, not over France'.[10] In essence, Dowding was hoping that by using British bombers against targets that had nothing to do with the battle on land, the Germans would feel obliged to do likewise.

At the midday cabinet meeting on the 14th, the question of air support was not discussed. Early that evening, however, Reynaud, the French Prime Minister, telegrammed Churchill with news that an irresistible combination of Stukas and tanks was overwhelming the French Army at Sedan. He appealed for a further ten fighter squadrons to be dispatched to France immediately. The British War Cabinet met again that evening to discuss the request.[11]

Newall assured the cabinet that Bomber Command 'heavies' would continue to hit communication targets behind the northern sector, as required by the French High Command (these were the targets in western Germany that Bomber Command was attacking). As no official request had come to retarget these bombers, he suggested that perhaps commanders at the front were not as concerned by developments around Sedan as Reynaud appeared to be. Sinclair emphasised how difficult it was for night bombers to hit troops and bridges and reminded everyone of the magnificent targets offered by oil refineries in Germany. However, the cabinet could not be persuaded. Newall explained that if the French wanted Bomber Command to attack targets further south, he would need twenty-four hours to draw up a plan. It was agreed that Newall should arrange for a joint study by the Air and General Staffs.[12]

It scarcely seemed the time for joint studies. A quick look at the map would have instantly revealed targets more useful than Mönchengladbach; it did not require twenty-four hours to order attacks on Sedan. In the March 1918 offensive, RFC and Army commanders had not retired for a day to draw up detailed plans. A line was drawn on the map and bombers were told to attack anything moving to the east of that line.

The next morning, a dejected Reynaud telephoned Churchill with the news that the French had suffered a major defeat at Sedan. The bomber and fighter support Reynaud wanted was now all the more urgent. That morning, the cabinet met to discuss Reynaud's appeal and also to decide whether the time was right for Bomber Command to launch its offensive against the Ruhr. As both Newall and Dowding emphasised, the two issues were very closely linked. Opening a bomber offensive meant a strong fighter force had to be kept in Britain to deal with the retaliation. Much was made of the fact that neither Gamelin nor General Georges, the commander of the French armies on the north-eastern front, had formally asked for more fighters—only the French Prime Minister was claiming they wanted more.[13]

What Dowding said at the meeting is not recorded, but plausible later accounts stated that he claimed that at the current rates of wastage, his entire Hurricane force—both in Britain and France—would be wiped out in a fortnight. This was certainly what he believed.[14] Put like that, there seemed very little to debate. There was unanimous agreement not to send any more fighters.[15] Nobody seemed to question Dowding's figures; in fact, he was just counting any Hurricane that crossed the Channel as a loss. Actual Hurricane losses in combat were undoubtedly serious; the figure available to Dowding at the time put Hurricanes destroyed or irreparably damaged at fifty.[16] The actual figure was probably worse—around eighty fighters lost or badly damaged, with forty-four pilots killed, wounded, or missing.[17] With production running at about forty a week, these were very serious losses. However, even at this rate, the Hurricane force was not going to disappear in two weeks. With such a crucial battle underway, losses were bound to be heavy on both sides. The Luftwaffe had lost forty-five Bf 109s and twenty-six Bf 110s in the same period.[18]

On the question of bomber support, the cabinet was equally united. The pros and cons of tactical and strategic bombing were again discussed. One of the reasons for delaying the strategic offensive had been the fear that the bombers might be needed tactically if the battle on land was going badly. It was now going very badly.

However, Newall and Sinclair again emphasised how difficult it was to attack troops moving along roads and pontoon bridges by night. Oil plants, on the other hand, were 'targets of huge dimension' that were easy to find in moonlight and highly inflammable. Four of these alone turned out 2 million tons of oil a year. Peirse assured the cabinet that the bombing of oil refineries would 'unquestionably' slow down the German advance.[19]

The daylight losses of the 14th seemed to underline how pointless any tactical bombing was. Even those who had felt that Bomber Command should be held back for possible tactical missions had changed their minds. Chamberlain now believed bombing would make no difference on the battlefield. Tactical bombing had failed; it was time to give strategic bombing a chance.[20]

Newall now promised 100 planes would take part in the initial attack. There was concern within the cabinet that the ruthless application of air power on this scale might induce revulsion in neutral countries. Britain could not afford to alienate public opinion in the United States. However, the cabinet noted that the bombing of Mönchengladbach and Aachen had raised no protests. It was agreed that Americans would probably quietly approve of this resolute show of force.

Ironside made a half-hearted appeal for the bombers at least to focus on oil in transit to the front rather than the oil refineries, thereby ensuring that the effects were more immediate, but he felt obliged to bow to Air Ministry insistence that the attack should be at the source of output. In the end, there was surprisingly little disagreement. The cabinet decided that Bomber Command should implement Plan WA4(c) on the night of 15–16 May. This would mutate into Plan WA6 (the plan to bomb oil targets throughout Germany) at the Air Staff's discretion. The pretence of disrupting the enemy's rear had been dropped.[21]

For Portal and the Air Staff, the proper war was finally about to start. Dowding felt the cabinet had decided on the 'soundest action which [they] could take in the present situation'. It was left to Dudley Pound, the First Sea Lord, to articulate what everyone was thinking. The possibility of German retaliation would provide 'a convincing and conclusive reason' for not sending any more fighters to France.[22]

There was a genuine feeling that the Allies were taking the initiative for once. A resounding victory was expected, forcing the Germans to rethink their entire strategy. Churchill rushed off a note to Reynaud that explained how Britain would play its part in the ongoing struggle in France by bombing the Ruhr and drawing the German attack on to Britain. He could not send any more fighters to France as it would be 'short-sighted' to 'squander, bit by bit, day by day, the fighter squadrons which are our Maginot Line'. If this line was 'ruptured', German bombers would 'strike a blow' at the British war industry, potentially irreparably damaging the Allied cause.[23] Churchill hoped by drawing parallels with French Army strategy, he would make the policy sound more reasonable.

On the night of 15–16 May, Bomber Command opened its strategic air offensive against Germany. The gloves were off. Bomber Command could now show the German nation what modern warfare was all about. In the largest Bomber Command operation of the war so far, around 100 planes attacked sixteen targets in the Ruhr, most of which were oil plants. Three were bombed by nine planes; an average of five planes was considered adequate for the remaining thirteen targets.[24] Only twenty-four crews claimed to have found their primary target, although all but sixteen found something worth bombing—more bombs were dropped on the Ruhr that night than the Luftwaffe had dropped on Rotterdam. The next day, the cabinet was told that the Duisburg, Ramen, and Sterkrade-Holten refineries were left blazing. The plant at Homberg blew up violently. Over Dortmund, aircraft flying at 10,000 feet were shaken by the blast of the exploding refinery.[25] Britain had thrown down the gauntlet. Dowding and Fighter Command braced themselves for the German response.

The beginning of the strategic air offensive was not announced with the sort of public fanfare that might accompany a new offensive on land. The official Air Ministry communiqué was very downbeat, making no mention of oil whatsoever. Instead, the targets were stated as roads and rails communications 'east of the Rhine … which are supporting [German] forces in the invasion of Luxembourg and the Low Countries'. This included mechanised columns, one of which was reported to be 2 miles long.[26] The astute reader might have wondered what such columns were doing east of the Rhine and, if they were there, how their destruction might help Allied troops engaged in a desperate struggle 150 miles to the west of the Rhine. It seemed the Air Ministry had decided that the British public would have as much trouble as British and French Army commanders appreciating the value of attacking oil plants in the current crisis.

There was one member of the public who might have been expected to read between the lines and appreciate the significance of this development. Indeed, he might be expected to rejoice at the news. The RAF was finally fighting the sort of independent war Trenchard had always wanted. However, far from feeling any satisfaction, the RAF's father figure had experienced an extraordinary conversion. He suddenly realised a huge mistake was being made; his mind was transported back to the German offensives of 1918, when the determined application of tactical air power had saved the day. With German armies advancing once more over the same territory, this was no longer the time for attacks on German cities. He hurriedly rushed off a dire warning for Churchill:

With the attack on France which has now developed, it is absolutely essential … that all the aircraft should be used not as I previously advocated but in order to delay and hold up the German Army and win the battle … All the air must be used on concentration[s] of troops, communications, bridges and ammunition dumps behind the frontline to prevent or help to prevent the German army being able to bring up supplies, its reserves, and its reinforcements[27].

He did not regret his earlier pronouncements; nor did he want to modify his views on air warfare in general. If cities like Essen had been destroyed before the Germans launched their offensive, as he had been demanding, it would have seriously undermined the morale of the German Army and people. Once the summer campaigning season was over, the opportunity for the bomber to play a crucial part in the defeat of Germany would return. However, now the land battle was underway, the destruction of Essen and its armament factories would mean nothing if the struggle on the battlefield were lost.[28]

While his disciples attempted to practise what Trenchard had always preached, the ex-Air Force chief was left rueing his legacy. Beneath the politicking, Trenchard had always known what was required. With the reality of a desperate battle in France to focus his mind, it all became blindingly clear again. The Air Force he had nurtured and shaped did not have the equipment, tactics, or mind-set to deliver the tactical counter air offensive that his own RFC had delivered so successfully in 1918.

Trenchard was not the only one questioning the strategy. No sooner had the opening shot in the strategic air offensive been fired than the cabinet also began having second thoughts. By 16 May, both Gamelin and Georges were formally requesting—indeed, pleading—for the immediate dispatch of another ten fighter squadrons. Barratt was demanding at least four more. The Belgians also wanted fighters. There could be no doubt now that more fighters really were desperately needed. Churchill was due to fly to meet Reynaud that day and was anxious not to arrive empty-handed. He asked the cabinet to approve a further six Hurricane squadrons for France. Newall objected, but it was eventually decided to send the four Barratt had requested and have another two on standby.[29]

Once in France, Churchill began to appreciate how serious the situation was. Reynaud and his generals were clearly shaken by the events that were unfolding. They renewed their appeal for more fighter and bomber support. Churchill argued that only ground forces could stop the Panzers. However, he was persuaded that unless the Luftwaffe could be neutralised, the French would never be able to get those forces into place. Churchill, now warming to the challenge, envisaged a brief but powerful intervention by British fighters over the shattered front. If the skies could be swept clear of the Luftwaffe for three days, the morale of the French Army could be restored. The situation could then be retrieved by a counterattack from north and south, cutting off the German Panzer spearhead. That evening, Churchill instructed his cabinet to consider the immediate dispatch of the full ten squadrons the French had requested. The Prime Minister also told Newall to switch bomber effort from the Ruhr to tactical targets.[30]

Churchill's thinking was sound. If the skies above the battlefield could be cleared of the Luftwaffe, even for just three days, the prospects of the Allied armies would be immeasurably improved. Whether ten Hurricane squadrons could achieve this was another matter. The fighter was simply not good enough. Neither Churchill, Reynaud, nor his generals appreciated that it was a question of quality as well as quantity. Even ten squadrons of Spitfires might now struggle to reverse the momentum the German forces had established.

The cabinet approved Churchill's request, but the fighter squadrons would not be sent to France on a permanent basis. Newall argued moving another ten squadrons to France would just add to the confusion. It would be better if they operated from Britain and just refuelled in France. It was not ideal. The front line was a long way from Britain.

Newall also seemed to be having doubts that this was the right time for strategic bombing and had no major objections to the change in bombing policy. Churchill's instruction had come too late to affect operations for the night of the 16th–17th, although there were few operations to affect—following its exertions the previous night, most of the force was rested. Twelve 'heavies' attacked oil targets and another nine sorties were flown against communication targets in Western Germany. On 17–18 May, Portal met Churchill's demands by sending fifty-three 'heavies' to attack communication targets between Gembloux and Dinant, but another seventy-two renewed the offensive against oil targets.

The battered Battle squadrons did their best to contribute by attempting to bomb the Meuse bridges under cover of darkness. The training in the spring for the proposed Rhine mining operation should have been of some benefit, although by the accounts of the aircrews, it had not helped that much. Positive identification of targets was often not even attempted. Most crews simply dropped their bombs when their stopwatches told them they might be in the target zone.[31] It was not surprising the Air Staff were sceptical about tactical night bombing achieving anything.

It need not be so haphazard. In the First World War, both sides had discovered that bombing by night had its advantages.[32] Looking for targets of opportunity just the other side of the front line was easier than looking for a factory deep inside Germany, and planes could fly as low as they liked without worrying about barrage balloons. Anti-aircraft defences were often less well-organised in the battlezone. French night bombers generally flew low enough to bomb and strafe. Guy Gibson, flying Hampdens, described how he bombed both ends of a railway tunnel with a train inside.[33] This might have involved a little artistic licence, but it showed a willingness to do more than drop bombs on 'estimated time of arrival'.

However, the major effort had to come by day, which meant ways had to be found of reducing losses. It was not too difficult to see how this could be done. On the 15th, twelve unescorted Blenheims from No. 2 Group lost three of their number, while another twelve escorted by French Hawks returned unscathed.[34] On the 16th, the heavy losses—20 per cent of the sorties so far flown—led to No. 2 Group being rested, but the next day twelve more No. 2 Group Blenheims were ordered to attack German columns in the Gembloux area. Hurricanes were to patrol the target area, but the Blenheims were intercepted long before they got this far. Eleven were shot down. The next day, more Blenheims were supposed to pick up a French escort in France. When the escort did not appear, the Blenheims attacked anyway. Three of the six Blenheims were lost.[35] On the 19th, the Group was rested once again. Without fighter escorts, it was impossible for the bombers to sustain the pressure.

Focusing effort where it was most needed was another problem, On the 17th, Air Component Lysanders and Blenheims were thrown into the battle in a ground-attack role against columns reported approaching Le Cateau and much further south-west, on the St Quentin-Peronne road. On the 19th, AASF Battles returned to day operations, attacking columns spotted by air reconnaissance north-east of Reims. Thirty-three set off in small flights covered by twenty-six Hurricanes flying in the general area. There was little of the focus that had characterised the counter air offensive in March 1918, when the Royal Flying Corps had been switched from one sector of the front to another as required. It focused its effort along short, well-defined stretches of the front and operated immediately behind the front line. In 1940, targets were anywhere between Mönchengladbach, Peronne, and Reims; it was all far too spread out to have any impact, so scattergun that the columns attacked around Le Cateau and St Quentin were probably French. Inadequate aerial reconnaissance made it more difficult to know where the enemy was and where he was going, but even with this handicap, the RAF had to focus its efforts where ground forces could take advantage. This did not come naturally to the RAF. Cooperating with the Army had become such an alien concept that the Air Staff tended to see the RAF role as stepping in when the Army had failed rather than helping the Army to succeed.

The command structure and the different agendas of the various commanders made it even more difficult to achieve any focus. The Army had control over Blount's Air Component, based north of the breakthrough. Barratt was doing his best to use the AASF to support the Army, but he had been forced to move to Coulommiers, south of the breakthrough. He was also no longer working alongside d'Astier; Portal and most of the Air Ministry wanted to focus effort on the Ruhr. No. 2 Group was half BAFF and half Bomber Command. Dowding and Fighter Command was concentrating on defending Britain. On the French side, there was more divided command. Somehow, from this chaos, the available resources had to be focused where they might make a difference.

Portal had his own very clear idea of how the RAF could make a difference. 'We could do so much more to help the land forces if our efforts were a little less direct,' Portal perversely insisted. Bombing the Ruhr would force the Germans to transfer their fighters and flak from the front to the rear and use their bombers to attack Britain instead of Allied armies, he claimed. Tactical day bombing meant misusing fighters for escort when they should be shooting down bombers and 'free to dispute air superiority', although this was surely what escort fighters were doing. 'Bombing movement does not affect the air situation … which I understand is the root cause of the crisis on the ground,' he suggested intriguingly.[36] Group Captain Baker, the Deputy Director of Plans, rejoiced at how fortunate Britain was that 'in the most decisive week of the war' the full moon would make it so much easier to find the oil plants.[37] Peirse thought if tactical bombing was required, Coastal Command should do it.[38] The consensus was that the 'heavies'— and preferably the Blenheims too—should concentrate entirely on oil.

Confronted by this united front, Newall felt compelled to agree. The 'heavies' would be used solely against oil targets. The Blenheims would continue to attack tactical targets, but these too would only operate by night. However, Newall insisted a caveat was added to the instruction. Churchill had promised the French that Bomber Command would support the Allied armies and this promise had to be honoured. Any French requests *via* Barratt for more direct support must be met. On the evening of 19th, the instruction went out to Bomber Command and BAFF— without Newall's caveat.[39] The Air Force chief was losing control of his ministry.

The following evening, German armoured forces reached the Channel, cutting off forty British, French, and Belgium divisions.

Relearning Old Lessons

For Air Component squadrons, the first ten days of the German offensive had been a harsh introduction to the realities of modern war. Losses had been heavy, but lessons had been learned and a more experienced and flexible force was beginning to emerge. Fighters were still flying in tight 'vic' formation, but they were beginning to fly in greater numbers. Some squadrons were beginning to use flights at higher altitude to cover those flying lower. The pilots in France were relearning the lessons of the First World War.

By the morning of 16 May, half of the 200 Hurricanes sent to France had been put out of action. Over fifty pilots had been killed, were wounded, or were missing. More reinforcements sent out on the 16th and 17th and the fighter squadrons operating from Britain and refuelling in France helped make up for these losses. There seemed to be some justification that basing more squadrons permanently in France would add to the confusion. There were some dangerously overcrowded airfields. On the 18th, bombers and strafing Bf 109s and Bf 110s destroyed seven Hurricanes from the six squadrons operating from Vitry.[1] There was no shortage of space in the swathe of territory north of the breakthrough, but there was a reluctance to disperse the fighters and operate them from more basic airstrips.

The newly arrived pilots had to start learning the tactical skills their comrades in France had been acquiring. Often the Hurricanes they flew had no rear armour, and some still had fixed two-blade wooden airscrews. Even the twin-engine Bf 110 posed problems for the struggling Hurricane pilots. Five out of nine patrolling Hurricanes were shot down on the 18th in a clash with I/ZG 26; three of the casualties were newly arrived Canadians.[2] Nevertheless, if they could avoid the Messerschmitts, the Hurricanes could still be very effective. On 17 May, No. 151 Squadron, operating from Abbeville for the day, shot down seven Ju 87s from III/ StG 51.[3] The Component Hurricanes were a very real presence; on the 19th, they managed around 250 fighter sorties. In particularly fierce clashes over Lille, KG 54 lost fourteen He 111s to Hurricanes. For those who had time to gain experience, the Bf 110 and even the Bf 109 were not posing quite the same degree of difficulty.

The Air Component was becoming more flexible. Despite the desperate shortage of fighters, reconnaissance Blenheim and Lysander sorties were now sometimes getting a close escort. If Hurricanes were going to accompany the Blenheim or Lysander anyway, there seemed to be a case for the fighter carrying out the mission. They were not equipped with cameras; the only information they could provide was what the untrained eye of the pilot might see, but that was often enough. On the morning of the 20th, it was Hurricanes sent out on reconnaissance missions that reported enemy columns were advancing towards Arras from Cambrai.[4] These reports led to another step on the path towards a more versatile tactical air force. The Merville ground controllers, whose normal task was to direct the fighters towards bombers, instructed Hurricanes already on patrol to strafe these columns. Other Hurricanes were ordered into the air to join them. Squadrons on escort or fighter patrols began to use any ammunition they still had at the end of their mission on any suitable ground targets.[5] After years of being frowned upon by Fighter Command, ground strafing had suddenly become an accepted part of the fighter's role.

The fighter pilots were scarcely prepared for this new role. They flew ground-staffing sorties as they flew any other fighter mission—in tight formations. These proved as unsuitable for ground strafing as they did for air combat. Sqn Ldr Kayll of No. 615 Squadron led his twelve Hurricanes in four sections of three and lost three to ground fire.[6] Of the fifty-odd ground-strafing sorties flown on the 20th, six were shot down by flak, with three pilots lost. In a day of intensive interception, escort, reconnaissance, and ground-attack missions, mostly in the Arras region, thirteen Hurricanes were lost, but forty enemy planes were claimed as destroyed or damaged and several enemy columns were shot up. In the heat of battle, the versatility the single-seater fighter had displayed in the First World War was being rediscovered.

It was not a versatility Dowding wanted rediscovered. Escort, reconnaissance, and ground strafing were not what his fighters were supposed to be doing. He did not even want them protecting the Army. On 16 May, he demanded to know how low the Air Staff was willing to let Britain's fighter defences run down before turning off the 'Hurricane tap'. Operations in France meant his remaining thirty-six home-based squadrons were already seriously understrength. Remarkably, Dowding was already contemplating French defeat; Britain had to look forward and consider how she could survive alone, he argued. As long as Fighter Command and the Royal Navy remained capable, defeat in France would not bring the defeat of Britain. If, however, Fighter Command was consumed in an effort to keep France in the war, 'defeat in France [would] involve the final, complete and irremediable defeat of this country'.[7] The Army was not mentioned. Apparently, ground forces were not essential to Britain's survival.

Newall agreed. The Chief of Air Staff could not see how a few more squadrons could make any difference in France. Newall presented these arguments, with Dowding's note, to the Chiefs of Staff Committee. They in turn recommended that no more fighter squadrons should go to France. On 19 May, Churchill agreed. This was not good news for the troops fighting in France, and what followed was even worse. Panic set in.

Churchill was not contemplating pulling the Army or the RAF out of France at this point. On the 20th, he asked Newall to make preparations in case the RAF had to be pulled out, but that was all.[8] He still envisaged the BEF breaking out to the southwest to rejoin the French Army, as Ironside wanted and Gamelin was planning. On the evening of the 19th, he dispatched Ironside and Slessor to France to make this clear to Gort. The BEF commander, however, was already planning to retreat northwards to Dunkirk. Indeed, Blount, with Gort's approval, was already sending his Air Component reconnaissance squadrons back to Britain. It was Gort who set in motion the evacuation of the RAF from France, not the Air Ministry. As Slessor left Dover for France, retreating Air Component squadrons were already landing at airfields a few miles away. By the time Slessor reached Gort's headquarters, all the Blenheim and Lysander squadrons—apart from one squadron and a flight of Lysander at Gort's headquarters—had left.

Churchill's decision that no more fighters should go to France was interpreted rather liberally by the Air Staff. Squadrons operating from Britain stopped using bases in France to refuel, and the half-squadron reinforcements sent on the 16th and 17th were also pulled back to Britain. This was perhaps not quite what

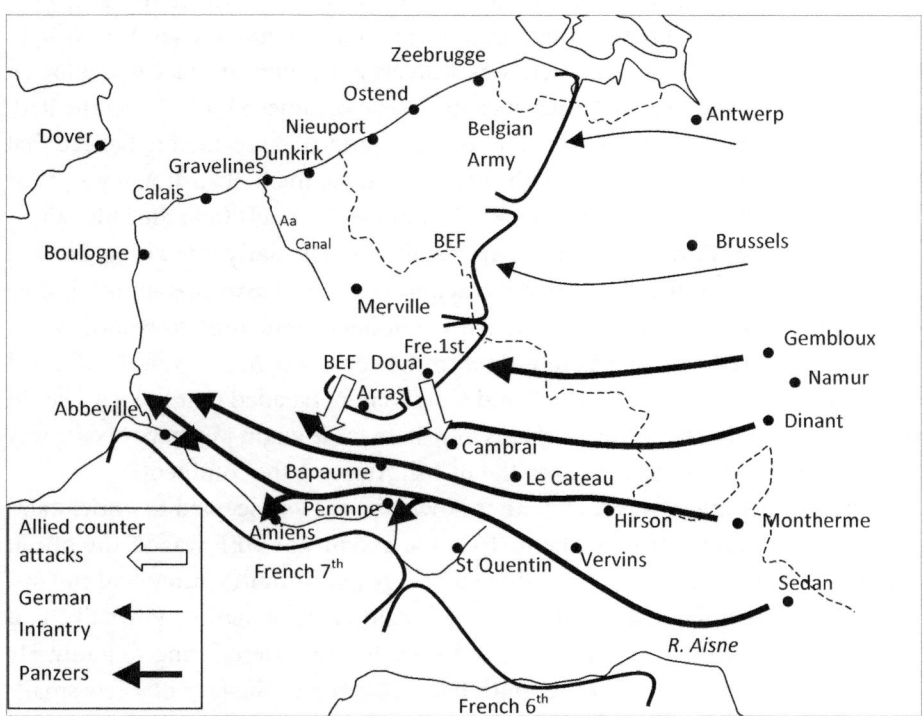

Arras on 21 May 1940.

Churchill meant. Slessor, however, took the policy a stage further by taking it upon himself to organise the withdrawal of all Air Component fighter squadrons. At 4 p.m. on 20 May, the Air Component flew its last fighter patrols from French bases. By the evening, the only RAF fighter squadrons in France were the three with the AASF south of the breakthrough.

There was an air of haste about the decision and panic about its implementation. Masses of equipment was abandoned, unserviceable aircraft were destroyed, and brand new aircraft suffered a similar fate if no pilots were around to fly them away. Hurricanes at storage parks were hauled into groups of three, nose-to-nose, and set alight.[9] Others were lined up and destroyed by anti-aircraft guns.[10] Elsewhere, transport planes were flying over to France to collect pilots with no planes to fly.[11] If air transport was not available, RAF personnel were told to make their way back to Britain as best they could. Some fled as far as Cherbourg, nearly 250 miles behind the French front line, to find a boat back to Britain.[12] On hearing that tanks were approaching, the staff of the Merville operations room clambered through the toilet window at the rear of the building and fled across the fields. The nearest German forces were over 20 miles away at the time, and they were not heading for Merville. The staff made their way to Boulogne and back to England.[13] They were actually fleeing towards the German forces; Boulogne would fall into enemy hands several days before Merville.

The evacuation was premature to say the least. Over forty Allied divisions were north of the German breakthrough in a pocket that extended from Abbeville in France to the Scheldt estuary. There was scarcely a shortage of space to deploy an air force. Blount and the Air Ministry seemed to be in rather a hurry to get the RAF back to Britain and Gort did not seem to mind; indeed, he seemed to believe that the sooner the BEF followed them, the better. Between them, British Army and Air Force commanders had scattered the RAF far more effectively than the Luftwaffe.

The attitude of Pownall, Gort's chief of staff, is particularly intriguing. He had spearheaded the pre-war Army drive to acquire more effective air support, but he seemed to raise no objections to the Air Component returning to Britain. Even if Gort's preferred option was to retreat to the coast, his Army would still need air support. It may be that Pownall and Gort were persuaded that the RAF could operate just as effectively from airfields in Britain, or it might just have been a way of pre-empting any decision to keep the British Army on the continent.

Part of the problem was that neither Pownall nor Gort seemed to understand what was happening around them. To some extent, the BEF was in the eye of the storm. British troops were only facing German infantry; they had not yet experienced the full ferocity of the air/tank blitzkrieg combination. Pownall could not understand why Dutch, Belgian, and French forces were faring so badly. He was convinced the French in the south had collapsed in the face of a few small-scale raiding parties. He did not think the main German Army had even been committed yet; he was so consumed by contempt for Britain's allies that he could not see that the way they were being defeated proved he had been right all along about the importance of air power.[14]

While the Air Component fled northwards, the Army it was supposed to support was preparing to strike southwards. The last squadron of Lysanders departed on the morning of the 21st, leaving just a single flight. Having gone to so much trouble to design an army-cooperation plane that could operate from any convenient open space close to the front line, most of his Lysanders would now be operating from airfields on the other side of the English Channel. The transformation could not have been more striking. The previous day, the skies above Arras had been the scene of furious battles between the RAF and the Luftwaffe; now there was not an RAF plane in sight.

Gort was about to discover the limitations of air support from 100 miles away. The 'Back Component' (as the Air Component was renamed) was no longer solely an Army force—its Blenheims and Lysanders were now controlled jointly by the War Office and Air Ministry. The Hurricane squadrons went straight back to Fighter Command. From now on, they would be used as Dowding saw fit. The retreat of the Component was a disaster for the BEF.

Dowding, however, saw it as a disaster averted. Indeed, to reduce losses further, he wondered if the three remaining Hurricane squadrons with the AASF could also return to the UK. For Dowding, the problem was not how to protect the British Army; in fact, the problem was the British Army. He did not measure the success of his force by how effectively it enabled the Army to operate—he measured it by how many enemy planes were shot down, and he believed that his fighters could shoot down more bombers and suffer lower losses when operating over Britain. Fighters that crashed could be repaired, not abandoned; pilots who baled out would land in friendly territory; and, most importantly of all, radar could direct the fighters to the bombers. He was sure that the best place to fight the war was over Britain.[15] However, this analysis ignored the fact that the war was being fought in France. Fighters might well be more efficient fighting a defensive war over friendly territory, but it was scarcely worth losing allies, abandoning armies, and taking your country to the brink of defeat to gain this tactical advantage.

Remarkably, Dowding's greatest fear was that the Allied armies surrounded in the north might successfully counterattack and re-establish contact with the bulk of the Allied forces in the south. If this were to happen, they would inevitably start asking for fighters again. As he put it: 'They will be unable to continue the battle without wrecking the Home Defence Units.'[16] As far as Dowding was concerned, the sooner the Allied armies in France were defeated, the better it would be. If losing France as an ally kept his Fighter Command intact, it was a price that he was willing to pay. It was the tunnel vision of a commander who could not see beyond his assigned mission of defending British airspace.

Dowding left Sinclair in no doubt about what was at stake:

I earnestly beg, therefore, that my commitments be limited as far as possible, unless it is the intention of the Government to surrender the country in the event of a decisive defeat in France.

For good measure, he also 'earnestly recommended' that Bomber Command be allowed to focus on oil plants and aircraft factories rather than wasting its time on communication targets that could be 'very quickly repaired'.[17] Dowding desperately needed the Luftwaffe to attack London. It was an interesting role reversal for Bomber Command; it had been set up to deter attack, but Dowding wanted to use it to encourage one.

Unfortunately, the German High Command was stubbornly refusing to comply with Dowding's vision of how the war should be fought. In five nights, the RAF had launched around 250 sorties against oil installations, yet still the Luftwaffe showed no inclination to retaliate. There was so little news emerging from Germany about the bombing, Duff Cooper, the Minister of Information, decided that the German authorities must be going to extraordinary lengths to 'hush up' the raids. Their single-minded determination not to be goaded into retaliating was impressive.[18]

In fact, the Germans faced no such dilemma. The bombers used in the initial strike on 15–16 May might have delivered more bombs than were dropped on Rotterdam, but the results could not have been more different. The Rotterdam raid had shocked the world, whereas Bomber Command's effort against the Ruhr merely sparked curiosity among the residents. The night of the 15th–16th had been no different to the previous four nights. A few bombs had fallen in built-up areas, but they were so scattered that it was impossible to work out what the intended targets might have been. There was speculation that the British raids were navigational training exercises flown by inexperienced crews, with a few bombs dropped randomly as an afterthought.[19] On the first night of the strategic air offensive one person was killed and at least seven were wounded.[20] It never occurred to the Germans that a full-scale air offensive had been launched. The need for retaliation was even further from their thoughts.

On the night of 17–18 May, the offensive was extended to oil targets outside the Ruhr. It was at least clear which towns were the targets. A fertiliser factory in Hamburg was gutted and 160 buildings damaged; thirty-four people were killed, and another thirteen died in Bremen. In terms of number of bombs landing in a built-up area, this was a more successful effort, but oil production was totally unaffected. The Germans were not even aware that oil plants were the target. The distress that the civilian casualties generated at a personal level did not affect a country enthralled by the staggering successes of its Army. To the Germans, Bomber Command's best efforts appeared to be indiscriminate terror raids that were so poorly executed they did not merit retaliation. Dowding would have to wait.

While Dowding marshalled his resources for the air attack that would never come, Gort was trying to deal with a German offensive on land that showed no signs of relenting. On 20 May, General Weygand replaced Gamelin as overall Allied commander and began organising the Allied breakout. The British would attack south from the Arras region and the French from Douai towards Cambrai. Weygand hoped to have forces for the main push ready for the 26th; in the meantime, preliminary raids were to prepare the way and hopefully knock the Germans off-balance. Gort was already planning a counterattack as a defensive measure, to slow the German drive past Arras. This now became the first instalment of Weygand's counterattack. Major-General Franklyn would command the British force, which would be spearheaded by two battalions of tanks, with seventy-four Matildas, led by Major-General Martel. Two battalions of infantry would accompany the tanks. This small force would need all the air support it could get.

It was unlikely to get any if Dowding and Portal got their way. Portal, however, was being forced to back-pedal. On the evening of the 19th, with the Air Ministry decision to cut back tactical air support still making its way to BAFF HQ, Barratt contacted Bomber Command about future bomber support. He was horrified to hear that there would not be any by day and only Blenheims by night. Furious, he immediately contacted Douglas; within hours, Newall's deleted caveat, guaranteeing Barratt's demands for direct support would be met, had been issued.

Georges was soon making it clear what he wanted. At midday on the 20th, the French requested maximum RAF effort by day and night to halt the tanks threatening Arras, with the focus in the Cambrai-Arras-Peronne triangle. General Dill, Ironside's deputy, backed the French request. Barratt and the French made 'tentative enquiries' about using the Wellingtons and Hampdens by day. In their reply, the Air Ministry went out of their way to explain they could not use the aircraft unless they had an escort.[21] It was a somewhat defensive explanation; the Wellington and Hampden were day bombers, and there was no reason why they could not have an escort—apart from the Air Staff's firm conviction that this was a misuse of fighters.

Slessor was busy organising the evacuation of the Air Component from France, but even he could see the need for more bomber support, insisting that No. 2 Group return to day operations. Portal had no choice but to sanction the use of Blenheim by day, but they would now get a close escort. There would be no more talk of clearing the air ahead of the bombers or meeting the escorts over the target; the Blenheims would fly to the fighter airfield and wait for the escort, after which the whole formation would fly to France, with the fighters 1 mile behind and 1,000 feet higher. The Blenheims flew around seventy sorties on the 20th, mostly south and east of Arras, as Dill and Georges had requested, and no aircraft were lost. It was a remarkable reversal of fortune. Cynics in the Air Ministry pointed out that no enemy fighters had been encountered. Instead of taking satisfaction on a mission successfully completed, it was felt that the escorting fighters had simply wasted their time. Perhaps a more useful conclusion would have been that it was time for escorted Wellington and Hampden missions.

On the night of 20–21 May, the night before the British attack, Bomber Command was ordered to suspend the oil offensive and strike much further west, in the Cambrai-Hirson-Vervins region. French bombers would operate in the St Quentin-Bapaume-Arras triangle. The French did their best to fly as many sorties as possible, with some planes flying two missions during the short summer nights. Fifty-nine sorties were squeezed out of the thirty-seven available planes. In its assigned area, Bomber Command used just seventy 'heavies' out of an available 250; Portal insisted that any more was impossible in such a small area. Eighteen Blenheims, flying their first nocturnal missions, attacked targets west of Brussels. Thirty-eight Battles continued their nightly offensive against the Meuse crossing points. At such a crucial time, the Allies could not afford to spread their meagre resources so thinly.

For Martel's counterattack, little if any reconnaissance had taken place since the Hurricane sorties the previous morning. Lysanders based in Britain were sent off to reconnoitre a swathe of territory between the coast and Arras to establish how far the German advance had reached. The flight of Lysanders left at St Omer flew eight missions along the southern flank of the BEF. Their reports include tanks spotted south of Boulogne, which suggests that these too were being used for strategic rather than tactical reconnaissance.[22] There do not appear to have been any sorties in the Arras region. Gort believed the counterattack would be striking in the gap between the armoured spearheads and the supporting infantry; as it turned out, the British forces would run into elements of Rommel's 7th Panzer Division preparing to strike to the north-west of Arras.

On the morning of the 21st, the Air Ministry instructed Fighter Command to supply three Hurricane squadrons for escort duties and three for sweeps in the area Arras-Cambrai-Le Cateau.[23] This was unnecessarily too far east for fighters that would struggle to patrol the Arras region for long from airfields in Britain. Again, the Blenheim escorts did their job—just two bombers being lost in fifty-eight sorties. The targets, however, were enemy columns advancing up the coast, towards Boulogne. As dangerous as these advances were, a choice had to be made between halting the advance in the rear or making it irrelevant by severing the German spearhead. Weygand had decided on the latter, but the RAF was attempting the former. The temporary disruption they caused might have been of more value south of Arras, where British troops could take advantage.

The instruction to fly fighter sweeps in the Arras area does not appear to have been acted on. No. 151 Squadron had already been ordered to fly a morning patrol along the Arras front, but the nine fighters were flying at 20,000 feet and spotted nothing. More fighters flying at a lower altitude were needed to tackle the German observation planes that seemed to be permanently hovering above the battlefield. This, however, proved to be the last fighter patrol for some time at any altitude.[24] Reports were coming in that the aerodromes at Calais and Boulogne were being bombed, so Park ordered his squadrons to try and include these areas in their patrols.[25] Given that they were nearer to Fighter Command airfields, it is not surprising that it was here that British fighters were involved in combats. Pilots were not going to take their fighters to the edge of their endurance by flying another 60 miles inland when there were enemy planes to deal with nearer the coast. At 10.00 a.m., a frustrated Gort demanded an intensification of fighter activity in the Arras area,[26] but no British fighters were in the region when the attack was launched at 2.30 p.m.

Initially, Martel's force made good progress. The standard German anti-tank gun failed to make any impression on the heavily armoured Matildas, and the Germans were soon in retreat. Ominously, however, the advance was taking place under the watchful eye of Henschel HS 126 observation planes. After advancing for about 5 miles, the advance was brought to a halt by a combination of air attack and 88-mm anti-aircraft guns firing over open sites. The German Army had used the same emergency measure in the First World War to stop tanks. In 1918, the Tank Corps had been allocated army-cooperation planes specifically to spot the guns and fighter-bomber Camels to destroy them. In 1940, the tanks had neither. This did not bring any protest or complaint from Gort or Pownall; even Martel seemed to have forgotten such air support once existed. The textbook Army solution was to wait for the artillery to move up to support the next stage of the advance.

If the Air Component had still been in France, it might have been different. The ground controllers would have been able to direct fighters to the area to provide some protection from German bombing and keep the prying Henschel spotter planes away. It is even possible they would have ordered fighters to attack the German positions holding up the advance. Even without any air support, the counterattack startled the Germans. Rommel reported hundreds of tanks were striking his flank, and the German High Command temporarily halted the advance westwards. Just the day before, there had been enough air strength in France to ensure the attack would have made an even greater impression on the enemy.

Renewed requests for air cover brought no response until 6 p.m., when patrols from Nos 253, 229, 146, and 601 Squadrons were dispatched to the Arras area. It is not clear whether they actually reached their destination. A couple of He 111s were claimed over Calais, an Hs 126 was shot down near Abbeville, and another was claimed near Amiens. All these were 40–50 miles from the scene of the Arras counterattack. Meanwhile, Franklyn did not feel he could hold the gains made. As he pulled back, the Stukas provided a reminder of how lacking fighter cover had been and how valuable close air support could be. Given that so much was at stake, the 142 sorties flown by Fighter Command on all fronts that day was scarcely an adequate response.

As Martel pulled his forces back, 20 miles north of Arras, at the now abandoned Merville Airfield, the commander of the air forces that should have been supporting the counterattack was searching for a means of escape. Blount worked his way through the disabled aircraft scattered around until he found a Tiger Moth that had been missed. In the early hours of 22 May, the Air Chief Marshal set course for England. The commander of the Air Component could claim, like any good captain, that he had been the last to abandon ship. The next day, the RAF sheepishly returned to Merville. Ten aircraft fitters flew in to see if they could salvage any of the abandoned aircraft.[27] It was not until a week later, with the Dunkirk evacuation in full swing, that the airfield fell into German hands.

On 22 May, it was be the turn of the French to attack southwards. As preparation, the French continued to use their worn-out Amiot 143s in the Arras–Cambrai area. Bomber Command, however, was back to attacking targets in Germany. If Portal could not attack oil targets, he would at least make sure that his bombs were falling on German soil. Bomber Command sent 124 Wellingtons, Hampdens, and Whitleys to the Aachen-Mönchengladbach region, more than 150 miles to the east of the French attack. Barratt switched his AASF squadrons from nocturnal attacks on the Meuse crossings to daylight armed reconnaissance missions in the Arras-Abbeville-Amiens region. This might help slow the German advance northwards, but it was too far west to help the French.

In the early hours of the 22nd, the Air Ministry warned Portal that escorted Blenheim missions would be required the following day to support the Allied armies. Dowding was told the protection of Calais and Boulogne was his priority. Where possible, however, fighter patrols should extend inland to support troops in the Arras-Cambrai area. A short while later, a revised, more strident message was passed on. Dowding was told that the future of the British armies in France depended on the success of the counterattack being prepared. German spotter planes were observing the Army all along the front, and troops were being exposed to fierce dive-bomber attacks. Dowding was informed that the Army was anxious to know what the Air Force could do about it.[28] Newall was not demanding action, merely passing on the message.

Dowding ordered No. 11 Group to switch two fighter squadrons from the Calais-Boulogne area to Arras. It was hardly an all-out effort. It seems that most fighter sorties were still flown around the coast.[29] In the afternoon and evening, flights from five squadrons were supposed to operate in the Arras-Cambrai region. The enemy planes the fighters claimed included seven of the troublesome Hs 126 observation planes, but it would seem none were lost around Cambrai.[30] The Army continued to complain that the German observation planes were operating unhindered.[31]

It was not easy for Fighter Command to do much about it. It was a very small sector of the front, a very long way from airfields in southern England, and patrols were likely to encounter enemy planes before they got anywhere near. Ironically, they had to fly over Merville and other abandoned airfields to reach their patrol lines. A much more focused effort would have been possible from airfields in France. With less than 200 sorties flown in the day, Fighter Command was still not committing sufficient resources either to protect the ports or defend the front line. For Dowding, this was not an oversight or misjudgement—it was policy.

The Blenheims were used throughout the day solely to slow down the German advance northwards along the Channel coast. Lysanders operating from Britain also attacked columns advancing towards Boulogne. This was perhaps the ultimate irony. The one plane the Air Ministry had designed to operate with the Army, under the control of the Army, was being used by the Air Ministry to supplement the efforts of Bomber Command. Twenty-four hours earlier, those Lysanders could have been supporting the Arras counterattack.

On the night before and day of the French counterattack, British bombers attacked nothing within 20 miles of Cambrai. There was little to support Peirse's assurances to the British War cabinet that everything possible was being done by night and day to support the British and French counterattacks.[32] Indeed, as Peirse spoke, Bomber Command was planning to reopen its offensive on oil targets by dispatching thirty-six Hampdens over 250 miles inside German territory to bomb the oil refinery at Merseburg, near Leipzig.

At 9 a.m. on 22 May, French tanks supported by motorised infantry began advancing towards Cambrai. The Germans were taken by surprise again, and their light defences were brushed aside. Anti-aircraft guns and repeated low-level strikes by Bf 109 fighters and 200-mph Henschel Hs 123 ground-attack biplanes eventually brought the advance to a halt just short of Cambrai. Despite Air Staff claims to the contrary, it seemed air support could help in defensive situations. Ironically, the Hs 123 was the sort of plane the War Office had been demanding during the winter of 1939–40.

By the 23rd, the British forces in the Arras region had been forced to withdraw northwards by Panzers swinging around to the north-west of the city. At this point, Blenheims were used against German columns in the Arras region. Not for the last time in the Second World War, RAF bombers were being called in to slow down an enemy advance when, just hours before, in support of a British advance, those same bombers might have been paving the way for a victory.

Weygand was still hoping to launch a major push southward from the Douai region. However, on the 25th, the British contribution to the attack had to be used to counter a German breakthrough further north on the Belgian front. On the 26th, Weygand's plan was abandoned. Gort was already pulling back to the Channel by this time.

This did not necessarily mean evacuation. The pocket contained very substantial Belgian, French, and British forces; the initial plan was to fall back and hold a bridgehead from Calais to Ostend.[33] This would tie down considerable German forces and give the French further south more time to establish a new defensive line along the Somme and Aisne. However, both wings were already in trouble. In the west, Boulogne had fallen on the 25th and Calais was already surrounded; in the east, the Belgians were struggling to hold the line. Gort was in no doubt that evacuation was the only option.

Preparations had been underway since Gort had first suggested the possibility of evacuation on 19 May. On the 23rd, Dowding was instructed to prepare a 'strong covering operation' for a possible evacuation of the BEF.[34] Non-essential personnel were already leaving France. On the 26th, it became a full-scale evacuation. What exactly the Belgian and French armies were supposed to do was not clear, but from the British perspective they would serve the useful role of covering the British withdrawal. Dunkirk was the only major port in the British zone; if it fell, evacuation would not be an option. The Aa canal running to Gravelines, just 12 miles from Dunkirk, represented the best and last hope for establishing a defensive line to the west of Dunkirk.

It was a desperate race to man the line before the Panzers breached it. The Army needed the Air Force to buy them some more time. From the 24th, Fleet Air Arm Swordfish and army-cooperation Lysanders and Hectors joined No. 2 Group Blenheims in attacks on German columns advancing along the coast. It seemed that even the 'heavies' would finally be used by day. For the 25th, four Hampden squadrons were told to prepare for a low-level daylight strike on armoured forces west of Gravelines. A Hurricane escort would be provided.[35]

Given Portal's attitude, it is surprising that the plan got as far as this. The attack did not take place. Instead, the Hampdens bombed communication targets in western Germany under cover of darkness. Only Portal knew how this was going to help save the BEF. It seems extraordinary that the crisis should see Naval biplanes used by day while so many of the RAF's specialist day bombers were only used by night. The Swordfish, Lysanders, and Hectors did their best; the Swordfish attack on the 25th ran into sixteen Bf 109s and Bf 110s, but the escort fought them off and no planes were lost. With fighter escort, daylight bombing was perfectly possible.

It will never be known whether these efforts would have been enough to halt the Panzers. The German advance was halted not by air attack or the defences on the ground, but by the German High Command, who feared the tanks might get bogged down in the marshy terrain; the Panzer divisions would soon be needed to strike at the main body of the French Army, along the Somme and Aisne. After two weeks of continuous advance, units were at 50 per cent strength and in need of rest. The Panzers were ordered to halt on the Aa Canal. Hermann Göring assured Hitler his bombers could finish the job. It would be two days before the order was rescinded and the Panzers tried to resume their advance; by that time, the defences were ready. Göring would have to deliver on his promise.

As the battle shifted to the Channel coast, encounters between the Luftwaffe and Spitfires (still under orders not to cross the coast) became more frequent. The British pilots seemed to have learned something from their earlier unsuccessful encounters off the Dutch coast. JG 27 lost five Bf 109s over Calais on the 23rd in clashes with Spitfires, and the next day another four were lost and two more damaged. The Spitfire was by no means superior to the Bf 109E—most were still handicapped by their fixed-pitch wooden propellers—but it was superior to anything most German pilots had encountered before. As soon as they could break free from their restrictively tight 'vic' formation, the Spitfires were formidable opponents.

German bomber losses were on the rise again, with at least four Ju 87s shot down over Calais by Hurricanes on the 25th. The RAF's own attacks on Wehrmacht columns were now only suffering light losses. For the first time, RAF bomber efforts could be sustained day after day. On the 24th, General von Kleist, the overall commander of the Panzer forces closing in on Dunkirk, reported—perhaps rather melodramatically—that for the first time in the campaign, the enemy had air superiority. On the same day, Guderian reported that enemy fighter activity had become so strong that reconnaissance was practically impossible once again.[36] Two days later, he was complaining that RAF fighter activity was intense and friendly fighter cover was completely lacking. The German commanders were perhaps exaggerating the extent of the problem, as commanders of all armies are inclined to do, but the RAF was making its presence felt. It was unfortunate that the Spitfires had not been able to do this sooner.

The BEF had secured Dunkirk, but the situation was still desperate. It was challenging enough to evacuate an entire army from a single port without any interference from the enemy; under air attack, it might be impossible. With the future of the entire British Army at stake, it seemed there could now be no excuse for Fighter Command holding back. Newall understood this. He gave Dowding very clear instructions that his command must provide continuous and powerful protection throughout the long, late-May hours of daylight. This would have been difficult enough if Calais was being used. Dunkirk was well within range of Fighter Command, but the distance fighters would have to fly to reach Dunkirk reduced the amount time that they could patrol for. Maintaining continuous, powerful protection would require a lot of fighters. It was more frustration for Dowding; his fighters were being misused yet again.

The Germans also had problems. The fighting had been tough, operations continuous, and losses heavy. Fighter units were, on average, down to 50 per cent serviceability rates, and the pilots were weary. German fighter units would be operating from captured and sometimes basic French and Belgian airstrips. These were not necessarily any closer to Dunkirk than RAF airfields. Accepting second-rate airfields, with pilots living rough, ground crews working in the open air, and supplies being brought in by transport plane, was all part of being a mobile tactical air force. It was what the German Air Force was used to. Even so, with their permanent bases and more secure lines of communication, RAF fighters seemed to have an advantage.

However, over-reliance on well-equipped permanent bases is also a disadvantage. There was no shortage of airfields in Kent that Dowding could use, if Fighter Command had been willing to match the flexibility of the German fighter force. Most of them were not part of the Fighter Command system, but being wired into the radar air defence system was not needed for operations over Dunkirk. If Fighter Command was going to put enough fighters over Dunkirk, it would need to improvise.

The Admiralty was showing the way; it was willing to risk its priceless destroyers to rescue the Army. More stirringly, Admiral Ramsay, in charge of the evacuation, assembled an improvised fleet of fishing boats, pleasure cruisers, and other privately owned craft to help lift the troops from the beaches to the larger ships offshore. Many of these would be piloted by their civilian owners. It perhaps behoved Fighter Command to match this courageous enterprise by throwing all it had into defending this band of civilian volunteers, not to mention the precious Royal Navy warships and soldiers trapped on the beaches.

It was not just Dowding who was reluctant to do this. Even at this moment of extreme peril, with Britain in danger of losing its entire Army, the bomber threat still dominated. Churchill had already asked his Chiefs of Staff to consider the worst-case scenario of a French collapse. Even with good fortune, it was estimated that Britain would do well to evacuate 45,000 troops of the 300,000 British troops in France. The generals saw no way for what was left of the British Army to be able to drive out an invading German Army. The Navy did not believe it could prevent it from getting ashore unless the RAF had control of the skies. Fighters would also be needed to protect ports and secure the supply of food and raw materials. The civilian population would only be willing to carry on the struggle if enemy bombing could be reduced to an acceptable level. The aircraft factories that supplied Fighter Command also had to be protected. All these responsibilities rested on the shoulders of Dowding's fighters. Britain could only survive if Fighter Command remained intact.[37]

Churchill agreed; he saw air attack as at least a great a danger as losing the British Army. It was a line of thinking that came very close to arguing Britain could afford to lose her Army, but it could not afford to lose Fighter Command. There was a genuine fear that if left unguarded, even for the briefest period, Britain (and particularly its aircraft industry) might suffer an instant and fatal blow. Given recent events in Rotterdam, this did not seem like an extravagant claim. It was, after all, what everyone believed British bombers were already doing to German industry. If Dowding did not overexpose his Command defending the troops at Dunkirk, there would not be too many objections from the politicians.

Similarly, Bomber Command did not want to be distracted by the plight of the British Army. Portal believed that his bombers were already winning the war, even though there was no concrete evidence of this. Photo-reconnaissance Spitfires had been dispatched to photograph the extent of the damage inflicted; unlike the low-level reconnaissance after the Sylt raid, the Spitfires were flying at 25,000 feet, and nobody was sure what could be seen from this altitude. When no damage was discernible, it was assumed that it must be technically impossible to see any damage at that altitude. It was better to believe the bomber crews.[38] 'We have already made progress in the systematic elimination of the key objectives', the Air Staff claimed. 'Shortage of lubricating oils and petrol may have a very important effect on the intensity of the air offensive against this country in the ensuing months'. On

26 May, the day the full evacuation started, Portal was trying to get the Blenheim effort reduced.[39] He could not afford to lose the bomber crews that would one day fly the next generation of heavy bomber. If the trapped Army needed bomber support, they would have to rely on Fleet Air Arm Skuas, Albacores, and Swordfish, or Air Component Hectors and Lysanders—not his bombers.

Despite Portal's protests, Blenheims continued to fly around fifty sorties each day. He was also forced to use his precious 'heavies' to ease the pressure on the Dunkirk defences, although he still insisted that this could be best done by bombing communication targets in Germany. On the night of 25–26 May, a Whitley impressed the residents of Cologne by defying the cloud to bomb a bridge and ignite a gasworks below. The bridge was closed for one and a half hours.[40] Troops falling back on Dunkirk might be forgiven for wondering how closing a bridge in Cologne was going to help them.

The heavies did also provide some closer support. On the same night as the Cologne attack, Wellingtons bombed German positions in the battlezone. Once the Dunkirk perimeter defences were established and the fighting more static, it became easier to define targets. Results were inevitably mixed, but any bombs dropped in the battle area at least had a chance of making a contribution and it was certainly encouraging for the trapped troops. The total effort against battlefield targets and communications in Germany was still only around fifty sorties per night. Raids on oil targets continued. On the night of 27–28 May, twenty-four Hampdens tried to hit oil refineries in Hamburg. The bombers managed to get seven bombs and a few incendiaries to fall within the city limits, starting one small fire.[41]

As the bombers were returning from their attack, news was breaking that Belgium had surrendered. Sir Roger Keys and Lt-Col. Davy, who had both been liaising with the Belgian forces, made it clear to the cabinet that the principal reason for the collapse of the Belgian Army had been Luftwaffe dominance in the air, not weakness on the ground.[42] The message was the same from every sector of the front—there were not enough fighters. Keys presented a heroic picture of Hurricanes trying and failing to break through the German escorts,[43] but there had been no major RAF fighter support for the Belgian Army since the Air Component pulled out of France. In other circumstances, it might have seemed strange that Britain did not just give the Belgian Air Force replacements for the Hurricanes and Gladiators that had been destroyed on the ground, instead of leaving the pilots without aircraft. It would not have turned the tide, but it would have shown a willingness to help and given the Belgians some hope. Given the attitude of Dowding and the Air Staff, it is not at all surprising that such a move was not even considered.

As soon as the surrender was announced, British and German forces rushed to fill the vacuum created. A fierce battle was soon underway for the coastal town of Nieuport, the last defensible position to the east of Dunkirk. It was a crisis within a crisis. For the next two nights, Bomber Command focused all its efforts on direct support for the Dunkirk garrison. By the 30th, however, the Air Ministry considered the crisis to be over; it reassured the War Office that 'in the event of a further critical situation arising in the land Battle', all effort once more would return to tactical missions. On 30–31 May, more Hampdens were dispatched to attack oil refineries in Hamburg.[44] It seemed the ongoing evacuation from Dunkirk was not crisis enough for the Air Staff.

While Portal deemed the crisis over, the British and French were grimly hanging on all along the perimeter defences. No. 2 Group was still fully committed to the Army's cause, with sorties rising to nearly 100 on the 31st. That evening, the day bombers made one of their more telling contributions; an attack by six Fleet Air Arm Albacores and eighteen Blenheims dispersed German forces gathering for another attempt to break though the increasingly shaky British defences around Nieuport.[45] Such timely interventions were still a matter of luck rather than judgement, but the bombers had to be operating in the right area before luck could even come into play. Ever fewer of the night bombers were in the right area. Wellington nocturnal sorties on German positions around the perimeter dropped from the forty-seven on the night of 28–29 May to just sixteen on the night of 2–3 June.

Fighter pilots were under clear instructions not to intervene on the ground. This was frustrating for some. It was obvious that their comrades were in enormous difficulty, and there seemed plenty of attractive targets.[46] Air defence was quite rightly the priority, but there was no reason why they could not expend any unused ammunition on ground targets before heading for home.

Dowding could claim that he had too few fighters to waste any strafing the enemy. Park, whose No. 11 Group was solely responsible for protecting Dunkirk, would not dispute this—he had just sixteen of the available forty-five squadrons. Park was also only allowed his fair share of the Spitfire squadrons, even though his were the only fighters that could possibly encounter the Bf 109. The defences of the rest of the country would not be weakened by concentrating the Spitfires in the south-east.

On 26 May, Park used eleven single-seater squadrons over Dunkirk. Reinforcements from neighbouring Groups increased this to nineteen on the 28th, and it stayed at around that level until daylight evacuation ended. Dowding could claim that thirty-four of his squadrons were involved over Dunkirk at one time or another; this sounded impressive, but nine squadrons were only used on one day, and only one squadron, No. 17, was used on all eight days. It was not an all-out effort and it was certainly not sufficient to protect the beaches 'from first light to darkness with continuous fighter patrols in strength', let alone escort planes attacking German positions.[47] Only around 250–300 sorties were flown over the beaches each day. To protect shipping crossing the Channel, a miscellaneous collection of Naval planes had to be used. While Hurricanes and Spitfires sat on airfields up and down the country, a motley collection of Hudsons, Rocs, Ansons, and Blenheim 1Fs were sent off in flights of three to patrol the sea-lanes. None of them would stand any chance if they encountered German fighters. Fortunately, the Luftwaffe would concentrate its efforts on Dunkirk.

In order to provide the continuous cover expected, Park had to use single-squadron patrols. On the 27th, the Luftwaffe launched a series of heavy attacks. Port facilities were so damaged that for a time, all troops had to be embarked from the beaches. The fighters, however, took a heavy toll. The vulnerable Ju 87 dive bombers managed to evade the high-flying RAF patrols, but twenty-four out of 225 medium bombers—over 10 per cent—were shot down. In response, the Luftwaffe stepped up its fighter cover[48] and the lone RAF squadrons often found themselves hopelessly outnumbered.

Park had to start using multi-squadron formations to combat the stronger German escorts. Initially two squadrons were used, often with a higher Spitfire squadron covering a lower Hurricane squadron. Later, formations of up to four squadrons were used. Some squadrons also began copying the looser German formations, with fighters working together in pairs. Even with the larger formations, the RAF fighters were still outnumbered, and there now had to be long stretches during the day when there was no fighter cover at all.

This was not what Newall wanted. He made it very clear to Dowding that he had 'to maintain continuous patrols in strength over Dunkirk and the beaches three miles east and west of it; to provide escorts for bomber sorties, and support the B.E.F'. Dowding insisted this was quite impossible. The air defences of Britain were at 'cracking point', and following these orders would lead to 'a dangerous situation'. It was a difficult argument to sustain when there were no attacks on the UK. Newall was not persuaded, and he essentially told Dowding to do what he was told.[49] However, if Newall wanted continuous cover in strength, he had to order Dowding to disregard temporarily the danger to the rest of the country and move more squadrons into the south-east. He chose not to, and Dowding essentially ignored the order to provide continuous cover.

Fortunately for the BEF, on the 28th, the morning of the 29th, and the 30th, Luftwaffe operations were severely hampered by poor weather. Luftwaffe bombing operations picked up during the afternoon of the 31st. The clear skies on 1 June meant that nearly 500 bombers, covered by over 500 fighters, were able to attack the port and transports. Fighter Command used fifteen squadrons and managed just 270 sorties. Even when the attacks coincided with RAF patrols, the fighters rarely broke through to the bombers. The RAF lost sixteen fighters, the Luftwaffe twelve, but only four bombers were lost, including just two of the 325 vulnerable Ju 87s.[50]

Three British and one French destroyer were sunk, along with a dozen other craft. So heavy was the bombardment that the British were forced to abandon the evacuation by day. It was a victory for the Luftwaffe. On 2 and 3 June, the Luftwaffe continued to bomb the encircled troops. The total number of sorties flown by Fighter Command dropped to just 147 on the 2nd, while the Luftwaffe was still using 500 fighters to escort their bombers. Throughout the evacuation, the number of RAF fighter sorties on any one day never exceeded 300.

The evacuation was another chance to see if the Defiant could be used offensively. No. 264 Squadron flew missions over Dunkirk on the 27th, 28th, and 29th, and appeared to be doing well, claiming eleven victories. On 31 May, however, the squadron lost seven planes in a single engagement. As compensation, the gunners claimed an extraordinary thirty-seven enemy planes shot down. In a little more than a fortnight, the unit was credited with the destruction of no less than sixty-five enemy aircraft. With several gunners firing at the same plane and all claiming the victory, Defiant claims were inevitably more suspect than most; even so, the over-claiming was extraordinary. The claims for 31 May comfortably exceeded Luftwaffe losses on all fronts for the entire day. The battered squadron again had to be withdrawn to rest and reequip, but the claims the crews were making kept alive the dream that the turret fighter could be a success. It was just a question of finding a way to reduce losses.

Fighter Command squadrons had made an impact from the 23rd to the 27th, but on subsequent days the Luftwaffe reasserted itself. Even the Spitfire did not seem to be posing the problems it had a few days before, as German pilots became more familiar with the strengths and weaknesses of the plane. Forty British fighters were lost on the three days between 31 May and 2 June, compared to seventeen German fighters and just fourteen bombers. Tactically, the Luftwaffe ended the battle on top.

Nevertheless, Göring had failed to deliver on his promise. Not even the all-conquering Luftwaffe could wipe out an army; even when it turned its attention to the ships, rather than the troops on the beaches, it could not destroy enough to prevent huge numbers escaping. The British were just as surprised. The number of soldiers rescued rose from under 8,000 on the 27th to nearly 50,000 on the 29th. From 30 May, the British agreed to take off an equal number of French troops, a belated but just reward for the crucial part they had played in holding the perimeter. By the end of the evacuation, 225,000 British and 100,000 French troops had been plucked from the beaches.

The Admiralty and War Office had good reason to celebrate, but the feeling of goodwill did not stretch to the RAF. From Ramsay and Gort at the top, right down to the humble private on the beach, there was fury at the scale of the RAF effort. Pilots unfortunate enough to be shot down over Dunkirk experienced the full wrath of the soldiers and sailors first-hand; some were denied access to the boats evacuating the troops.[51] In Britain, it was considered unwise for anyone in Air Force blue to venture out alone. At what point exactly the Royal Air Force was rechristened the 'Royal Absent Force' is not clear, but post-Dunkirk that was the sentiment.

Soldiers on the front line are scarcely best-placed to be aware of all the facts. It was a very easy to draw the wrong conclusions when bombs were raining down and there was not a single RAF machine in sight. Nevertheless, some of the attempts to justify the apparent absence are scarcely convincing. Some fighters did have to fly at high altitudes, and they did have to try and intercept the bombers before they reached Dunkirk, but with limited endurance, patrolling too far inland was not a sensible tactic. The Spitfires were still under orders not to cross the coastline. The Air Ministry excuse that Dunkirk was beyond their air defence system again underlines how the Air Staff had allowed radar to become a crutch that Fighter Command believed it could not do without.[52]

One of the particularly disappointing features of the RAF operation was the relatively few highly vulnerable Ju 87s shot down. Leaving aside the extraordinary claim of the Defiant squadron on the 29th (eighteen claimed destroyed when the Luftwaffe only lost two on all fronts) RAF pilots only claimed twenty destroyed during the entire evacuation.[53] The actual Luftwaffe losses were just ten.[54] With such strong escorts, the fighters attempting to tackle the bombers needed cover above them, but often even the lower fighter formations were flying too high to deal with the Stukas. Low-level fighter cover had been poor throughout the campaign. In tactical operations, the RAF had to be effective at all altitudes, which meant fighters operating at low as well as high altitudes.

The soldiers and sailors may not have had all the evidence, but they were essentially correct. There is no denying that the fighters that were used made a difference. As the Army had discovered in Norway, opposed bombing was far less effective than unopposed bombing. However, there were times when there were no fighters at all, and when they were present, there were not enough of them. Even if all the Spitfire and Hurricane squadrons available had been used, they could never have prevented bombs falling on Dunkirk. No doubt the soldiers and sailors would still have complained. Nevertheless, if the Air Staff and Dowding had so wished, Fighter Command could have done more.

The pilots were not entirely convinced by the orders they were following. Flying so high puzzled some when they could see the Stukas below.[55] Bomber pilots were also troubled. Guy Gibson, flying Hampdens, described how the aircrews in his squadron agonised over the logic of striking at industrial targets inside Germany when the soldiers on the ground were quite clearly in need of more direct support.[56] Such doubts were arising at a time when bomber crews still firmly believed their strategic operations were inflicting enormous damage on the German war machine.

Churchill tried to restore Fighter Command's reputation by claiming that RAF fighters had achieved a victory within the defeat. Not many were persuaded. It was unfortunate that it was often the brave pilots who flew in this unnecessarily unequal battle that bore the brunt of the soldiers' and sailors' ire. It was the Air Staff and politicians, chief among them Churchill, who were responsible for misjudging the bomber threat and holding back too many fighters. They were the ones who deserved the criticism.

It was not just RAF commanders who were getting it wrong; Göring also had an exaggerated idea of what bombers could achieve. Air forces could not destroy armies. German victories had been achieved by the Panzers and Air Force working together. It seemed that air power worked best when it was supporting forces on the ground.

The Luftwaffe could not win wars, or even battles, on its own; the failure to appreciate this would have fatal consequences for the German cause later that summer.

The 225,000 British troops rescued from Dunkirk provided Britain with a nucleus of trained, battle-hardened troops around which a new Army could be built. Nevertheless, even with the manpower resources of an empire, the British could never hope to muster an army that could single-handedly drive the Wehrmacht from the countries Germany had occupied. Britain still needed France. Even after the May debacle, the French Army was still far larger than Britain's could possibly hope to be for some time to come.

The Dunkirk evacuation gave the French the briefest of breathing spaces to organise their defences along the Somme and Aisne. The thirty divisions the French Army had lost included their best-trained and best-equipped. Weygand realised that with the Luftwaffe ruling the skies, he could not fight a mobile battle. Instead, he created a defence in depth, with every village and hamlet turned into a strongpoint that would continue to resist even if surrounded; he hoped that these strongpoints would suck the momentum out of any new German assault. If the French could hang on, their defences could only get stronger. The 100,000 troops rescued at Dunkirk were on their way back to France. In the air, there were already signs of a revival. The Martin 167 (Maryland) bomber squadron flew its first mission on 22 May, followed by the Douglas DB7 (Boston) squadron on 31 May. At the beginning of June, the French had seventeen day bomber squadrons equipped with modern planes and eight fighter squadrons reequipped with the Dewoitine D.520. French troops would now get more support from their air force, and at least the Stuka and the tank would no longer be a surprise.

Churchill was determined to give the French all the help he could. The newly formed 1st Armoured Division was already on the way to France to join the sole remaining division of the BEF. Britain's only two fully trained divisions would follow. In terms of land forces, Britain was literally committing everything. However, the fear of a German bomber offensive ensured air support was treated very differently. Given the importance of the battle that was about to open, the French saw no reason why every one of the 680 fighters they believed Fighter Command had should not be transferred to France. If that was expecting too much, half this force could be sent at the very least. Given that Fighter Command had scarcely put half its available strength over the British Army evacuating from Dunkirk, it was a request that was unlikely to cause much soul-searching in the Air Ministry, and none at all at Fighter Command Headquarters.

Barratt was more realistic about what reinforcements might arrive, but even his modest requirements were unwelcome in Air Ministry circles. Barratt now recognised how unbalanced his original force had been; it had far too few fighters for the number of bombers and reconnaissance planes. Losses had reduced his AASF to just six Battle squadrons, but even this reduced force needed more than the three fighter squadrons he had. Barratt's message was simple; either recreate a more balanced force with a higher proportion of fighters, or pull back the entire force to the United Kingdom. The latter, he emphasised, was unthinkable. If fighter reinforcements were sent, they had to arrive before the Germans launched their offensive—not in the middle of a retreat.

The cabinet discussed the matter on 3 June. The debate generated some curiously cunning arguments from the Chief of Air Staff. Churchill noted that the number of RAF squadrons available to support the Allied armies in France was now substantially fewer than at the beginning of the campaign and wanted British air support for the French to match the scale, and indeed the risk, being taken with ground forces. Newall, however, insisted that Churchill was getting his figures wrong; the Prime Minister was including the AASF and the fighter squadrons attached to it. This was 'an integral part of the Metropolitan Air Force, which had been located in France for operational convenience', Newall explained. The bombers belonged to Bomber Command, and the fighter squadrons attached to it were there to protect the bombers, not France or the French Army. As a concession, he suggested that these squadrons should be allowed to stay in France and form the reinforcement Churchill was asking for. It was an argument that stretched credulity to its limits—the AASF Battles had been part of the tactical BAFF since January.[57]

As for fighters, Newall and Dowding repeated the usual arguments about fighters achieving better results guided by radar over home territory. Dowding produced a graph showing that in the week following the German offensive, Hurricane squadrons in France were losing an average of twenty-five planes per day, while production was only four per day. If this loss rate had been allowed to continue, the entire RAF Hurricane force would already have ceased to exist.[58]

Dowding's attempt to portray Command on the brink of collapse relied on a rather creative use of the figures. It seems that he had spotted an old production programme that had anticipated only seventeen Hurricanes would be built in the four days following the 13 May bank holiday. Even before Churchill had appointed Lord Beaverbrook to pep up production, fighter output was exceeding these expectations. No less than forty had actually been built in the week in question, and in the week preceding the cabinet debate, ninety-two had rolled off the production lines.[59] The loss figures Dowding was using were also misleading; he seems to have arrived at a figure of twenty-five per day by counting as 'lost' the fifty-odd Hurricanes still serving with the three AASF squadrons in France. The figure also included the 100 or so abandoned or deliberately destroyed when the Air Component fled France. Dowding could, of course, claim that it did not matter how the plane was lost—a loss was a loss—but it also seemed reasonable not to expect a panicky retreat from France to happen every week.[60]

Dowding made much of the huge burden the ongoing air battles over Dunkirk involved. As he spoke, he melodramatically told the cabinet that the very last three squadrons were flying down to take part in the Dunkirk evacuation. This gave a rather misleading idea of the intensity of Fighter Command operations in defence of the evacuation. Squadrons were so under-strength, he insisted, the resources of eight squadrons had to be combined to form one 'strong' patrol. This was just a reference to the multi-squadron formations Park had started using over the beaches to combat the German escorts.

Even if no more fighters were sent to France, Dowding warned the cabinet, if the Luftwaffe turned its full weight on Britain, he could only guarantee to maintain air superiority for forty-eight hours. Churchill pointed out that the German Air Force was by all accounts suffering heavy losses too, but Dowding claimed the Luftwaffe's vast numerical advantage meant that only a victory-loss ratio of 8:1 would do. British fighters in France had only managed 1.5:1. Even in the Dunkirk evacuation, Fighter Command had only managed 4:1.[61]

As far as Dowding was concerned, the role of the Air Force was not to help win a battle, halt an enemy advance, or protect an evacuation. The only measure of success was the victory-loss ratio. For a force that was determined to fight its wars independently of what was happening on land or sea, it was an entirely logical way of measuring who was winning—indeed, arguably the only way. Victory-loss ratios are a useful way of assessing how an air force is faring, but it is not a measure of victory or defeat.

Hurricane losses had been serious—323 Hurricanes had been lost in May and only 226 delivered.[62] Nevertheless, Dowding's admission that Fighter Command had over 500 serviceable fighters seemed to the cabinet rather at odds with his gloomy prognosis. He countered by insisting that the real problem was pilots. Again, losses had been heavy, with over 200 killed, wounded, or captured since the beginning of the battle.[63] Nevertheless, the pilot situation was still not a crisis. On 15 June, Fighter Command had over 1,000 pilots in front-line fighter squadrons, which was not ideal—each squadron was supposed to have twenty-two pilots, so there was a deficit. However, Dowding cleverly managed to make the deficit more striking by increasing the pilot strength of each squadron from twenty-two to twenty-six. At a stroke, this increased the deficit from 134 to 362 pilots.[64]

Britain's apparent difficulties were not going to look so serious to her struggling ally. As Churchill pointed out, Britain had 'some 500 fighters of incomparable quality which we would be withholding at a moment when they would be making a supreme effort on land'. Nevertheless, he agreed that any military help Britain could provide in the immediate future was so limited that it would almost certainly make no material difference to the outcome of the battle in France. The morale-boosting impact of a British contribution would be enormous, but Britain should send the minimum to achieve this. France would either stop the Panzers with what she had left or be defeated, regardless of what Britain sent. The French were told the RAF fighter force would stay at just three squadrons because this was the maximum that could be maintained by existing production,[65] which must have left the French wondering why British fighter production was so low.

Bomber support provoked an equally vigorous debate. Even the Minister of War, Eden, insisted that the French campaign had shown the pointlessness of attacking bridges and troops. The most useful contribution British bombers could make to French success on the battlefield would be to continue to attack oil targets in Germany. Eden was only being critical of Allied efforts at tactical bombing; no one was suggesting that German efforts had been pointless. Atlee supported Eden, but Churchill insisted that once land operations began, Bomber Command must turn its efforts to supporting the French and British Armies more directly. Once again, the bombers would only be committed when things started to go wrong. The Germans were massing equipment in the bridgeheads they had established over the Somme at Abbeville, Amiens, and Peronne, and it was these targets that Bomber Command should have been attacking, before the offensive began—not oil refineries in Germany.

One of the reasons Newall gave for not deploying more RAF squadrons in France rather summed up British priorities. The servicing units more reinforcements required would be needed for Operation Haddock, a plan that was to be put into effect as soon as Italy declared war (which was expected to happen very soon). RAF bombers using airfields in France would strike targets in Italy. As always, Churchill was anxious to go on the offensive, and he had managed to persuade Reynaud that bombing Italy was a good idea.[66] A token raid against a possible future enemy can scarcely have seemed a high priority to the French as they prepared to meet an imminent German offensive.

While the French and Germans packed their front lines for the decisive battle, the Luftwaffe tried its hand at independent strategic bombing. On 3 June, the German Air Force launched 640 bombers against the French capital, ten times the number that had struck Rotterdam just three weeks earlier. It was not an indiscriminate terror raid—airfields and factories were the target—but it was hoped that the attack would weaken the French will to resist. Several factories were damaged and twenty French aircraft were destroyed on the ground. Two hundred civilians and fifty servicemen were killed. Even a nervous French government could take this level of intimidation in its stride.

On 5 June, the real battle began. The thrusts from the Amiens and Peronne bridgeheads posed a direct threat to Paris. This was where French defences were strongest and where the French Air Force made its greatest effort. The Abbeville front was closer to Britain and the French hoped the RAF could help cover this. The only British division in the front line was the 51st Highlanders, on the coast near Abbeville.

No reinforcements had arrived for the AASF. The three Hurricane squadrons mustered just eighteen serviceable planes. By this time, the AASF had retreated to the Le Mans region, 100 miles west of Paris. They were further from the front line than squadrons in Britain. On the first day of the offensive, the only air support from Britain was one escorted raid by Blenheims. The Highlanders were immediately under enormous pressure, and they appealed to London for fighter cover to fend off the continuous Stuka attacks. From the 6th, two squadrons from Fighter

Command operated over the division, using Rouen to refuel. This was increased to four squadrons from the 7th. The three AASF Hurricane squadrons also finally got some reinforcements to bring them up to full strength. Blenheim support slowly increased, with thirty-six sorties on the 6th and fifty-four on the 7th. No. 2 Group then maintained this level for a week. Dowding and Park were again dismayed by the way their fighters had to be used to escort these raids; Park was still trying to persuade everyone that single-seaters were quite unsuitable, and he suggested that the Defiant would be more successful.[67] It was a claim that was hardly borne out by the success of the German single-seater escorts over Dunkirk and the failure of the Defiant to deal with them. By night, Bomber Command gradually switched some of its effort from oil to the Abbeville front, but nearly 50 per cent of sorties flown were still against targets inside Germany. Once again, the effort in the tactical zone was belated and half-hearted.

French resistance on the ground was stubborn and German progress was initially slow. It briefly seemed that the French might have done enough to halt the German juggernaut. For three days, French bombers managed around 100 sorties a day against the German forces edging forward. French cannon-armed fighters were thrown into the ground-attack role. They were supported by Barratt's Battles, now benefitting from fighter escorts, although the shortage of fighters meant many Battles had to operate by night.

While the French focused their efforts on the Peronne and Amiens front, Rommel, almost unnoticed, broke through just south of Abbeville. By the 7th, his Panzers were racing westwards, outflanking the French forces still holding the Germans further south. On the 9th, a second German offensive across the Aisne shattered the French resistance. The next day, Mussolini declared war on France. The military situation in France was now hopeless. The transfer of reinforcements to France was halted, and the evacuation of all remaining British personnel began. From 14 June, the remnants of the AASF began leaving for Britain. On their return, the fighters went back to Fighter Command and the AASF became No. 1 Group Bomber Command again. The BAFF, the RAF's first Second World War tactical air force, had ceased to exist.

Despite the imminent collapse of French forces in France, Churchill still hoped that France would fight on with her navy and forces in North Africa. With Italy now in the war, the British would need all the help they could get in the Mediterranean, and the longer the French Army could hold on in France, the more time Britain would have to organise her defences on the home front. It was not an argument many Frenchmen sympathised with after the British evacuation from Dunkirk. However, Reynaud was still determined that France should fight on. Churchill set off for France yet again to bolster his efforts.

The French were trying to evacuate as much equipment to North Africa as possible. From 16 June, instructors, ferry pilots, and even partially trained pilots flew as many aircraft out of the country as possible. Aircraft were flown straight from factories without so much as a test flight. No less than 650 aircraft crossed the Mediterranean. With a secure supply of aircraft from the United States, the French Air Force had the means to support their Army in North Africa.

Reynaud was doing his best to persuade the growing number of doubters in his cabinet that it was worth fighting on. At this point, the Air Ministry blundered in with 'Operation Haddock'. It was a complication Reynaud did not need. It seemed the British were willing to go to enormous trouble to bomb Italian cities but far more reluctant to use these same bombers to support the French Army, which was still heroically fighting on. To the French, the operation just seemed like an invitation to the Italians to retaliate against French cities. Frantic appeals from French Army and Air Force generals to call off the raid were disdainfully dismissed. With Churchill's backing, the Air Ministry insisted that the French government had given the go-ahead two weeks beforehand, and there was therefore no reason not to proceed.

On 11 June, two Wellington squadrons arrived in Salon, in the south of France, to refuel. As they were preparing to set off for Genoa, the local French authorities took matters into their own hands by parking trucks on the runway. If Churchill had appreciated how little damage these bombers could inflict, he might have adopted a different attitude. However, he was still convinced even a handful of RAF 'heavies' could cause untold devastation. He was sure the impression made on the Italian nation would make up for any political disadvantages. He persuaded Reynaud to allow the mission to go ahead. Reynaud's acquiescence did nothing to strengthen his position; most of his cabinet believed only Britain had anything to gain by France continuing the struggle.

On the night of 15–16 June, eight Wellingtons headed for Genoa. Only one managed to drop bombs on the city. The following night, the force did better— fourteen managed to find Genoa and Milan. In the meantime, Reynaud had been forced to resign. Petain took over and immediately began negotiating a surrender. The Wellingtons beat a hasty retreat back to Britain. Operation Haddock may not have played a major part in the French decision, but it was at the very least insensitive. On 25 June, all French forces in France and North Africa laid down their arms. Britain was on her own.

The Luftwaffe had lost nearly 1,500 planes in combat during the two-month campaign; the RAF and French Air Force had each lost nearly 1,000 planes. In purely arithmetic terms, the Allied Air Forces did not seem to have done so badly. The figures, however, meant nothing. The RAF and French Air Force had completely failed to provide the Allied armies with adequate protection and support. The heavy losses suffered by the Luftwaffe were a small price to pay for the elimination of the French Army and nation. The Allies would have happily accepted far higher losses if it had meant halting the German advance.

Lessons had been learned. Forty per cent of all Blenheim bomber losses had occurred in the first eight days of the battle. Combat experience and fighter escorts had both helped to reduce losses dramatically. The Battle loss rate dropped from

50 per cent in the first few days of the campaign to 9 per cent in June.[68] This was still high, but once self-sealing tanks were fitted, losses could be expected to fall further. Fighter pilots too were beginning to acquire the tactical skills that would enable them to tackle fighters as well as bombers. The pilots and even some of the Air Force commanders directly involved in the fighting had begun to appreciate what was required of a modern tactical air force. Whether the lessons had been learnt in time was another matter. Within two months, Britain had gone from being a member of a powerful alliance with the potential to achieve victory to being alone and on the brink of defeat.

In London, the Air Staff did not see it this way. Far from being overwhelmed by the enormity of the task ahead, there was a sense of relief within the Air Ministry that the French had been eliminated. This was not just sheer bravado in the face of imminent catastrophe; there was a genuine feeling that with the land battle in France now over and its endless air-support requirements redundant, the RAF could finally get on with the task of winning the war.

In the midst of defeat, the Air Staff were already plotting how victory would be achieved. According to the experts in the Ministry of Economic Warfare, Germany was already close to collapse. The country would soon be facing crippling shortages of vital raw materials, especially oil. There would also soon be widespread shortages of food in much of Europe, including Germany. By the winter of 1940–41, the shortage of oil would already be loosening Germany's military grip on Europe. By the summer of 1941, a large proportion of European industrial plant would stand idle and Germany would have to cope with large-scale unemployment.[69] These were remarkable conclusions given that an isolated Britain was no longer in a position to enforce an economic blockade and Germany now had access to the resources of a continent.

Nevertheless, there was enough in the report for Churchill to set out his master plan. For Churchill, there was 'only one sure path' to victory. He had spent the 1930s mesmerised by the destructive power of the bomber, and this weapon would now be Britain's salvation. The RAF would win the war by delivering an 'absolutely devastating exterminating attack by very heavy bombers'.[70] The destruction of economic targets in Germany and the weakening of German morale would ultimately create the circumstances for a widespread uprising in German occupied territories and the downfall of Hitler; it was just a question of surviving until the bomber fleet had been built.

Faith in the power of the long-range bomber had contributed much to the crisis Britain now found herself in, but at least it now offered the country hope. Victory by aerial bombardment seemed a plausible strategy. For the Air Staff, the only fly in the ointment would be if the Germans upset the master plan by invading Britain and involving the RAF in yet another messy, distracting, unnecessary land battle.

Desperate Measures: Wasted Resources

On 18 June, Winston Churchill stated, 'What General Weygand called the "Battle of France" is over. I expect the "Battle of Britain" is about to begin.' At this stage, however, Churchill was not envisaging the purely aerial 'Battle of Britain' that now fills our history books. The Prime Minister was anticipating a battle fought on the beaches, landing grounds, fields, and streets of Britain, as well as in the skies. This was not the battle he had foreseen as a maverick backbencher in the mid-1930s. Bombers, not invading armies, had been the danger. In the early summer of 1940, even hard-line bomber advocates found it difficult to believe Germany would not follow up her success in France with an invasion of Britain.

The German invasion of Norway had already set alarm bells ringing. The Home Guard had been set up to guard the coast and the air equivalent, the Banquet Scheme, would see RAF trainers, flown by instructors, thrown against any surprise invasion. These forces would not now be an insurance against an unlikely event—they were a key element of Britain's attempt to deal with what seemed a certainty, fighting alongside an army that had abandoned most of its equipment at Dunkirk. Twenty-seven divisions existed in some form or other, but there was scarcely enough to equip two of them. They had just 167 anti-tank guns between them. To replace the 45,000 cars and trucks lost in France, the Army was reduced to scouring scrap yards for any ancient vehicles that might be made serviceable. There were two armoured divisions with around 250 tanks, most of which were only armed with a machine gun. It was not much with which to take on the all-conquering Wehrmacht.[1]

Ironside, now commanding British forces in the UK, was still expecting the invasion to come along the east coast. This had been the only possible route before the German occupation of France and the Lowlands, and with its attractive landing sites and flat country beyond to exploit, it still seemed the most likely. Ironside could not see how the British forces could be mobile enough to challenge a German invasion on the coast, and the Luftwaffe would probably make movement impossible anyway. It seemed best to try and make a stand inland, on the shortest line of defence, and he started establishing defences from Bristol to London and north to the Wash. Churchill thought that it would be catastrophic to gift the

German forces a solid footing in the country, arguing that a German invasion would have to be defeated on the beaches. This was where the Navy could intervene and the Air Force could bomb the forces disembarking invasion 'without fear of endangering the lives of our own forces or of the civil population'.[2] Churchill replaced Ironside with General Alan Brooke, someone more in tune with this approach. However, appointing a new commander did not make the British Army any more mobile or the Luftwaffe any less of a threat. The flaws in both strategies underlined how desperate Britain's situation was.

If Britain's makeshift army was to succeed, it would need all the support the RAF could provide. The War Office was not optimistic about getting it. Following the debacle in France, relations between the Air Ministry and War Office had fallen to an all-time low. There was considerable and open resentment within Army circles at the failure of the RAF to do more in the French campaign. As far as the War Office was concerned, a very high price had been paid for the Air Ministry's obsession with its independent bombing strategy and its stubborn refusal to prepare and equip the RAF for tactical air operations. Reports that Newall had been deprecating the 'frittering away of resources in the land battle' fanned Army fury. The Luftwaffe had spent the previous three months demonstrating what tactical airpower could do; surely there could now be no doubt that air support was an essential part of modern warfare. The Army expected the RAF to focus its efforts closer to the front line. During the retreat to Dunkirk, reports troops had heard on the radio of the Ruhr and Hamburg being bombed had been 'cold comfort'. The Army expected changes, and with invasion of the United Kingdom imminent, they expected them quickly.[3] There was no longer time for tact or diplomacy.

The War Office demand was very straightforward. It wanted no less than 'the elimination of a separate Air Staff and Air strategy divorced from the other two services'. Col. Festing, in the Directorate of Military Operations, had particularly good reasons for having strong views on the subject. He had been the Army/Air liaison officer in the Norwegian campaign and was all too familiar with what current Air Staff policy meant for the troops on the ground. He believed the only solution was a combined Air/War Ministry. The current crisis facing the country scarcely seemed the time for such a radical reorganisation; that was one for the future. However, the Army had to have more say in the type of aircraft equipping the RAF and more control over their use. Multi-purpose 'army-cooperation' planes were not enough—the Army needed bombers and fighters under its direct control. If the RAF did not have the right planes, Festing suggested, then the Air Ministry should buy them from the United States.[4]

A joint Air/War Ministry could not have been further from the thoughts of the Air Ministry, but criticism of the RAF was rife and the pressure for some sort of change was intense. The Air Ministry solution was to create a new post, the 'Director of Military Cooperation'. This was supposed to improve cooperation between the Army and Air Force. In practice, it was just a department for dealing with War Office complaints about the lack of cooperation.[5]

Festing dispatched a scathing critique of RAF air support in France to Sinclair. The enemy 'was able to establish air superiority over the whole front for the whole period', he fumed.[6] The Air Ministry was infuriated at this 'unbalanced' report. The new Director of Military Cooperation, Group Captain Fraser, was called in to refute the claims; he claimed that even before reinforcements had been sent, there had been more fighters in France than in Britain. This puzzled the War Office, but it was just about true if French, Dutch, and Belgium fighters were taken into account. 'At any time attacks might have been turned on Britain', Fraser desperately argued, claiming that 'history [would] relate that the disposition of fighters represents a proper balance'.[7] Unfortunately, history would also record that Britain had not been bombed, the British and Allied armies had, and Britain was now facing defeat alone.

The good news for the War Office was that the Air Ministry was no longer solely responsible for Air Force equipment. Churchill had never had much faith in the organisation. One of his first acts as Prime Minister was to create a Ministry of Aircraft Production, which took aircraft design and production out of Air Ministry hands. The dictatorial press baron Lord Beaverbrook was put in charge and given a clear mandate to do whatever was necessary to increase production. He pursued this mission with ruthless zeal. Lord Nuffield believed the country owed him a debt of gratitude for taking on responsibility for developing the Castle Bromwich Spitfire factory. When Beaverbrook criticised the running of the plant, Nuffield dared Beaverbrook to accept his resignation. It was accepted on the spot.

Beaverbrook's uncompromising style did not go down well in the Air Ministry or the War Office—Brooke personally detested the man[8]—but the new minster recognised the Army's need for air support and would prove to be a useful ally. In some respects, he was too radical for the War Office; he was soon suggesting that air support should be the responsibility of an 'Army Air Arm' within the Army, along the lines of the 'Fleet Air Arm'. It was what the War Office had always wanted, but taking over full responsibility for raising, training, and developing an Army Air Arm from scratch was a little too ambitious in the desperate days of 1940.[9] They would be quite happy with an 'Army Cooperation Command' within the RAF, which would give Army support equal status to the work of Bomber, Fighter, and Coastal Command. It seemed a modest enough request, but it received short shrift from the Air Ministry. A puzzled Air Staff managed to see 'no operational purpose' for such a command.[10] The gulf between the two services could not have been wider.

Beaverbrook's efforts to rationalise aircraft production tried to take War Office requirements into account. After consultation with the Air Ministry, Beaverbrook chose to focus on five key types—the Spitfire, Hurricane, Wellington, Blenheim, and Whitley. The Blenheim was a concession to Army requirements. However, there was still space for the Whitley, the plane that could contribute least to defeating an invasion. The higher-performance Hampden did not make the cut. The latest Whitley V was slower than the Hampden and could only operate by night, but it could carry more bombs further, and this was what the Air Staff (and indeed the offensive-minded Churchill) wanted. Even at this critical stage of the war, the strategic air offensive had to be maintained.[11]

Beaverbrook did, however, make sure that fighter production still had priority.[12] Given the insatiable demand for fighters for interception, escort, and tactical air cover—not to mention entirely new roles such as reconnaissance and ground attack—it seemed like a very straightforward decision. The Air Ministry, however, was aghast. In a logical but (in the circumstances) perverse analysis, the Air Staff argued that the German defeat of France made long-range bombers even more important. RAF bombers no longer had French airfields to use and therefore had even further to fly to reach German targets. Beaverbrook's proposals, the Air Ministry warned, meant that there was a grave danger that in August 1941 the German bomber fleet might still outnumber the British bomber fleet by two to one. This would have fatal consequences for the country.[13] Fortunately for Britain, Beaverbrook recognised that without fighters, Britain might lose the war long before August 1941.

Beaverbrook also went some way towards meeting the Army's need for bomber support. The War Office needed army-cooperation squadrons with more teeth. It had won approval for thirty-eight Army squadrons worldwide, but it did not want them all equipped with the traditional Lysander-type army-cooperation plane. Seventeen would be specialist close-support squadrons (seven in the UK, six in the Middle East, and a reserve of four).[14] For these aircraft, the War Office wanted something more like the Ju 87 Stuka. With a sympathetic Beaverbrook in charge of ordering equipment, there was a much better chance of getting them.

This time, the Army was determined not to be thwarted by Air Ministry talk of the time required to develop such a plane. The existing Hawker Henley was fine. The last of the 200 built were just coming off the production lines and were on their way to training schools to serve as target tugs. The War Office demanded that the Hawker light bomber be put back into production immediately.[15]

There was no reason why this could not happen. The Hurricanes the Gloster plant was now producing instead were desperately needed, but the parallel production line being set up to build the struggling Albemarle might have been more usefully employed building Henleys. It might be a while before any more were delivered, but a start could be made by converting the initial batch of 200 back to light bombers. They would have been ideal equipment for the specialist close-support squadrons the Army wanted. Instead, Beaverbrook ordered 1,000 American Vultee Vengeance and Brewster Bermuda dive bombers. These had a similar performance to the Henley, but they could not arrive until 1941. For the coming battle, it seemed the Army would have to continue relying on Blenheims and Battles.

It was easy to dismiss the Battle as obviously obsolete following its catastrophic losses during the first few days of the French campaign. However, subsequent losses on daylight missions had been far lower, and with more armour, stronger escorts, and self-sealing tanks, losses ought to be even lower. The Battle was far from ideal, but it was also far from useless.

Meanwhile, the Air Ministry was being forced to consider how these bombers and the Air Force in general might support the Army more effectively. War Office complaints had led to Sinclair setting up an internal Air Ministry enquiry into the performance of the RAF in France. Brooke-Popham was given the task of leading the investigation; his conclusions would perhaps be a little more hard-hitting than the Air Ministry was anticipating.

His report noted how the Germans seemed to be able to call in air support immediately, whereas it took the Allies at best four to five hours, sometimes as long as twelve hours, to respond. Brooke-Popham argued that if fighters could scramble quickly in response to approaching bombers, so could Battle squadrons to attack ground targets—it was just a question of mentality and expectation.[16]

In fact, it was only squadrons based in Britain that had taken excessively long to respond. Before the German offensive, systems had been set up in France that enabled requests for air support to be acted on almost immediately. Human hesitancy rather than inadequate systems had been the problem. During the German advance towards Arras, ground controllers had used the systems developed to vector fighters towards bombers, to direct patrolling fighters towards ground targets. The systems needed already existed.

Col. Woodall, who had served as a staff officer at BAFF headquarters, presented a brief paper to the Air and General Staffs outlining procedures that could be used to direct close-support bombers to their targets more speedily.[17] The proposals were not that radical; they suggested that Army officers in armoured cars at the front should signal requests for air support to control centres in the rear. These would be manned by Army and Air Force officers, who would then pass on instructions directly to the close-support squadrons. These procedures were similar to those that had been used in colonial conflicts during the 1930s, and indeed the system Barratt had developed in France. It was agreed that full-scale trials should take place in Northern Ireland from September, with two Battle squadrons and the 53rd Infantry Division.[18]

Whether it was the time for lengthy reports and methodical trials was debateable. With an invasion imminent, improvising systems seemed more useful than setting in motion a lengthy development programme. It seemed more a way of shelving the close air support issue. The process needed one of Churchill's stirring 'Action this day' decrees, but it was not a topic that attracted the Prime Minister's attention. The lack of urgency contrasts strikingly with the haste with which semi-developed airborne radar systems were rushed to operational units to deal with the night bomber. Improving ground/air cooperation was nowhere near as crucial as stopping the long-range bomber.

Brooke-Popham also thought it was time for a rethink on the multi-purpose army-cooperation plane. The low-performance Lysander was fine for short-range observation and even short-range ground attack, but Brooke-Popham did not believe it could be expected to penetrate deep into enemy airspace. It could certainly not go on long tours of the enemy rear in search of information. In future, all reconnaissance missions had to have a specific objective and the plane had to spend the minimum time in enemy airspace. Brooke-Popham mentioned the limited but successful use made of the Hurricanes in the low-level tactical-reconnaissance role during the fighting in France.[19]

This was indeed the way forward, as the unarmed photo-reconnaissance Spitfires of No. 212 Squadron had perhaps even more persuasively demonstrated. Up to the end of June, the squadron had flown nearly 300 photo-reconnaissance sorties for the loss of just three Spitfires.[20] These included sorties flown at low altitude, when cloud prevented high altitude missions. The medium/low-level Spitfire Type G was developed specifically for the purpose. It kept its armament, but there was the addition of two cameras for vertical photography from 10,000 to 2,000 feet and an oblique camera for work under 2,000 feet.[21] The problem was that Dowding wanted every available Spitfire, and Beaverbrook, worried by the vulnerability of his aircraft factories, was reluctant to deny him.[22] Only two low-level tactical Spitfire Gs were delivered during the summer of 1940.[23] For too many in the Air Ministry, reconnaissance came a very distant third after bombing and interception, 'a purely negative contribution to war winning and an impossible drain on limited resources', as Harris had once put it.[24] In fact, knowing where the enemy is and what he is doing was, and still is, the most important contribution an air force can make.

The main problem with the Lysander was that it was a rather expensive way of performing the more limited role Brooke-Popham was envisaging. Major Bazeley had a cheaper solution for at least one of the Lysander roles; for some time, the Major and fellow artillery officers had been pushing their Air Observation Post concept, which involved using light, low-powered, unarmed planes flown by artillery officers to direct fire. The Air Ministry had always scoffed at the idea of a plane with the same performance as a First World War B.E.2 playing any part in a modern war. However, with the decision to expand the Army, the Air Ministry was anxious not to waste its shrinking share of production capacity on the Lysander. If the War Office really believed the Army could use cheap, light planes, the Air Ministry was now more than happy to let them try.

Trials went ahead in France with a two-seater developed by Taylorcraft, and these were reasonably successful. Now it was the War Office that seemed reluctant to push ahead with what was available. Bazeley, somewhat contradicting the thinking behind the concept, decided that the Taylorcraft design had inadequate lifting capacity, climb, and take-off performance. He wanted a plane that was twice as powerful and twice as big. The American Stinson Vigilant was ordered, but deliveries could not be expected to begin until the end of 1940.[25] It was an unfortunate decision as the Taylorcraft plane, in the form of the more advanced Auster, would eventually become the standard Army artillery observation plane. In truth, there was still not that much interest in the Air Observation Post concept outside artillery circles. It was an idea that seemed to be associated with an outmoded era of trench warfare and observation balloons. Close air support was the way forward. The blitzkrieg had been spearheaded by Stukas, not artillery. The War Office was far more interested in acquiring dive-bombers.

The threat posed by the other key element of the German blitzkrieg, the tank, did provoke some hasty improvisation, which gave the Lysander an entirely new role. On 11 June, William Petter, designer of the four-cannon Whirlwind, approached Beaverbrook with a proposal to give the Lysander a tank-busting capability by arming it with the 20-mm Hispano Suiza HS 404 cannon. Nobody even knew how thick German armour was, but the French had claimed that their fighters had found the less well-protected rears of German tanks were vulnerable to 20-mm cannon fire (in fact, the lighter Panzer I and II were vulnerable. It would need a lucky shot to knock out a Panzer III or IV). Beaverbrook backed the scheme, and within days, trials had demonstrated the cannon could penetrate 20-mms of armour.[26]

Not everyone in the Air Ministry was enthusiastic about the idea,[27] but Douglas gave it his backing. 'We have got to get down to this question of attacking enemy tanks from the air by cannon guns seriously,' he implored.[28] The cannon was fitted to a Lysander. There were no technical problems, although aiming was not easy.[29] Late in July, Churchill saw the combination in action and was impressed. This seemed to trigger an immediate decision to issue Lysander squadrons with cannon conversion kits. Churchill also quizzed Dowding about what else he was doing to create an anti-tank force. No. 19 Squadron was about to be reequipped with cannon-armed Spitfires and No. 151 Squadron had been trying out a cannon-armed Hurricane. Dowding found himself committed to holding these back for ground-attack duties.[30]

The invasion panic that was gripping the country was focusing Air Ministry minds. After insisting it was the job of the Army, not the Air Force, to stop the tanks, officers were now rushing forward with responses to Douglas's plea. Hawker was asked if they could modify another thirty Hurricanes to carry a couple of cannon.[31] Bristol was asked to try fitting a couple to the Blenheim. Douglas even wondered if training aircraft could lift a cannon into the air. The use of the twin-engine Airspeed Oxford trainer was seriously considered.[32]

Portal entered into the spirit by suggesting that the sixty old COW 37-mm cannon still in stores could be mounted on obsolete bombers such as the Virginia, Sidestrand, or Overstrand. Protected by substantial armour, these could hunt down German tanks that had broken through the lines. It turned out that only three Virginias and six Overstrands were in a flyable condition, and the 10,000 rounds of 37-mm ammunition that still existed in stores was so old that there were doubts it was safe to use.[33] The idea got no further. On the face of it, 100-mph armoured Virginia bombers flying above the treetops, taking pot shots at German tanks, seems somewhat absurd, but the idea of just getting an anti-tank gun 100 feet or so into the air and giving it the mobility to move quickly to the enemy tanks had advantages even the Air Ministry could see. One day, equally slow helicopters would perform this role. The Virginia and Sidestrand were planes from the past, but the concept was one for the future.

These ancient biplane bombers were not the only obsolete planes being considered for anti-invasion duties. In the desperate straits Britain now found itself, the Banquet Scheme had a crucial role to play. By the end of May, plans already existed for flights of six trainers to operate from Bomber Command's main and auxiliary airfields, and stocks of the bombs they would carry were already in place. By the end of June, No. 6 Group (Bomber Command's operational training unit) and No. 22 Group (Army Cooperation) had around 200 planes available for ground-attack duties. These ranged from Blenheims and Hampdens to Hawker Hinds and Harts. Instructors and any sufficiently proficient pupils would fly the planes. Armour and self-sealing tanks were to be fitted if possible, but the crews would have to fly without if necessary.[34]

Another 500 De Havilland Moth, Miles Magister, and Avro Cadet trainers at elementary training schools were also being equipped with racks for eight 20-lb bombs. The instructors would fly the planes and pupils would accompany them as gunners. These 'light strike' flights were supposed to 'dive bomb' the invasion beaches. The Fleet Air Arm chipped in with aircraft from its training schools.[35] There would inevitably be a delay while all these trainers were readied for action. To fill the gap, there were plans for a special quick-reaction force of ten squadrons, each with twelve 'Hart variants', flown by older pilots (over forty). The force would be permanently on call, ready to strike at the invading forces wherever they might land.

No stone was left unturned in the search for aircraft that might be capable of attacking a German invasion. Even converting civil airliners to bombers and arming liaison planes was considered.[36] In a scheme every bit as desperate as the Virginia cannon-armed tank-busters, Britain's fighter defences were to be bolstered by Miles Master advanced trainers flown by instructors. One hundred were to have six machine guns fitted; when the invasion came, they would fly to Fighter Command airfields and operate alongside Hurricanes and Spitfires.[37]

These were indeed desperate measures, typical of the time. The public was asked to hand in any weapons they might have so that the Home Guard could be armed with something better than improvised pikes. The Royal Family led the way by going through their gunroom. The government was asking the public to hand in their aluminium saucepans so that they could be recycled into Spitfires. No means of improving the country's defences was overlooked—or so it seemed. While the Air Ministry was arming Tiger Moth and Master trainers and toying with the idea of sending ancient Virginia bombers into combat, an Aladdin's Cave of modern planes was beginning to accumulate. Roosevelt's self-styled 'arsenal of democracy' was coming to Britain's rescue.

Unlike the French, Britain had not so far made much use of American industrial might. Lockheed Hudson coastal patrol bombers were in service with Coastal Command. In December 1939, 120 Brewster Buffalo fighters and 300

L7026
V PS

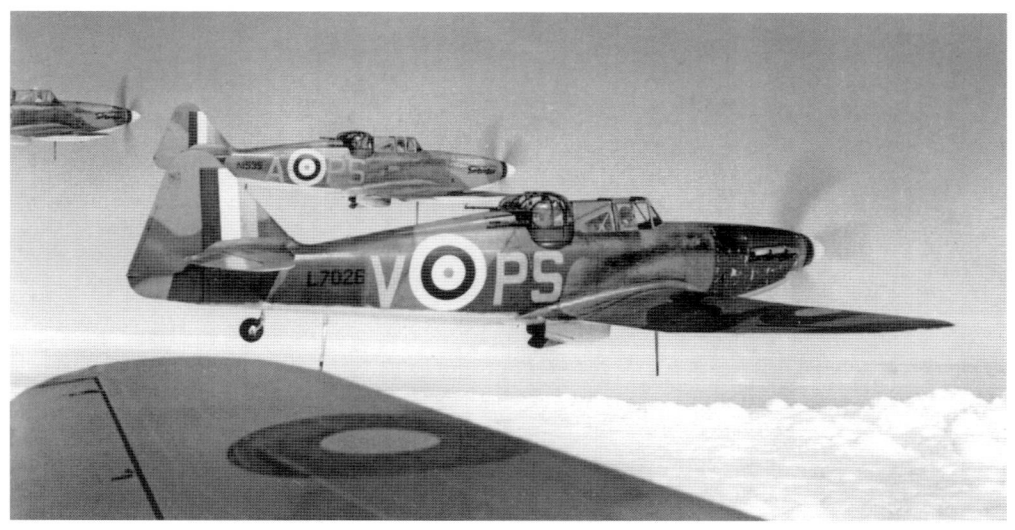

The Boulton Paul Defiants of No. 264 Squadron in the summer of 1940. Designed as a bomber interceptor, it was hoped that the aircraft's turret would make it ideal as an Army air superiority fighter. (*Crown*)

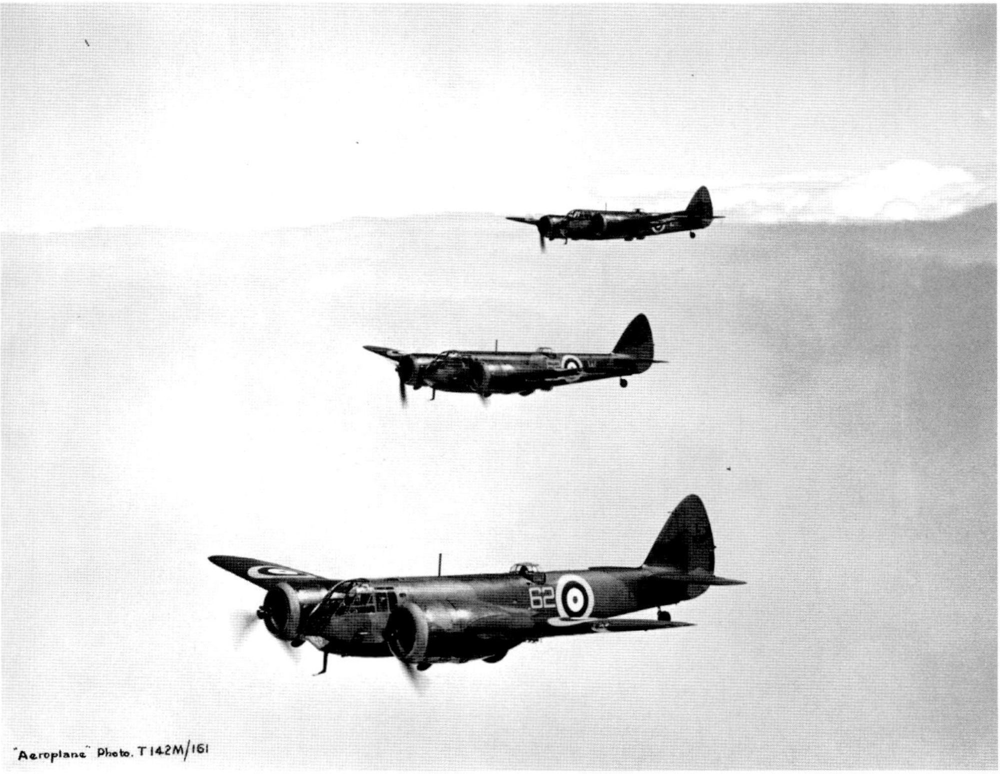
"Aeroplane" Photo. T142M/161

While the RAF were awaiting delivery of the Defiant, a makeshift fighter version of the Blenheim I bomber was supposed to provide air cover for the Army. (*T. Buttler*)

Air Vice-Marshal Douglas, Assistant Chief of the Air Staff and, from April 1940, Deputy Chief of the Air Staff. (*Crown*)

Air Chief Marshal Ludlow-Hewitt, head of Bomber Command until April 1940. (*Crown*)

Air Commodore Slessor,
Director of Plans. (*Crown*)

Air Marshal Peirse, Deputy Chief of
the Air Staff and, from April 1940,
Vice-Chief of the Air Staff.

Above: Spitfire Is of No. 65 Squadron. The RAF took pride in the ability of its fighter pilots to fly in close formation. The bulged cockpit was introduced to help improve rearward view. (*Crown*)

Below: A Hurricane 1 of No. 615 Squadron. Powered by the same engine as the Spitfire, the bulkier Hurricane was far slower. (*Crown*)

Three twin-engine cannon fighters were lined up to replace the Spitfire and Hurricane. This is the sleek Westland Whirlwind, with its four cannon protruding from the nose. (*T. Buttler*)

Above: The far larger Bristol Beaufighter was an adaptation of the Beaufort torpedo bomber. It eventually served as a specialist night fighter. (*Crown*)

Below: The five-cannon Gloster F.9/37 was pencilled in to join the Whirlwind and Beaufighter. (*T. Buttler*)

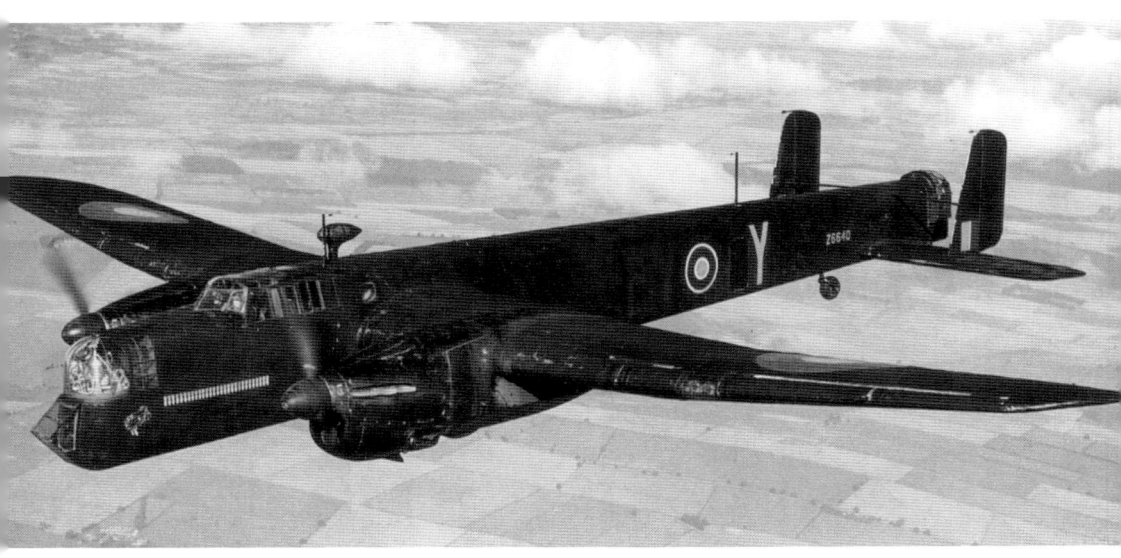

The rather ungainly Armstrong Whitworth Whitley was the RAF's standard night bomber. (*Crown*)

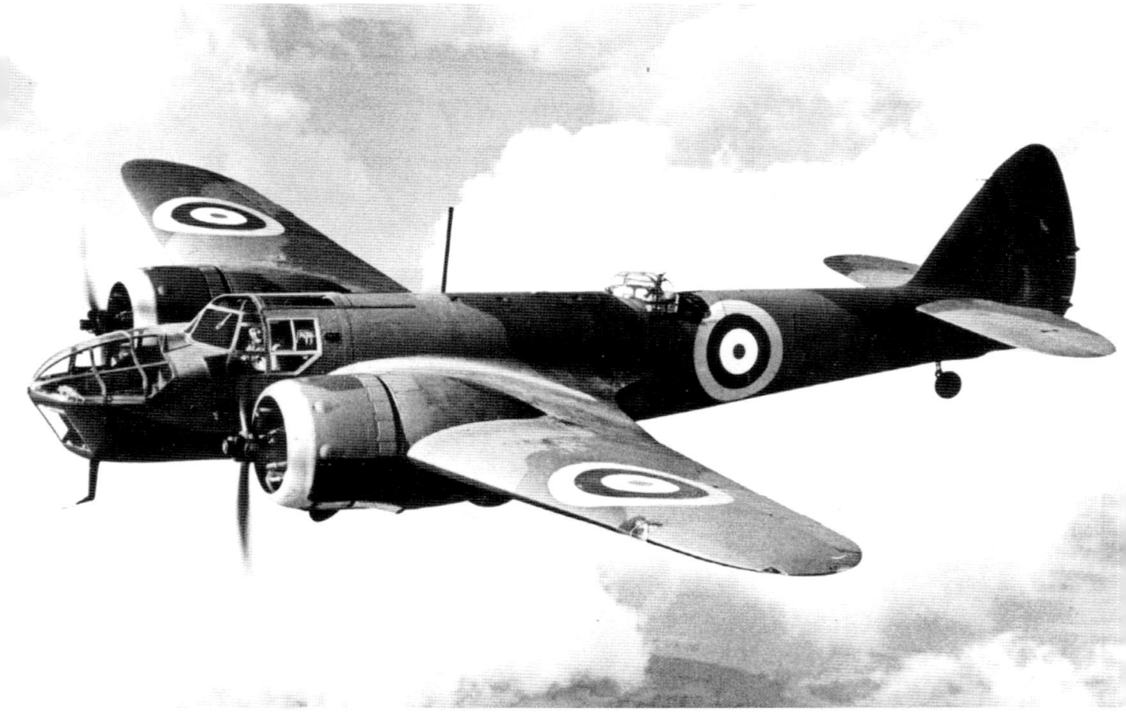

The Blenheim IV. With a twin-gun dorsal turret and a ventral chin turret, it was reasonably well-armed. (*T. Buttler*)

Above: The Handley Page Hampden. (*Crown*)

Below: The Wellington 1c with improved Nash and Thompson power-operated turrets. The beam guns fired through the triangular transparent section of the fuselage. Both the Wellington and the Hampden were designed for day operations, and they were as capable of filling this role as any bomber of that era. (*Crown*)

The larger the bombers became, the less suitable they were for daylight tactical operations. The Avro Manchester was larger and much heavier than the Wellington. (*T. Buttler*)

Above: The Handley Page Halifax. Four-engine bombers were expensive; five Spitfires could be built for the price of one Halifax. (*Crown*)

Below: The twin-engine Armstrong Whitworth Albemarle was added to the bomber programme as a way of keeping costs down. (*T. Buttler*)

Above: The Short Stirling was designed for day and night operations. There were fears its machine-gun defensive armament would not be adequate for daylight operations. (*T. Buttler*)

Below: A model of the proposed Blackburn B.1/39 bomber with the low-profile four-cannon dorsal turret. It was hoped that this turret could be grafted onto the Short Stirling Handley page Halifax and Avro Manchester; it was also going to be used in the twin-engine Boulton Paul P.92 fighter. (*T. Buttler*)

A flight of Fairey Battles. It was believed that by flying in formation, their combined firepower could beat off fighter attacks. (*Crown*)

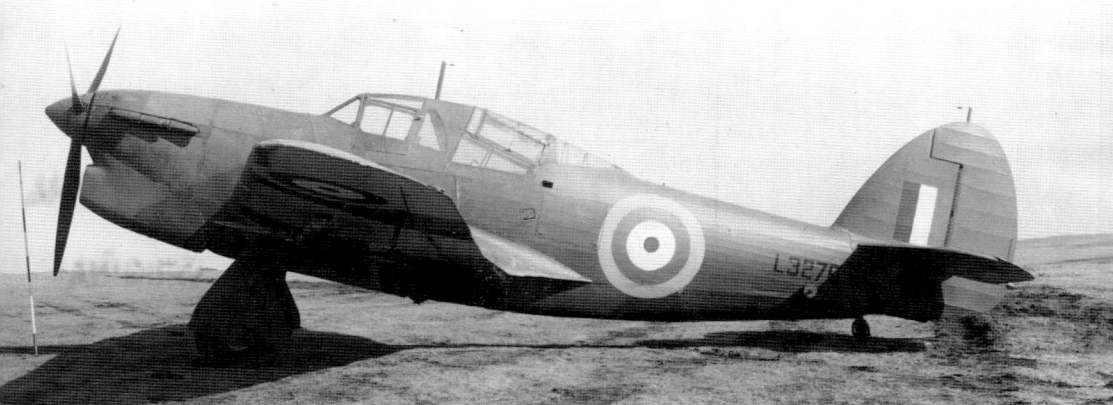

Above: The faster and more agile Hawker Henley would have made a better tactical bomber. (*Crown via P. Butler*)

Below: The sophisticated high-wing Westland Lysander showing off its excellent view down. With an 870-hp supercharged engine, it was not cheap. (*Crown*)

The Taylorcraft Plus C/2, which had an engine rated at just 90 hp, was a cheap way of peeping over the frontline. (*Crown via P. Butler*)

Above: The American Lockheed Hudson. Both the Hudson and the Beaufort would have been among the first planes to attack an invasion fleet. (*T. Buttler*)

Below: The Bristol Beaufort torpedo bomber. (*T. Buttler*)

Left: A Henschel HS 126 hovers above an advancing German column. Army commanders were constantly complaining about the inability of the RAF to drive these spotter planes away.

Below: A Ju 87 Stuka flies low over German paratroopers. For German ground forces, air support was very visible.

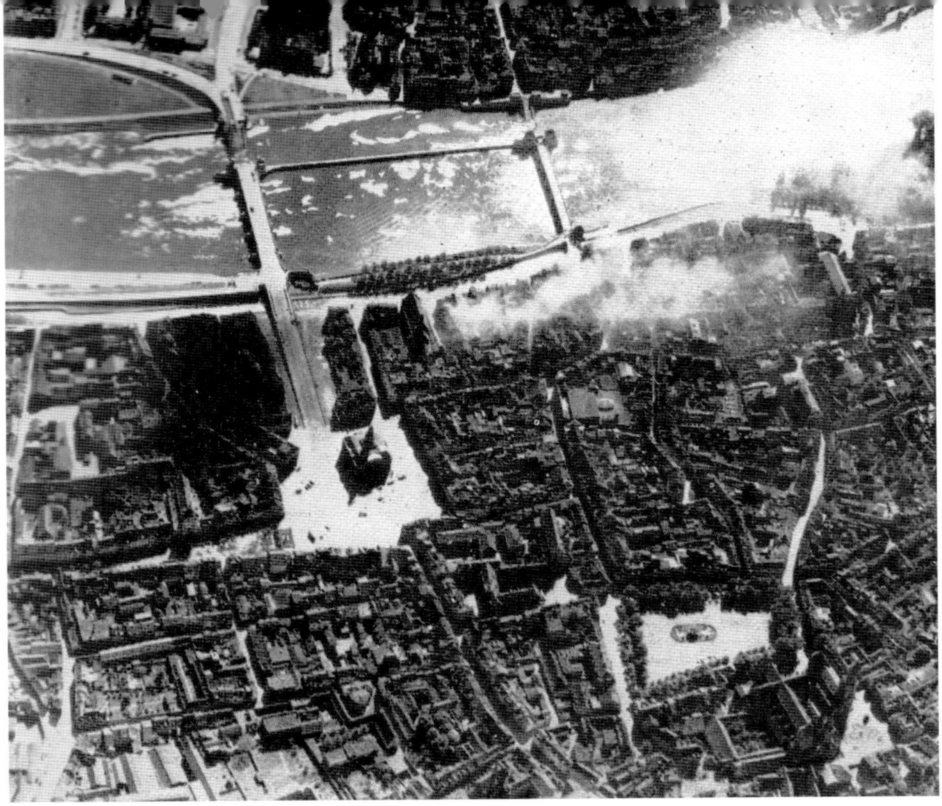

Above: The St Servatius Bridge in Maastricht, photographed during a Blenheim raid on 12 May. The demolition of part of the bridge carried out by the Dutch is clearly visible.

Below: Rotterdam after the raid. The Dutch were holding the north bank of the river. German paratroopers were holding a small bridgehead at the north end of the bridge visible at the bottom of the photo.

Top and middle: To attack the invading German Army, the Tiger Moth (above) and the Miles Magister trainers (below) were fitted with racks for 20-lb bombs.

Bottom: There were plans to arm ancient Vickers Virginia bombers with 37-mm cannon and use them to hunt down German tanks. (*Crown*)

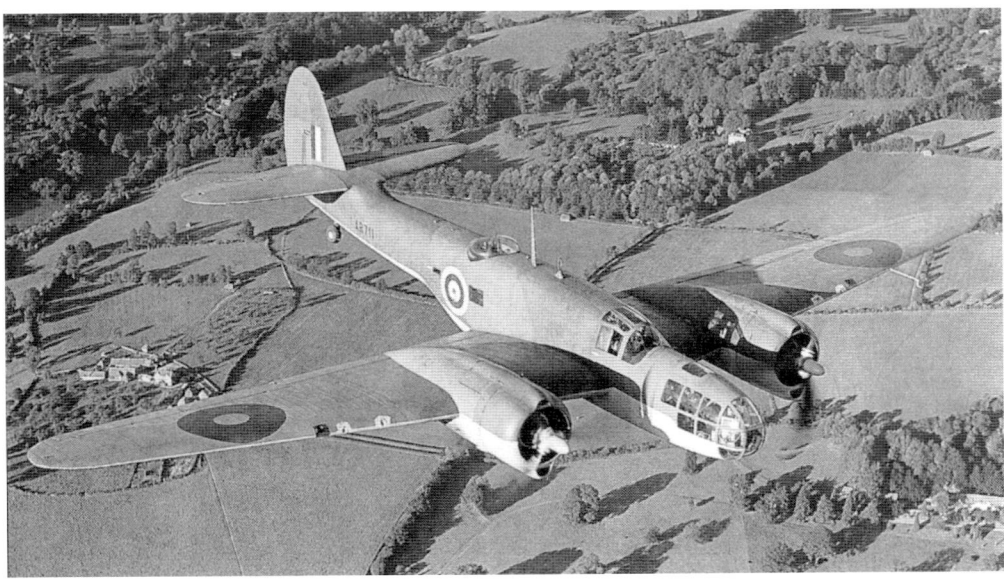

Above: The American light bombers the RAF decided not to use—the Northrop A-17 Nomad (*Crown via P. Butler*), the Douglas DB7 Boston (*T. Buttler*), and the Martin Maryland. (*T. Buttler*).

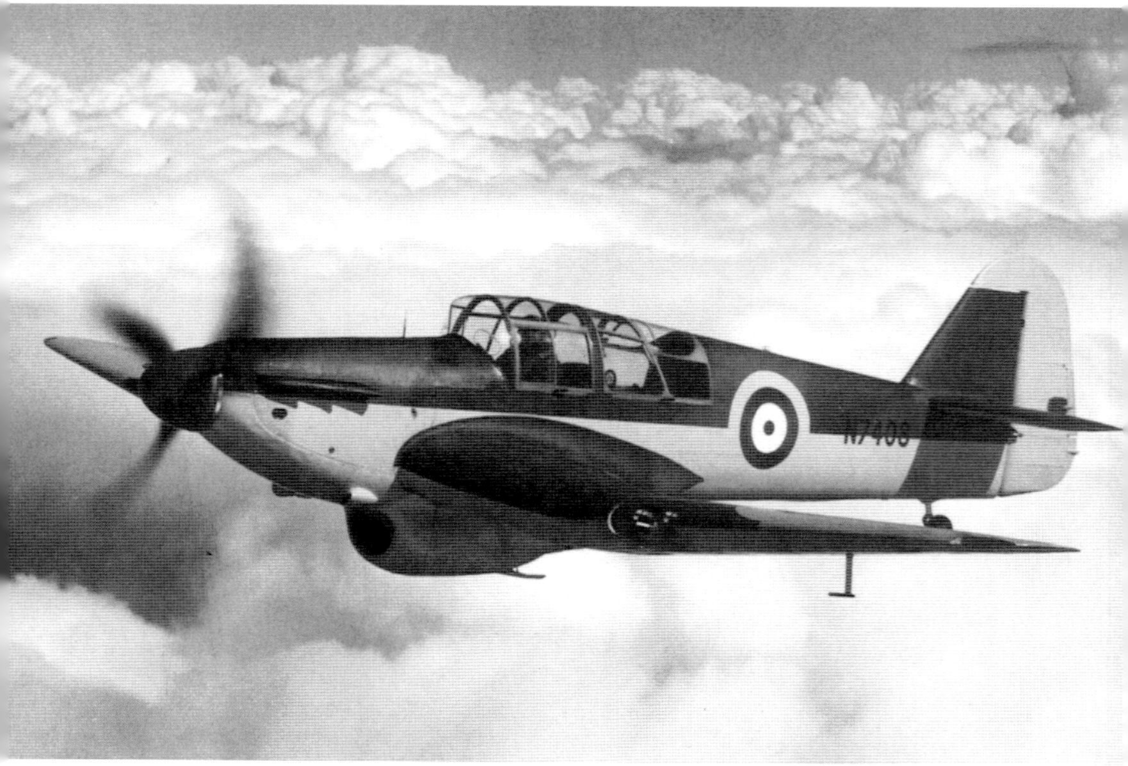

Above: The Miles Master trainer was turned into a fighter by being armed with six machine guns. (*Crown*)

Below: An ex-French Curtiss P-36 A-4 Hawk. This became the Mohawk IV in RAF service. (*Crown*)

Above: The rotund but manoeuvrable American Brewster Buffalo. These were on their way to Belgium before being diverted to Britain.

Below: Curtiss P-40s started reaching Britain in the autumn of 1940. An offer to deliver them earlier was politely declined. *(T. Buttler)*

Air Chief Marshal Hugh Dowding. (*Crown*)

The underground operations room at Fighter Command HQ, Bentley Priory. (*Crown*)

Air Vice-Marshal Trafford
Leigh-Mallory,
the commander of
No. 12 Group. (*Crown*)

Air Vice-Marshal Keith Park, the commander
of No. 11 Group, in flying gear. During the
Dunkirk evacuation, he occasionally flew his
Hurricane over the port. (*Crown*)

Air Marshal Charles Portal. The commander of Bomber Command from April 1940. (*Crown*)

Archibald Sinclair, the Secretary of State for Air from May 1940, with Air Marshal Cyril Newall, the Chief of Air Staff. (*Crown*)

Above and right: Two ex-Chiefs of Air Staff, Marshals of the Royal Air Force John Salmond (above) and Hugh Trenchard (below) both tried to influence policy from behind the scenes. (*Crown*)

Above: Unprotected fuel tanks were not the only problem Battle crews faced. Many crash landed relatively intact after the engine radiator system had been holed. (*Crown*)

Below: With two dorsal guns and a nose chin turret, the Blenheim IV had a reasonable defensive armament. (*Crown*)

Above: A close-up of the transmitting aerial in the nose of the Blenheim. (Crown)

Above: The AI receiving aerials above and below the wing. When the signal from each was equal, the plane was climbing towards its target. (*Crown*)

Right: There were two receiving aerials outboard of each engine. When the signal from each was equal, the plane was on the right bearing for the target. (*Crown*)

Above: The Beaufighter was far too large to be a successful day fighter, but it was ideal for carrying the bulky AI equipment. (*Crown*)

Below: The Handley Page Harrow was used to drop mines on parachutes in the path of the approaching bombers. (*Crown*)

Above: The Air Staff were reluctant to use the Douglas DB-7 as a bomber, but they were quick to adapt it to the night fighter role. (*Crown*)

Below: A Boulton Paul Defiant Mark II of No. 151 Squadron. The switch to night fighting enabled the Defiant to be used as its designers intended. (*Crown*)

Above: A pall of smoke rises above London Docks on the afternoon of 7 September 1940.

Below: Coventry the morning after the raid of 14–15 November 1940.

Douglas DB7b (Boston III) light bombers were ordered.[38] There was little enthusiasm about acquiring either. The Douglas order was soon cut to 150 when it was discovered the plane was more expensive than expected.

The French, however, persuaded the British it might be a good idea to have a back-up source of supply, safely situated in the neutral United States, in case the German bomber fleet wiped out the British and French aircraft industries. The Air Ministry agreed that in a crisis, American planes might be better than nothing. Both countries placed massive orders for a range of combat planes. The Air Staff was not the least bit impressed by attack bombers like the Martin 167 Maryland, which the French had bought in large numbers. The four-engine Consolidated B-24 Liberator heavy bomber looked a bit more like what was required.[39] American fighters were capable of impressive speeds; the Curtiss P-40, a more powerful version of the French Curtiss Hawk, was credited with a top speed of 360 mph, the strange twin-boom Lockheed P-38 was capable of 400 mph, and the equally odd Bell P-39 Aircobra, with the engine behind the pilot, had managed 390 mph. The British and French ordered large numbers of all these planes.

None of these orders could help Britain in 1940 as deliveries could not begin until 1941.[40] A month after the orders were placed, the Germans launched their offensive in the west, and Dowding was soon warning Churchill that his fighter force was close to collapse. A startled Churchill decided he had to have American reinforcements long before 1941. On 15 May, Churchill made contact with Roosevelt for the first time as Prime Minister. Dowding's and Newall's warnings at that day's cabinet meeting were still ringing in his ears. Instead of waiting for the aircraft ordered in the United States to be built, Churchill pleaded for 'several hundred of the latest types of aircraft' to be diverted from the US Army Air Corps to Britain in lieu of these contracts.[41] Five days later, with Dowding's warning becoming ever more dire, he asked Roosevelt for as many Curtiss P-40 fighters as possible to be delivered to Britain as quickly as possible.[42] The first of these were just being delivered to the USAAC, and Air Force generals were not going to take kindly to having their latest fighter taken away from them; nevertheless, Roosevelt promised to do his best.

At the end of June, the first American aircraft started to arrive. They were not a response to the orders placed in the spring or Churchill's appeals to Roosevelt, but deliveries which had been on their way to countries that had now been occupied by Germany. Just hours before surrendering, the French had hastily transferred all the contracts they had placed to the British. At a stroke, this increased British orders to over 6,000 planes.[43] Shipments on their way to France were diverted mid-Atlantic to Britain. By the end of June, twenty-six Martin 167 Maryland and sixteen Douglas DB7 Boston light bombers had already reached the UK. In July, they were followed by another twelve Marylands, thirty-two Curtiss Hawk fighters, sixty-one Northrop A-17 Nomad attack bombers (all ex-French contracts) and twenty-one Belgian Brewster B-339 Buffalos. There were already over 150 combat planes in

Britain, and more were crossing the Atlantic.[44] It was a veritable windfall. Instead of waiting until 1941 for its first Boston, the RAF had them in June 1940. The first assembled Buffalos and Bostons were delivered to the RAF in the second week in July; the first Hawks, Marylands, and Nomads followed the following week. The 7 July meeting of the ERPC (Expansion and Re-equipment Policy Committee) decided that it probably made sense to ship future deliveries directly to overseas commands, but while the threat of invasion remained, deliveries to the UK should continue.[45] Clearly the intention was to make full use of these planes.

Britain was being gifted some excellent tactical warplanes. The Maryland had suffered the lowest loss rate of any day bomber serving with the French Air Force. Just a couple of months before, two RAF pilots had tried out a French Douglas DB7 and were impressed by the speed and manoeuvrability of the plane.[46] Both American planes were superior to the Blenheim. Arguably, they were the best light bombers in the world at that time.

The Air Ministry also knew all about the superbly agile Curtiss Hawk. The Brewster Buffalo had the same impressive qualities. It lacked speed at high altitude, but at low/medium altitudes it could dive, climb, and fly faster than the Hurricane. Like the Hawk, it was more manoeuvrable than the Hurricane and Spitfire, especially at high speed. It came with back-seat armour and, the cockpit provided the pilot with an excellent view.[47] The Northrop Nomad was not modern. Those on their way to Britain had been hurriedly taken out of USAAC stores and refurbished when the French, in desperation, had asked the Americans to send everything and anything they had. It was slower than the discredited Battle, but it was smaller and more manoeuvrable, and with four fixed machine guns, it at least had a built-in ground-strafing capability.

Even in the dark days of July 1940, these planes were not greeted with much enthusiasm. Some of the early deliveries necessarily arrived with the instrumentation and equipment that was required by the continental air forces they were intended for. These were not necessarily trivial differences; the French, for instance, required the throttle stick to move in the opposite direction. Nevertheless, given the gravity of the situation facing Britain, it was perhaps not really the time to be complaining about this or altimeters that read metres rather than feet. Complaints that some of the planes lacked armour and self-sealing tanks seemed particularly harsh given these were only just being introduced to British planes. The planes did not arrive complete, but it only took 300 man-hours to complete a Curtiss Hawk, compared to the 15,000 required to build a Spitfire or Hurricane.

At a time when it was thought necessary to arm Magister trainers as emergency fighters and attach bomb racks to Tiger Moths, the American planes seemed worth having by any standards. However, the Air Ministry struggled to think of any way of using them. The Hawk and Buffalo might be useful as a desperate, last-ditch reserve, but that was about all. The bombers did not have the range or bomb load to be used against Germany. The single-engine Northrop Nomad was considered so inadequate that those still in the United States were redirected to training schools in Canada. Judgements were made before the planes even arrived. The Air Ministry did not even bother to find out what the Buffalo was capable of until November. Despite Britain's desperate situation, the Air Ministry seemed to consider these American arrivals as more trouble than they were worth.

In fact, they were exactly what Britain needed. Low-level cover had been poor during the fighting in France, and the War Office had constantly demanded manoeuvrable fighters to deal with observation and ground-attack planes operating low over the battlefield. The Mohawk (as the RAF renamed the Hawk) and Buffalo were ideal for this role. They also provided an immediate way of implementing Brooke-Popham's idea of using single-seater fighters for tactical reconnaissance. During the summer of 1940, there were occasional references in Air Ministry files to the possibility that 'suitable fighter types' might have to replace the Lysander,[48] but nobody seems to have thought of using the American fighters. They could even have been used to equip the 'close-support' army-cooperation squadrons the Army wanted. Not so long ago, the War Office had suggested that planes the RAF no longer wanted could be used for ground attack, and both the Buffalo and Hawk could carry bombs.[49]

None of these uses was considered. Instead, once erected, the fighters just sat there doing nothing. Martlesham Heath pilots had claimed the Hawk was so easy to fly 'anyone who could fly a Hart could be sent off in one of these'. A few of the instructors earmarked to attack the German bridgeheads with their Hawker Harts might have appreciated the opportunity to find out if this was true.

It seemed that the Maryland and Boston would make it to front-line squadrons. With the Battle being phased out of production, the ERPC decision taken on 25 July to reequip No. 1 Group with Bostons or Marylands seemed the obvious step to take. The committee ordered any planes already available should be sent 'at once' to get some training going. Portal, however, had other ideas. He did not want bombers that could play no part in his strategic air offensive. When the battered AASF Battle squadrons returned to the United Kingdom, Portal's immediate reaction was to disband them all and use their aircrews to reinforce his 'heavies'. With an invasion expected at any moment, the War office was not going to accept the disbanding of half the available tactical bomber force. However, with the Battle being phased out of production and insufficient Blenheims being built, Portal hoped he could claim that he had little choice but to reequip the group with 'heavies'.[50] The arrival of American Douglas and Martin light bombers upset his plans; nevertheless, he managed to persuade the committee that if sufficient American bombers did not arrive in time, he could reequip the Group with Wellingtons.[51] It was a concession he would exploit to the full.

By the end of August, sixty Bostons and forty Marylands had arrived and many hundreds more were on their way. Forty-three had been assembled, fitted with armour, British guns, and bombing equipment and made ready for operations.

None of them, however, had reached No. 1 Group, not even to get some training going. An alarmed Douglas suggested a start should be made, and specified Nos 12 and 142 Squadrons should start replacing their Battles with the American bombers. Still no attempt was made to deliver any. Nevertheless, time was found for aircrews from these squadrons to visit Wellington squadrons so they could familiarise themselves with the bomber. The only American bombers to become operational in the summer of 1940 were six Marylands dispatched to Malta for reconnaissance duties. The first operational sortie by an RAF Maryland was flown from Malta in September.[52]

Even the Northrop Nomad might have been useful. It was not as obsolete as the Swordfish and Hectors that had been used in France or the Harts that were going to be used against an invasion. It was certainly not as inadequate as the Tiger Moth trainers that were supposed to dive-bomb the invasion beaches. If instructors were going to risk their lives repulsing enemy landings, they might have wished the Northrop planes had been sent to their training schools rather than those in Canada. Most of those that arrived in Britain had been assembled by the end of August.[53] They were briefly considered as interim equipment for the proposed 'close-support' army-cooperation squadrons while they awaited the delivery of the Vengeance and Bermuda dive-bombers,[54] but nothing came of this idea. It seemed that all the American planes would remain an unused stockpile for which there was no need, no use, and no pilots.

However, it was not just aircraft that were arriving from abroad. At the same 7 July ERPC meeting that first discussed what to do with the American aircraft, Douglas drew the attention of the committee to the large number of foreign aircrews that were also arriving. Most of these were Poles and Czechs, 'many of which [had] useful fighting experience'.[55] In the summer of 1940, there could not have been a more valuable human resource than experienced, battle-hardened combat pilots.

The Poles and Czechs arriving in the wake of the French defeat were not the first to set foot in Britain. With the occupation of Czechoslovakia and the defeat of Poland a few months later, thousands of airmen from these countries had made their way to Britain and France. The vast majority chose France, as that was where the action was likely to be. The French Air Force was so overwhelmed by the numbers arriving that it asked the British to take some off their hands. The Air Ministry reluctantly agreed to take half and, being principally interested in expanding Bomber Command, they insisted on bomber pilots and aircrew.

As the British would later discover, they also netted a number of fighter pilots who preferred to retrain as bomber pilots rather than wait for the French to use them as fighter pilots. Some 2,000 pilots, aircrew, and ground crew (but mostly flying personnel) began arriving in Britain in December 1939. It was planned to use these to form two Wellington squadrons. When more waves of volunteers turned up in France, the French insisted the British continue to take half. The Air Ministry was not at all happy at this French attempt to stretch the original agreement, but the Foreign Office was anxious to avoid a row on the matter and persuaded the Air Ministry to take them.[56] Neither the French nor the British appeared to be especially keen about this apparently priceless windfall of partially and fully trained pilots and aircrew.

The Poles found the British were even slower than the French at organising them into fighting squadrons. On the eve of the German offensive in France, the plans to form two Polish Wellington squadrons had still not got going.[57] Some of the exiles were still waiting to fly a plane for the first time since they had fled their country. The only excuse the British could offer was that there was a shortage of aircraft. To the frustration of these exiles, on the other side of the Channel many of their compatriots were finally serving with front-line French squadrons.

In fact, Bomber Command was fast losing interest in its Polish reinforcements. The commander of No. 6 Group (OTU) thought the Poles were far too individualistic for the teamwork required by a Wellington crew. There was a shortage of Wellingtons anyway. With the Allied armies in retreat in France, he suggested the Poles could be given Battles and sent off to France to support the Army. If the British Army did not want them, the French Army would no doubt be more than happy to have them.[58] It was perhaps ironic that this was written on the day after the British launched their Arras counterattack without any air support. It seemed tactical air support was just a way of making use of inadequate aircraft and second-rate aircrews. The two Polish Battle squadrons began forming, but France was defeated before they could move to the continent.

The Poles in these Battle squadrons were just the tip of the iceberg. The failure to do anything with the large number that were still unemployed was becoming an embarrassment to the British authorities. It became even more of an embarrassment as reports began arriving of how well the Poles and the Czechs in the French Air Force were doing. The Polish authorities were also asking awkward questions, not least concerning why trained Polish fighter pilots in the United Kingdom were being retrained to fly bombers. A rapid census of the Poles in the UK revealed not only that there were 140 trained fighter pilots in the country, but that twenty-five of them had fought the Luftwaffe in September 1939. There were, it was felt, enough pilots for at least one fighter squadron, and a substantial reserve.[59]

Meanwhile, the defeat of France had triggered an even greater influx of foreign volunteers. Again, the vast majority were Poles and Czechs. By 6 July, it was planned to have one Polish fighter squadron, one Czech fighter squadron, and one Czech bomber squadron in addition to the two Polish Battle squadrons. This soon looked inadequate as the Poles and Czechs continued to pour in. Between 10 June and 14 July, over 200 Czech and over 700 Polish pilots arrived in Britain, along with 450 pupil pilots.[60] Many more thousands of aircrew and ground crew were said to be on the way *via* North Africa. On 11 July, it was agreed that a second Polish fighter squadron should be created, but clearly far more pilots had arrived than would be required by three fighter and three bomber squadrons.[61] An element of the Banquet Scheme had involved an instant reaction force of ten Hart squadrons, ready to strike an invasion wherever the enemy landed. Perhaps they could man these squadrons, it was suggested, but this idea came to nothing when it was discovered that most of the Hawker Harts had been sent overseas.[62]

There should have been no problem making use of the fighter pilots. Dowding claimed to have a deficit of over 300. Fighter Command also needed to expand to protect the country from raids that could now come from any direction, from Norway to Brittany. No. 13 Group had to cover Scotland, and the newly created No. 10 Group extended Fighter Command's defences along the south coast. Before the defeat in France, the 'staggering, possibly impossible' target of eighty fighter squadrons by the spring of 1941 had been set as the ideal figure to deal with an attack from German bases. With France defeated, Douglas and Stevenson put the required figure at no less than 120 squadrons.[63] Despite the loss of around 500 fighters and 300 pilots in Norway and France, Dowding was demanding another ten squadrons immediately[64] and the original target of eighty achieved as soon as possible after that. To try and meet this target, pilots were transferred from army-cooperation squadrons and retrained as fighter pilots—a somewhat questionable policy considering the imminent invasion. Douglas thought the pool of trained Polish and Czech fighter pilots was a far more obvious way of filling the gap.[65] Others did not seem to be quite so enthusiastic.

Part of the problem was that there was no more confidence in the quality of these foreign volunteers than there was in aircraft manufactured in the United States. Reports written by the reception centres that greeted the first batch of Poles to arrive from France emphasised the lack of discipline and low morale. It was perhaps what the British wanted to believe; the German threat looked less formidable if Allied defeats could be put down to incompetence and inefficiency rather than superior German equipment and training. This prejudice seemed to be taken to extremes in the case of the Poles. As soon as they got some RAF pay in their pockets, one report claimed, they lost their enthusiasm for taking on the Germans and seemed only interested in having a good time. If the Poles were able to mix with RAF personnel, the report patronisingly suggested, they might eventually come to realise the high standards that were expected in the RAF. This, however, would take time—perhaps six to nine months, the report suggested.[66] In the summer of 1940, Britain did not have six to nine months to find out how prejudiced these comments were.

If anything, Czechs were viewed even less favourably. They also brought delicate political problems with them. Their country had never been at war with Germany. Indeed, their country no longer existed; Bohemia was a protectorate of the Third Reich, which technically made some of the Czech exiles German citizens. The names of Czech airmen often appeared on lists of potential fifth columnists.[67]

Language was an obvious problem for fighter pilots expected to function in a tightly controlled air defence system. As well as learning the language, they also had to learn how to fly in tight 'vic' formations and master all the numerous intricate attack patterns Fighter Command had come up with for shooting down unescorted bombers. The Air Ministry seemed particularly doubtful about their eastern European allies' ability to cope with all these complexities.

Given the assessments of their capabilities, it is surprising that Dowding wanted the Poles and Czechs at all. However, times were desperate, and Dowding was willing to make a concession for 'old' Poles—those who had arrived in Britain before the French defeat. The large number of 'new' Poles and Czechs—those who had fought in France and lost—were not so welcome. He did not want the high morale of his Fighter Command squadrons disturbed by pilots from 'failed air forces'. Dowding did not seem to mind Belgian and French pilots joining RAF squadrons, despite the fact were also from 'failed air forces'. He was willing to accept thirty-one French and twenty-nine Belgian pilots, along with the sixty-three 'old Poles'. However, he warned that if they were not up to it, Bomber Command would have to take them; if they were not good enough to fly bombers, they could perhaps become ferry pilots or fly target tugs. If this was too difficult for them, they would have to be sent back to their respective authorities for deployment as they saw fit.[68] It was scarcely a ringing vote of confidence in their capabilities.

It was no doubt frustrating for pilots trained in the Polish and Czech air forces to be retrained by the French Air Force before being retrained yet again by the Royal Air Force. The victories many of the pilots had gained in Poland and France should have been sufficient proof that they were ready for front-line duties. Unfortunately, these skills counted for nothing. They had to learn how to be part of an integrated air defence system. The RAF was trying to deskill them. They were, however, more fortunate than the 209 fully trained 'new' Czech and Polish fighter pilots. Dowding was adamant that he would rather disband a squadron than use them to replace losses.[69]

Dowding's preferred solution for the 'new' Poles and Czechs was to form entirely new squadrons, where they would not be able to contaminate the rest of Fighter Command. Having British officers share command positions would overcome the problem of communicating with ground controllers. This approach dovetailed nicely with the desire of the Polish and Czech authorities to reform in some way their own air forces.[70] This approach created yet more problems; there were issues around the status of these reconstituted 'foreign' air forces within the RAF, and in particular over who the airmen owed their allegiance to. Governments in exile might decide to use the participation of their squadrons to extract concessions, choosing to withdraw them if they disapproved of a particular British government policy. British Dominions might expect their air forces to have a similar status. These issues caused more delay, but Dowding would rather wait for these problems to be resolved than have the 200 'new' Poles and Czech pilots posted to RAF squadrons. Indeed, he would not even allow training to begin until they were sorted out. The Poles and Czechs would have to carry on waiting for their chance to get into an OTU and discover the mysterious ways of British fighter tactics.

Even when compromise arrangements with the Polish and Czech governments in exile were hammered out early in August, there was still no rush to get these pilots into combat. Two Polish squadrons (Nos 302 and 303) and one Czech squadron (No. 310) began to form. It was generally agreed that there were already enough pilots and ground personnel to form at least another three Polish and one Czech squadron, but it was claimed that there were no fighters for them to fly. There were not even enough fighters to get some training going.[71]

The Air Ministry seemed to have forgotten about the American fighters. The unused Mohawks were the fighters the Czechs had been flying in combat in France. Until they were diverted to Britain, these ex-French planes were on their way to the very pilots who were now left kicking their heels at various airfields up and down the country. The Poles and Czechs would have had no problems with the French instrumentation and reverse throttles. No doubt the Polish and Czech bomber pilots would have been equally happy to do some training on the Northrop Nomads that were also left scattered around various airfields. Indeed, they would have happily flown them in action against an invasion if required. They could only have been an improvement on the Hawker Hart it had been suggested they use.

It was all very different for the Dutch naval reconnaissance squadrons that had retreated to Britain in May 1940. They brought their Fokker floatplanes with them, and within a couple of weeks No. 320 Squadron Coastal Command was formed and operational with Fokker T.VIII torpedo bombers. The fact that there were only eight of these floatplanes and no spares did not stop the squadron flying them on coastal patrols until the end of September. The Anson-equipped No. 321 Squadron became operational in July with the remaining Dutch personnel. Incorporating Dutch airmen into Coastal Command seemed remarkably swift and painless. The crucial battle might be over before Polish and Czech fighter pilots made it to the front line. It was a potentially fatal waste of resources.

Preparing for Invasion

In the early summer of 1940, it seemed very likely that the crucial battle would be an invasion. Churchill expected it. Even the Air Staff were resigned to it. Hitler might hope for a political solution, and Göring might believe his Air Force could deliver outright victory, but the German High Command knew that victory would only come after the British Army had been engaged and defeated.

Brooke was far from confident his Army could avoid defeat. He demanded the maximum air support for his forces. RAF commanders seemed willing do their best. All Air Force Commands were given clear instructions about what their role would be; Coastal Command was to disrupt German preparations, give warning of an approaching invasion fleet, and attack it as it approached. The two Beaufort torpedo-bomber squadrons would spearhead these efforts. There were also a couple of Fleet Air Arm Swordfish torpedo bomber squadrons to hand. The recently arrived American Hudsons and the rather less capable Ansons (bomb load just 360 lbs) would join in these attacks. The Army's own army-cooperation squadrons would be among the first planes to attack the invading forces as they landed. Up to two-thirds of available Lysanders would be used for ground attack, their efforts helping to fill the anticipated one-hour gap between the initial landings and a full response from Bomber Command.[1]

This sounded impressive, but Coastal Command squadrons were necessarily spread around the British coastline and the nine army-cooperation squadrons were all attached to the various Army corps. Only a very small proportion of these squadrons would be close enough to the scene of any invasion to intervene. To make matters worse, in July, the Beaufort's troublesome Taurus engines grounded these squadrons.[2] Soon afterwards, the two Swordfish squadrons were transferred to HMS *Courageous* for duties in the Mediterranean, leaving no specialist anti-shipping force.

The Banquet force was standing by to back-up the efforts of the regular squadrons. By early July, 1,000 training school planes (ranging from Tiger Moths to Wellingtons) were ready to strike the invasion beachheads. It was hoped that the final figure would be approaching 2,000.[3] Operating slow biplanes in the battlezone might seem to be inviting a massacre; however, low-performance planes like the Dutch Fokker C.X, the German Henschel HS 123, and the British Hawker Hector had all been used in the recent fighting in the low-level ground-attack role without suffering excessive losses. Against forward troops with less organised anti-aircraft defences, even slow biplanes had a good chance of hitting their targets and making their escape. A bridgehead in the process of being established might or might not be such a place.

The main problem was actually concentrating the Banquet force where the invasion was likely to occur. Most of the training schools were not close to the scene of a likely invasion. Moving the elementary training schools closer was considered, but it seemed unnecessarily disruptive and risky. Flying in hundreds of planes to airfields in the confusion of an invasion might not be practicable; the airfields would almost certainly have been damaged by bombing, and the resources of these airfields would already be fully stretched by the regular squadrons operating from them.[4] Bomber Command thought it was more efficient to use the resources of No. 6 Group (OTU) as straightforward replacements for losses in regular squadrons.[5]

In the end, it was decided that four flights of basic trainers would be attached to Army Cooperation, Coastal Command, and Bomber Command bases. Each flight would consist of five or six planes. Initially, the first two flights would be deployed; it would be up to the commander of the base to decide if his airfield could accommodate any more. As the instructions for deployment to army-cooperation squadrons grimly put it: 'This number (of flights) may be increased if casualties in the A.C. squadrons have reduced the risks of congestion.'[6]

At what point the Air Ministry would have ordered the Banquet planes into action was never definitively decided. It would have been a drastic step to take, given that the losses inflicted on instructors and pupils would have wrecked the training programme for some time. It was still planned to use the Banquet elements if there was a landing in an unexpected stretch of the coastline—in Scotland, for example, where no substantial forces were immediately available. Elsewhere, it would depend on the circumstances. Douglas did not think it 'should be used at the first sign of an enemy landing.'[7] Indeed, the basic trainers could not be kept permanently ready to intervene without interfering with the training programme. Where substantial regular forces existed, it would seem the Banquet forces would have been held back as an option of last resort. Its deployment would depend on how quickly the situation became serious enough to warrant it; given the state of the British Army at the time, this might not have been very long.

If the plan had been put into effect, it is doubtful that the invading German forces would have found a hornet's nest of Banquet aircraft swarming over them. The flights would have been as widely spread as the Coastal Command, Army Cooperation, and bomber bases they were attached to. All in all, the combined efforts of Coastal and Training Commands and the army-cooperation squadrons might not have amounted to much. The main blow would have to be delivered by Bomber Command.

Newall may have infuriated the War Office with his reported comments on the frittering away of bomber resources, but he was trying to strike a balance between the strategic aspirations of the Air Staff and tactical responsibilities of the Air Force.

In the days following the French collapse, with the RAF coming in for some heavy criticism, even Portal felt the need to give ground. He assured Brooke there would be a powerful response against any beachhead, even agreeing that as soon as the invasion was underway, half of Nos 1 and 2 Groups (two Battle and seven Blenheim squadrons) would be at the disposal of the Army. Indeed, if, in the confusion of an invasion, communications were to break down between the two Groups and the Air Ministry, all these squadrons would be available to the Army. It was quite a coup for the War Office, although it still meant that the Army would start the battle with a smaller bomber force than the BAFF had possessed in France. Douglas also made it clear to Portal that his 'heavies' would have to attack targets assigned by the Army.[9] Each Army Command would have a Combined Operations Room (COR), which would pass on requests direct to Nos 1 and 2 Groups and to Bomber Command HQ if 'heavies' were required.[10]

Portal had the forces for a powerful intervention. The 'heavies' of Nos 3, 4, and 5 Groups had only suffered minor losses during the French campaign, and the Blenheim squadrons of No. 2 Group were back to full strength after their heavy losses. Only the decimated Battle-equipped No. 1 Group was still in the process of recovering. With the two Polish squadrons, the number would be up to six by late summer, with two more in the process of forming.

Portal, however, was far less inclined to commit his bombers to support the Army than his assurances to Brooke might have suggested. It was with some relief that on 17–18 June, with the land battle on the continent effectively over, he was finally able to focus on oil targets again. Approximately 100 bombers set off, and once again numerous fires and explosions were reported in the target areas. The strategic bombing offensive was back on track.[11] Unfortunately, the scale of destruction Bomber Command was inflicting existed solely in the vivid imaginations of the Air Staff and bomber commanders. There was far too much willingness to accept the reports of aircrews, who wanted to believe their bombs were hitting their targets.

In the face of this apparent success, Newall feared that equally destructive raids would soon be raining down on British targets. He ordered Bomber Command to switch its focus to the factories building German bombers.[12] Portal was furious; it was not the job of his bombers to bolster Fighter Command.[13] Aircraft factories were also much further east and far harder to find than oil plants; they tended to be in isolated areas, meaning bombs that missed would be completely wasted. This rather alarmed an Air Staff already anxious that their strategic air offensive should not degenerate into indiscriminate bombing. There was no inkling of how indiscriminate it already was.

Portal managed to get some oil targets reinstated. Invading land, sea, and air forces would all need petrol, he argued, and there was a case for not letting the good work already done go to waste by relaxing the pressure. So much damage had been inflicted already that even light attacks ought to be worthwhile. A small number of bombers would also continue to attack communication targets leading to the ports an invasion fleet might use. It was believed that previous attacks on communication targets were already making it difficult to supply German forces in occupied territories. Even a relatively small effort would ensure communications remained disrupted.

The Air Staff was trying to be realistic about what bombing was achieving. There were concerns that bomber crews might just be damaging rather than destroying their targets. Limiting the number of targets would ensure their complete destruction. The final plan called for the main effort to be against ten aircraft assembly plants and depots and five oil targets, with a small effort devoted to communications. These attacks might not have an immediate effect on German Air Force operations, it was conceded, 'but the effect when felt would be permanent'.[14]

The success Portal thought his long-range bombers were having was going to make it even more difficult for him to agree to use his bombers tactically. Initially, he seemed committed to doing everything to defeat an invasion; all his instructions ended with a reminder that once the invasion was underway, Bomber Command would be expected to switch its entire attention 'at short notice' to invasion targets. These would include 'points of embarkation, craft crossing the Channel and later the landing grounds'.[15]

Ports offered the perfect bottleneck, and they were also relatively easy to attack by night. Sinking ships before they discharged their contents was the most efficient way of reducing the strength of the invading forces.[16] Indeed, there was an element of relish within the Air Ministry about the prospect of taking on the invading armada at sea: it was a chance to prove the claim that the Air Ministry had made so often that air power could dominate the oceans in a way that would make navies obsolete. However, there was little evidence that British bombers could do this; Bomber Command had not yet managed to sink a single German ship. Much was expected of the 'buoyancy bomb' that had just entered production. The bomb was dropped ahead of an approaching ship and supposed to rise slowly to the surface, detonating against the more vulnerable hull as the ship passed over it. However, relying so heavily on an unproven weapon seemed risky.

Plans at the time called for Wellingtons to attack ships with these buoyancy bombs while Hampdens and Whitleys showered smaller craft and the forces that had landed with 20-lb and 40-lb General Purpose bombs.[17] This sounded impressive, but much would depend on whether the Wellingtons and Hampdens attacked by day. The more these two bombers flew by night, the more Portal and the Air Staff viewed them as specialist night bombers. A dawn invasion might mean these attacks would not come until darkness fell, giving the Germans an entire day to consolidate a beachhead.

It was only a few months since they had switched to night operations, so there was no question of aircrew having lost the art of formation flying. No. 3 Group was upbeat about the prospects of operating by day, provided their Wellingtons were equipped with the promised beam guns. The Air Staff was generally in favour of improving defensive firepower of the 'heavies', mainly because nocturnal missions would be ending in daylight due to the short summer nights. There was, however, little urgency. At the end of July, Wellingtons were still coming off the production lines without the beam guns.[18] At No. 5 Group, Harris was not willing to wait for officialdom to take its course. He got his technicians to devise a beam position for a machine gun and asked the local manufacturer Rose and Company to design a new ventral mounting and a dorsal turret to improve the field of fire. The Air Ministry were not the least bit impressed by this 'backdoor' approach, but by June all the modifications were approved. By this time, fifty Hampdens already had the beam-gun position, the dorsal turret was being modified, and Harris had ordered 100 of the new ventral mounts and sent the bill to the Air Ministry.[19]

At a time when Tiger Moths were being readied for action against an invasion, it seemed even more reasonable to expect bombers designed for day operations to operate by day. Whether they would have done is not clear—the Air Staff and Bomber Command were curiously vague on the issue. Documents at the time refer to their use 'by day or night'. Throughout the summer months, all Bomber Command Groups held a certain number of flights on standby from the early hours, bombed up and ready to go, so that any approaching invasion armada could be attacked as soon as it was sighted. Even the commander of No. 4 Group could get no assurance that his Whitley night bombers on standby would not be called upon after dawn.[20]

Portal was not happy that any part of his force had to be on permanent standby, and therefore not available to bomb targets in Germany. He also insisted, quite reasonably, that any daylight operations would require fighter escorts. However, there were no discussions or attempts to try out escorted Wellington or Hampden missions; it was almost as if there was an understanding between Bomber and Fighter Command not to pursue the escort option. Dowding did not want its efforts diverted from its primary air defence role, and Portal needed a good reason for not being diverted from his strategic offensive. Doing nothing about the escort issue suited both Commands. When daylight bombing appeared on Air Ministry agendas, it seems to have been viewed as a last resort.[21] There was no definitive decision, but the evidence suggests that, as in France, on tactical missions the Wellington and Hampden would only have been used by night.

This left the Blenheims and Battles. The Army did have some control over these—initially, at least. The Air Staff Memo issued on 30 July was quite specific about Bomber Command duties. During the actual landing, the beaches would become 'the decisive point of action', and Coastal, Fighter, and Bomber Commands were to focus all their efforts there and the immediate sea approaches.[22] Portal however, did not want his command included in the list. His bombers were no good at 'beach fighting', as he put it. Once enemy troops were on the beaches, it would be up to the Army to deal with them, along with the Hart and Audax 'anti-tank dive-bombers'.[23] The Air Ministry agreed. Even the Blenheims were entirely unsuitable for the close-support role—they would be far more effective against German shipping moving across the Channel.[24]

Portal was now regretting that he had agreed to hand over half of Nos 1 and 2 Groups to the Army. He claimed the War Office had taken advantage of his offer, which was only ever intended as a way of dealing with a surprise invasion. The Army were wrong to assume that it was an automatic transfer as soon as enemy forces were landing or about to land. With this interpretation, he claimed, a few thousand parachutists landing in the Shetlands would immediately justify the Army taking over half of Bomber Command's medium bomber force.[25]

Portal listed all the disadvantages of the Army controlling any bombers. The Army commander would inevitably hold them back until the landings had taken place so that his forces would benefit the most. Under Air Force control, a more balanced decision could be made about how they could best be used. With Army and Air Force commanders both ordering bomber attacks, there would also inevitably be confusion and possibly duplication.[26]

Portal won the argument; the Army lost its nine Blenheim and Battle squadrons, and Bomber Command assumed responsibility for coordinating all heavy and medium bombing missions. Temporary exceptions to this would be made only if there was a genuine 'surprise invasion',[27] which was carefully defined as a landing that was taking place without an official twelve-hour warning signal. In these circumstances, the local Army commander could 'apply' for the use of one bomber squadron, but he had to prove he had a worthwhile target.[28] This might have provoked a smile from the now-retired former Army chief, Field Marshal Milne. In 1926, Milne had been discussing Army/Air Force cooperation with Trenchard, and the former Chief of Air Staff had poked fun at Milne's attempts to establish clear guidelines for when the Army could expect air support. The two ministries were not departments of lawyers, Trenchard had insisted.[29] In 1940, the War Office might have felt it needed a good lawyer to 'apply' for air support.

Rather than preparing his command to help the Army defeat an invasion, Portal spent the summer trying to increase the long-range capability of his force at the expense of his tactical medium bombers. The role of his bombers was to lead the fightback by striking at targets in Germany, not compensate for the inadequacies of the Army by helping out on the battlefield. By bombing Germany, he would be helping to defeat an invasion and taking the first steps towards victory. This sort of talk went down very well with the Prime Minister, who, despite the desperate military situation, was already insisting everything should be done to increase the production of heavy bombers.[30] Portal's offensive spirit so impressed the Prime Minister that he was already pencilling in the Bomber Command chief as Newall's successor.

To boost the strategic air offensive, Portal could not get rid of his medium bombers quickly enough. He wanted No. 1 Group to convert from Battles to Wellingtons, not Bostons or Marylands. In mid-August, he suggested that fifteen of the medium bomber squadrons should be converted to eight heavy bomber squadrons, because, as he put it, the Blenheim was 'not pulling its weight',[31] by which he meant it was not capable of contributing to the strategic air offensive. The plane was not remotely suitable for the ground-attack role; it could not even ground strafe, he insisted. This may have been true, although it was hardly consistent with the Air Staff decision to develop the Bisley ground-attack version of the Blenheim.

To justify converting medium bomber squadrons to heavy bomber squadrons, Portal pointed out that the twenty-three operational Blenheim and Battle squadrons that existed exceeded the 250 bombers the Army had asked for before the campaign in France. Furthermore, this commitment had been made with a thirty-two-division army in mind. A smaller army was envisaged for some time to come. Some might argue that this was a reason for increasing air support, but not Portal; he managed to persuade the ERPC that the smaller British Army only needed eight squadrons. The committee approved Portal's plan in principle—only heavy bomber production would delay implementation in practice. As American aircraft became available, the tactical day bomber force would, at some distant point in the future, eventually be restored to twenty-five squadrons, but in the short-term, building up the long-range heavy bomber force had priority.[32] With an invasion imminent, it was not a particularly sensible decision.

If Bomber Command had an anti-invasion policy, it was not to waste too much effort dealing with it. As far as Portal was concerned, supporting the Army was not his responsibility—it was a task for the army-cooperation squadrons, Coastal Command, or even Training Command Harts and Tiger Moths. In other words, anybody but Bomber Command. Bombing targets on the battlefield would not make any difference, whereas his offensive against German industry would. Newall tended to agree; he accepted that Bomber Command had to use all its resources to 'frustrate' an enemy invasion. However, he stated 'this does not imply bombing operations will be restricted to the actual invading forces on land or at sea'.[33] In the midst of an invasion, Bomber Command would continue to bomb industrial targets deep inside Germany, just as it had done during the Battle of France.

For Dowding's Fighter Command, the difference between its intended air defence role and an anti-invasion role was not quite so marked. Either way, the battle would be fought over Britain and the type of aircraft required need not be so radically different. Nevertheless, with single-seater escorts now within range, even dealing with a purely aerial assault required a significant shift in thinking. An invasion would again force Dowding to use his fighters for roles he did not believe they should perform.

At the end of June, Stevenson, the Director of Home Operations, outlined what the fighters would have to do. First priority would be the destruction of the transports carrying the much-feared airborne troops; the second priority would be bombers. Some fighters would operate at altitude to provide cover, but the majority would have to operate at low-level, where the ground-attack planes, observation planes, dive-bombers, and troop-carrying transports would be. RAF bombers attacking the invasion fleet would also need an escort.[34] It was a formidable set of tasks. A puzzled Dowding was relieved that he did not have to protect the Royal Navy as well, but this oversight was soon put right. In July, protecting the Fleet was added to the list and assumed absolute priority. Without air cover, the fleet would not be able to intervene.[35]

Ground attack was another potential role for Fighter Command. The Air Ministry was constantly stressing that strafing was better than bombing as a way of supporting ground forces. This was mainly to ensure Bomber Command was not burdened with the role, but the corollary was that fighters were very suitable.

Hurricanes had been used in this role in France and some pilots were keen to continue the experiment—some even asked if their planes could carry 20-lb bombs, but the request was curtly turned down.[36] Fighters had to concentrate on their primary task of shooting down bombers.

Nevertheless, as the first German troops came ashore, fighters might also make a significant contribution by attacking the invading forces when they were at their most vulnerable. It was not a role that came naturally to Fighter Command. An Air Component controller in France might order fighters to strafe ground targets, but a Fighter Command sector commander had different priorities. It was the difference between an air force used to working with an army and one trying to fight an independent air war.

It did not make sense to have a blanket ban on ground strafing. Churchill made sure an exception was made for cannon-armed fighters. Dowding had promised the Prime Minister that the cannon-armed Spitfires delivered to No. 19 Squadron would be held back for attacks on the landing craft as they came ashore, but that was the only firm Fighter Command commitment.

Even this small commitment was a diversion Dowding felt he could not afford; he could not forget that his primary duty was to defend Britain. Even with a German army massing on the other side of the Channel, Churchill, Beaverbrook, and the Air Staff were still mesmerised by the prospect of the German bomber fleet wiping out the British aircraft industry at a stroke. Dowding thought the Luftwaffe would be unlikely to divert effort to attacking factories in the midst of an invasion. Peirse, however, insisted the Army and Navy could stop an invasion, but only Fighter Command could defend Britain's aircraft factories.[37] This had to be Dowding's priority. Fighter Command's role was to defend the country, not to establish air superiority over a battlefield. Its squadrons would continue to be spread fairly evenly amongst the twenty-odd sectors that protected the country from every direction.

Dowding knew that this was a problem. He rather desperately hoped the Germans would land all along the coastline, from Scotland to the West Country, and then develop any landings that proved successful. This was what he mistakenly believed the Germans had done in France, and it was the strategy that his widely spread fighter force would best be able to deal with. Equally likely, however, was a landing along a narrow stretch of coastline. Dowding had to admit that Fighter Command was not capable of concentrating its resources in a single region, although it was only fear of the knockout blow and the Command's own self-imposed rigid Group/sector structure that was stopping it.[38]

Air Vice-Marshal Leigh-Mallory, the commander of No. 12 Group, believed that the Germans would seek to establish air superiority before attempting any invasion, with an offensive against RAF airfields lasting a week or so. Dowding hoped they would, as this would give the RAF a chance to wear down the Luftwaffe before the 'serious business' started. Indeed—rather prophetically, as it turned out—Dowding believed that if the Luftwaffe persisted with an air campaign lasting a month, there would be no invasion. He feared, however, that any pre-invasion air offensive would probably be no longer than twenty-four hours.[39] This scenario would place the

Fighter Command Groups and sectors, August 1940.

greatest pressure on his command. As soon as the invasion was underway, Fighter Command would have to divert resources to protect the Army and Navy, escort bombers, and still have squadrons available to defend British cities and industry. From Fighter Command's point of view, the longer it stayed a battle between the two air forces, the better. Indeed, it was arguably Britain's only chance.

When the invasion came, Dowding instructed his group commanders to use 'pretty big units', although at this stage that only meant nothing below squadron strength. The early warning radar chain would not help much, he conceded. The action would be continuous, with formations of three squadrons being thrown against the invading forces at one, one and a half, or two-hour intervals for the eighteen hours of daylight. Pilots would be flying up to six sorties per day. Each 'wave' of fighters would consist of one squadron flying high, acting as cover, and two heading for the transports and bombers.[40]

The range of the German fighter force pretty much dictated where the invasion would come. The Bf 110 could cover landings from just south of the Wash to a little east of Weymouth. Apart from the southernmost sectors in No. 12 Group and one in No. 10 Group, this lay entirely within the area No. 11 Group was responsible for. If the Bf 109 was to be involved, the invasion would have to take place well south of the Wash, taking No. 12 Group out of the equation completely. Whether the Germans took the obvious invasion route across the Channel (as, indeed, they planned to) or struck along the east coast (as Brooke still expected), No. 11 Group would bear the brunt of the assault.

Sectors were smaller where the population density was higher, so it was fortunate that the invasion would come close to the capital. Park's Group was the strongest in Dowding's Command, but even so it only had about a third of the available fighter squadrons. It was not enough to deal with an invasion. Nevertheless, Dowding was adamant that Park had to see the requirements of the country's air defence as a whole. No one group could expect special treatment, and he would not get any priority in terms of quality of equipment or personnel. The Spitfire squadrons and the experienced pilots would continue to be shared evenly around the various groups.

The mistakes made in France were being repeated. Two thirds of the available fighters would be outside the battlezone, and No. 11 Group would be outnumbered just as the Air Component and AASF fighters had been. It was a daunting prospect. Park told his pilots they would probably have to fly eight sorties per day; targets would be so plentiful and sorties so brief that fighters would often be landing to rearm, but not to refuel. Park realised that this intensity could not be maintained for long. The invasion would have to be defeated in twenty-four hours, or forty-eight hours maximum.[41] Even with pilots flying eight sorties per day, Park did not have enough to protect the troops defending the beaches and the warships taking on the invasion fleet, escort the bombers and 'helpless and defenceless' Banquet Scheme trainers, and still defend London and the aircraft factories in his region.

Fighter Command needed the German High Command to adopt a strategy its squadrons could handle. The possibility that the Luftwaffe might attempt to defeat Britain on its own was a prospect that could only provoke apprehension. It did, however, limit the task, and it was what Fighter Command was prepared for. Perhaps a prolonged air assault would precede an invasion. The Air Staff managed to persuade itself that invasion was 'not a practicable operation of war' until the German Air Force had defeated Fighter Command. Even air superiority would not be enough. The Air Staff decided that nothing short of 'virtual air supremacy' would be necessary 'in the vital areas'.[42] Before embarking on an invasion. the Germans would have to destroy Fighter Command, and all Britain had to do to avoid invasion was to make sure Fighter Command was not destroyed. Put like this, the task seemed achievable. Dowding's aim would not be to defeat the Luftwaffe, but merely to avoid being defeated. This actually turned Fighter Command's widely spread deployment into an advantage—if squadrons could not be committed, they could not be defeated. It was a dangerous game to play.

There was no evidence from previous German operations that they would seek air supremacy or indeed even superiority before invading. This was not how the Wehrmacht had won its victories. There had been no attempt to destroy the Polish Air Force or Allied air forces in France before launching a ground offensive—the assault on land and in the air had been simultaneous. The Air Staff was making a rather convenient assumption, reassuringly pushing the possibility of the ill-equipped British Army taking on the Wehrmacht a little further into the future. Whatever happened, a battle would be fought in the skies first, either to pave the way for invasion or simply to defeat Britain outright.

There was indeed no need for Germany to adopt this strategy. Success had come in Poland, Norway, Holland, Belgium, and France because the different arms of the Wehrmacht had worked together. The Luftwaffe had kept the enemy air forces at bay and helped the Army advance, and the disruption caused by this advance had enabled the Luftwaffe to tighten its control of the air. There were good reasons to believe that the same cooperation would enable an invasion of Britain to succeed. The invasion fleet would give the German fighter force the same opportunity to inflict heavy losses on RAF bombers as the bridges over the Meuse. Luftwaffe air support would help the German Army establish a bridgehead and, incidentally, punch a hole in the early warning network. Even a small bridgehead would give German pilots somewhere closer to head for than the French coast when they were in trouble. It might soon expand enough to accommodate temporary airstrips, increasing the support the Luftwaffe could offer German ground forces. Once again, the success of one would contribute to the success of the other.

Obligingly, however, the German High Command decided to change its strategy. The German Army wanted to strike quickly, before the British Army could recover some of its fighting capability. However, before any invasion was attempted, Grand Admiral Raeder, the commander of the German Navy, insisted not just on air superiority over the Channel, but also the elimination of the RAF. It was not British bombers Raeder was worried about; his concern was the Royal Navy.

This was not the first time the German High Command had considered a preparatory air-only offensive; it had been an option before the offensive against France.

Lieutenant General von Manstein, the architect of the German victory, was very concerned by the disruption Allied bombers might cause as his columns made their way through the Ardennes, and he wanted the Luftwaffe to achieve air superiority before he advanced. Hitler, however, feared this would turn into a lengthy war of attrition and become 'a Verdun in the air'.[43] The Army was overruled. The attack on the ground and in the air was simultaneous. For the invasion of Britain, Raeder was not overruled. Hitler would get his 'Verdun in the air'.

Göring, who was still unaware how unsuccessful his Luftwaffe had been at Dunkirk, would get another chance. The air offensive alone, he hoped, might even be enough to finish Britain off. A provisional date of 15 September was pencilled in for the invasion, with landings between Brighton and Deal.[44] The Luftwaffe would have until then to destroy Fighter Command. It seemed more than enough time. The feeling was that two weeks of good weather ought to be sufficient. It was an extraordinarily ambitious aim. Even after the crushing victory over France, the French still had nearly 600 fighters in front-line squadrons.[45] The French Air Force had been heavily defeated, but it had not been wiped out; if the German Army had waited until the French fighter force ceased to exist before attacking, the aerial Battle of France would still be raging.

The stage was set for a Battle of Britain that would not involve fighting on the beaches or in the streets. It would only involve air forces. For Dowding, it was the perfect scenario; there would be no bombers to escort, no fleets to protect, and no armies to worry about. The enemy target would not be British towns and cities, nor even aircraft factories. The target was Fighter Command. It was not quite the battle his Command had been created for, but it was close enough. It would be fought over British soil, with all the advantages that he had so often listed. It was a battle his Fighter Command was organised and trained to fight, and radar would finally be able to play a full part. The miracle was not that Britain had radar, but that the German High Command had adopted a strategy that enabled the RAF to make maximum use of it.

For the Luftwaffe, it would be a struggle for air superiority, a battle between the two fighter forces. For Dowding, it was a battle against the German bombers. If escorts got in the way, they would have to be dealt with, but the bombers were the priority. It was not just the best strategy for the RAF to adopt—it was the only strategy. Fighter Command did not have sufficient fighters of sufficient quality, nor did its pilots have the tactical skill to defeat the German fighter force. The Bf 109s were not vulnerable, but the bombers were, and it was bombers RAF pilots were trained to shoot down. The more Fighter Command could keep the battle between British fighters and German bombers, the better it would be for the RAF and Britain. Dowding's tunnel-vision obsession with the bomber was now precisely what Britain needed. Fighter Command would be fighting the battle on just about the most favourable terms possible. Even so, victory was still far from certain.

Dowding's Battle

Dowding might be fighting the battle on his terms, but he would also be fighting it with all the limitations of the air defence system he had helped create. To keep interception time down to a minimum, squadrons took off and attacked singly. Arguably, organising larger formations to respond as quickly was just a matter of training, but one squadron was what Fighter Command was used to. On 1 August, Park had nineteen squadrons, and Dowding could claim this was close to the maximum the Group could handle. Each sector could vector three formations towards the enemy; at a pinch, four was possible. This meant Park's seven sectors could comfortably handle twenty-one squadrons and might just about manage twenty-eight. It was very much a self-imposed maximum. There was no limit to the number of squadrons that could simply be told to patrol a given area.

The sector system was more flexible than it had once been. The range of the latest radios meant a squadron could be vectored towards an enemy formation in a neighbouring sector. Inter-group cooperation was more complicated. While the Group commander had full control over all the squadrons in his zone, support from neighbouring groups could only be requested, and these squadrons had to be controlled by their own Group system. Cooperation between Groups relied on the goodwill of the commanders involved.

The Group commanders did their best to pick their way round the limitations of the system. Initially Brand at No. 10 Group had only four day fighter squadrons, but he kept two of them at Middle Wallop, right on the border of No. 11 Group. It was a strange deployment if Brand was really trying to cover the coast from Bournemouth to Plymouth, but a perfectly logical one if he was to use his squadrons to reinforce the defences of Southampton and Portsmouth, just over the boundary in No. 11 Group. By 1 August, the number of No. 10 Group single-seater fighter squadrons had increased to six, but half of them were still at Middle Wallop or Warmwell, a little further south.

Leigh-Mallory's No. 12 Group was supposed to be protecting the east coast almost as far as Middlesbrough, with the Midlands and Merseyside key targets to his rear. The way No. 11 Group sectors radiated out from London meant

No. 12 Group's southernmost airfields were not far from London. The most southerly sector had originally been intended to protect London from attacks coming from around a neutral Holland. It was now pointing the wrong way. Instead of providing protection for London, it had been split into two sectors that formed a backstop for No. 11 Group. Like Brand, Leigh-Mallory understood the key battle would be in the south-east. Despite the length of coast No. 12 Group had to cover, half of its single-seater fighter squadrons were based at either Coltishall or Duxford, which was as close to No. 11 Group as it was possible to get.

Just 20 miles across the Channel, the Luftwaffe suffered from no such self-imposed geographical restrictions. In the Calais region, the Luftwaffe had concentrated four fighter wings with around 500 fighters in an area about the size of Kent. Further west, another three fighter wings were operating from the Le Havre and Cherbourg areas. These would be supported by 350 longer-range Bf 110 fighters. Park's 300 fighters would be far more heavily outnumbered than they need have been.

As if numerical inferiority was not a sufficient handicap, Park's pilots were still trying to work out how to deal with enemy fighters. Park had been well-aware of the problem for some time. In a report on No. 11 Group's involvement in the French campaign, he freely admitted his pilots had no training in fighter-*versus*-fighter combat, dealing with escorted bombers, or flying in wing or any multi-squadron formations. Nor were they prepared for combat at high-altitude or skilled in basic deflection shooting. It was a formidable list of deficiencies, although Park still managed to conclude that 'the average German fighter pilot [was] not as well trained as his British counterpart'.[1] Park did not mean these comments as criticisms; he was merely highlighting the folly of employing his fighters over France in a role it was not trained or prepared for. Unfortunately for Park and his pilots, there was now no way of avoiding a battle with the opposing fighter force. His pilots would have to acquire skills not taught in the training schools.

There was little attempt amongst the top RAF commanders to provide any guidance. It took time just to appreciate the scale of the problem. At the beginning of the French campaign, Park had described how fighter-*versus*-fighter combat in France was 'degenerating' into dogfights at an early stage. He likened it to the primitive tactics used in the early stages of the First World War, before the importance of maintaining formation had been established. Fighter units were criticised for not carrying out organised formation attacks on opposing fighters.[2] By the end of May, he was beginning to accept that individual dogfights might be inevitable, but squadrons should at least try and maintain sections or, as a last resort, pairs.[3]

By this time, some squadrons were coming to the conclusion that far from being a last resort, the pair their German opponents were using, with one fighter attacking and the second covering, was the ideal tactical combat formation.[4] In No. 10 Group, it soon became standard practice, but no official instruction was ever issued by Dowding to Fighter Command or by Park to No. 11 Group. Squadrons were allowed to decide their own tactics and some continued using the standard, inflexible 'vic' formations throughout the summer of 1940. Tail-end Charlies were also still used. Some still thought the Defiant could provide cover.[5] Looser 'vic' formations made it slightly easier to scan the skies for the enemy without crashing into your neighbour, but old habits die hard; years of training could not be simply deleted at the drop of a hat. Less excusably, training schools continued to teach the same old tactics. When the pilots were posted to operational squadrons, it seemed that they had enough to worry about without being told to forget a lot of what they had been taught.

It was not just the tactics that were wrong; the fighters themselves had not been designed with fighter-*versus*-fighter combat in mind. The Merlin engine tended to cut out when the pilot threw the plane into a dive. Sudden manoeuvres were not required for bomber interception, but they were when engaging fighters. The poor handing of the Spitfire and Hurricane at high speed was another disadvantage; pilots often found that it was difficult to aim their guns accurately, never mind evade a chasing enemy fighter.[6] Acceleration was also not a major issue for bomber interception, but British fighters struggled to match the acceleration of the much lighter Bf 109. Its low weight also gave the German fighter better climb and performance at altitude. Trials with the captured Bf 109E demonstrated that even the Spitfire was outclassed by the Bf 109E above 15,000 feet.

Defensively, seat armour had already been fitted to give pilots some protection from attacks from the rear. Using 100-octane petrol helped improve performance. It was found that high-speed handling could be improved simply by using metal instead of fabric to cover the ailerons. Constant-speed propellers, which automatically adjusted the pitch at all speeds, provided a way of improving acceleration and climb. On 9 June, de Havilland was asked to investigate the possibility of fitting British fighters with their constant-speed airscrew. Tests with a Spitfire were completed on 20 June.[7] Conversion of all aircraft was immediately ordered, with priority going to Spitfire squadrons. By the end of July, all Spitfires had been modified—a demonstration of how fast the Air Ministry could get things moving when it wanted to.

Dowding would start the battle with fifty-seven squadrons. Plans to increase the number were shelved; these would require a nucleus of experienced pilots from existing squadrons, and it was not the time to weaken the front line. Instead, it was decided to form an extra flight of four fighters in thirty Hurricane and six Spitfire squadrons, enabling these to put sixteen rather than twelve fighters into the air. Although Dowding saw it as a rather unsatisfactory emergency measure, in fact it made the individual squadron a much more formidable fighting formation.

The fifty-seven squadrons consisted of seven Blenheim squadrons, twenty-nine Hurricane squadrons, nineteen Spitfire squadrons, and two Defiant squadrons.[8] Dowding had actually wanted one third of his force to be capable of carrying AI for night defence, but problems with the Beaufighter and the shortage of Blenheims meant there were less than half the required number. This might be worrying for those concerned about the state of the night defences, but it was a stroke of good fortune for the battle for daylight air superiority. Problems with the Defiant and Whirlwind were equally fortuitous. The Air Staff had wanted a third of the day fighter force equipped with the turret fighter, and as many as possible of the rest were supposed to be equipped with the twin-engine Whirlwind and, indeed, the Beaufighter. Again, production problems came to Britain's aid. Only two squadrons had reequipped with the Defiant, and the Whirlwinds were only just arriving. Britain was lucky that the planes that would have been the least useful in the summer of 1940 had the most development and production problems. If everything had gone to plan, Fighter Command could have entered the Battle of Britain with fewer than twenty Hurricane and Spitfire squadrons; instead, it had nearly fifty.

The Luftwaffe opened its daylight operations against Britain early in July with fighter sweeps over the south-east of England and attacks on coastal shipping along the south and east coast. Dowding had no intention of challenging German fighter sweeps, although as radar could not distinguish between bomber and fighter formations, this was not always easy to do. Dowding was, however, under pressure to protect the convoys. Once again, he felt he was being forced to fight a battle that was not necessary and in circumstances that did not favour his fighter force. Radar could not give sufficient warning of Luftwaffe attacks, which meant the convoys could only be properly protected by standing patrols. Pilots shot down would also have to bail out over the sea. The Channel and North Sea was not where Dowding wanted to fight his battle; he could not understand why the goods could not go by rail. For Churchill, it was a matter of principle and national pride that British shipping should be free to use a stretch of water that he considered to be British.

Churchill's argument was perhaps more emotional than reasoned, but his instincts were right. The Luftwaffe only needed to control the skies over the Channel to launch an invasion. Allowing the Luftwaffe to gain the impression that they had achieved this was a dangerous policy; a reluctance to commit Fighter Command over the Channel could easily have been interpreted by the Germans as confirmation that their intelligence estimates were right and the RAF was a fading force. The last thing Britain wanted to do was to encourage the Germans to take a chance on an early invasion.

The first attack on a convoy took place on 1 July. Three Hurricanes were dispatched to provide protection after the convoy reported it was being dive-bombed, but they arrived too late to help. The scale and the timing of the intervention reflected Dowding's reluctance to get involved. On 4 July, the Luftwaffe claimed its first victim—a merchant vessel that had to be beached after a direct hit. Hurricanes trying to intervene were beaten off by the Bf 109 escort. On the 7th, No. 11 Group flew 215 sorties in defence of one convoy. The Luftwaffe did not attack until the convoy reached the Straits of Dover, when forty-five Do 17Zs sank one ship and damaged three more. Fifteen Spitfires were sent to intervene. One flight of three Spitfires was caught by high-flying Bf 109s and the formation was wiped out. None of the attacking bombers were shot down. Altogether, six Spitfires and a Hurricane were lost that day. The Luftwaffe lost no fighters. The destruction of three reconnaissance planes shadowing the convoy was little consolation for Dowding; it was not a good start.[9]

Shipping losses rose as the Luftwaffe became more proficient at hitting naval targets. On 25 July, eleven out of a convoy of twenty-one ships were either sunk or badly damaged by a combination of air attack, E-boats, and artillery fire from the French coastline. Two of the badly damaged ships were destroyers—warships that were expected to play an important part in defeating a German invasion. Following these attacks, convoys through the Channel were temporarily suspended in daylight. Instead, the ships crept along the coast during the short summer nights, putting into port during the day. The Luftwaffe was beginning to establish the air superiority an invasion required. On the 27th, one destroyer was sunk off the Suffolk coast and another in a raid on Dover harbour. As a result, destroyers were withdrawn from Dover to Harwich and Sheerness. It was another small victory for the German bomber force.

If the British fighters could break through the escorts, the German bombers (especially the Ju 87) were proving vulnerable. On the 29th, within the space of a few minutes, four dive-bombers were shot down and one damaged by Spitfires of No. 41 Squadron and Hurricanes of No. 501 Squadron. The Luftwaffe lost eighty-three bombers on daylight operations in the period of 1 July–4 August, a worryingly high 7 per cent of sorties flown. However, the small British fighter patrols also suffered heavily at the hands of the high-flying German patrols and close escorts. In the same period, Nos 10 and 11 Groups lost eighty-five fighters, while the Luftwaffe fighter force lost forty-two.[10] If it was to be a war of attrition between the fighter forces, the Luftwaffe was winning. If it was a battle between Fighter Command and the German bomber force, the RAF was winning.

The battle of the convoys reached its peak on 8 August with a series of furious Luftwaffe attacks on convoy C.W.9 as it made its way from the Medway to Swanage. The Hurricanes of No. 145 Squadron distinguished themselves by shooting down seven Ju 87s and damaging four more in two missions. Five Hurricanes were lost in combat with Bf 109 escorts, but the pilots of No. 145 Squadron claimed at least three of the Messerschmitts. During the day, Fighter Command lost seventeen fighters; on the German side, eleven Bf 109s, one Bf 110, and eight Ju 87s failed to return. Of the twenty ships that had set out, only four reached their destination. Seven had been sunk, and the rest, all seriously damaged, had been forced to make for other ports.

These early battles demonstrated that both sides had problems. On 9 July, the Luftwaffe committed the Bf 110 over the Channel for the first time. Hurricanes from Nos 43 and 151 Squadrons shot down three and damaged one. Two days later, another four were shot down by Hurricanes. Even the Hurricane had mastered the German twin-engine fighter. Although used in much smaller numbers than the Bf 109, about half the German fighter losses in the period up to 4 August were Bf 110s.

On the British side, the Defiant continued to suffer heavy losses whenever it encountered enemy fighters. The fact that the turret fighter was being used over the Channel at all demonstrated just how much confidence some still had in the Defiant's ability to cope with fighters. Advocates of the fighter insisted trials with a Bf 109E proved their point; the squadron commander of No. 264 Squadron had taken on the captured German fighter in mock combat and claimed the Defiant was just as fast at low-level and at least as manoeuvrable. Any German fighter pilot would find it difficult to follow the Defiant in a tight turn, and even if he did, he would be vulnerable to the rear turret.[11] It was a demonstration of how these trials could be set up to favour one's own fighter.

A more searching examination took place on 19 July, when nine Defiants of No. 141 Squadron were surprised by Bf 109s. Five were shot down, a sixth crashed at its base, and a seventh was so badly damaged it had to be written off. It is likely that the entire formation would have been lost had it not been for the timely arrival of Hurricanes of No. 111 Squadron. For Park, it was final confirmation that the Defiant could not operate when enemy fighters were likely to be met.[12] The squadron moved north, out of German fighter range, where it could be used against unescorted bombers, which was what it was designed to do. Unfortunately, the personnel of the squadrons were determined to develop tactics that would enable it to take on fighters. More disasters lay ahead.

The vulnerability of the Bf 110 was a much more serious matter for the Luftwaffe than the Defiant's problems were for Fighter Command. Only two squadrons had the turret fighter, while the Bf 110 equipped a quarter of the German fighter force. The Germans had been relying on the twin-engine fighter for long-range escort; the Bf 109 could only manage twenty minutes' combat time over England, and London was at the extreme limit of its range.

Although Fighter Command had come off worse in these opening exchanges, the Luftwaffe had made little impression on overall RAF fighter strength. From the beginning of July until 10 August, around 200 Spitfires and Hurricanes had been destroyed or seriously damaged, but nearly 600 had been built.[13] At the beginning of August, Fighter Command had more pilots than it had at the beginning of July.[14] In the war of attrition, the Luftwaffe was not making any headway. Nevertheless, the Luftwaffe was dominating the Channel. Arguably it was doing enough for an invasion to succeed. German bombers had suffered some heavy losses, but so had they in the French campaign. With every week that passed, more RAF fighter pilots were gaining the experience they needed. It was not going to get any easier for the Luftwaffe. There is sometimes a fine line between inspired decisions and good fortune; if the Germans had thrown caution to the wind and invaded in the early summer of 1940, Dowding's decision to hold back might have proven to be a serious mistake. Fortunately for Dowding and Britain, the Germans had decided that only the complete destruction of Fighter Command would do.

To achieve this, German bombers would have to fly deeper into British airspace. This brought the radar chain into play. With no need for standing patrols, there would be less strain on man and machine, and the defending fighters would also have more time to climb to more favourable altitudes. As the attacking German formations grew in size, more time would be needed to assemble the formations, giving Home Chain operators more time to follow the build-up on their cathode ray tubes. It was soon no longer a case of scrambling squadrons at the first sign of attack, but rather judging the right moment to order them up. Scrambled too soon, they might start running low on fuel before the bombers even arrived.

To make sure the offensive got off to a good start, Göring wanted a minimum of three days of guaranteed continuous good weather. The plan was simple—two days of intensive operations would suck all Fighter Command's reserves into the battle in the south, and on the third day, units in Scandinavia would strike the undefended North East of England. It would be a powerful demonstration of the Luftwaffe's total domination. It was 13 August before the German meteorologists were confident the Luftwaffe would get its three days, although this did not prevent some fierce clashes occurring in the meantime.

On the morning of the 11th, seventy-four bombers escorted by sixty-one Bf 110s and thirty Bf 109s attacked Portland Naval base. Park and Brand, in charge of No. 10 Group, kept in close contact as the raid developed on the RDF screens. Five squadrons from No. 10 Group and three from No. 11 Group, with sixteen Spitfires and fifty-eight Hurricanes, were directed towards the German formation. They soon found themselves entangled with the escorts. It was a bad day for the Hurricanes; No. 145 Squadron lost four out of twelve to German fighters in fifteen minutes. Nos 238 and 601 Squadrons suffered equally heavily; twelve out of thirty-five Hurricanes had been lost. The German escorts also suffered, losing six Bf 109s and six Bf 110s, but they succeeded in keeping bomber losses down to six.[15] A couple of hours later, over the Thames Estuary, No. 111 Squadron lost five Hurricanes in fifteen minutes in a clash with Bf 109s while attempting to protect a convoy. Of the thirty-two Fighter Command losses on the 11th, twenty-five were Hurricanes. Total German fighter losses were thirteen Bf 109s and eleven Bf 110s, but again they had done a reasonable job protecting the bombers. Only twelve were lost.

Spitfire losses on the 11th were broadly in line with production, but Hurricane losses amounted to about half a week's output. Nevertheless, reserves were still substantial. On 10 August, there were 160 Hurricanes and 132 Spitfires available. Casualties had reduced the number of pilots, but on 10 August, Fighter Command still had nearly 1,400, which was 300 more than it had on 15 June.[16] Dowding, always one to be creative with his statistics, managed to massage this down to around 800. He was already suggesting the pilots of Battle squadrons should be retrained as fighter pilots; he could not imagine what possible use these squadrons could be. Using Battles on operations would simply be throwing away the lives of experienced pilots.[17] Some in the Air Ministry saw this as a rather premature and panicky move, but Dowding insisted he was just 'thinking ahead'. Douglas considered the idea most 'unpalatable', partly because the squadrons would be needed to help deal with an invasion. Looking further ahead, however, like Portal, Douglas did not want to lose the pilots that would one day fly the Manchesters, Halifaxes, and Stirlings.[18]

Park was more concerned with the quality rather than the quantity of his pilots. The loss of four experienced pilots, he claimed, could reduce the efficiency of a squadron by 50 per cent. He wanted the experienced pilots he was losing replaced by equally experienced pilots from other Groups. It was effectively another way of concentrating quality where it was needed. However, Dowding was not persuaded; he feared that if squadrons lost their best pilots, morale would suffer. If squadrons were seriously weakened by losses, it would be better if entire squadrons were withdrawn and replaced by fresh squadrons from other groups.[19]

On the 12th, 100 Ju 88s of KG 51, escorted by 120 Bf 110s and twenty-five Bf 109s, struck Portsmouth. Again, there was good coordination between Nos 10 and 11 Groups. Anti-aircraft fire and fighters accounted for ten of the German bombers. The twin-engine Bf 110s struggled again; they did not have the manoeuvrability to take on the single-seaters and were reduced to flying a defensive circle above the bombers in the hope of drawing off the intercepting fighters.

Fighter Command airfields and the early warning system throughout the south of England were now priority targets. The Ju 88s of KG 51 had the only success against Home Chain radar stations, knocking out Ventnor, on the Isle of Wight, with a particularly accurate attack. Elsewhere, the lattice structure of the towers proved impervious to the blast of bombs. The Germans were not even aware of the success they had achieved at Ventnor, as engineers had quickly rigged up a transmitter that broadcasted similar signals.[20] Manston Airfield was severely hit and Hawkinge and Lympne also suffered damage, although few aircraft were destroyed. The RAF lost twenty-one fighters in the air; the German losses were thirty-one planes (fourteen bombers and seventeen fighters).[21] The Luftwaffe was edging ahead in the battle between the fighter forces, but it was still a very slow process, and it would be a very long time before the cumulative effect became significant. Göring needed something much more decisive, and he expected his three-day 'Eagle Attack' assault to provide it.

This assault finally began on 13 August. It got off to the worst possible start when continued poor weather caused a last-minute postponement; the order did not get through to all units, and some bomber formations set off without their fighter escort. Most got some protection from the bad weather, but KG2 lost five Do 17s in a raid on Eastchurch Airfield. When the full offensive got going, Fighter Command airfields continued to be the main objective, but German intelligence was poor and many of the airfields were not fighter bases. The German Air Force flew around

500 bomber sorties, escorted by 1,000 fighters.[22] Fourteen medium and seven dive-bombers were lost. These losses included eight Ju 88s, with eleven more damaged. The Luftwaffe's latest and fastest bomber was proving just as vulnerable as the older types, and it was just as much in need of an escort.[23]

Fighter Command losses were just thirteen fighters, but twelve of them were Hurricanes. There were days when Spitfire losses could be just as heavy, especially as it was often tasked to deal with the more dangerous Bf 109E escorts, but it was obvious to all that the Hurricane was struggling. The only instant solution was to upgrade the Hurricane with the Merlin XX. Both the Spitfire and Hurricane were due to get this engine, but the Hurricane needed the extra power more urgently, so Camm's fighter got priority.[24] The first Hurricane IIs were rushed to the squadrons in September. The RAF was getting a fighter that was still slower than the Spitfire I, and it was using the engine the vastly superior Spitfire III needed.

On 14 August, cloudy weather again confounded the Luftwaffe weather experts. The third day of Göring's offensive was therefore a rather premature climax. Nevertheless, the planned *coup de grace*, with bombers from Scandinavia attacking the North East, still went ahead. An all-out attack from all directions would, it was hoped, stretch Fighter Command to breaking point. Dowding's determination to spread his defences thinly might have had its disadvantages but on 15 August it was responsible for inflicting a huge psychological blow on the enemy. Göring was convinced Dowding only had 400–500 fighters and that they were all in the south.[25] On 15 August, seventy-two He 111s escorted by twenty-one Bf 110s set off from Norway and Denmark for airfields and other targets in the Newcastle, Middlesbrough, and Sunderland areas. Further south, fifty unescorted Ju 88s attacked Driffield Airfield. Squadrons from No. 13 Group intercepted the former and No. 12 Group tackled the latter; it was the first time either Group had been involved in a major action. To the consternation of the Luftwaffe crews, they were met by Hurricanes and Spitfires from no less than six squadrons. Eighteen bombers and eight of the escorts were shot down. It would be the only major raid flown from Scandinavian airfields. For the Luftwaffe, it was the first inkling that destroying Fighter Command was an impossible task.

Further south, 1,800 Luftwaffe fighters and bombers were met by 650 fighters from No. 10 and 11 Groups. Another twenty-seven bombers were shot down. The Ju 87 was suffering particularly heavily, with seven lost during the course of the day. The day was a disaster for the Bf 110. No less than twenty-seven failed to return. The Whirlwind and Beaufighter would have suffered similar fates if Fighter Command had been using these as day fighters.

The 15th was the Luftwaffe's 'Black Thursday'. Sixty-seven planes were lost at a cost to Fighter Command of eleven Spitfires and eighteen Hurricanes. It was the first and only occasion that the Command was able to use all four Groups, and it proved how effective Dowding's force could be against bombers operating outside the range of the Bf 109. In southern England, however, only ten twin-engine bombers and seven Bf 109s had been lost. Most of these failed to return from raids on Portland and airfields near Southampton, which were only just about within range of the escorting Bf 109s. The losses among unescorted and dive-bomber units was distorting the overall picture. Even on this blackest of days, escorted medium bombers were still able to operate well inland of where the Germans planned to invade.

The overall bomber losses were high enough to alarm Göring. He insisted that closer escorts had to be provided, especially for the Ju 87. The dive-bomber was a particularly difficult plane to escort, needing protection at medium altitude (before it dived) and at low altitude (after it dived). Göring's solution was have one fighter group at altitude, a second to accompany the Ju 87 in the dive, and a third to deal with any enemy fighters waiting at low altitude. It was a lot of escorts for one bomber formation. It was a major change in emphasis; the German fighters were being forced to focus more on defending the bombers rather than destroying Fighter Command.

On the 16th, Stukas carried out a devastatingly effective raid on Tangmere, but they suffered heavy losses despite the accompanying Bf 109s. Spitfires occupied the escort while Hurricanes took on the Stukas. Of the nine shot down, seven were victims of Hurricanes.[26] Losses as heavy as these were acceptable if it meant breaking Belgian resistance at Eben-Emael, helping the German Army cross the Meuse, or indeed establishing a bridgehead on the English south coast. However, they were excessive if the only end result was a damaged airfield. Another fifteen bombers either failed to return or were so damaged they had to be written off; seventeen Bf 109s and seven Bf 110s were also lost, making it another costly day for the Luftwaffe. It was a very reasonable return for the eleven Hurricanes and ten Spitfires that Fighter Command lost.[27]

After a day's pause, the battle was resumed on the 18th. Again, Luftwaffe losses were heavy. Another eighteen Ju 87s out of a force of eighty-five were lost. This was the last straw—the dive-bomber units were pulled out of the battle. The Ju 87 was ideal for attacking tactical targets near the front line, but it was not capable of operating deeper inside enemy airspace. The aircraft would now be held back for the invasion, when their contribution would be worth risking heavy losses.

Seventeen medium bombers were also lost, along with fifteen Bf 110s and eighteen Bf 109s, out of the 240 medium bombers and 460 fighters committed. It was perhaps not quite as bad as it looked. The bomber losses included seven out of nine Do 17s involved in an unescorted low-level strike on Biggin Hill. At medium altitude, with substantial escort, bombers were not suffering nearly as heavily as the low-level and dive-bombing attacks. On the other hand, bombing from medium altitude caused less damage. Fighter Command losses were rising too; thirty-six were lost on the 18th in air combat, with another six Hurricanes destroyed on the ground.[28]

Although heavy, Luftwaffe losses were still nowhere near as high as they had been on 10 May. On the first day of the offensive against France, no less than eighty-eight bombers had been written off. These losses, however, had heralded a spectacular advance on land and ultimately complete victory. In the battle over Britain, the Luftwaffe was no closer to achieving the long-term aim of an outright victory in the air. The losses on 10 May were justified, but the losses in August were not. Hitler was getting the 'Verdun in the air' that he had always feared, and, as at Verdun, Germany was not gaining any ground; indeed, the Luftwaffe was being forced on to the defensive. German fighter pilots were instructed to abandon their independent offensive sweeps and provide the bombers with closer escort. In so doing, German pilots conceded some of the initiative to their opponents. German fighter pilots riled at this restriction, but it was a necessary retreat. The bombers needed as many close escorts as possible.

Despite the heavy losses some RAF squadrons had suffered, Fighter Command as a whole was holding up well. Dowding had more serviceable planes available in the middle of August than at the beginning of the battle.[29] Even where losses had been heavy, the morale of the pilots was buoyed by the success they seemed to be achieving. On 15 August, Fighter Command claimed an astonishing 182 enemy aircraft,[30] and another 126 were claimed on the 18th.[31] These were extraordinary figures. Dowding knew that his pilots were not doing this well. There were simply far too few enemy aircraft coming down on British soil, and it was improbable that the balance could be made up by aircraft crashing in the sea. Nevertheless, the figures were good for morale.

Park's No. 11 Group seemed to be bearing the brunt well. On the evening of the 17th, the serviceability rate was 77 per cent, compared to 78 per cent in No. 10 Group and 83 per cent in No. 12 Group.[32] There were some ominous signs; in the week leading up to the 17th, both Hurricane and Spitfire losses exceeded production for the first time. Hurricane losses were twice output. Fighter Command was slowly eating into its reserves. However, it was a very slow process; on the 17th, there were still around 200 Hurricanes and Spitfires to call on.[33]

Despite this, Dowding remained as pessimistic as ever. On 17 August, he claimed that the number of replacement pilots arriving was less than half the actual losses.[34] Again, he seems to have been exaggerating the problem, but losses were exceeding replacements. In a rather desperate move, the OTU course was reduced from four to two weeks. In future, replacement pilots would be even less ready for combat. Strangely, there were not enough British pilots considered good enough to fill the fighter OTUs. Dowding again insisted that more pilots from other Commands should be retrained as fighter pilots, and this time he won the argument. Five volunteers from each of the four Battle squadrons and three from each of the eleven Lysander squadrons were sent on a two-week conversion course.[35] The RAF was eating into the resources it would need to resist an invasion.

It was scarcely sensible or necessary. As experienced as these pilots were, they were not likely to be adequate replacements for combat-experienced fighter pilots. The pool of Polish and Czech fighter pilots was a far more suitable source of reinforcement. Around 100 of these had already claimed victories in the skies over Poland and France and were desperate to avenge the German occupation of their countries. Dowding now decided that those who had served with the defeated French Air Force were not such a bad bunch after all; spaces in OTUs would be filled by Poles and Czechs, and they would be allowed to join British squadrons, but only as a short-term measure for the duration of the 'invasion season'.[36] After sitting around doing nothing for weeks (months, in some cases), some were now sent on an abbreviated two-week OTU course. By the end of August, forty Poles and Czechs had been posted to Fighter Command squadrons, but it was still only a small fraction of the number available. Authorisation was also now given for another three Polish and one Czech fighter squadrons in addition to the two Polish and one Czech squadrons already forming.[37]

Even as the battle reached its most critical phase, there were objections to these attempts to reinforce and expand Fighter Command. Courtney claimed that it was delaying the expansion of Bomber Command. The new squadrons could not possibly become available for another four to six weeks and would therefore be unlikely to influence the current battle. Using these resources to expand Bomber Command would be far more productive.[38] Sometimes, the battle the Air Ministry was waging with its own wayward thinking was as fierce and as crucial to Britain's survival as the battle being fought in the skies over southern England.

Despite Dowding's constant complaints that pilots were the problem, it was fighters Britain was actually short of. Hurricanes reserves had dropped from 164 on 3 August to ninety-eight on 17 August.[39] This was still a reasonable cushion for existing squadrons, but clearly not enough to form seven Polish and Czech squadrons. There were actually more Spitfires immediately available to issue to squadrons than Hurricanes, even though there were fewer Spitfire squadrons to maintain. It would have made more sense to form at least one of the Polish or Czech squadrons on Spitfires. Dowding, however, was adamantly opposed to equipping any foreign squadrons with his best fighter. When it emerged there were spaces in the Spitfire-equipped No. 7 OTU, he insisted that the Czechs and Poles posted there should train on Hurricanes, despite the servicing problems involved in operating two different types.[40]

The shortage of Hurricanes meant the four new Polish and Czech squadrons would get just half a dozen Hurricanes each to get some training going. If sufficient Hurricanes could not be made available, then the squadrons might have to reequip with Defiants. There were no plans to reequip any more RAF squadrons with the turret fighter, but it seems they were considered good enough for the Poles and Czechs. Asking battle-experienced fighter pilots to drag a gunner with a four-gun turret through the air would have been a serious misuse of resources.

If Dowding could not bring himself to allow these foreign pilots to use Spitfires, he could at least let them use American fighters. The declining rate at which these planes were being assembled reflected the lack of interest in them. The first batch of thirty-two Buffaloes had been delivered by the middle of August, but after assembling nineteen in July, no more were assembled until the end of September. Eighty-three Mohawks had arrived by 4 September, and another seventy-six followed in the next two weeks. After reaching a peak output of eighteen Mohawks in the second week of August, deliveries declined to zero in the first week of September.[41] It was a shocking waste, especially as there were Czech pilots who had already flown the Mohawk in combat. The Czechs would have surely preferred their familiar and trusted Hawk to the Defiant.

There could have been a lot more American fighters available. Roosevelt had responded to Churchill's May appeal for as many Curtiss P-40s as possible, as quickly as possible. If Britain's need really was desperate, the Americans would be willing to divert the 200 P-40s being delivered to the USAAC to the UK. It was a magnificent gesture. Ironically, at the very same meeting the problems of equipping the four new Polish and Czech squadrons was discussed, the ERPC decided there was no urgent need for the Curtiss fighters. The American offer was politely declined.[42]

This was another missed opportunity. A single example of the Curtiss P-40 arrived for trials in August, but it seems to have stayed in its crate. In fact, the fighter was far superior to the Hurricane I at low and medium altitudes, but the RAF did not find this out until they tested the plane in December. The American fighter would have been a useful addition to Britain's air defences as an interceptor, and an absolutely priceless asset in the low/medium-altitude battle for air superiority over an invasion beachhead. There is no reason why they could not have arrived in time. The A-17 Nomads that arrived in July were the result of a phone call by the French Prime Minister on 5 June.[43] Within weeks, the Americans had taken the A-17s out of stores, refurbished them, and sent them on their way across the Atlantic. The brand new P-40s could have been on their way even faster.

The experienced Poles and Czechs that were now being posted to existing squadrons were a very welcome reinforcement. Fighter reserves were still reasonable. Even if the Germans were able to maintain the intensity of operations and continue to inflict the same losses, it was going to take a very long time to destroy Fighter Command. The weather alone made it difficult to maintain the pressure. More poor weather from 19–23 August brought a much-needed respite to both sides, but it favoured the defence more. Time was on the side of Fighter Command.

The weather cleared on 24 August and the Luftwaffe was able to launch a new wave of attacks. German intelligence was now beginning to understand better how Fighter Command was operating. In truth, in the early stages of the battle, Fighter Command's radar early warning and vectoring system had its advantages for the Luftwaffe. The Germans had no desire to avoid combat; their fighter pilots wanted to be found as quickly as possible so they could take on the RAF fighters before their Bf 109s started running low on fuel. As the battle became more desperate, so German pilots became more anxious to negate the advantage radar offered the defence. Radar stations might be difficult to put out of action, but by flying formations parallel to and 20 miles from the coast, the German Air Force could

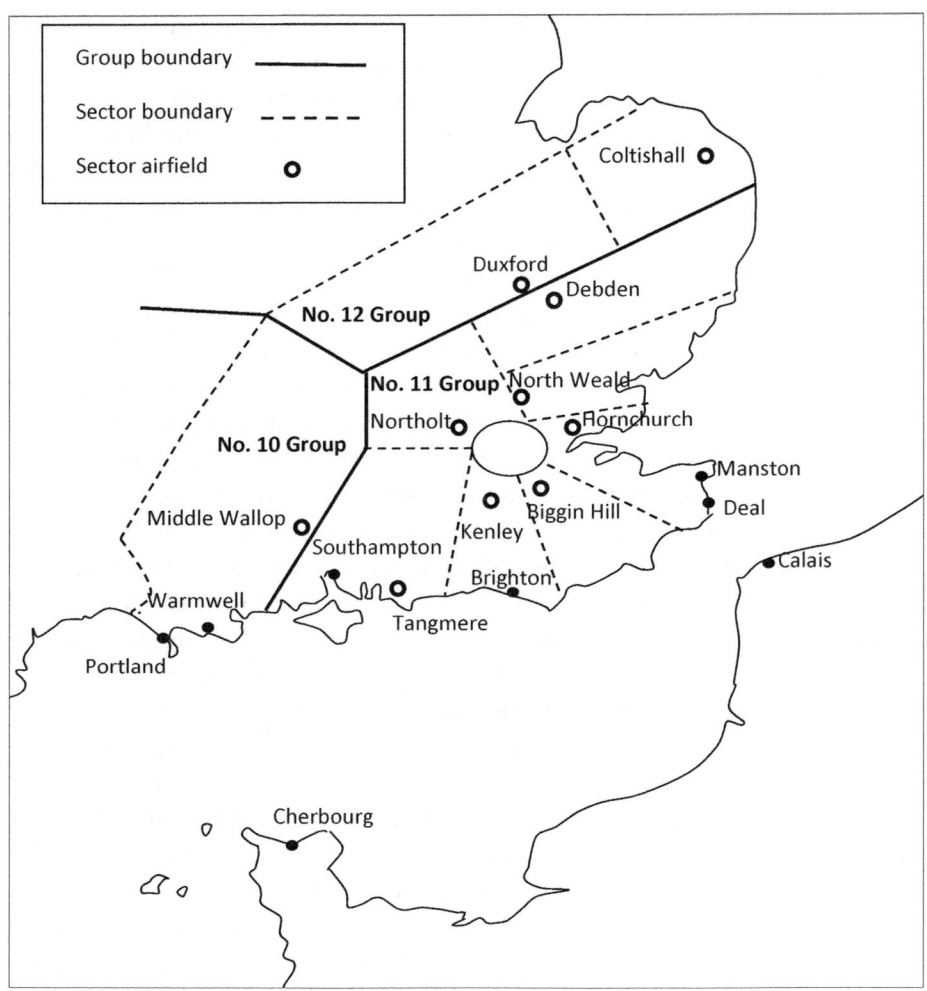

No. 11 Group.

keep Fighter Command controllers guessing. The planes would start to turn inland and then withdraw in the hope of causing squadrons to scramble prematurely and open the way for others to attack while they were landing to refuel. It was the beginning of the cat-and-mouse radar countermeasures war, with each side trying to turn a technical advantage held by the enemy into a tactical weakness.

With time running out, the Luftwaffe needed to force the pace. All the Bf 109 units around Cherbourg were now moved to the Calais area. Park's No. 11 Group now faced nearly 700 fighters.[44] With the Luftwaffe now focusing all its efforts further east, Brand's No. 10 Group squadrons were too far away to help much. Dowding, however, continued to insist that the whole country had to be covered and Park's No. 11 Group should not get special treatment. Even the new Czech and Polish squadrons were to be shared equally amongst the various Groups. The only increase in strength Park could look forward to was No. 303 (Polish) Squadron.

Exhausted squadrons were replaced, but this did not always help much. After suffering heavy losses, No. 266 Squadron (on Spitfires) was rested and the Defiants of No. 264 Squadron took its place. With German escorts increasing, it was a catastrophic decision. Ideas about making best use of the turret fighter were getting desperate; the commanders of both Defiant squadrons suggested fixed forward-firing guns should be added so that the Defiant could be used like the Bristol fighter of the First World War.[45] However, there was no point in weighing down a fighter with a heavy power-operated turret if it was not going to be the main offensive weapon.

No. 264 Squadron were convinced that new tactics involving fighters flying in descending circles would be enable the rear gunners to beat off fighter attacks. These tactics did not help much in No. 264 Squadron's return to action on 24 August. They thought they had made it through to a group of He 111 bombers unnoticed, but they were then surprised by the Bf 109 escort. Three Defiants were immediately shot down. It would be the last attempt to use the turret fighter in No. 11 Group in daylight. Dowding was also worried about how the other great hope for Fighter Command, the cannon-armed twin-engine Whirlwind, would fare in the Bf 109-infested skies of southern England. He feared it would only ever be able to operate if it had its own personal fighter escort.[46]

On the 24th, airfields along the coast were hit. Manston was bombed again and so badly damaged that it had to be abandoned. Despite this success, the Germans now appreciated it was the sector stations directing the fighters that were key. Hornchurch and North Weald were the targets on the 24th, with the latter suffering particularly heavily. Enemy activity was relatively light on the 25th, but two major raids resulted in the loss of another sixteen fighters, with thirteen pilots killed or missing. The next day, the sector stations at Kenley, Biggin Hill, Hornchurch, North Weald, and Debden were all targeted. Fierce opposition managed to disrupt all these attacks, and only Debden was badly hit. There was another pause on the 27th, and on the 28th the sector airfields were spared. However, worryingly, the ever-increasing fighter escorts were beginning to make it much more difficult for the fighters to get through to the bombers.

On the 29th, the Luftwaffe attempted to lure Fighter Command into a decisive battle by employing 700 fighters in huge sweeps across the southeast. As soon as the intercepting fighters saw the formations were merely high-flying fighters, combat was avoided. German fighter pilots took some consolation from this apparent lack of fighting spirit, but Dowding and Park were not going to be tempted into a battle they did not want or need to fight. If the Germans wanted British fighters to engage, they would have to put their vulnerable bombers in the air and attack targets Fighter Command felt it had to defend.

There would now be no more pauses for Fighter Command to catch its breath. Each day brought powerful attacks on the sector airfields. The defending fighters were still reducing the severity of the raids, even turning the bombers back on occasion. Nevertheless, German bombers inflicted severe damage on Biggin Hill on 30 and 31 August and 1 September. For long periods, all its communication systems were knocked out. On 31 August, it was the turn of Hornchurch; three out of nine Spitfires taking off were blown off the runway, with all three pilots miraculously escaping unhurt. Debden was severely damaged on 31 August and 2 September, and North Weald suffered heavy damage on 3 September.[47]

These raids on the very heart of Park's command and control system were a severe test for the Group's nerve. Dowding was convinced his force was in terminal decline. Whatever the German fighter pilots felt about Göring's insistence that they stay closer to the bombers, it was reducing bomber losses. Dowding's fighters found themselves increasingly caught up in dogfights with the escorts. In the period of 8–18 August, as many enemy bombers as fighters had crashed on British soil, but from 24 August to 6 September there were only two bombers for every five fighters. A frustrated Dowding wanted to know why pilots were not obeying instructions and concentrating on the bombers, but with such massive escorts, the pilots had no choice. Fighter Command's claim-loss ratio fell from 3:1 in early August to 2:1 in late August. There were days early in September when Fighter Command claims for enemy aircraft shot down barely matched its own losses. Dowding was well-aware how exaggerated RAF claims were. Fighter Command was losing the battle.[48]

The strain was beginning to tell on his pilots. The shortened training programmes meant replacement pilots were even less ready for combat. For hard-hit squadrons, the need to complete their training made these pilots more of a burden than a source of reinforcement. The constant alerts meant little real relaxation, and being thrown into combat in small, squadron-strength formations increased the mental strain. The RAF fighters were always going to be outnumbered, but to the pilots of an individual squadron, often flying understrength, the situation always looked even more daunting than it actually was. On 3 September, Dowding ordered the Group to abandon any pretence at maintaining reinforced squadrons at four flights of four. All squadrons returned to an establishment strength of sixteen, with twelve as the target operational strength.[49] However, with raids penetrating further inland, there was more time to organise squadrons into pairs. Park's sector commanders were keen to do this; Park himself worried about the delays involved, but his controllers were given permission to use pairs of squadrons as long as this did not stop the bombers being engaged before reaching their target.[50]

There was also a growing frustration within Park's own headquarters about the failure to concentrate more squadrons in the southeast, especially as the German Air Force was now attacking on such a narrow front. Dowding still stubbornly refused any weakening of Groups in unthreatened parts of the country. The sector stations the German Air Force was now targeting were, however, much further inland—most of them were in a ring just outside London. This brought the German formations closer to No. 12 Group, making these squadrons a natural source of reinforcement. As far as Leigh-Mallory was concerned, it was a long-overdue call to battle. Apart from the raids by Luftwaffe on the east coast on 15 August, there had been very little for his Group to do. Unfortunately, relations between Park and Leigh-Mallory were not good. Leigh-Mallory was, according to some, pompous and difficult to get on with; Park, for his part, was a proud and somewhat vain person who did not take too kindly to criticism or interference.[51] The fact that Leigh-Mallory felt he should have got command of the key No. 11 Group—rather than Dowding's choice, Park—did not help the relationship.

On 19 August, Park asked Leigh-Mallory to have his squadrons ready to patrol No. 11 Group airfields should all his fighter squadrons be involved in action.[52] It was a perfectly logical way of employing squadrons that were based to the north of London. Perhaps understandably, it was a secondary role that was not likely to find much favour with the pilots or the Group commander, who were all desperate to contribute to the crucial battle that was obviously taking place a little further south.

On 24 August, Park asked No. 12 Group to cover North Weald and Hornchurch, but its squadrons failed to prevent the damage inflicted on the former. On the 26th, the Group was asked to cover Debden, but by the time No. 19 Squadron reached the airfield, German bombers had already attacked and departed. No. 312 Squadron, the first mission flown by the Czechs, gave chase and claimed three of the fleeing raiders.[53] The enterprise shown by the Czechs was not appreciated by Park, who was furious. He suspected Leigh-Mallory's squadrons had left their assigned patrol line and gone looking for action. He made it clear to Dowding that he was not getting from Leigh-Mallory the cooperation he had been getting from Brand.

The relationship between No. 11 Group and its northern and western neighbours was always bound to be different. Nos 11 and 10 Groups were both facing south and fighting side-by-side; No. 12 Group was to the rear, and geography dictated a covering role. As for the actions of the pilots, there is always a very fine line between using initiative and not following orders. No. 12 Group pilots may on occasion have 'gone looking for a fight', but it was going to be very difficult to stop aggressive pilots doing just that. Cruising at 250 mph (4 miles per minute), it did not take fighters long to travel some way from their assigned patrol line. Park fanned the flames by telling his controllers not to make requests directly to Leigh-Mallory's Group but to go through Dowding's HQ at Bentley Prior instead.[54] No doubt Park hoped that the authority of the request would induce more discipline in No. 12 Group, but he also wanted to make sure Dowding knew what was going on.

The animosity between Park and Leigh-Mallory exposed the fault lines in the Group organisation. A more centralised air defence system would not have had to contend with the personal rivalries of its commanders. It was perhaps Dowding's responsibility to impose more central control. The desire of No. 12 Group pilots to play a more active role in the battle should have been used more positively. Dowding's opponents in the Air Ministry, which by now meant nearly everyone, were becoming increasingly frustrated at his failure to get the best out of not just the resources available to him, but also the commanders under him.

Park further escalated the conflict by expressing his displeasure at the standard of some of the replacement squadrons sent by Leigh-Mallory. To support his complaint, he drew up a table comparing the victory-loss ratios for fighter squadrons transferred into No. 11 Group from Nos 10, 12, and 13 Groups.[55] Taking a leaf out of Dowding's book, Park's figures were somewhat selective. In fact, most squadrons transferred into No. 11 Group struggled to adapt; No. 603 Squadron joined No. 11 Group from No. 13 Group on 28 August and lost nine pilot and sixteen aircraft in nine days. No. 253 Squadron, also from No. 13 Group, lost thirteen aircraft and nine pilots in seven days.

The point that Park should have been focusing on was that the policy of replacing exhausted squadrons with fresh squadrons was not working. Instead of giving weary squadrons a four-to-six-week break, their less-experienced replacements were scarcely lasting a week, forcing the more experienced squadrons to return. An exhausted but battle-hardened squadron was a more effective fighting unit than a fresh inexperienced one.[56]

The Polish and Czech squadrons were different. Their pilots were fresh and experienced, but there seemed no rush to get them into action. No. 303 Squadron had started forming on 2 August. It was packed full of battle-hardened pilots, but the squadron was still laboriously practising Fighter Command's methodical interception routines at the end of the month. On 30 August, the squadron was performing yet more practice attacks on a formation of Blenheims when one of the pilots noticed a Do 215. This seemed a far more worthy target to practise on, and the German bomber was soon shot down. The Polish pilot was reprimanded, but the point had been made. The next day, the squadron was declared operational.

In its first seven days, the squadron claimed no less than forty enemy aircraft. Despite their late start, the squadron went on to become the highest-scoring squadron in the Battle of Britain. Their success was hardly a surprise; the pilots were the survivors of combats with the Luftwaffe in obsolete PZL P.11 fighters and not-so-obsolete but scarcely high-performance French M.S.406 fighters. The squadron was what the British disdained so much, and sought to avoid—a crack unit full of particularly experienced and successful pilots. Meanwhile, the equally experienced Polish No. 302 Squadron had also become operational. Instead of being thrown into the crucial battle in the south, it was confined to flying patrols over the east coast, between Grimsby and Scarborough. Their sole task was to investigate the odd suspected enemy reconnaissance plane, which, more often than not, turned out to be a returning British bomber.

Park needed such squadrons further south. The battle seemed to be drifting away from his overstretched and exhausted squadrons. The last day of August was the worst yet for Fighter Command, with the loss of thirty-five fighters and twenty-three pilots killed or wounded. Fighter reserves were at their lowest point, down to seventy-eight Hurricanes and seventy-three Spitfires.[57]

On the Brink?

Despite the losses, Fighter Command was hardly wasting away. There had been some difficult times during August, but taking the month as a whole, the factories had turned out 251 Hurricanes and 163 Spitfires to replace the 253 Hurricanes and 137 Spitfires lost. On 1 September, the Command still had more fighters than it had at the beginning of the battle, and, for all Dowding's concerns, more pilots to fly them. The main problem was still the self-imposed handicap of operating a relatively small proportion of the available fighter force in the crucial battle area. Fighter Command had nearly 900 fighters on 1 September, but less than 350 were in Park's No. 11 Group.

Many of the squadrons stationed outside No. 11 Group were units recuperating from losses in the south, but many could have been used in the south east. The battle-experienced squadrons of No. 10 Group had been side-lined by the Luftwaffe's shift to the east, and many other squadrons—such as the Polish No. 302 Squadron and Czech No. 310 Squadron, not to mention No. 242 Squadron and its redoubtable commander Douglas Bader—were only able to operate on the fringes of the battle, if at all. On 30 August, No. 11 Group commanders again voiced the general feeling that more fighter squadrons should be moved to the south east,[1] but Dowding felt he had no choice but to stick to his policy. Beaverbrook was again sounding the alarm about the vulnerability of British aircraft factories. Dowding still had visions of the German bomber fleet descending on British factories and wiping them out in a single blow. As a reminder of what the German Air Force could do even in the well-protected south, on 15 August a daylight attack on the Short's factory in Rochester had caused severe damage. Six of the first four-engine Stirling bombers to come off the production line were destroyed—an especially severe blow for an Air Staff that still saw increasing the striking power of the bomber fleet as the priority. On 4 September, Park tentatively asked Dowding for two more squadrons to strengthen two of his sectors. He received one.[2]

Despite the handicaps, Park's Group was grimly hanging on—indeed, perhaps even doing a little better than this. On the evening of the 1 September, after another fierce day's fighting, his squadrons mustered on average sixteen pilots, excluding those fresh out of OTUs. Each squadron had around fifteen serviceable fighters, which, after the ground crews had got to work on the machines they could patch up on base, was expected to rise to an average of seventeen the following morning. Some squadrons had been particularly badly hit. No. 85 Squadron had lost five planes in two missions during the day's fighting and was down to just nine serviceable fighters and nine operational pilots. No. 616 was also down to just nine pilots. Interestingly No. 303 (Polish) Squadron was overflowing with pilots, with twenty-one fully operational and no less than thirteen non-operational.[3] The latter were probably not the typical green British pilot straight out of an OTU. Despite the fierceness of the struggle, Park's command was still an effective fighting force.

Nevertheless, the pressure was mounting. The first week in September was another tough one for Park's squadrons. The escorts were now virtually impossible to break through; the Luftwaffe only lost around twenty bombers on missions in the first six days of the month, and many of these were victims of anti-aircraft fire. Attempts to intercept the bombers were turning into the fierce fighter-*versus-*fighter battles that the Luftwaffe wanted and Dowding did not. Losses on both sides were heavy. Again, fresh squadrons moving into No. 11 Group suffered some of the heaviest losses. On 4 September, No. 66 Squadron, which had just arrived from No. 12 Group, lost five Spitfires in combat with Bf 109s. The next day, it lost another three. No. 41 Squadron, from No. 13 Group, lost five Spitfires on the 5th. The experience of the Polish pilots of No. 303 Squadron could not save them on the 6th, when they were caught climbing by Bf 109s and lost five of their Hurricanes in a single engagement. In the first six days of September, 140 Hurricanes and Spitfires were lost or badly damaged, losses that were well in excess of production. However, the German fighter force was also losing heavily; in the same period, just over 100 Bf 109s and Bf 110s failed to return or were written off on return.[4]

The failure to pass on the lessons being learned in the south did not help squadrons fresh to the battle. Leigh-Mallory complained about the lack of information on tactics being used by Park's No. 11 Group or Brand's No. 10 Group.[5] Perhaps justifiably, Park was too concerned with mere survival. There was, however, no overall direction from Dowding about the best tactics to use; squadrons still had to work it out for themselves.

In the relative calm of Leigh-Mallory's No. 12 Group, there was more time to do this and ponder alternative tactics. So far, Park had used mainly single squadrons, sometimes pairs, to ensure the bombers were intercepted as far forward as possible. So far, this tactic had paid off; German attacks had been disrupted, sometimes to the extent that the raid was completely ineffective. Leigh-Mallory, with his more northerly squadrons, had more time to assemble larger formations. Douglas Bader, the commander of No. 242 Squadron at Coltishall, was very keen on what would become known as 'big wing' formations. Bader was a charismatic and pugnacious leader. The loss of both his legs in a flying accident had forced him out of the service, but his relentless determination had seen him readmitted on the outbreak of war, initially as a ferry pilot, but eventually as a combat pilot. His enforced absence had left him well behind many of his contemporaries on the career ladder, and at the age of thirty, he was relatively old to be given the command of his first squadron. He was, therefore, by no means an ordinary Squadron Leader. He was not lacking in self-confidence, and his age lent his opinions a certain authority. Like all the pilots in No. 12 Group, Bader was hugely frustrated that his squadron was not involved in the fierce fighting taking place further south.

On 30 August, Bader's squadron finally got the chance for some action, being ordered to fly south and cover Park's airfields. His squadron intercepted a formation of He 111 bombers escorted by Bf 110s and claimed twelve without loss. It would seem to have been a particularly extreme example of over-claiming; his squadron had probably only shot down two German bombers. However, Bader insisted that if he had possessed twice the number of fighters, he could have inflicted twice the losses. It was a simple enough argument, and his Group commander did not need much persuading. Leigh-Mallory had always believed it was the total number of planes shot down that counted, not whether they were shot down approaching or leaving the target. The aim was not to prevent a particular attack on a particular target, but rather to halt the offensive by inflicting the highest possible losses. If using larger formations meant intercepting the bombers later—even possibly after they had delivered their attack—then so be it.

There were other advantages to flying fighters in larger formations. The general expectation in No. 11 Group was that the Spitfires would deal with the escorts while the Hurricanes went for the bombers, but this was difficult to put into practice when all the squadrons were operating individually and often far apart. Flying as part of a much larger formation, it was much easier for the Spitfires to provide protection. With calls to action still rare, Bader had the time to practise his Wing tactics with the Spitfire-equipped No. 19 Squadron, the Hurricane-equipped No. 303 Squadron, and his Hurricane-equipped No. 242 Squadron. The wing used Duxford as its rendezvous point and the formation became known as the 'Duxford Wing'. Bader would soon have the opportunity to try out his wing in combat.

Across the Channel, minds were also focusing on how more decisive results might be achieved. Outright victory seemed as far away as ever. The numbers of enemy fighters rising to meet the Luftwaffe attacks did not seem to bear out the intelligence estimates that Fighter Command was on its last legs. To try and stop the apparently endless flow of replacement aircraft reaching RAF squadrons, the German Air Force was instructed to target aircraft factories more vigorously. On 2 September, the Luftwaffe bombed the Vickers and Hawker factories at Brooklands. The long-awaited and much-feared offensive against the British aircraft industry seemed to have begun.

An alarmed Dowding instructed Park to make sure the Hurricane factories at Kingston, Langley, and Brooklands and the Spitfire plant in Southampton were covered. No. 10 Group was given the task of patrolling these areas whenever

No. 11 Group was involved in major operations.[6] On 4 September, the Luftwaffe returned to Weybridge; in a low-level attack on the Vickers plant, just six bombs killed eighty-eight and injured many hundreds. Two days later, it was the turn of the Brooklands Hawker factory, on the other side of the airfield.

The death tolls were heavy, but the actual damage to the plant was not as devastating as many had feared. It was not as easy as it seemed to knock out aircraft factories. Just one bomb exploding in the middle of the factory might be expected to cause mayhem; the initial destruction looked serious and the casualties were shocking, but once the rubble had been cleared away, it was often found that machine tools had survived and production resumed remarkably quickly. The apparently hugely successful attack on the Vickers plant on the 4th only stopped production for four days.[7] The raid on the Hawker factory caused no loss of output at all.[8]

To have any chance of success, you also have to know where the factories are. The Supermarine factory at Southampton was particularly vulnerable, but it would seem that the Germans were not aware that this was where nearly all the Spitfires were being built. The Castle Bromwich Spitfire plant in the Midlands opened with such public fanfare in the summer of 1938, was the target of some nocturnal raids. According to the management, these worried the workers enough to reduce production on the night shift by 50 per cent.[9] However, the plant was only producing a trickle of planes anyway; the apparently unfortunate publicity given to the opening of the Castle Bromwich plant was perhaps paying dividends. The plant had effectively become a decoy. Overall, German bombing was having very little effect on fighter production.

The battle in the air was causing far more concern. The Prime Minister grimly reported to his cabinet that the battle was becoming precisely what Britain did not want—a contest between the two fighter forces. Losses on both sides were now approximately equal, and the RAF was getting through its reserves of aircraft 'at a dangerous rate'.[10] In truth, a reduction in the Hurricane/Spitfire reserve from 190 to 151 during the last three weeks of August scarcely seemed to spell imminent disaster. Nevertheless, Dowding continued to spread gloom. On 7 September, he called an emergency meeting with No. 11 Group and Douglas, representing the Air Ministry. Dowding quite bluntly described his command as going 'downhill'. The purpose of the meeting, he explained, was to decide how best to manage this decline.

Dowding used an array of arguments to demonstrate how desperate the situation was. As always, he was happy to put the worst possible spin on the facts. He claimed that requests for replacement aircraft had not been met; on 4 September, for example, he had wanted fourteen Hurricanes and twelve Spitfires, but none had been delivered.[11] The complaint infuriated those responsible for issuing reserves. Dowding had simply chosen the only day when there had been a temporary problem; on every other day, all requests for replacements had been met immediately.

Dowding insisted that squadrons were so weak they were having to pair up to form effective fighting units. This might have been true in some cases, but using pairs of squadrons was actually a positive decision to give intercepting formations more punch. He suggested the situation was so serious that squadrons not in the battlezone might have to give up their Spitfires and Hurricanes and reequip with American Mohawks and Buffaloes. It seems to have been the first time anyone suggested using the American fighters. There was no relief that such a useful reserve existed; the suggestion was merely supposed to underline how desperate the situation was. He was also worried about pilots. He predicted that at current loss rates, there would be a deficit of sixty-eight over the next four weeks. This scarcely suggested a force with 1,300 pilots was likely to collapse before the autumn.

Douglas refused to accept the picture was as bleak as Dowding was claiming. He pointed out that in August, Hurricane and Spitfire production had far exceeded losses, and Air Ministry figures showed there were nearly 300 fighters in reserve. There was much consternation on both sides that each should see the situation so differently. In fact, both Dowding and Douglas were playing rather free and easy with the figures. Douglas's loss figures did not include the seventy-odd fighters that were so seriously damaged they had to be sent to the maintenance units for repair. The reserves he quoted included fighters being repaired, most of which would not be available for some time. At the time of the meeting, reserves had dropped to 127 Spitfires and Hurricanes. It was dropping, but there was a reserve, and it was still adequate to cope with losses. The number of serviceable fighters the Command could put into the air had never slipped below 600 during the entire battle, and on 4 September it stood at 700. There were, on average, twenty-two pilots in each squadron, although there were undoubtedly problems with the quality of those straight out of OTUs.[12]

The situation was not as rosy as the Air Ministry was insisting, but it was not nearly as bad as Dowding was claiming. The main problem was still the self-inflicted disadvantage of not focusing the available resources where they were needed. Dowding had to admit his squadron-rotation system was not working; rather reluctantly, he decided to adopt Park's preferred option of replacing pilots rather than squadrons. Experienced pilots would move from squadrons stationed outside the battlezone, and pilots from OTUs would replace them. Gradually, squadrons outside the south east would lose all their experienced pilots and effectively become Operational Training Units. This had the added advantage of relieving front-line squadrons of the task of inducting OTU pilots. The sectors flanking No. 11 Group in No. 10 and No. 12 Groups were in the front line, so these would also be kept at full strength.[13]

The result was the ABC system. No. 11 Group and the flanking sectors from No. 10 and No. 12 Groups would be entirely equipped with full-strength category-A squadrons. There would be a small number of category-B squadrons, which would be outside the battlezone but kept at full strength, serving as replacements for squadrons needing a rest. The majority of the squadrons outside the south east would be category C. These would guard the less-vulnerable parts of the country, but their main task would be to complete the training of pilots emerging from OTUs.[14] As far as Dowding was concerned, it was a desperate measure for desperate times; in fact, by the back door, Park was beginning to get the concentration of resources he needed. Fighter Command finally had its best pilots where they were needed.

Not that Dowding thought this would make much difference. During the course of the 7 September meeting, he repeatedly emphasised to Douglas that Fighter Command was losing the battle. This was the message he insisted Douglas had to take back to the Air Ministry. Dowding saw no reason why the German offensive would not go on until his force was wiped out. Park, on the other hand, felt sure the Germans would not be able to sustain the existing intensity of operations for more than another three weeks. Dowding was not persuaded; he could see no light at the end of the tunnel. No. 11 Group would do its best—his pilots would fight until the last Spitfire and Hurricane, and then fight on with anything that could fly. It was a grim scenario.[15]

Dowding's pessimism stemmed from his failure to appreciate the nature of the battle Fighter Command was engaged in. Both Dowding and Park believed they were facing an open-ended air offensive, for which seasons made no difference. The air battle would rage through the autumn and winter until one side or the other was exhausted. This was not the situation—the Luftwaffe was trying to pave the way for an invasion. They did not have even three weeks; the invasion had to be launched before autumnal storms made it impossible, and the last possible date was supposed to be 15 September. The Germans were running out of time, and Dowding was far closer to the finish line than he believed.

The Luftwaffe had the upper hand, but it was still a long way from defeating Fighter Command. It was perhaps easier to come to this conclusion from the distance of a detached Air Ministry, with just the cold figures to analyse. Understandably, the battle looked very different from Dowding and Park's perspective. Airfields were being bombed, hangars were being smashed, and Air Force personnel were being killed. The pilots were exhausted. However, the squadrons continued to function. Fighter Command was adapting: aircraft were no longer kept in vulnerable hangars, instead being dispersed around the airfields; ground crews became used to working in the open; and bombed airfields were soon made serviceable again, with only two airfields—Lympne and Manston—put out of action for more than a few hours.[16] Engineers, sometimes working in appallingly dangerous conditions, repaired smashed cables and got power running again to airfields and sector control centres. Bombed-out sector stations started up operations from wherever it was possible—on one notable occasion, in a local village shop.[17] In the most difficult of circumstances, Fighter Command was battling through, on the ground and in the air.

The heavier escorts were making life much more difficult for Dowding's fighters, but even this represented a victory of sorts. The higher proportion of escorts meant the German Air Force was using fewer and fewer bombers. At the beginning of August, on average, the Luftwaffe was flying two and a half escorts per bomber. By the end of August, this had gone up to nearly four and a half. The weight of attack had effectively been halved. The very accurate Ju 87 had been driven from the skies and low-level bombing had proven too risky. These were all very significant achievements.

Who was actually winning the battle depended on which battle was being considered. The Luftwaffe was a long way short of destroying Fighter Command. However, Luftwaffe fighters were succeeding in protecting the bombers. As long as they had an escort, German bombers could operate over the entire south-east corner of England without suffering unacceptable losses. A degree of air superiority had been established; Park was nowhere near defeat, but his force had been worn down. If the invasion had been launched in early September, his squadrons would not have been able to continue defending their airfields and sector stations, protect the Royal Navy, provide air cover for the Army, and escort the Battles, Blenheims, and Banquet bombers.

The Germans had all the air superiority they needed to invade, but the German High Command still wanted more. The Luftwaffe had been set the task of destroying Fighter Command. It had failed to achieve this, and it seemed unlikely that the Air Force would succeed in this aim before the weather broke and invasion became impossible. It was not obvious that the German fighter force could maintain the offensive much longer. Operating over enemy territory in a fighter with a very limited endurance imposed an enormous strain on the pilot. A close eye had to be kept on the petrol gauge and there was always the possibility of having to fly back over the Channel in a damaged machine. The defending fighters had all the advantages Dowding had always insisted he needed. Every time a German fighter was shot down over Britain, the pilot was lost as well, whereas a British pilot was often back with his squadron the same day. RAF fighters that crash-landed could be repaired, but Messerschmitts that were forced down were lost. Production of the Bf 109 was actually running at a lower level than Spitfire/Hurricane production. Ironically, while Dowding was considering the possibility of using the French Curtiss Hawks to reequip squadrons in the rear, the Germans were seriously considering reequipping some of their squadrons in the rear with captured French Bloch 152 fighters.[18]

The battle in the skies was becoming a stalemate. The German Air Force was no nearer to its goal of eliminating Fighter Command, but RAF fighters were not making any substantial inroads into the German bomber force either. On 3 September, with air supremacy still not established, Hitler put the invasion date back a week to 21 September. The British were unaware of this postponement; they were only aware an invasion was imminent. Reconnaissance planes were picking up the movement of invasion barges making their way to the Channel ports.

While the air forces battled it out, the respective armies prepared as best they could. From nothing, the German Navy conjured up an invasion fleet with all manner of improvised landing craft. There were even submersible tanks and a primitive artificial harbour.[19] The British Army was still in a desperate state, but the American government had responded magnificently; the US Army pulled hundreds of thousands of obsolete rifles, tens of thousands of machine guns, and hundreds of artillery pieces and mortars out of stores and shipped them across the Atlantic.[20] Even so, only four of the twenty-seven divisions were considered to be fully equipped. There were just two armoured divisions and six independent tank brigades, with no more than 600 tanks in the entire country. Churchill remained bullishly optimistic any invasion would be defeated, but Brooke was not so confident; he did not think his forces were sufficiently trained, powerful, or mobile to defeat the mighty Wehrmacht. He desperately hoped his forces would at least get a winter of training before being put to the test.[21]

With air reconnaissance picking up barges heading for the Channel ports, it seemed Brooke was not going to get his wish. It was only now that the British Chiefs of Staff realised the invasion was likely to come along the south coast rather than the east. From the night of 6–7 September, the Battles and Blenheims of Nos 1 and 2 Groups, supported by Fleet Air Arm and Coastal Command squadrons, began bombing the ports where the barges were congregating. The following night, twenty-six Hampdens joined them, but the threat of imminent invasion was not allowed to disrupt the heavies' offensive against German industry. On 8 September, Invasion Alert No. 1 was released, but it was another week before Nos 3, 4, and 5 Groups switched all their efforts to the Channel ports.

When cloud cover allowed, Blenheims attacked by day, but coastal targets are always relatively easy to find by night, and the growing mass of invasion barges made for an attractive target. In ten days, around 1,000 sorties were flown against the ports. Up to 21 September, air and sea attack resulted in about 10 per cent of the invasion fleet being destroyed or damaged.[22] The number that survived was another reminder of how surprisingly little damage bombing can inflict even on such an apparently vulnerable target. The bombers had made a useful contribution, but ample craft remained to set course for Britain.

There was never any doubt that the Navy would have risked all to sink the invasion fleet in transit and bombard any forces that landed. The time it took for Bomber Command to switch its main effort from German industry to invasion ports did not suggest the Air Force response would be so spontaneous. In the three months since the defeat of France, virtually no progress had been made in preparing the RAF to support the Army any more effectively than it had in May and June. If anything, the Air Force was less prepared. Tactical air support was going backwards.

There was no equivalent to the tactical BAFF that had existed in France. The Air Ministry had refused to create an Army Cooperation Command. The Combined Operations Room existed to pass on requests for fighter and bomber support, but Fighter and Bomber Command had not made any serious preparations to prepare their squadrons to respond. Early in September Fighter Command was reminded of its bomber escort and fleet defence responsibilities; at the very bottom of the list of priorities came protecting the troops from the Stukas.[23] It rather underlined how short of fighters the RAF was. To have any chance, the RAF needed to mobilise every available fighter pilot and fighter in the country, regardless of their country of origin.

On 14 September, with the invasion expected any day, the Air Ministry was reminded that Fighter Command cannon-armed fighters must be held back for ground-attack duties; unfortunately, Fighter Command no longer had any. No. 19 Squadron had the cannon removed from their Spitfires because they jammed so often, and nothing came of the plan to arm Blenheims with them. Plans to equip more Hurricane Is with cannon had been postponed until the Hurricane II became available, and the four-cannon Whirlwind was still struggling with its unreliable Peregrine engines. Fighter Command did not have an anti-tank capability.

Slessor's Plans department did not see this as an Air Force problem—it was the Army and 'its Lysanders' that must first deal with tanks once they got ashore.[24] Unfortunately, these were not armed with cannon either. The army-cooperation squadrons were still administratively part of Fighter Command, so it was Dowding's responsibility. When Douglas quizzed Dowding, he claimed to be completely unaware and very 'perturbed' that this instruction had not been carried out.[25] He might argue that nobody in Fighter Command had the time to worry about army-cooperation squadrons or any cannon ground-attack capability. It would be difficult to dispute that, but it was also a rather obvious example of why the 'Army Cooperation Command' the War office wanted was so necessary.

Bomber Command had grown in strength during the summer. No. 2 Group had thirteen squadrons, with over 200 Blenheims immediately available. The four Polish Battle squadrons being formed brought the number available to No. 1 Group to eight, but no effort had been made to improve their ground-attack capabilities by adding armour or increasing their ground-strafing capability. The Battles had still not been equipped with self-sealing tanks. Instead of getting Bostons or Marylands, the first two squadrons (Nos 103 and 150) had begun converting to the Wellington.[26]

The fate of the American combat planes was bordering on a scandal. American aircraft companies were modifying the ex-French aircraft to British standards and rushing them across the Atlantic as fast as they could, along with any artillery, machine guns, and rifles the American Army could spare. Obsolete artillery was gratefully received and distributed amongst the divisions. Equally obsolete rifles were handed out to the 500,000-strong Home Guard. Brand new, modern American combat planes, however, were left unused. Around 300 had arrived by the end of August, of which only half had been assembled.[27] Bomb racks for Tiger Moth trainers and constant-speed propellers for Spitfires had been conjured up and fitted in weeks, but not a single American bomber or fighter reached a front-line squadron.

What the Prime Minister would have made of it can only be imagined. Churchill had told Sinclair how 'shocked' he was to see so many communication aircraft on a visit to Hendon. He felt these and their pilots could form 'two good fighter or bomber squadrons of the reserve category', which could be used in an emergency.[28] Churchill might have been even more shocked if he had known about all the unused American combat planes and the unemployed Polish and Czech pilots who might have flown them.

The resources existed for a useful tactical air force, but too many within the Air Force did not believe it was their duty to provide it. In September 1940, the RAF had no specialist close-support capability and no high-speed tactical-reconnaissance planes. Bomber Command was focusing on Germany, and Fighter Command was totally consumed by its battle for survival. Winning this battle was becoming the only opportunity for the RAF to make a significant contribution to stopping an invasion. It need not have been so; Fighter Command's furious defence of British skies should have been just the first RAF obstacle the Germans had to overcome. Instead, it was the RAF's last stand. For the Luftwaffe, invasion would have meant a welcome return to its more familiar Army-support role. For the RAF, it was a transition the force was incapable of making. The air battle Fighter Command was engaged in was even more crucial than it need have been. The RAF might be able to prevent an invasion, but it could do very little to help defeat one. For the RAF, there was no Plan B.

That air battle was now reaching its climax. At the beginning of September, after a month of intense fighting, both sides were looking for new solutions to break the deadlock. To win the battle, the Luftwaffe needed to shoot down more RAF fighters. To achieve a decisive victory, Fighter Command needed to shoot down more bombers. Avoiding defeat, however, might be enough—provided the German High Command did not change its mind about requiring air supremacy. In this respect, the battle was still on a knife-edge. Britain needed Germany to stick to its plans.

Luftwaffe commanders were divided about how close to defeat Fighter Command was. Figures of British fighter strength produced by German intelligence fluctuated between 100 and 350. Field Marshal Sperrle, the commander of Luftflotte 3, believed Fighter Command still had 1,000 planes.[29] Field Marshal Kesselring, at Luftflotte 2, insisted Dowding's force was almost finished and one final push would see total victory achieved—it just required the last remnants of Fighter Command to be induced into the air. Circumstances conspired to give Kesselring the decisive battle he wanted. On the night of 25–26 August, German aircraft dropped some bombs on central London by mistake. Whitleys retaliated with an attack on Berlin. Neither of these raids caused much damage, but Hitler's pride was hurt. He wanted retaliation, and this gave Kesselring his opportunity. Surely the British could be relied on to throw in every last reserve in defence of their capital—the destruction of Fighter Command would still be the objective, but London would be the battleground.

The attack was launched on 7 September. The sudden change in focus took Fighter Command controllers by surprise. Squadrons had to be hurriedly switched from blocking the path to their airfields to the bombers heading for the London Docks.

Once again, the escort bore the brunt of the Fighter Command assault. Fourteen Bf 109s and seven Bf 110s were lost, but only eight of the attacking 348 bombers. With Fighter Command losing thirty-seven Hurricanes and Spitfires destroyed or seriously damaged, it was another tactical victory for the Luftwaffe.[30]

The bombing was concentrated and heavy. In ninety minutes, 300 tons fell on the East End. Warehouses, gasworks, and oil depots from Tower Bridge to Thames Haven were left blazing, and although the targets were legitimate, there was heavy loss of life. For London, it was just the beginning—the blazing fires clearly marked the way for the night bombers that would follow—but London's suffering was Fighter Command's salvation. The immense pressure of operating from airfields that were constantly under attack was lifted. Fighter Command stations had the respite they desperately needed. It was one of the great ironies of the war; the Command had been set up to defend London, but in the end, it was London that saved Fighter Command.

Too many advantages now lay with the RAF fighters. The Bf 109 would be operating at the very limit of its range; it was now a very long return flight. Park had more time to pair up his squadrons and get them into position at adequate patrolling altitudes. London was also reasonably close to where both No. 12 and No. 10 Groups converged with No. 11 Group, which would now allow Dowding's fighters to be concentrated in a way that had not previously been possible.

The next day, there was a noticeable relaxation in Luftwaffe pressure. For the first time in many days, not all squadrons were placed on readiness. In the operations that were flown, there was a growing wariness amongst the German fighter pilots as they sought to counter the high-flying British fighters by flying well above the bombers they were supposed to be escorting. It was a defensive move by the fighters that left the bombers more exposed.

On the 9th, the German escorts again absorbed a lot of the Fighter Command effort. Fighter Command pilots attempted to counter the freer, high-flying German fighter formations by flying higher themselves. Altitude was everything; controllers were adding a few thousand feet to be on the safe side, and squadron commanders would invariably add a few thousand more. Bomber formations at medium altitude were getting through unhindered. Dowding ordered his sector controllers to stick to the altitudes radar was indicating. Eighteen escorts were lost, but the defending fighters probably only shot down five enemy bombers. Another twenty-three Hurricanes and Spitfires were lost.

Poor weather on the 10th prevented much activity and provided yet more time for Fighter Command to catch its collective breath. On the 11th, the premature departure of the escorting Bf 109s of LG 2 and JG 51 through lack of fuel emphasised how stretched the German fighter force now was. Hurricanes and Spitfires took advantage, shooting down seven bombers and damaging ten.[31] Two days of relatively light activity kept German losses to a minimum but also provided yet more time for Fighter Command to prepare for the climax of the battle.

The more relaxed atmosphere at sector stations was in stark contrast to the growing tensions between Park and Leigh-Mallory. Bader had led his Duxford Wing into action for the first time in the 7 September raid on London, with No. 19 Squadron (Spitfires) covering the Hurricanes of Nos 242 and 310 Squadrons. By the time they reached their patrol altitude, the German bombers were starting to head for home, and Bader's fighters only engaged the rear-guard escorts. On the 9th, his wing was called on again; this time, they claimed an astonishing nineteen Do 17 bombers. This seems to have been a gross exaggeration; German records do not actually record any Dorniers lost that day.[32] More successes were claimed on the 11th, with elements from four squadrons forming a three-squadron-strong wing. Bader still felt there were insufficient fighters to take advantage of the disorder the initial attack had caused, and that more than one squadron was needed to keep off the German escort. Five squadrons was a more satisfactory number, with two Spitfire squadrons to take on the escort and three Hurricane squadrons to deal with the bombers.

Park did not take kindly to Leigh-Mallory's claim that his tactics were better than those that No. 11 Group was using. He blamed the late arrival of Leigh-Mallory's fighters on the need for these cumbersome wings to form up and made it clear he would prefer one squadron patrolling his airfield in fifteen minutes rather than several arriving too late. If wings had to be used, they should form up over the airfields he had asked them to defend.[33] It was a tetchy response, demonstrating the strain Park was under. He correctly felt that winning the battle was his and No. 11 Group's responsibility. Perhaps understandably, he saw any unsolicited help or advice that he should be fighting the battle any differently as a suggestion that his Group was not coping and evidence of personal weakness.

In practice, there was not a great deal separating the fighter formations the two Groups were using. Park seems to have been won over by his commanders' insistence that squadrons should go into action in pairs. By 11 September, Park was instructing his controllers to use pairs whenever possible.[34] Ideally, Park wanted a pair of Hurricane squadrons to be covered by a pair of Spitfire squadrons operating 5,000–8,000 feet higher.[35] This was not as closely coordinated as Bader's idea of two Spitfire squadrons 3,000–4,000 feet above a wing of three Hurricane squadrons, but the principle was the same.[36]

Bader did not agree that using larger formations wasted valuable time, partly because he saw no advantage in the tight, rigid formations that were still common in Fighter Command. Any 'forming up' could be done on the way to the designated patrol zone. If his wings arrived too late, it was only because they had not been scrambled in time. With radar providing plenty of early warning, there was nothing to stop Bader getting the extra time he wanted.

Dowding saw no reason to intervene in the dispute, but giving his Group commanders free rein looked like tacit support for Leigh-Mallory, which must have offended his protégé, Park. To his critics in the Air Ministry, it looked like a lack of leadership. In the Park/Leigh-Mallory dispute, the ministry tended to side with the latter; there was growing frustration at the cantankerous commander-in-chief's failure to make better use of No. 12 Group. It was all rather unsavoury, but for the RAF it all worked out well for the decisive assault on 15 September.

On this day, the Luftwaffe launched two raids on London. Both were relatively small compared to previous raids, but both also had massive escorts. The German crews set off, encouraged by claims that Fighter Command was down to just a handful of fighters. The first raid consisted of fifty bombers and 150 escorts. Park's squadrons engaged as soon as the formation crossed the coast, harassing the bombers all the way to London.[37] Up to this point, the escorts had done a reasonably good job, but over the capital, four more Hurricane squadrons and Bader's wing of two Spitfire squadrons and three Hurricane squadrons hit the German formation simultaneously. The remaining escort was swamped and the closely packed bomber formations scattered. The crews dropped their bombs haphazardly and headed for home as best they could.[38]

In the afternoon, a second wave of bombers had no better luck. One hundred and fourteen bombers with around 500 fighter escorts crossed the Kent coast and headed for London. On the approach, German escorts again successfully fended off the efforts of No. 11 Group but they burned precious fuel in the process. Over London, six squadrons from No. 11 Group, two sent over from No. 10 Group, and the five squadrons of No. 12 Group's Duxford Wing broke through the now scattered German escort. Once again, the bombers hurriedly dumped their loads on the suburbs before being chased back to France. Demoralised bomber crews described how formations of eighty enemy fighters had met them over the capital. The Luftwaffe lost sixty-four planes; these losses were serious, but the psychological blow of meeting such formidable formations of fighters was even greater. It was now clear to Luftwaffe aircrew and their commanders that Fighter Command was still a very effective force. On 17 September, the invasion was postponed indefinitely.

As RAF reconnaissance followed the transfer of the invasion barges from the exposed Channel ports to safer inland waterways, the Army and country breathed a collective sigh of relief. Brooke had no illusions—it was no more than a postponement. With the return of favourable weather the following spring, the invasion threat would be renewed. Britain had won a valuable six-month breathing space, but that was all. Nevertheless, Brooke would now get the winter he needed to train his army.

Britain had been fortunate. The German Navy had never required air superiority over central London—for an invasion to be successful, the Luftwaffe merely had to control the skies over the Channel and the German bridgeheads. Arguably, the Luftwaffe had long since achieved this objective. Fighter Command would never have been able to achieve the degree of concentration over a beachhead as had been possible over London, and German fighters would not have been operating in such difficult circumstances.

For the Luftwaffe, it was another failure. The German fighter force was good enough to establish a degree of air superiority, but eliminating Fighter Command had proven impossible. Fighter Command ended the summer of 1940 tired and battered, but it had more pilots and planes than at the beginning of the battle. The Luftwaffe had not even come close to destroying it. For the second time in a matter of months, the Luftwaffe had been set the task of achieving results on its own; just as had happened over Dunkirk, it failed. Fighter Command had done well in a battle where it only had to focus on the enemy air force. How well it would have done dealing with an enemy invasion will never be known.

With hindsight, the retreat of the invasion fleet signalled the end of the immediate danger, but this was not how it was seen at the time. The withdrawal of the invasion barges was a relief, but invasion was only one of the threats facing Britain, and for many it was not the most feared; the bomber still remained.

Dowding was in no doubt that the danger had not passed. The air offensive against Britain had not been halted. It was merely evolving. There had always been reasonable confidence that a daylight offensive could be dealt with, but it had always been assumed that once defeated by day, the enemy would merely turn to bombing by night. This would not be some futile act of despair by a defeated and bewildered enemy, but rather a natural progression to an offensive that posed even greater danger. Douglas had no doubt that bombing alone could bring Germany victory. At a dinner party, he was appalled by the naivety expressed by a prominent politician who claimed the bomber was overrated as a weapon of terror and could never bring any country to its knees. Douglas put the counterargument to him so strongly he found himself reported to Churchill for defeatism.[39]

For Dowding, Douglas, and many in the Air Ministry, the battles of July, August, and early September were just the prelude to the main event. The long-awaited assault on British cites was finally underway. The civilian population would now become the principal target. This was the air war the Air Staff had always predicted, the battle they and the politicians had always most feared. It was far more dangerous than mere invasion and the German Panzer blitzkrieg; indeed, the air element of the German blitzkrieg was so prominent in the public mind that the new strategy was seen as merely an extension of the old, a purer form of the strategy with the irrelevant Panzer element removed. The transition was so smooth that the British public and press kept the same name—the German bomber offensive was referred to as the 'blitzkrieg', soon abbreviated to 'the Blitz'.

As far as the Air Staff were concerned, the real war was just beginning.

Bomber Theory Put to the Test

For the German military, the course of events in the summer of 1940 was rather perplexing. Their relentless advance through Europe had taken even Germans by surprise, as every nation that had stood in its way was swept aside with astonishing ease. Suddenly, and equally surprisingly, the German war machine had been brought to a halt by an enemy that appeared to be on the brink of capitulation. Still, it seemed only the English Channel had saved Britain from immediate defeat. The country was isolated and in desperate straits; it was surely just a question of time before Britain succumbed.

The fundamental mistake of expecting air power to achieve results on its own was not identified. Throughout the summer of 1940, the hope that the aerial offensive alone might be sufficient to bring Britain to her senses was never far from Göring and Hitler's minds. A complicated, messy, and even risky invasion of Britain might not be necessary. Now that the onset of autumn had ruled out an invasion, there was time to give the theory a longer run. Germany had a large bomber fleet, excellent bases in Northern France, Belgium, and Holland to operate from, and no alternative way of using these bombers. If bombing by day was too risky, then Britain would have to be bombed by night. The aim was not to bring the RAF into battle and defeat it, but to avoid the RAF and strike the British nation. Suddenly, Germany was following a military strategy Britain understood.

It was the nightmare scenario that had haunted a generation of politicians—1,300 bombers based on airfields in the Lowlands, just 200 miles from London, a target so near and so big it was almost impossible to miss. The apocalyptic predications of the Air Staff throughout the 1920s and '30s seemed about to come to pass. In the early '20s, it was believed that 50 tons per day would make the capital untenable.[1] By the eve of the Second World War, it was estimated the German Air Force could deliver 700 tons per day; by May 1940, it was up to a staggering 4,800 tons a day.

This was the threat that Churchill had spent so much time and energy in the 1930s criticising governments and the Air Ministry for underestimating. Ironically, Churchill was now rather anxious to tone down the dire forecasts. He suggested the 4,800-ton figure the Air Staff had presented him with was unnecessarily alarmist, and he asked for it to be reconsidered, to which the Air Ministry agreed. The Luftwaffe had been engaged in intensive operations throughout the summer and serviceability rates were probably low, so a figure of 1,800 tons per day was probably more reasonable.[2] This was scarcely encouraging. Using the standard fifty-casualties-per-ton estimate, the country could expect 30,000 dead and 60,000 injured each day. There would be 630,000 casualties in the first week. Britain was prepared for the worst; 750,000 beds were ready to receive the injured. Churchill had no reason to doubt that bombing was a strategy that could lead to Britain's defeat—it was, after all, the only strategy he had for defeating Germany.

The incendiaries the Luftwaffe had dropped in the late afternoon of 7 September were a beacon for the waves of night bombers that would prolong the bombardment of London throughout the night. In less than twelve hours, nearly 600 bombers would drop 700 tons of high explosives and incendiaries on the Port of London and surrounding area.[3] It was far less than the Air Ministry's lower, revised figure, but it was nonetheless frightening.

Given this was the moment the defences had been anticipating for so long, the initial response was remarkably feeble. The day defences were understandably caught out by the change in German strategy on 7 September, but they still managed to put up some resistance. By night, just four Blenheims and a single Beaufighter took to the air to defend the capital. Not one of them made contact with the enemy.[4] Many of the anti-aircraft defences had been switched to defend the aircraft factories everyone was so worried about; the few that remained blazed wildly and hopefully and hit nothing. The defences could not claim a single success. With the nights rapidly lengthening, the advantages would be stacked even more in favour of the attackers. It seemed the German Air Force would be able to repeat this scale of attack as often as it liked.

It was a huge challenge, but it was at least a challenge that took Fighter Command back to its original purpose. By night, there was no need to worry about escorts and fighter-*versus*-fighter combat—it was back to the straightforward duel between the interceptor and the bomber. Dowding had no doubt that radar was key; since the first demonstration of airborne radar, he had been fascinated by its potential, and he believed all fighters should be equipped with it. He was willing to accept Blenheim and Beaufighters, with a pilot and separate AI operator, as an interim measure, but he made sure the AI Mark VI system had priority so that one day all single-seaters would have AI radar as standard.[5]

Even better results were expected with the new centimetric systems that were emerging. Dowding was already envisaging a fully automated air defence system where radar information on the location of the target would be fed directly into an autopilot that would not just fly the plane to the vicinity of the target, but also take it into a firing position. The autopilot would even decide when the target was close enough for the guns to open fire. For Dowding, the pilots had always been the weak link in the system, especially with their notoriously poor ability to judge distances.

Radar could do this very precisely, removing the human element from the interception process. The pilot would just be required to get the plane off the ground and land it;[6] for the rest of the mission, he would just need to monitor the systems. It was the ultimate air defence system. While Dowding could scarcely contain his excitement, the scientists pondered the difficulties. They doubted that existing technology would allow anything this sophisticated, even with centimetric radar. Only a shotgun-type dispersion could ever hope to score any hits.[7] Nevertheless, the scientists set to work on what would become AI Mark IX.[8]

Whether this was the most urgent need of Fighter Command or the country was another matter. The fear of bombing was concealing how crucial the struggle for air superiority by day had been. It was the restrictive air defence system, and the equipment, tactics, and training that came with it, that had been such a disadvantage in fighting these battles. The more the bomber threat dominated thinking, the more emphasis there would be on tightly controlled interception systems rather than battlefield air superiority fighters.

Meanwhile, the results achieved with the first 1.5-metre AI systems were not justifying Dowding's faith in radar. The equipment remained as unreliable and as difficult to use as ever. It did not help that the sets were still using components designed for cheap domestic television sets, rather than the rigours of air combat at 15,000 feet.[9] Some of the problems were overcome by trial and error; the problem of the target appearing on one side of the plane when it was on the other side was solved. The engineers tried turning the aerials round, more in hope than expectation, but it did the trick. All the receivers were now placed well away from the fuselage and engines to avoid bogus reflections. Placing the vertical and horizontal receivers at a diverging angle also helped prevent stray signals being picked up.[10] EMI developed a new transmitter that in tests had a maximum range of 5 miles and a minimum range of 400 feet.

All these improvements were incorporated into AI Mark IV, which began to appear in the summer of 1940. It was the first half-acceptable airborne radar. In service, a range of 3.5 miles was a more reasonable expectation. There was still a gap between this and how close ground radar could get the fighter. Ground reflections still reduced range at altitudes lower than 18,000 feet, and the equipment was still temperamental and difficult to use. Coordination between the pilot and the AI operator in the rear, huddled over his flickering screen, was still difficult. Somehow, these problems had to be overcome; the stakes could not be higher. It was genuinely believed that if these problems could not be solved, the Luftwaffe would bomb Germany to victory.

The changeover from daylight to nocturnal bombing was not sudden. As early as May, the occasional raider had been flying over Britain; they appeared to be aiming at military targets, but their efforts seemed strangely scattered, with the most serious loss of life being nine killed in Cambridge. Initially, it seemed existing fighters might be able to cope. Around half the sorties were flown by

AI-equipped Blenheims and the remainder by single-seater fighters. There was nothing odd about using single-seaters—both the Hurricane and Spitfire had been designed to operate by day and night. With German bombers flying at 10,000 feet or lower, searchlights were much more successful than radar at picking up the enemy. In June, Fighter Command was able to claim an impressive sixteen victories. However, German crews soon realised that flying above 10,000 feet put them beyond the range of searchlights, and in July, Fighter Command interceptions dropped to just four.[11]

Even more worrying was the growing evidence that the Luftwaffe was using radio waves to help bombers find their targets. Terms like '*Knickebein*' and '*X-Gerät*' kept cropping up in documents found in crashed German bombers and loose talk among captured German airmen. The terms seemed to refer to navigational systems; R. V. Jones, in charge of Air Ministry intelligence, was asked to investigate. By 20 June, sufficient evidence had emerged to justify a briefing session at 10 Downing Street, with Newall, Dowding, and Portal in attendance.[12] Portal and Newall were somewhat puzzled by the whole affair; they could not understand why German bomber crews would need such devices when Bomber Command crews were managing perfectly well without them.

The next day, an Anson sent up to search for evidence picked up the characteristic dots and dashes of the widely used Lorenz short-range blind-landing system. The fact that the Anson was detecting these signals over East Anglia suggested the Germans were using it for much more than helping their bombers to find their own airfields.

The Anson had in fact picked up *Knickebein*, the second of two blind-bombing systems developed in Germany. The first, X-Gerät, was an upgraded version of the Lorenz blind-landing system and had been available since 1938. It steered bombers along a cone that was 400 yards wide over targets 180 miles away. At two points 12 miles and 3 miles short of the target, beams intersecting the *X-Gerät* transmissions measured the speed of the bomber and calculated when the bombs should be released. The system required specialised equipment and training and was therefore restricted to the elite Kampfgruppe 100. The system picked up by the Anson, *Knickebein*, was a less sophisticated version; it used the standard Lorenz equipment installed in all German bombers and could get a bomber to within 1.5 miles of a target 270 miles away.

It was all rather ironic. The Luftwaffe was an air force that was dedicated to army support, yet it was preparing to carry out long-range raids under cover of darkness with far more sophistication than the supposedly more specialist Bomber Command could muster. The irony was not yet appreciated in Air Ministry circles. Indeed, the Air Ministry would have wondered what the point was of a system that could only get the bomber to within 1.5 miles of the target.

In July, as the crucial struggle by day grew in intensity, 20 per cent of all German bomber sorties were already being flown by night. It still seemed a rather haphazard affair. The British were as puzzled as the Germans were by RAF nocturnal efforts;

Dowding could not understand why the Luftwaffe was not already using beams and bombers to pulverise British cities. The only explanation he could come up with was that Bomber Command raids on German cites must be so devastating that Hitler dare not risk provoking similar raids against Berlin.[13] Others suggested that the bombs falling in open countryside might be practice runs for invasion parachute drops, or perhaps they were just partly trained aircrew.[14] This last explanation was remarkably similar to German efforts to explain Bomber Command inaccuracy.

During the course of 400 nocturnal bombing sorties in July, 258 British civilians lost their lives.[15] It was scarcely the fifty casualties per ton anticipated by pre-war estimates, but it was still more than had died in air raids on the United Kingdom in the first year of Zeppelin raids in the First World War. Dowding warned Churchill that the night defences were still inadequate and German bombing might seriously affect civilian morale. Once a country's industries had been destroyed, it would 'be possible to apply to the enemy population that degree of misery by which alone a modern war between determined opponents can be won'.[16] No one was more sensitive to the danger of bombing than Churchill. Beaverbrook needed little reminding about how vulnerable his aircraft factories might be if night defences were not strengthened.

Douglas was another expressing his concern. 'The problem of the night fighter is still far from being solved,' he reminded everyone. The Blenheim was obviously too slow and the Beaufighter was not showing much promise. In any case, both were merely makeshift adaptations of aircraft designed for other roles. There was not much optimism at Supermarine or Hawker about fitting AI into the Spitfire and Hurricane. Rowe's AMRE doubted if a single-seater would ever have enough space.[17] In any case, for all the ingenuity of the fully automatic AI Mark VI, a dedicated operator was having enough trouble getting useful information out of AI Mark IV; it seemed a little optimistic to expect a pilot to fly the plane and use the AI equipment.

With a long war in prospect and the bomber so crucial to the outcome, Douglas did not believe it was too late to start from scratch with a purpose-built night-fighter. With Beaverbrook's drive, he suggested, it might be in production in as little as a year to eighteen months. Work began on formulating specification F.18/40, a specialist twin-engine, two-seater night-fighter armed with six cannon.[18] There was no parallel talk of needing to start from scratch with a purpose-built single-seater air superiority fighter. Nobody was suggesting that the thinking behind the Tornado/Typhoon bomber interceptor should be reviewed. On the other side of the North Sea, a much clearer idea of what was required from a fighter was emerging—the Focke-Wulf FW 190 was about to go into production.

On the night of 23–24 July, an AI Mark III-equipped Blenheim of the Fighter Interception Unit was directed close enough to an intruder for the on-board radar to pick it up. Conditions were particularly good that night. The Blenheim caught sight of the Dornier 17 against a clear moonlit sky and, approaching from below, achieved the first AI-assisted victory of the war. It was a success that proved difficult to replicate. Even when the AI equipment picked up an intruder, the signal was nearly always lost before visual contact was made. The equipment's inadequate minimum range was the prime suspect. Some thought the Blenheim was simply too slow to keep up with the bomber; the much faster Beaufighter was expected to solve this problem. The first examples of this fighter reached the F.I.U. in August and regular squadrons in September.

Meanwhile, as the number of bombers used by day decreased, so the scale of bombing by night increased. On the night of 13–14 August, a raid on the Shorts factory in Northern Ireland destroyed five almost-complete Stirling bombers. On the same night, in cloudy conditions, nine He 111 bombers from the elite Kampfgruppe 100 attacked the massive Castle Bromwich Spitfire factory. Eleven 250-kg bombs hit the plant. The damage was not great, but the accuracy was impressive. General Pile, in charge of the country's anti-aircraft defences, could not believe that bombs were hitting factories from aircraft that were apparently at 20,000 feet in cloud by sheer chance.[19] He was right; it was, in fact, the operational debut of the *X-Gerät* blind bombing system.[20]

Countering planes guided by radio beams had been on the RAE agenda for many years.[21] As soon as the existence of the German navigational beams was confirmed, No. 80 Wing was set up to jam them. The *Knickebein* system was the first to suffer. Signals were picked up and retransmitted from another site, and over Britain, these fake beams were the stronger signal. The first 'masking beacon' or 'Meacon' was set up at the end of July. By the middle of August, there were nine in place.

The end of August saw a sharp escalation in German bombing. On four nights from 28–29 August, German attacks were directed at Liverpool. Around 600 sorties were flown, but accuracy was so poor it was not until the fourth night that it even became clear that Liverpool was the target.[22] Night fighters flew around 100 sorties, but only one bomber was sighted and even this escaped.[23] Civilian casualties were also rising; in August, the civilian death toll exceeded 1,000.

Within the Air Ministry, there was a growing frustration at Dowding's apparent fixation with AI as the only way of tackling the night bomber. Douglas was reminding Newall how successful the single-seater Camels had been as night fighters in the First World War and he saw no reason why Hurricanes could not be just as successful.[24] With so many of Dowding's squadrons dotted around the country and doing little else, there seemed no reason why they should not try. Dowding, however, insisted that using single-seaters without AI was a waste of time.

Douglas also wanted Dowding to get rid of the turret on the Blenheim to improve speed. Again, Dowding refused. On this issue, Dowding perhaps had a stronger case; on the two occasions in August that Blenheims claimed victories, the fighter had flown alongside the bomber and completed the destruction with aimed fire from single machine gun in the turret. It was a reminder that the Defiant turret fighter was a perfectly sound concept when used as intended. Indeed, with this in mind, Dowding switched the two Defiant squadrons to the night-fighting role even though the AI Mark V they were supposed to use was not yet ready. This was as far as Dowding was willing to go with non-AI-equipped fighters. To the frustration of the Air Staff, Dowding also doggedly refused to show any interest in other, more unorthodox solutions. Lindemann's aerial minefields or Helmore's nose-mounted searchlight were, he believed, not even worth investigating. It was not an attitude that was likely to improve his standing in Air Ministry circles.

Even if airborne radar worked, the shortage of Blenheims and the delays with the Beaufighter meant Dowding had relatively few specialist night fighters. There were two AI Blenheim squadrons with each of Nos 10, 11, and 12 Groups, and a single squadron in No. 13 Group. The addition of the two Defiant squadrons (one in each of Nos 12 and 13 Groups) brought the total available to nine. London's defences consisted of just two Blenheim squadrons.

The sprawling mass of London, at the end of an estuary that funnelled the bombers towards their target, was one of the easier targets for the Luftwaffe to find. On the night of 7–8 September, with the huge fires started by the day bombers to guide them, it was impossible to miss. When the last German bomber headed for home, the carnage inflicted was every bit as grim as the pre-war prophets of doom had predicted. The contents of the London Dock warehouses burned with such intensity that the heat blistered paint on the fire tugs pouring water into the blazes from 300 yards away. The rescue services were overwhelmed by 1,000 small fires, fifty-four large blazes, and nine conflagrations. Over 400 Londoners died and 1,600 were injured; it was not the 35,000 that the fifty-casualties-per-ton ratio would have predicted, but it was a chilling loss nonetheless. The population of the East End was badly shaken. There was an understandable clamour from those whose homes had been damaged or destroyed to get out of the area as quickly as possible.

In the days that followed, attempts to bomb London by day were comfortably defeated, but by night German bomber crews encountered virtually no opposition. Despite this, the number of sorties soon dropped off as wear and tear took its toll. The 350 tons of high explosive and incendiaries dropped during the course of the 7–8 September raid dropped to just over 220 on the second night of the offensive and an average of just over 165 tons for the next eight nights. Once the daylight offensive was called off, the entire fleet could be used by night. On the 17th, the tonnage increased to 375, and 350 tons was maintained for the next three nights. However, it then dropped to an average of just over 200 tons.[25] This was a formidable tonnage, but nowhere near as high as pre-war predictions. It had been assumed that all bombers would be available to deliver their maximum bomb loads on the first night. This would drop to 50 per cent on the third night, but this rate would then be maintained night after night. The drop-off rate was broadly correct, but the 200 tons the Luftwaffe was able to maintain was 15 per cent of its potential maximum, not 50 per cent. This was not much better than the 10 per cent Trenchard's Independent Force had managed in 1918. Instead of conjuring up hypothetical estimates based on theoretical guesswork, the pre-war experts would have done better to examine the hard evidence of the First World War.

It may not have been what the experts had predicted, but it was still a huge quantity of high-explosive and incendiary bombs. On 7 September, the Germans had dropped on London nearly twice the weight of bombs dropped on all targets in the United Kingdom in the entire First World War. For the citizens of London, the sense of helplessness was deepened by the apparent lack of any defence. Anti-aircraft guns defending aircraft factories were rushed back to defend the capital. Pile issued orders to let fly with every available gun at every opportunity. The defensive fire was largely indiscriminate, but the 180 German bombers that attacked London on the night of 11–12 September were greeted by a thunderous barrage that sometimes drowned the explosions of the falling bombs. It may not have destroyed many bombers, but it lifted the spirits of the civilian population enormously. At the cabinet meeting on 13 September, Malcolm MacDonald, the Health Minister, was able to report a 'remarkable improvement' in morale. Indeed, many of those who had been anxious to leave the area were now determined to stay.[26]

It was difficult to judge how long civilian morale could be maintained. The assault was relentless in a way the First World War air attacks had never been. Night after night, the bombers came. By the end of September, over 5,000 tons had fallen on the capital. Businesses and livelihoods were destroyed and homes smashed. Nearly 7,000 men, women, and children had been killed, and over 10,000 injured. There seemed no end to the bombing. There were fears that smashed mains supply water and sewage pipes would result in widespread epidemics, with the crowding together of so many in the only genuinely bombproof shelter—the London Underground—helping to spread disease. As the nightly bombardment stretched into October, Churchill feared it would continue until there was only rubble left to bomb.[27]

However, despite the heavy loss of life, the citizens of London were not cowering. The propaganda slogan 'We Can Take It' both encouraged and reflected the genuine mood of defiance. As is so often the case in such crises, very ordinary people proved capable of quite extraordinary resilience. At the beginning of October, the police reported that morale was still good. There was no hint of any desire to topple the government or surrender; the most powerful emotion was the desire for revenge.[28]

Once it became clear that London was the main target, there was some effort to concentrate fighter resources around the capital. Dowding moved one flight from each of the two Defiant squadrons south to No. 11 Group. At No. 10 Group, Brand moved his two Blenheim squadrons to the very edge of his group boundary so they would be better placed to help. With the Fighter Interception Unit also operating from No. 11 Group, London now had the lion's share of the country's night defence force. Beaufighters were beginning to arrive to replace the slower Blenheims. The problems and delays with the Beaufighter led to the American Douglas Boston being drafted into the night-fighting role as the Havoc. The bomber threat caused these excellent planes to reach front-line squadrons far more quickly than fear of an invasion.[29]

The main problem was not the performance of the available aircraft, but how to get any fighter within AI range of the target. The Home Chain stations could not get the AI-equipped night fighters close enough. Some experiments with the shorter-range but more-accurate low-level CHL 1.5-metre systems suggested that these could cover the gap. The Chain Home could pass the target over to a CHL radar when it passed within its 50-mile range. This could direct the fighter until AI could take over. It was extravagant in terms of resources as it meant each intercepting fighter would require its own dedicated ground station. A switching device enabled the same array to transmit and receive signals, and the array rotated automatically; it was beginning to look like a modern-day radar system. A height-finding capability was added and a neat system developed that enabled both the intercepting fighter and approaching bomber to appear as dots on the same screen. For the first time, the operators had a presentation system that actually mirrored, in the horizontal plane at least, what was physically happening in the air. This became the basis for the GCI (Ground Control Interception) system. The first experimental set was trialled in October. Before the trials were even complete, 120 hand-built sets were ordered. Deliveries were expected before the end of the year.[30]

As a makeshift arrangement, Dowding acquired ten examples of the 1.5-metre GL gun laying radar used by Anti-Aircraft Command. These had a range of 7 miles and were set up in the Kenley sector, the most common approach route for German bombers. Information was sent to the sector operations room, where the position of the bomber was chalked on a blackboard along with the position of the intercepting fighter. The controller then guided the fighter towards the bomber.[31]

Still success did not come. Even if the AI operator picked up the echo of a bomber and the equipment did not break down, the signal would often be lost before the minimum range of the equipment was reached. Morale in the AI-equipped squadrons hit rock bottom. The AI operators were frustrated with the equipment and the pilots did not know whether to blame the equipment or the operators. Some operators pretended that they were still getting an echo, even when they had lost it, for fear of incurring the wrath of the pilot.[32] With the faster Beaufighters also losing the signal, speed did not appear to be the problem. Some suspected that the Germans knew all about AI and were engaging in violent evasive manoeuvres as soon as they detected AI transmissions.

It was not German countermeasures that were causing the problem, nor the speed of the Blenheim. Most German bombers were not that fast. Eventually, it was realised that the main problem was the tendency of pilots to overcorrect to such an extent the tell-tale reflections of target planes were lost. Tactics slowly evolved whereby instead of rushing to close the gap as quickly as possible, the fighter would approach the target slowly. As the gap closed, instead of telling the pilot where to steer, the AI operator told the pilot where to look. If the pilot did not spot the bomber and the operator lost the signal, it was best to drop back until contact was re-established and start again.[33] Eventually these tactics would become standard practice, but not in time to help much with the Blitz of 1940–41.

The problem with operator/pilot communications underlined the need to move to the AI Mark V, where the pilot had his own display, and the Mark VI, where no operator was required. With Dowding under pressure to use his single-seaters, he too was rather anxious for some progress. Trials with AI Mark V began in October 1940 and with the fully automatic Mark VI in December. In December, forty-eight handmade versions of the Mark V (initially known as AI Mark IVA), were ordered. Once these proved satisfactory, full-scale Mark V production version would go ahead. The Air Ministry instructed EMI to get twelve prototypes of the completely automatic AI Mark VI ready and tested by the end of the year. By this time, preparations were underway for the production of no less than 2,000.[34]

The technology was ingenious, but, as was so often the case with radar, what worked well in the laboratory did not always work so well in the air. The automatic strobe with AI Mark VI had an unfortunate tendency of locking onto the ground reflections instead of one of the detected planes.[35] The dot on the display screen tended to wander, jitter, and become ill-defined. Switching from the glare of the cathode ray tube to the murk outside made it impossible for the pilot to see the bomber the radar told him was there; an observer was still required to actually see the plane. A first victory with AI Mark V was achieved in June 1941,[36] but the equipment was far too temperamental to become standard equipment. Dowding's dream of equipping all single-seater fighters with radar would take a little longer. In the end, the Mark IV proved to be the best that 1.5-metre systems could do. Dowding was right about the long-term value of airborne radar, but for all the ingenuity and perseverance shown, none of systems tried was ever able to make a decisive contribution to defeating the German Blitz.

Dowding's absolute faith in AI was causing as much frustration in the Air Ministry as the capricious AI equipment was inflicting on night fighter aircrews. Dowding was already under fire for the way he was running day defence. His opposition to the aerial mines proposed by Lindemann, Churchill's personal advisor and friend, did not help his cause. As well as the hostility of the current Air Staff, Dowding also had to contend with former Chiefs of Air Staff Trenchard and John Salmond sniping from the wings. Salmond had retired in 1934 but was now working in the Ministry of Aircraft Production, where Beaverbrook was becoming increasingly alarmed by reports that night shifts in aircraft factories were spending half their time in air raid shelters.[37]

Salmond fuelled Beaverbrook's concerns by writing a report criticising the way Dowding was running the night defences. Beaverbrook was impressed and instructed Salmond to head a committee on Night Defence. Dowding was expected to cooperate with this committee, but he was not part of it. The committee did not waste any time; it had its first meeting on 16 September and drew up its conclusions at its second meeting the following day. These were presented to Dowding for comment on the 18th.[38] The recommendations were scarcely startling, calling for the production of AI Mark IV, Beaufighters, and GIC sets to be stepped up. However, the committee also recommended that more use should be made of single-engine fighters in the night-fighting role.

The Defiant was already demonstrating that fighters could achieve success without AI. The turret fighter achieved its first nocturnal success on 17 September. Victories were few and far between, but they were more frequent than AI-radar-directed victories. As the invasion fleet dispersed, there was no reason not to switch more day fighters to night defence, but Dowding did not see it like this.

For Dowding, the dispersion of the invasion fleet was irrelevant. The German air offensive by day had not yet been defeated. Fighter Command's fighters still had to deal with hit-and-run raids often flown at high altitude. To prove Dowding's point, as soon as the invasion was cancelled, the Luftwaffe launched a couple of heavy daylight attacks on the Bristol Filton and Supermarine Southampton factories. The loss of life at both was heavy, and the Supermarine works was completely gutted. No. 10 Group, leaning eastwards to help cover London, had been caught out. Brand hastily moved a Hurricane squadron westwards to cover the Bristol area, and the next attack on Filton was not so successful. Nevertheless, the danger of leaving aircraft factories exposed to daylight attack was clear.

Criticism of Dowding continued to grow—even the Admiralty was getting involved. On 16 October, Admiral Philips, the Vice-Chief of the Naval Staff, sent a memo to Churchill accusing Dowding of lacking imagination and flexibility. He declared the Defiant to be a failure and the AI-equipped Beaufighter as yet-unproven, and he wanted at least three single-seater fighter squadrons to be assigned to the night-fighter role. That Churchill expected Dowding to answer Admiralty criticisms about air strategy gives some idea of how low Dowding's stock had now fallen. In response, Dowding reaffirmed his faith in the AI-directed night fighter and repeated his belief that there was no point in using fighters not equipped with AI. Two days after Philips's memo, Newall, under pressure from Churchill, instructed Dowding to assign three Hurricane squadrons to the night-fighter role.[39] Dowding put his objections on record. He claimed that the extra strain put on his command by the high-flying hit-and-run raids and the continual demands for convoy protection made the loss of three day-fighter squadrons totally unacceptable:

> Please do not say I agree, reluctantly or otherwise, to the diversion of Hurricanes. I am carrying out orders which I believe to be dangerous and unsound with our present strength of fighter squadrons.[40]

The facts scarcely supported Dowding. During October, nearly three quarters of all German bomber sorties were by night, yet day fighter sorties regularly exceeded 500, while night sorties rarely exceeded 50. With London being brutally bombed every night, it was scarcely an appropriate balance.

As well as switching Hurricanes to night defence, Dowding was forced to allow trials to begin with Lindemann's aerial mines. The obsolete Handley Harrow heavy bomber became the unlikeliest of night fighters. The idea was for the Handley Harrow to patrol ahead of the predicted path of the attacking bomber, parachuting 2,000-foot lengths of piano wire with a bomb attached to the top. When the bomber hit the wire, a parachute at the lower end opened, which dragged the bomb downwards towards its target. Dowding was also told to remove the turrets from the Blenheims to give the plane slightly more speed. His authority was being undermined; with both Salmond and Trenchard openly campaigning for his departure, Dowding's days were numbered.

Around mid-October, the Luftwaffe stepped up its campaign. On 15 October, over 500 tons were dropped on the capital, and an average of 350 tons was maintained for a week. Between 7 September and 13 November, London was bombed every night bar one. Londoners, however, were adjusting remarkably well to the horrors of modern war. Indeed, they were beginning to take pride in their resilience. There seemed no end in sight to the misery the bombers were inflicting, but equally there seemed no sign that the will of the people would crack. Churchill would often watch the gruesome spectacle from his rooftop balcony. London seemed like a 'huge prehistoric animal, capable of enduring terrible injuries, mangled and bleeding from many wounds, yet preserving its life and movement'.[41] Göring was also beginning to appreciate that London was simply too big to damage mortally. The Luftwaffe needed to concentrate its efforts on a smaller target, where the same damage might make more impact.

On the night of 14–15 November, He 111s of KG 100 used *X-Gerät* to mark the city of Coventry with incendiaries. Nearly 450 bombers homed in on the markers and delivered the most concentrated and effective attack yet. It was not a totally indiscriminate raid; the bombers were aiming at industrial plants, many of which were involved in aircraft construction. Nevertheless, even bombing far more accurate than was possible in 1940 was bound to cause serious civilian casualties. Large tracts of the city were gutted and over 4,000 homes destroyed. Nearly 400 civilians lost their lives. Twelve factories involved in aircraft production were severely damaged along with nine other plants, and the collapse of power supplies ensured no factories in the city opened the next day.[42]

The survivors emerged from the ruins dazed and shocked by their ordeal. There was again considerable resentment among the local population about the ineffectiveness of the defences. This time, however, Fighter Command could not be accused of not trying. Thirty-five Blenheims, twelve Beaufighters, thirty Defiants, forty-three Hurricanes, and even five Gladiators took to the skies—a total of 125 fighters. Seven enemy bombers were sighted and two were fired at, but none were claimed as destroyed. The sole success of the night was achieved by an anti-aircraft battery.[43]

Troops moved in the next day to help in the grizzly task of clearing the rubble and removing the bodies of the victims. Mobile soup kitchens arrived to feed the population. The King visited. Astonishingly, by the evening of the 16th, there were already signs of improving morale. Transport was provided to evacuate 10,000 citizens, but only 300 took up the offer. Shopkeepers and small businessmen sifted through the rubble to see what could be salvaged and opened for business in defiance of the carnage that surrounded them. Power lines were restored. Teams sifted through the debris of factories and once more found that many of the machine tools still functioned. Some factories began production just two days after the attack.[44]

The interwar prophets of doom can perhaps be accused for not looking closely enough at the evidence the First World War provided. The estimated casualties for a given tonnage of bombs were grossly exaggerated, and the problems of inflicting meaningful damage on industrial plants and the difficulties of maintaining a bombing offensive were underestimated. It is more difficult to criticise the prophets for their conclusion that the average citizen would not tolerate the horror and hardship bombing would impose. Nobody could have predicted that the human spirit could absorb such horrendous blows and still persevere. There were plenty of calls for retaliation, but no hint of any desire to surrender—just a grim determination to see it through.

The government did not normally announce the casualties for any particular raid. However, there were concerns that rumour might exaggerate the death toll. An exception was therefore made in the case of Coventry. In a bizarre reaction, the German authorities retaliated by announcing that 223 German citizens had been killed in a 'revenge' attack on Hamburg on the night following the Coventry raid.[45] The RAF attack was indeed one of the more destructive raids of the period, but in reality, only twenty-six German civilians lost their lives. In the quest for foreign sympathy, neither side saw any need to minimise the devastation being caused by the enemy. Indeed, the Germans felt compelled to exaggerate their own death toll to keep up. The propaganda war, however, was one battle Britain was winning; reports of the effects of German raids on British cities were making a huge impression in an increasingly sympathetic United States.

There were also lessons for the Air Staff. If British cities could survive and indeed recover from such devastating attacks, it had to be wondered whether Bomber Command could really ever hope to paralyse German industry. The Air Ministry defiantly insisted that the Luftwaffe had missed an opportunity, as repeat attacks might have finished the city off completely.[46] An equally valid question might have been that if it took repeated maximum efforts from the German Air Force just to eliminate one small city, how long would it take to wipe out all the cities? What if the country still refused to surrender? What was supposed to happen then?

As it turned out, the Coventry raid was the high point of the German bombing offensive. The Luftwaffe would never be able to repeat the devastation achieved. The raid had relied on the *X-Gerät* blind-bombing system, but No. 80 Wing was already working on an antidote. Equipment recovered from crashed German bombers had enabled No. 80 Wing to construct the 'Bromide' jammer. This was actually operating on the night of the Coventry raid, but on the wrong frequency. Five nights later, when the German bomber force tried to repeat its Coventry success against Birmingham, the 'Bromide' jammer successfully disrupted and dispersed the pathfinders. The raid was a complete failure. The German blind-bombing systems would never be as successful again.

Londoners had weathered the storm, and now the populations of other cities were showing they could match the resilience of the capital. In the war between the bomber and the people, the people had won, and Hitler knew it:

> The least effect of all (as far as we can see) has been made on the morale and will to resist of the English people. No decisive effects can be expected from terror attack on residential areas.[47]

Nor had the British aircraft industry been ravaged. The damage looked serious; early in October, Beaverbrook warned the cabinet that the German raids in September had reduced that month's output by 300 machines. However, the machine tools survived. New premises were found. The Supermarine factory was relocated, but this time it would not be a single target; dispersion was already a general policy, and German bombing simply accelerated the programme.[48] In the last quarter of 1940, aircraft production dropped 11 per cent, nearly 500 planes down on the third quarter. Output was restored by the first quarter of 1941, and it then continued to rise. The aircraft industry had emerged stronger from the ordeal.[49]

The Coventry raid brought about Dowding's downfall. The total failure of the fighter defences was the final straw for the Air Staff, and Douglas took his place. Park would soon follow, replaced by his arch-rival Leigh-Mallory. Douglas brought a new energy to the night defences of the country, and by May 1941, sixteen of the twenty planned night fighter squadrons existed (four Defiant, one Hurricane, three mixed Hurricane/Defiant, six Beaufighter, and two Havoc).[50] There was no reliance on radar-equipped fighters. The Defiant was undergoing a resurgence in fortune in its new night-fighter role, with more squadrons converting to the type. Douglas was anxious to prolong production, even accepting a reduction in Hurricane production to allow for the delivery of 200 of the improved Defiant II. The fighter was finally being allowed to do what it was designed to do—shooting down unescorted bombers. Turrets were now very much back in fashion, with the F.18/40 specialist night fighter amended to require one.[51] Bristol and De Havilland were asked to investigate fitting turrets to Beaufighters and Mosquitos respectively.[52]

Under Douglas's reign, the alternatives to AI that Dowding had disapproved of were given a chance. However, Douglas's predecessor proved to be right about most of them. A searchlight was mounted in the nose of a Havoc, but trials in the spring of 1941 were not encouraging.[53] No. 420 Flight, which had been experimenting with Lindemann's aerial mines, was now declared operational as No. 93 Squadron.

It claimed its first success on 22 December, but subsequent successes would prove to be very few and far between. Intruder missions against enemy airfields were a little more successful.

The Douglas Boston was in demand for all these roles. The chances of any being available to re-equip the light bomber squadrons of No. 2 Group was drifting ever further into the future. With attention once more focusing on turret fighters, the bomber threat was again drawing attention away from the need for bombers and fighters that could support the Army.

Airborne radar was slowly bringing more success. By the beginning of 1941, the first six hurriedly hand-built examples of the new GCI radar formed a belt from the Humber to Weymouth. The number of times the GCI control was able to bring the fighter within AI range of the bomber increased from forty-four in January to ninety-five in March. Even in March, there were only thirty-one actual combats. 'Cat's eyes' operations with non-radar-equipped aircraft provided the backbone of the fighter defences. These usually operated over the cities under attack, the only location where the fighters could be sure to find the bombers. Rather grimly, the fires below would sometimes help illuminate their targets. Percentage-wise, single-seater fighters did not get into position to attack as often as AI-equipped fighters, but there were more of them and they were responsible for a greater number of contacts.[54] Dowding was right about radar being the long-term solution, but he was wrong to ignore the contribution single-seaters could make in the short term.

After a relative lull in January and February, the next three months saw more punishing attacks. The German emphasis was now on attacking ports as a way of backing up the U-boat campaign. The loss of life was sometimes great, but the country could endure the ordeal with more confidence. Night defence quite rightly had a high priority; the government had a duty to preserve the lives of its citizens, and it needed to ensure production was not disrupted. Nevertheless, Churchill and his government now knew bombing British cities was not going to win Germany the war. Indeed, Churchill was beginning to think that bombing Germany would not win Britain the war either.

Despite all the efforts of Douglas, the scientists, and the pilots, the Luftwaffe was never seriously embarrassed by the defences. Bomber losses rose slowly, but they were never much higher than 1 per cent of sorties flown. The highest German loss was on the night of 10–11 May, when fourteen out of 571 bombers sent against London were shot down. It was never enough to force the Germans to call a halt to the offensive; instead, the Blitz ended because it was not achieving anything and the German High Command had better ways of using the Luftwaffe. The German Army and Luftwaffe were about to be reunited, and *blitzkrieg* was to be restored as the principal means of waging war.

The German bomber offensive did not even push Britain close to defeat. Once again, an air-only offensive had degenerated into a long, drawn-out battle of attrition.

It was responsible for much suffering, but it could not force a decision. All the Blitz had done was confirm that airpower, acting on its own, could not win wars.

In 1909, the Liberal MP Alfred Mond had attempted to calm the hysteria over the Zeppelin threat by assuring his colleagues that 'No nation would make peace because the enemy was killing civilians'.[55] He was right.

Conclusion

From Munich to the end of the Blitz, the RAF had gone full circle. In 1938, Britain had no plans for a European expeditionary force; instead, she would rely on the bomber. The government had then changed its mind and decided to build an army, but that army had been rather ignominiously evicted from mainland Europe. By the spring of 1941, the idea of winning the war with ground forces had been abandoned and Britain was back to relying on the bomber.

For the Air Ministry, the period from March 1939 to June 1940, when the Army became a major player, was just an aberration. For a while, the Air Ministry had been forced to consider how the Air Force could support the Army. It had genuinely tried to do its best, but it could not escape from the doctrinal straight jacket that successive Chiefs of Air Staff had constructed during the 1920s and '30s. The best the Air Staff could do was to impose their strategic template at a tactical level. Bombers remained the decisive weapon, but not on the battlefield. The Air Force could help best by attacking targets way beyond the battlezone; indeed, the closer the bombing got to the enemy's sources of production, the better. Defending the Army meant preventing the enemy air force from doing likewise with a Fighter Command-style air defence system in the rear. The evidence from Spain and Poland that aviation could be used to great effect on the battlefield was ignored or distorted to fit the Air Staff's preconceived ideas.

The realities of war forced the RAF to become much more involved in the battle than the Air Staff wanted. It soon became clear that the aircrews had neither the equipment nor the training for tactical air operations. When Britain's allies asked for support for their armies, the Air Ministry was unwilling and the RAF unable to give it. One by one, Britain's allies fell by the wayside.

Involvement in the land battle had forced the Air Force to adapt. While the squadrons based in Britain fought the war very much as the Air Staff wanted it to be, in France, away from Air Ministry dogma, the beginnings of a flexible tactical force began to emerge. However, before these could take root, the RAF was back in Britain. During the disastrous Battle of France, the RAF was moving in the right direction. During the Battle of Britain, tactical air support was going backwards.

Faith in strategic bombing was so set in stone that evidence was irrelevant. Early attempts at long-range strategic and short-range tactical bombing both resulted in equally heavy losses. For strategic bombing, this was not taken as evidence that it might not work; rather, it just meant that another way of pursuing the theory had to be found. Heavy losses supporting the Army, on the other hand, were immediately used by the Air Staff as conclusive proof that tactical air support did not work.

Inconveniently for the Air Staff, the Luftwaffe was proving the contrary—something the Air Staff struggled to explain. The Luftwaffe could do it because it had air superiority, which seemed to be something only Germans could possess. No-one in the Air Ministry was trying to work out how RAF might develop the fighters and tactics needed to win air superiority over the British Army. Indeed, the Air Staff definition of air superiority was still having more bombers than the enemy, not having a superior fighter force. The argument that Luftwaffe air support only worked because the German Army was advancing seemed to be confusing cause and effect. Believing that it did not work for retreating armies was a self-fulfilling prophecy; without adequate air support, armies were more likely to be in retreat. With the support of the Luftwaffe, the German Army had conquered half of Europe, but as far as the Air Staff was concerned, the Germans did not really understand how to use air power.

Ironically, having lost all her allies, Britain had no choice but to believe the bomber was the only way to win the war. Britain could not build a big enough Army on her own, so bombing Germany into defeat seemed the only remotely plausible strategy for winning the war.

Before even contemplating victory, Britain had to avoid defeat. Alone and isolated, it seemed only a miracle could save Britain from becoming Germany's next conquest. That miracle proved to be the German decision to take a leaf out of the British book of strategy. Three times the Germans decided to rely on air power operating independently of ground forces to gain victory. Three times it failed. First, the Luftwaffe failed to stop the British Army escaping from Dunkirk. Then it failed to destroy Fighter Command in the Battle of Britain. Finally, it failed to break the morale of the British people with the Blitz. The strategy used on these three occasions was not how Germany had conquered most of Europe.

For the Air Staff, this was rather reassuring. German strategy was conforming to their view about how wars should be fought. The British approach had the German stamp of approval; the bomber was the decisive war-winning weapon the Air Staff had claimed it to be throughout the interwar years. German bombers might have failed, but British bombers would show how it should be done.

In fact, the first eighteen months of war had demonstrated how flawed the theories of the interwar years had been. Land battles were supposed to degenerate into the stalemate that had characterised most of the First World War. Independent air action was supposed to bring swift results. Bombers would end wars in weeks, if not days. The reality was quite the opposite. The battles on land developed with a speed that took the British and French commanders by surprise. Once the ground element was removed and the air forces were on their own, the engagements turned into ponderous battles of attrition spread over months, with little progress being made by either side. It was the Battle of Britain and the Blitz that resembled the trench warfare of the First World War. On its own, air power was not the decisive weapon many had predicted.

The Air Staff, however, remained convinced that avoiding defeat was about shooting down bombers and that winning wars was about building more heavy bombers than the enemy. Britain's only victory so far was the aerial Battle Britain. Sticking to an aerial war could lead to more victories, or so the Air Staff believed. In October 1940, Portal replaced Newall to give the bomber offensive more focus. Under his direction, the Air Staff would move even further from understanding what was required for victory.

Germany took a different course. The aberration had been the Luftwaffe's unsuccessful venture into independent strategic air warfare. The Luftwaffe and German Army were about to resume their partnership and their victorious march across Europe. The next assault on Britain might be a joint land and air assault, and the RAF might have to defend the Navy and support the Army, not just avoid being defeated.

However, this was not what the Air Ministry expected. Come the spring of 1941, the German Air Force would resume the bomber offensive by day in what would be a rerun of the Battle of Britain.

The Air Staff was still preparing for the wrong war.

Endnotes

Unless otherwise stated, files are from the National Archives.

Chapter 1

1. AIR2/2634 (November 1935–January 1936).
2. WO106/1578 (2 April 1937).
3. WO106/1588 (April–May 1938).
4. WO106/1583 (May 1938).
5. Baughen, G., 'Chapter 13', in *Blueprint for Victory* (2014).
6. WO193/685 (early 1938).
7. AIR2/2634 (October 1937).
8. AIR2/2634 (October 1937).
9. WO193/685 (early 1938).
10. *Ibid.*
11. WO193/685 (June 1938).
12. Baughen, G., *The Rise of the Bomber* (2015), pp. 227–231.
13. AIR2/2825 (20 October 1938).
14. CAB53/48 (4 August 1938).
15. AIR2/2964 (25 August 1938).
16. AIR2/2964 (20 June 1938).
17. AIR2/2964 (27 June 1938, 2 July, 20 July, 19 August 1938).
18. AIR6/33 (3 February 1938).
19. AIR2/2964 (27 June 1938).
20. AIR6/33 (3 February 1938).
21. AIR6/32 (1 February 1938).
22. AIR6/32 (18 January 1938).
23. AIR6/34 (12 April 1938).
24. AIR2/2824 (25 March 1938).
25. T161/923 (30 September 1938).
26. AVIA46/175, p. 33.

27. James, T. C. G., *The Growth of Fighter Command 1936-1940* (2012), p. 41.

28. AIR14/225, (28 September 1938).

29. AIR41/39, p. 242.

30. AIR41/39, Appendix 2.

31. AIR41/39, p. 239.

32. AIR2/1798 (14 June 1938).

33. AIR9/90 (13 April 1938).

34. AIR14/433 (24 May 1938).

35. AIR2/2821 (12 July 1938).

36. AVIA46/122, Introduction section IV.

37. AIR2/3075 (22, 29 November 1938).

38. AVIA46/108 (1 February 1939).

39. AVIA46/256, p. 74.

40. AVIA46/96 (23 March, 11 May 1939).

41. Goulding, J., *Interceptor* (1986), p. 118.

42. AIR2/2964 (2 July 1938).

43. Clarke, R. W., *British Aircraft Armament Vol. 2* (1994), p. 70–71.

44. AIR9/77 (30 March 1939).

45. Buttler, T., *British Secret Projects, Fighters and Bombers 1935–1950* (2004), p. 43.

46. AIR14/433 (May 1938)/AVIA65/1868 (6 July 1937).

47. AVIA7/2009 (18 November1938).

48. AVIA7/2009 (15 March 1939).

49. AIR41/88, p. 112/AVIA7/2009, (15 June 1939)/AIR2/3276, (16 June 1939).

50. AVIA7/2009 (3 July 1939)/Bowen, *Radar Days* (1987), p. 70.

51. AVIA7/2009 (15, 22 June 1939).

52. AVIA7/2009 (3 July 1939).

53. AIR2/2917 (10 July 1939).

54. AIR41/17, pp. 10–11.

55. Baughen, G., 'Chapter 5' and 'Chapter 7' in *The Rise of the Bomber* (2015).

56. Bowen, E. G., *Radar Days* (1987), p. 81.

57. AIR41/39, p. 241.

58. T161/923 (28 October 1938).

59. AIR2/3229 (10 May, 27 June 1938).

60. T161/923 (28 October 1938).

61. AVIA46/256, pp. 33–34.

62. AVIA46/256, p. 74.

63. AIR2/2677 (30 March 1937).

64. AIR20/12 (September 1938).

65. AIR14/154 (2 September 1939).

66. AVIA18/560 (27 August 1938).

67. AIR2/1964 (8 May 1939).

68. AIR2/3276 (14 April 1938).

69. AIR2/3276 (5 December 1938)/AIR2/1964 (8, 18, 23 May 1939).
70. AIR9/97 (8 December 1938).
71. AIR2/2955 (13 December 1938).
72. AIR2/2955 (13 July 1939).
73. AVIA15/118 (1, 28 March 1939).
74. AIR2/2059 (24 February, 16 March 1938).
75. AIR2/2059 (23 June 1939).
76. AIR2/2059 (29 June 1939).
77. AIR2/2613 (23 November 1936).
78. AIR9/97 (21 December 1938).
79. AIR2/3037 (1 April 1938).
80. AIR2/3037 (May 1938).
81. AIR2/2613 (March 1937).
82. AIR9/37 (8 December 1938).
83. AIR14/225 (30 August 1938).
84. AIR2/2613 (March 1937)/AIR2/2677 (9 June 1937).
85. AIR8/251 (19 January 1939).
86. AIR8/251 (21 January 1939).
87. AIR14/131 (13 February 1939).
88. AIR14/131/AIR2/2805 (20 February 1939).
89. AIR14/131 (27 March 1939).
90. AIR14/131 (17 May 1939).
91. AIR2/1964 (8 May 1939).

Chapter 2

1. AIR8/272 (21 April 1939).
2. Bond, B., *Chief of Staff Vol. 1* (1972), p. 143.
3. WO193/685 (29 April 1939).
4. Slessor, J., *Airpower and Armies* (London: OUP 1936) p. 3.
5. *Ibid.* p. 90.
6. AIR2/2059 (4 October 1938).
7. Boyle, A., *Trenchard* (1962), p. 711.
8. AIR9/132 (late 1939).
9. CAB56/5 (21 February 1939).
10. *Ibid.*
11. *Ibid.*
12. *Ibid.*
13. AIR14/818 (17, 21 April 1939).
14. AIR9/97 (22 April 1939).
15. AIR8/272 (probably May 1939).

16. AIR2/2059 (29 June 1939).

17. AIR2/4130 (3 June 1939).

18. AIR8/272 (May 1939).

19. Air2/2059 (9 July 1939).

20. AIR8/272 (12 June 1939).

21. Omissi, D. E., *Airpower and Colonial Control: The Royal Air Force, 1919–1939* (1990) pp. 74-75.

22. Slessor, J., 'Appendix B' in *The Central Blue* (1956), pp. 121–132.

23. Harris, A., *Bomber Offensive* (1990), p. 9.

24. Omissi, D. E., *Airpower and Colonial Control: The Royal Air Force, 1919–1939* (1990), p. 158.

25. Air Historical Branch N.S33143 (November 1934, 13 February 1935).

26. WO233/60, p. 97.

27. AIR16/123 (August 1939).

28. AIR2/3505 (November 1938–May 1939).

29. Air Historical Branch N.S33143 (November 1934, 13 February 1935).

30. CAB36/5 (21 February 1939).

31. AIR2/2964 (June 1938).

32. AIR2/2964 (22 June 1938).

33. AIR2/2964 (19 August 1938).

34. AIR2/2964 (16 November 1938).

35. AIR16/96 (18 July 1939).

36. AIR16/96 (13 March 1939).

37. AIR16/96 (4 May 1939).

38. AIR16/119 (6 April 1939).

39. AIR8/272 (21 April 1939).

40. AIR9/97 (8 May 1939).

41. AIR2/2895 (30 June 1939)

42. AIR8/272 (11 May 1939); James, T. C. G., *The Growth of Fighter Command 1936–1940* (2012), p. 56.

43. AIR16/190, p. 9.

44. AIR8/272 (12 June 1939).

45. James, T. C. G., *The Growth of Fighter Command 1936–1940* (2012), p. 55.

46. AIR16/119 (19 April 1939).

47. AIR16/258 (15 May 1939).

48. AIR16/258 (15 May 1938).

49. AIR16/1024 (31 May 1939).

50. CAB21/521 (12 June 1939).

51. *Ibid.*

52. *Ibid.*

53. *Ibid.*

54. AIR2/2895 (June 1939)/CAB21/521 (June 1939).

55. *Ibid.*

56. Baughen, G., 'Chapter 12' in *Blueprint for Victory* (2014).

57. Bond, B., *Chief of Staff Vol. 1* (1972), p. 142.
58. CAB21/521 (30 June 1939).
59. CAB21/521 (20 September 1939).

Chapter 3

1. James, T. C. G., *The Growth of Fighter Command 1936–1940* (2012), p. 78.
2. Latham, C., and Stobbs, A., *Radar: A Wartime Miracle* (1996), pp. 2–6.
3. Calder, A., *The People's War* (1969), pp. 35–36.
4. Webster, C., and Frankland, N., *The Strategic Air Offensive Against Germany 1939–1945 Vol. 1* (1961), p. 135.
5. AVIA10/19 (14 September 1939).
6. *Ibid.*
7. Boyle, A., *Trenchard* (1962), p. 712; Richards, D., *Portal of Hungerford* (1977), p. 146; AIR20/379 (16 May 1940).
8. WO193/678 (25 September 1939).
9. AIR41/21, p. 41.
10. AIR8/287 (28 September 1939).
11. AIR16/190, p. 26; James, T. C. G., *The Growth of Fighter Command 1936–1940* (2012), p. 75.
12. AIR16/190, p. 28.
13. AIR8/287 (5 October 1939).
14. AIR14/265 (31 October 1939).
15. AIR2/5251 (Barratt response to Brooke-Popham report).
16. CAB21/521 (20 September 1939).
17. CAB21/521 (3 October 1939).
18. *Ibid.*
19. AIR40/1400 (19 October 1939).
20. AIR41/21, pp. 99–100.
21. AIR40/1400 (September 1939).
22. *Ibid.*
23. AIR39/139 (21 November 1939).
24. AIR14/107 (11 November 1939).
25. AIR39/139 (21 November 1939).
26. Baughen, G., 'Chapter 13' in *Blueprint for Victory* (2014).
27. WO193/678 (25–27 September 1939).
28. WO193/678 (27 October 1939).
29. AVIA46/66 (16 October 1939); CAB66/3/27 (3 December 1939).
30. CAB66/3/27 (2 December 1939).
31. *Ibid.*
32. WO193/678 (8 December 1939).
33. WO193/678 (11 December 1939).

34. AIR41/21, pp. 180–181.

35. Bond, B., *Chief of Staff Vol. 1* (1972), p. 248.

36. AIR41/21, pp. 171–172.

37. *Ibid.* pp. 141–142.

38. AIR14/170 (18 September 1939).

39. AIR8/28, (28 September 1939).

40. Price, A., *The Spitfire Story* (1982), pp. 93–100.

41. AIR41/21, p. 77.

42. AIR9/137 (20 December 1939).

43. AIR2/3075 (December 1939).

44. AVIA15/362 (December 1939–February 1940).

45. AVIA46/125, p. 1.

46. AVIA15/227 (28 December 1939).

47. AVIA15/227 (10 January 1940).

48. AVIA15/227 (17 April 1940).

49. AIR2/3193 (12 December 1939).

50. AIR20/3461 (29 March 1940).

51. AIR20/3461 (3 May 1940).

52. AIR41/21, p. 139.

53. AIR2/3456, (27 October 1939, 6 November 1939).

54. AIR2/3456 (23 September 1943).

55. AIR4/412 (16 October 1939).

56. AIR16/123 (21 January 1940).

57. CAB21/521 (October 1939).

58. AIR16/140 (28 October 1939).

Chapter 4

1. Shores, C., *Fledgling Eagles* (1991), pp. 50–51.

2. *Ibid.* pp. 130–133.

3. *Ibid.* pp. 134–140.

4. AIR14/211 (Tactical Memo No. 10).

5. AVIA10/33 (13 November 1939).

6. AIR2/2613 (5 December 1939).

7. AIR20/12 (29 January 1940).

8. AIR14/283 (6 October 1939; AIR20/17 (1 December 1939).

9. AVIA15/142 (7, 12, 30 September, 27 October 1939).

10. AIR2/3126 (4 March 1940).

11. CAB65/11/14 (15 January 1940).

12. AVIA46/256 (July 1940).

13. AIR2/209 (16 November 1939).

14. AIR2/209 (25 November 1939); AIR14/251 (16 January 1940); AIR14/251 (12 December 1939).

15. *Ibid.*

16. AIR2/2059 (12 December 1939).

17. AIR2/2059 (16, 22 November1939).

18. AVIA46/175 (March 1940).

19. AIR14/251 (14 March 1940); AIR20/5553 (22 January 1940).

20. AIR2/3075 (12 March 1940).

21. *Ibid.*

22. *Ibid.*

23. AIR2/2822 (28 January 1940).

24. AIR2/3037 (27 February 1940); AIR2/2822 (February 1940).

25. AIR2/3037 (27 February 1940); AIR2/2822 (3 March 1940).

26. AIR9/97 (12 March 1940); AIR14/251 (7 April 1940).

27. AIR16/1024 (12 March 1940); AIR2/3075 (12 March 1940).

28. AIR2/3037 (12 March 1940).

29. Webster, C., and Frankland, N., *The Strategic Air Offensive Against Germany 1939–1945 Vol. 1* (1961), p. 139.

30. *Ibid.*

31. *Ibid.* pp. 139, 288–9.

32. AIR14/251 (January 1940).

33. Webster, C., and Frankland, N., *The Strategic Air Offensive Against Germany 1939–1945 Vol. 1* (1961) pp. 208–9.

34. Middlebrook, M., and Everitt, C., *The Bomber Command War Diaries* (1990), p. 28.

35. AIR41/21, p. 171.

36. AIR2/7189 (April 1940).

37. AIR2/7189 (30 March 1940).

38. Richards, D., *Portal of Hungerford* (1977), pp 64–65.

39. Webster, C., and Frankland, N., *The Strategic Air Offensive Against Germany 1939–1945 Vol. 1* (1961), p. 141.

40. Richards, D., *Portal of Hungerford* (1977), p. 146.

41. AIR16/190, p. 23.

42. AIR126/101 (20 September 1939).

43. Gunston, B., *Rolls Royce Aero Engines* (1989), p. 77.

44. AVIA46/66 (14 October 1939).

45. AIR6/40 (31 October 1939).

46. Bowen, E. G., *Radar Days* (1987), pp. 92–93.

47. AIR14/121/AVIA7/2009 (18 October 1939).

48. AVIA7/2009 (15 December 1939).

49. AVIA7/2009 (19 December 1939).

50. AIR2/2917 (October 1939); AIR2/8651 (24 February 1940); AIR2/3125 (December 1939).

51. AVIA15/136 (4, 5 January 1940).

52. AVIA7/2009 (2, 5 April 1940).

53. AVIA7/2009 (9 May 1940).

54. AVIA7/2009 (28 May 1940).

55. Hanbury Brown, R., *Boffin* (1991) pp. 59–61.

56. AVIA15/133 (7 May 1940).

57. AIR2/8651 (13 June 1940); AVIA15/136 (13 June 1940); AVIA15/133 (7 May 1940).

58. AIR2/8651 (6 March 1940).

59. AIR2/8651 (15 June 1940).

60. AVIA7/2009 (22 May, 28 May, 4 June 1940).

61. AVIA7/2009 (19 December 1939).

62. Bowen, E. G., *Radar Days* (1987) p. 142; AVIA7/2009 (21 January, 10 February, 29 March 1940).

63. AVIA15/136 (10 July 1940).

64. AVIA7/114 (9 October 1940).

65. James, T. C. G., *The Growth of Fighter Command 1936–1940* (2012), p. 76.

66. AIR41/21, p. 167.

67. Shores, C., *Fledgling Eagles* (1991), p. 147.

68. AIR20/12 (14 December 1939).

69. Richey, P., *Fighter Pilot* (1956), p. 39.

70. *Ibid.* p. 51.

71. AIR2/2037 (19 January 1939).

72. Cuny, J., and Danel, R., *L'Aviation de Chasse Francaise 1918–1940* (1973), p. 144.

73. DSIR 23/7798.

74. Baughen, G., *The Rise of the Bomber* (2015), pp. 1801–81.

75. DSIR 23/7798, (December 1939).

76. AIR35/121 (2 May 1940).

77. AIR20/279 (2, 25 April 1940).

78. AVIA46/66 (14 October 1939).

79. AIR2/3075 (6 December 1939); AVIA15/363 (9 November 1939).

80. AVIA15/142 (30 December 1939); AIR16/347 (March 1940).

81. AVIA15/363 (9 November 1939, 24 March, 1 May 1940); AIR16/361 (29 February 1940).

82. AIR2/2833 (4 January 1939); AVIA15/142 (7, 9, 12 September 1939).

83. AVIA15/142 (30 December 1939).

84. AIR2/3075 (4 March 1940).

85. AIR/16/347 (March 1940).

86. AVIA46/66 (28 October 1939).

87. AIR20/3461 (3 May 1940).

88. AIR20/3461 (22 January 1940).

Chapter 5

1. *The Times*, 5 April 1940.

2. Derry, T. K., *The Campaign in Norway* (1952), p. 16.

3. Shores, C., *Fledgling Eagles* (1991), p. 226.

4. *Ibid.* pp. 248–249.

5. Middlebrook, M., and Everitt, C., *The Bomber Command War Diaries* (1990), p. 33.

6. AIR14/418 (17 June 1940); Gibson, G., *Enemy Coast Ahead*, p. 64.

7. Shores, C., *Fledgling Eagles* (1991), p. 257.

8. *Ibid.* pp. 252–253, 259.

9. AIR41/20, p. 46.

10. Derry, T. K., *The Campaign in Norway* (1952), pp. 75–76.

11. *Ibid.* pp. 89–90.

12. AIR41/20, p. 5; AIR2/5116 (17 April 1940).

13. Shores, C., *Fledgling Eagles* (1991), p. 278.

14. Derry, T. K., *The Campaign in Norway* (1952), p. 117.

15. Shores, C., *Fledgling Eagles* (1991), p. 287.

16. *Ibid.* p. 292.

17. *Ibid.* p. 289.

18. Derry, T. K., *The Campaign in Norway* (1952), p. 119.

19. AIR2/5216 (28 April 1940).

20. WO106/1903 (15 May 1940).

21. Brown, D., *Naval Operations of the Campaign in Norway, April–June 1940* (2005), p. 60.

22. Shores, C., *Fledgling Eagles* (1991), p. 300; Brown, D., *Naval Operations of the Campaign in Norway, April–June 1940* (2005), pp. 133–134.

23. Shores, C., *Fledgling Eagles* (1991), p. 341.

24. Richards, D., *Portal of Hungerford* (1977), p. 147.

25. WO233/60, p. 107.

26. AIR14/107 (23 November 1939).

27. AIR2/3192 (11 November 1939, 3 January 1940).

28. AIR2/3192 (22 December 1939, 3, 16 January 1940).

29. CAB65/12/22 (12 April 1940).

30. WO106/1596 (20 April 1940).

31. CAB65/12/30 (21 April 1940).

32. WO106/1596 (20 April, 1, 5 May 1940).

33. WO106/1596 (20 April 1940).

34. WO106/1596 (5 May 1940).

35. WO193/678 (7 May 1940).

36. CAB65/13/4 (7 May 1940).

37. CAB65/13/5 (8 May 1940).

38. AIR41/21, p. 184.

39. AIR2/7265 (3 May 1940).

40. AIR20/2061 (2 May 1940).

41. *Ibid.*

42. AIR2/7265 (7 May 1940); AIR14/265 (7 May 1940).

43. CAB80/10 (3 May 1940).

44. AIR2/3192 (23, 30 April 1940).

45. AIR9/125 (4 May 1940).

46. *Ibid.*

Chapter 6

1. Horne, A., *To Lose a Battle* (1982), pp. 217-218.

2. Cuny, J., and Danel, R., *L'Aviation de Chasse Francaise 1918–1940* (1973), p. 181.

3. *Ibid.* 'Chapter 8', 'Chapter 9'

4. Icare, N., *La Bataille de France Vol. 9: L'Aviation Neerlandaise* (1977).

5. AIR14/773 (4 May 1940).

6. AIR41/21, p. 168.

7. Hooton, E. R., *Phoenix Triumphant* (1994), p. 242.

8. Icare, N., *La Bataille de France Vol. 9: L'Aviation Neerlandaise* (1977).

9. Hooton, E. R., *Phoenix Triumphant* (1994), pp. 240, 242.

10. AIR40/21, pp. 193–194.

11. Cull, B., Lander, B., and Weiss, H., *Twelve Days in May* (1995), pp. 55–56.

12. Icare, N., *La Bataille de France Vol. 9: L'Aviation Neerlandaise* (1977), pp. 38–41.

13. Offenberg, J., *Lonely Warrior* (St Albans: Mayflower Publishing, 1974), p. 13.

14. *Service Historique de a Defense Vincennes* (sorties May–June 1940).

15. Hooton, E. R., *Phoenix Triumphant* (1994), p. 247.

16. Bingham, V. F., *Blitzed* (1990), pp. 232–3.

17. AIR35/354, p. 15; Richey, P., *Fighter Pilot* (1956), pp. 92–93.

18. Simpson, W., *One of Our Pilots is Safe* (1942), pp. 54–7.

19. Icare, N., *La Bataille de France Vol. 9: L'Aviation Neerlandaise* (1977), pp. 38–40.

20. AIR35/326 (May 1940).

21. AIR20/2061 (10 May 1940).

22. CAB65/7/10 (10 May 1940).

23. AIR14/773 (10 May 1940).

24. Middlebrook, M., and Everitt, C., *The Bomber Command War Diaries* (1990), p. 41.

25. AIR35/326 (May 1940 report).

26. *Ibid.*

27. AIR41/21, p. 199; Cull, B., Lander, B., and Weiss, H., *Twelve Days in May* (1995), pp. 59–60.

28. WO208/714 (12 May 1940).

29. AIR41/21, p. 207.

30. Icare, N., *La Bataille de France Vol. 9: L'Aviation Neerlandaise* (1977), pp. 44–47.

31. WO208/714 (13 May 1940).

32. AIR41/21, p. 213.

33. Foot, M. R. D., *Holland at War Against Hitler: Anglo-Dutch Relations, 1940–1945,* (1990) p. 45.

34. WO208/714 (13 May 1940).

Chapter 7

1. CAB65/7/10 (10 May 1940).
2. Paquier, P., *Aviation de Bombardment Francaise* (1948), p. 232.
3. AIR41/21, pp. 196–197.
4. AIR41/6, p. 165.
5. Icare, N., *La Bataille de France Vol. 8: L'Aeronautique Militaire Belge* (1977).
6. Middlebrook, M. and Everitt, C., *The Bomber Command War Diaries* (1990), p. 42.
7. Paquier, P., *Aviation de Bombardment Francaise* (1948), p. 232.
8. Richards, D., *The Fight at Odds* (1974), p. 117.
9. Icare, N., *La Bataille de France Vol. 10: L'Aviation d'Assaut*, p. 24.
10. Galland, A., *The First and the Last* (1970), p. 13.
11. Ellis, L. F., *The War in France in Flanders* (1954), p. 54.
12. Chapman, G., *Why France Collapsed* (1968), pp. 104–105.
13. AIR41/21, p. 206.
14. Guderian, H., *Panzer Leader* (1976), p. 100.
15. AIR41/21, p. 207.
16. AIR41/21, p. 213.
17. Chapman, G., *Why France Collapsed* (1968), pp. 119–12.
18. AIR41/21, p. 212.
19. Shirer, *The Collapse of the Third Republic* (1970), pp 629–630.
20. Astier, *Le Ciel n'etait pas Vide* (1952).
21. AIR41/21, p. 220.
22. Shirer, W. L., *The Collapse of the Third Republic* (1970), pp. 629–630.
23. AIR41/21, p. 221.
24. Cull, B., Lander, B., and Weiss, H., *Twelve Days in May* (1995), p. 133.
25. *Le Service Historique de la Defense Vincennes*, Unit histories GC1/1, GCII/1, GCII/10, GC III/10.
26. Icare, N., *La Bataille de France Vol. 3* (1977), p. 63.
27. Bond, B., *Chief of Staff Vol. 1* (1972), p. 311.
28. Ellis, L. F., *The War in France in Flanders* (1954), p. 56.
29. Cull, B., Lander, B., and Weiss, H., *Twelve Days in May* (1995), pp. 137–138.
30. Middlebrook, M. and Everitt, C., *The Bomber Command War Diaries* (1990), p. 42.
31. Ellis, L. F., *The War in France in Flanders* (1954), p. 56.
32. Horne, A., *To Lose a Battle* (1982) pp. 383–387, 406–409.

Chapter 8

1. Richards, D., *Portal of Hungerford* (1977), p. 146.
2. CAB65/7/11 (10 May 1940).
3. CAB65/13/11 (10 May 1940).

4. CAB65/13 (12 May 1940).

5. *Ibid.*

6. AIR14/773 (13 May 1940).

7. CAB65/13/7 (13 May 1940).

8. *Ibid.*

9. *Ibid.*

10. AIR14/449 (14 May 1940).

11. CAB65/7/17 (14 May 1940).

12. *Ibid.*

13. CAB65/13/9 (15 May 1940).

14. Wright, R., *Dowding and the Battle of Britain* (1970), pp. 103–104.

15. *Ibid.*

16. AIR41/22, Appendix M.

17. Cull, B., Lander, B., and Weiss, H., *Twelve Days in May* (1995), pp. 55–56, 78–79, 96–97, 112, 137–138.

18. Bingham, V. F., *Blitzed* (1990), pp. 222–226.

19. CAB65/13/8 (14 May 1940).

20. CAB65/13/9 (15 May 1940).

21. *Ibid.*

22. AIR65/13/9 (15 May 1940).

23. CAB65/13/9 (15 May 1940).

24. Middlebrook, M., and Everitt, C., *The Bomber Command War Diaries* (1990), p. 43.

25. CAB65/13 (16 May 1940).

26. *The Times*, 17 May 1940.

27. AIR20/379 (16 May 1940).

28. *Ibid.*

29. CAB65/13 (16 May 1940).

30. Churchill, W., *Their Finest Hour* (1952), pp. 52–57.

31. AIR41/21, p. 461.

32. Baughen, G., *Blueprint for Victory* (2014), pp. 145–146.

33. Gibson, G., *Enemy Coast Ahead* (1955), pp. 84–86.

34. Bingham, V. F., *Blitzed* (1990), pp 77–78.

35. *Ibid.* p. 84.

36. AIR20/23 (17 May 1940).

37. *Ibid.* (18 May 1940).

38. AIR9/90 (19 May 1940).

39. AIR41/21, p. 276.

Chapter 9

1. AIR41/21, pp. 218–224.
2. *Ibid.* pp. 201–202.
3. Cull, B., Lander, B., and Weiss, H., *Twelve Days in May* (1995), pp. 193–194.
4. Ellis, L. F., *The War in France in Flanders* (1954), p. 81.
5. Cull, B., Lander, B., and Weiss, H., *Twelve Days in May* (1995), pp. 280, 283–285, 292.
6. *Ibid.* p. 292.
7. James, T. C. G., *The Growth of Fighter Command 1936–1940* (2012), p. 133–4.
8. CAB65/13/13 (20 May 1940).
9. Bingham, V. F., *Blitzed* (1990) p. 92.
10. Cull, B., Lander, B., and Weiss, H., *Twelve Days in May* (1995), p. 290.
11. *Ibid.* p. 288.
12. *Ibid.* p. 295.
13. *Ibid.* p. 303.
14. Bond, B., *Chief of Staff Vol. 1* (1972), p. 327.
15. James, T. C. G., *The Growth of Fighter Command 1936–1940* (2012), pp. 139–40; AIR16/347 (24 May 1940).
16. *Ibid.*
17. *Ibid.*
18. CAB65/13 (18 May 1940).
19. Speidel, W., 'The German Air Force in France and the Low Countries' in *USAF Historical Studies* No. 152 (unpublished), pp. 238, 257.
20. Middlebrook, M., and Everitt, C., *The Bomber Command War Diaries* (1990), p. 43.
21. AIR41/21, p. 286.
22. Ellis, L. F., *The War in France in Flanders* (1954), p. 116.
23. AIR20/2061 (21 May 1940).
24. AIR20/2061 (21 May 1940); AIR27/1018 (21 May 1940).
25. AIR16/900 (21 May 1940).
26. AIR20/2061 (21 May 1940).
27. Cull, B., Lander, B., and Weiss, H., *Twelve Days in May* (1995), p. 303.
28. AIR16/900 (22 May 1940).
29. *Ibid.*
30. Cull, B., Lander, B., and Weiss, H., *Twelve Days in May* (1995), p. 315.
31. AIR41/21, p. 300.
32. CAB65/13 (22 May 1940).
33. Bond, B., *Chief of Staff Vol. 1* (1972), p. 336.
34. AIR16/347 (23 May 1940).
35. AIR16/99 (24 May 1940).
36. Richards, D., *The Fight at Odds* (1974), p. 129.
37. CAB66/7/48 (25 May 1940); CAB66/7/49 (26 May 1940).

38. AIR41/6, p. 158; Webster, C., and Frankland, N., *The Strategic Air Offensive Against Germany 1939–1945 Vol. 1* (1961), pp. 211, 221.

39. AIR2/7218 (26 May 1940).

40. Middlebrook, M., and Everitt, C., *The Bomber Command War Diaries* (1990), p. 47.

41. *Ibid.*

42. CAB65/7/39 (28 May 1940).

43. *Ibid.*

44. AIR41/21, p. 330.

45. AIR41/21, p. 334.

46. Franks, N., *Air Battle for Dunkirk* (2006), p. 163.

47. AIR20/2061 (28, 29 May 1940).

48. Hooton, E. R., *Phoenix Triumphant* (1994), p. 259.

49. CAB65/7/39 (28 May 1940).

50. Hooton, E. R., *Phoenix Triumphant* (1994), p. 260.

51. Franks, N., *Air Battle for Dunkirk* (2006), p. 25.

52. *The London Gazette*, 15 July 1947.

53. Franks, N., *Air Battle for Dunkirk* (2006), pp. 170–184.

54. Hooton, E. R., *Phoenix Triumphant* (1994), p. 260.

55. Franks, N., *Air Battle for Dunkirk* (2006), pp. 163, 166, 156, 140.

56. Gibson, G., *Enemy Coast Ahead* (1955), p. 83.

57. CAB65/13/31 (3 June 1940).

58. *Ibid.*

59. AIR8/278 (20 May, 4 June 1940).

60. CAB65/13/31 (20 May 1940); AIR41/22, Appendix M.

61. CAB65/13/31 (20 May 1940).

62. AIR8/278 (4 June 1940); AIR41/22, Appendix M.

63. Franks, N., *Air Battle for Dunkirk* (2006), p. 186; Cull, B., Lander, B., and Weiss, H., *Twelve Days in May* (1995), p. 307.

64. Wood, D., Dempster, D., 'Appendix 10' in *The Narrow Margin* (1967).f

65. CAB65/13/31 (3 June 1940).

66. Churchill, W., *Their Finest Hour* (1952), p. 116.

67. AIR16/216 (15 June 1940).

68. AIR41/21, p. 476.

69. CAB66/7/48 (23 May 1940).

70. Churchill, W., *Their Finest Hour* (1952), p. 505.

Chapter 10

1. Collier, B., *The Defence of the United Kingdom* (1995) p. 130; Postan, M. M., *British War Production* (1952), p. 117.

2. CAB66/9/16 (30 June 1940).

3. WO106/1596 (June 1940); WO106/1757, p. 15.

4. WO106/1757 (10 June 1940).

5. AIR9/137 (22 June 1940).

6. WO106/1757 (10 June 1940).

7. WO106/1757 (20 June 1940).

8. Alanbrooke, *War Diaries 1939–1945* (2001), p. 100.

9. CAB66/11/50 (14 September 1940); WO193/678 (19 September 1940).

10. WO193/678 (9 October 1940).

11. AVIA46/68 (May 1940).

12. AIR16/347 (30 June 1940).

13. AIR8/258 (June 1940).

14. AIR8/892 (August 1940).

15. AIR39/139 (5 June 1940).

16. AIR2/5251 (16 July 1940).

17. AIR39/139 (August–September 1940).

18. WO233/60, pp. 123–124.

19. AIR2/5251 (16 July 1940).

20. AIR41/6, p. 183.

21. *Ibid*. p. 209; Price, A., *The Spitfire Story* (1982), p. 100.

22. AIR16/659 (8 July 1940).

23. AIR41/6 p. 209.

24. AIR9/37 (November 1935).

25. AVIA15/533 (28 May, 5 June 1940).

26. AVIA15/536 (14 June 1940).

27. AIR2/7230 (16 June 1940).

28. AVIA15/536 (13 June, 1940).

29. AIR14/267 (2 July 1940); AIR16/347 (3 July 1940).

30. WO193/678 (26 July 1940).

31. AVIA15/536 (12 June 1940).

32. AVIA15/536 (14, 17, 18 June 1940).

33. AVIA15/536 (14, 17 June 1940).

34. AIR14/266 (18, 22, 31 May 1940).

35. AIR14/265 (May–June 1940).

36. AIR14/266 (28 June 1940); AIR14/265 (June 1940).

37. AIR14/266 (28 June 1940).

38. AIR6/40 (12 December 1939, 2, 30 January 1940).

39. McVickar Haight, J., *American Aid to France 1938–1940* (1970), pp. 189–197.

40. AIR20/3461 (3 May 1940).

41. Churchill, W., *Their Finest Hour* (1952), p. 35.

42. *Ibid*. p. 60.

43. AVIA10/126 (16 June 1940).

44. AIR19/524.

45. AIR20/3461 (7 July 1940).

46. AVIA18/700 (22 April 1940).

47. AIR20/12762 (5 November 1940).

48. AIR9/137 (2 August 1940).

49. Cuny, J., and Danel, R., *L'Aviation de Chasse Francaise 1918–1940* (1973), p. 231; Green, W., *Warplanes of the Second World War Fighters Vol. 4* (1966), p. 30.

50. AIR20/5552, (29 May, 7 June 1940); AIR20/3461 (18 June, 23, 25 July 1940).

51. AIR20/3461 (25 July 1940).

52. AIR20/5777 (26 August 1940).

53. *Ibid.*

54. AIR20/5777 (30 August 1940).

55. AIR20/3461 (7 July 1940).

56. Brown, A., *Airmen in Exile* (2000), pp. 23–30.

57. AIR2/7196 (4 May 1940).

58. AIR2/7196 (22 May 1940.)

59. AIR2/7196 (1, 3 June 1940).

60. AIR14/1075 (14 July 1940).

61. AIR2/7196 (14 July 1940).

62. AIR14/266 (June 1940).

63. AIR16/347 (30 June 1940).

64. AIR20/5777 (1 July 1940).

65. AIR20/3461 (7 July 1940).

66. Brown, A., *Airmen in Exile* (2000), pp. 30–31.

67. *Ibid.* pp. 91–92.

68. AIR20/251 (20 July 1940).

69. AIR14/1075 (14 (July 1940); AIR20/251 (29 July 1940); AIR20/3461 (3 August 1940).

70. AIR2/5196 (20 July 1940).

71. AIR20/251 (29 July 1940); AIR2/5196 (20 July 1940).

Chapter 11

1. AIR25/578 (6 July 1940).

2. Bowyer, M. J. F., *Aircraft of the Few* (1991), p. 121.

3. AIR20/5298 (28 June 1940).

4. AIR14/266 (24 May, 2 June 1940).

5. AIR14/266 (28 June 1940).

6. AIR14/267 (1, 16 July 1940); AIR20/5298 (9 August 1940).

7. AIR14/267 (16 July 1940).

8. AIR2/7294 (25 June 1940).

9. AIR14/267 (29 June 1940).

10. AIR39/49 (2 July 1940).

11. AIR41/40, p. 110.

12. Webster, C., and Frankland, N., *The Strategic Air Offensive Against Germany 1939–1945 Vol. 4* (1961), p. 115.

13. AIR41/40, p. 117.

14. Webster, C., and Frankland, N., *The Strategic Air Offensive Against Germany 1939–1945 Vol. 4* (1961), p. 120.

15. AIR14/267 (25 July 1940).

16. AIR14/267 (25 July 1940); AIR39/49.

17. AIR14/266 (31 May 1940); MacBean, J. A., and Hogben, A. S., *Bombs Gone* (1990), pp. 252–3.

18. AIR14/385 (31 July 1940).

19. AIR14/283 (5, 17 May 1940); AIR14/418 (April–July 1940).

20. AIR14/267 (7 August 1940).

21. AIR14/265 (2 July 1940); AIR14/266 (1 July 1940).

22. AIR39/49 (30 July 1940).

23. AIR14/267 (2 July 1940); AIR8/272 (2 July 1940).

24. AIR2/7218 (15 August 1940).

25. AIR14/267 (24 July 1940).

26. *Ibid.*

27. AIR2/7294 (5 August 1940).

28. AIR20/5298 (18 August 1940).

29. Baughen, G., *The Rise of the Bomber* (2015), p. 80.

30. AIR20/5777 (23 July 1940).

31. AIR20/5777 (17 August 1940); AIR20/3461 (17 August 1940).

32. AIR20/3461 (17 August 1940).

33. AIR14/267 (19, 25 July 1940).

34. AIR2/7210 (29 June 1940).

35. AIR2/7210 (30 July 1940/AIR14/267 (25 July 1940).

36. AIR16/216 (20 June 1940).

37. AIR14/267 (26 July 1940).

38. AIR16/347 (3 July 1940).

39. *Ibid.*

40. AIR16/347 (3 July 1940).

41. AIR16/212 (8 July 1940).

42. AIR2/7210 (30 July 1940).

43. Speidel, W., 'The German Air Force in France and the Low Countries' in *USAF Historical Studies* No. 152 (unpublished), p. 42.

44. Schenck, P., *Invasion of England 1940* (1990), pp. 10–12.

45. Cuny, J., and Danel, R., *L'Aviation de Chasse Francaise 1918-1940* (1973), p. 190.

Chapter 12

1. AIR16/352 (8 July 1940).
2. AIR16/281 (17 May 1940).
3. AIR16/281 (23, 29 May 1940).
4. AIR16/281 (June 1940).
5. AIR16/216 (9 June 1940).
6. Franks, N., *Air Battle for Dunkirk* (2006), pp. 167–8.
7. Price, A., *The Spitfire Story* (1982), p. 82.
8. Mason, F. K., *Battle Over Britain* (1969), p. 130.
9. *Ibid.* pp. 133–146.
10. Hooton, E. R., *Eagle in Flames* (1997), pp. 14-15.
11. AIR24/526 (3 July 1940).
12. AIR16/216 (28 June 1940).
13. Mason, F. K., *Battle Over Britain* (1969), pp. 595, 598.
14. Wood, D., Dempster, D., 'Appendix 10' in *The Narrow Margin* (1967).
15. Mason, F. K., *Battle Over Britain* (1969), pp. 225–6.
16. Wood, D., Dempster, D., 'Appendix 10' in *The Narrow Margin* (1967).
17. AIR20/5777 (12 August 194); AIR20/251 (12 August 1940).
18. AIR20/251 (13 August 1940); AIR41/15, p. 222.
19. AIR20/251 (12 August 1940).
20. Bekker, C., *The Luftwaffe War Diaries* (1966), p. 147.
21. Mason, F. K., *Battle Over Britain* (1969), pp. 230–235.
22. Bekker, C., *The Luftwaffe War Diaries* (1966), p. 154.
23. Mason, F. K., *Battle Over Britain* (1969), p. 241.
24. AIR19/226 (27 August 1940).
25. Hooton, E. R., *Eagle in Flames* (1997), p. 20.
26. Mason, F. K., *Battle Over Britain* (1969), pp. 266–268, 273.
27. *Ibid.* p. 271–273.
28. Mason, F. K., *Battle Over Britain* (1969), pp. 280–84.
29. Wood, D., Dempster, D., *The Narrow Margin* (1967), p. 477.
30. Mason, F. K., *Battle Over Britain* (1969), p. 260.
31. Price, A., *The Hardest Day* (1979), p. 163.
32. *Ibid.* p. 189.
33. Mason, F. K., *Battle Over Britain* (1969), pp. 595, 598.
34. AIR25/197 (17 August 1940).
35. AIR41/15, p. 223.
36. AIR20/5777 (12 August 1940).
37. AIR41/15, p. 225; AIR20/3461 (17 August 1940).
38. *Ibid.*
39. Mason, F. K., *Battle Over Britain* (1969) p. 595.
40. AIR20/3461 (17 August 1940).

41. AIR19/524 (Deliveries of North American Aircraft)/Bowyer, M. J. F., *Aircraft of the Few* (1991), p. 245; Wood, D., Dempster, D., *The Narrow Margin* (1967), p. 475.

42. AIR19/173 (17 August 1940); AIR20/3461 (17 August 1940).

43. McVickar Haight, J., *American Aid to France 1938–1940* (1970), p. 252.

44. Mason, F. K., *Battle Over Britain* (1969) p. 294; Collier, B., *The Defence of the United Kingdom* (1995), p. 464.

45. AVIA15/600 (1 August 1940).

46. AIR16/330 (7 September 1940).

47. Wood, D., Dempster, D., *The Narrow Margin* (1967), pp. 321–329.

48. AIR41/15, p. 392.

49. AIR20/252 (3 September 1940).

50. Collier, B., *The Defence of the United Kingdom* (1995), p. 215.

51. Ray, J., *The Battle of Britain: New Perspectives* (1994), p. 96.

52. Wood, D., Dempster, D., *The Narrow Margin* (1967), p. 300.

53. *Ibid.* p. 315.

54. Ray, J., *The Battle of Britain: New Perspectives* (1994), p. 87.

55. AIR16/330 (26 August 1940).

56. AIR41/15, p. 396.

57. Mason, F. K., *Battle Over Britain* (1969) pp. 330–331, 595.

Chapter 13

1. AIR25/197 (30 August 1940).

2. AIR16/330 (4 September 1940).

3. AIR16/365 (1 September 1940).

4. Mason, F. K., *Battle Over Britain* (1969) pp. 334–357.

5. Ray, J., *The Battle of Britain: New Perspectives* (1994), p. 101.

6. AIR41/16, Appendix 11.

7. Mason, F. K., *Battle Over Britain* (1969), p. 348.

8. *Ibid.* p. 354.

9. Ritchie, N. S., *Industry and Airpower* (1997), p. 236.

10. CAB65/14/27 (30 August 1940).

11. AIR20/252 (4 September 1940).

12. AIR16/330 (7 September 1940).

13. *Ibid.*

14. AIR41/15, pp. 399–400.

15. AIR16/330 (7 September 1940).

16. AIR16/1067 (28 August 1940).

17. Mason, F. K., *Battle Over Britain* (1969) p. 337.

18. Hooton, E. R., *Eagle in Flames* (1997), p. 24.

19. Schenck, P., *Invasion of England 1940* (1990), pp. 19–144.

20. Postan, M. M., *British War Production* (1952), p. 117.

21. Alanbrooke, *War Diaries 1939-1945* (2001), p. 108.

22. Hooton, E. R., *Eagle in Flames* (1997), p. 28.

23. AIR41/16, Appendix 16.

24. AIR2/7210 (September 1940).

25. AIR16/330 (7 September 1940).

26. AIR20/5777 (26 August 1940); Bowyer, M. J. F., *Aircraft of the Few* (1991), p. 207–210.

27. AIR8/278 (3 September 1940); Wood, D., Dempster, D., *The Narrow Margin* (1967), p. 475; Bowyer, M. J. F., *Aircraft of the Few* (1991), p. 245.

28. Churchill, W., *Their Finest Hour* (1952), pp. 520–1.

29. Hooton, E. R., *Eagle in Flames* (1997), pp. 25–26.

30. *Ibid.* p. 26; Mason, F. K., *Battle Over Britain* (1969), pp. 365–9.

31. Mason, F. K., *Battle Over Britain* (1969), pp. 374–379.

32. *Ibid.* p. 374.

33. AIR16/330 (9 September 1940).

34. Ray, J., *The Battle of Britain: New Perspectives* (1994), pp. 102–104.

35. Newton Dunn, B., *Big Wing* (1992), p. 75.

36. Ray, J., *The Battle of Britain: New Perspectives* (1994), p. 180.

37. Hooton, E. R., *Eagle in Flames* (1997), p. 27.

38. Mason, F. K., *Battle Over Britain* (1969) p. 388.

39. Douglas, S., and Wright, R., *Sholto Douglas*, (1966), pp. 81–82.

Chapter 14

1. Baughen, G., *The Rise of the Bomber* (2015).

2. Cab66/9/35 (6 June, 9 July 1940).

3. Collier, B., *The Defence of the United Kingdom* (1995), pp. 237, 494.

4. *Ibid.* p. 239.

5. AIR2/7395 (18 September 1940).

6. AIR2/7395 (18 September 1940); AVIA7/251 (3 September); AVIA7/251 (23 October 1940).

7. AVIA7/251 (29 November1940).

8. AIR2/7395 (6 July 1941).

9. AIR15/133 (10 May 1940).

10. Hanbury Brown, R., *Boffin* (1991), p. 58.

11. AIR41/17, pp. 34, 40.

12. Jones, R. V., *Most Secret War* (1981), pp. 126–127.

13. *Ibid.*

14. AIR41/17, p. 33.

15. Mason, F. K., 'Appendix M' in *Battle Over Britain* (1969).

16. PREM3/22/2 (15 July 1940).

17. AVIA15/133 (June–July 1940).

18. AIR2/5170 (10 July 1940).

19. AIR2/7180 (29 August 1940).

20. Mason, F. K., *Battle Over Britain* (1969), p. 243.

21. Baughen, G., *The Rise of the Bomber* (2015), p. 183.

22. Collier, B., *The Defence of the United Kingdom* (1995), pp. 211–213.

23. AIR41/16, Appendix 16.

24. AIR16/1067, (28 August 1940).

25. Collier, B., 'Appendix 26' in *The Defence of the United Kingdom* (1995).

26. CAB65/9/11 (13 September 1940).

27. Churchill, W., *Their Finest Hour* (1952), p. 303.

28. CAB.68/7/16 (5 October 1940).

29. AIR16/380 (26 September, 24 October 1940).

30. AIR41/17, pp. 12–15, 59–63; Latham, C., and Stobbs, R., *Radar: A Wartime Miracle* (1996), pp. 60–62.

31. Price, A., *Blitz on London 1939–1945* (1976), p. 95.

32. Rawnsley, C. F., *Night Fighter* (1975), p. 61.

33. Hanbury Brown, R., *Boffin* (1991), p. 65.

34. White, I., *The History of Air Intercept Radar and the British Nightfighter* (2007), p. 102.

35. AVIA7/114 (December 1940–March 1941).

36. White, I., *The History of Air Intercept Radar and the British Nightfighter* (2007), p. 100.

37. Cab66/13/7 (27 October 1940).

38. Ray, J., *The Battle of Britain: New Perspectives* (1994), pp. 136–137.

39. AIR2/8420/AIR16/380 (18 October 1940).

40. AIR2/8420 (October 1940).

41. Churchill, W., *Their Finest Hour* (1952), p. 303.

42. AIR41/7, pp. 84–88.

43. Air41/17, p. 86.

44. AIR41/17, p. 87.

45. CAB65/10/10 (18 November 1940).

46. AIR41/17, p. 88.

47. Trevor-Roper, H., *Hitler's War Directives 1939–1945* (1973), p. 102.

48. CAB66/13/7; Price, A., *The Spitfire Story* (1982), pp. 115–118.

49. Ritchie, N. S., *Industry and Airpower* (1997), p. 235.

50. Collier, B., *The Defence of the United Kingdom* (1995), p. 509.

51. AIR2/517.

52. Sharp, C. M., and Bowyer, M. J. F., *Mosquito* (1971), p. 55; Buttler, T., *British Secret Projects, Fighters and Bombers 1935-1950* (2004), p. 63.

53. AIR20/2910 (23 April 1941).

54. AIR41/17, p. 110.

55. Baughen, G., *Blueprint for Victory* (2014), p. 16.

Appendix I: Aircraft Performance

Unless otherwise stated, mg refers to 0.303-calibre machine guns.

FIGHTERS	Prototype first flight	Engine	Speed (mph) at altitude (ft)	Range (miles)/ Endurance (hours)	Climb to (ft/min-sec)	Ceiling (ft)	Empty weight (lbs)	Loaded weight (lbs)	Wing area (sq ft)	Armament
Boulton Paul Defiant	11/08/1937	1,030 Merlin III	315/16,500	465 mi.	15,000/10-6	30,350	5,868	7,510	250	4 × mg
Boulton Paul F.11/37	project	2 × 1,710-hp Vulture	371/15,000					17,697	650	4 × 20-mm cannon
Brewster Buffalo	12/1937	1,200-hp Wright Cyclone GR-1820-G 205A	313/13,500	650 mi.		30,500	4,479	6,840	209	4 × 0.5 mg
Bristol Beaufighter	17/07/1939	2 × 1,590-hp Hercules	323/15,000	1,500 mi.	20,000/14-6	28,900	14,069	20,800	503	6 × mg 4 × 20-mm cannon
Bristol Blenheim IF		2 × 840-hp Mercury XV	260/12,000	1,460 mi.	15,000/15-0	24,600	9,200	13,800	469	6 × mg
Curtiss P-36 (Hawk A-3 / Mohawk III)		1,050-hp Pratt & Whitney R-1830-S1C3-	311/10,000	820 mi.	15,000/4-54	33,700	4,620	5,996	236	6 × mg
Curtiss P-40 (Tomahawk I)	10/1938	1,040-hp Allison V-1710-33	357/15,000	650 mi.	15,000/5-18	32,750	5,376	7,326	236	4 × mg 2 × 0.5 mg
Dewoitine D520	02/10/1938	910-hp Hispano-Suiza 12Y45	329/19,685	777 mi.	13,120/4-0	36,090	4,608	6,129	172	4 × mg1 × 20-mm cannon
Gloster F.5/34	12/1936	840-hp Mercury IX	316/16,000		20,000/11	32,500	4,190	5,400	230	8 × mg
Gloster G.39 (F.9/37)	03/04/1939	2 × 1,050-hp Taurus TE/1	354/16,000			30,000	8,828	11,615	386	5 × 20-mm cannon
Gloster Gauntlet	01/1930	775-hp Mercury VIS	223/15,000	425 mi.	10,000/4-12	33,200	2,823	3,937	315	2 × mg

	Prototype first flight	Engine	Speed (mph) at altitude(ft)	Range (miles)/ Endurance (hours)	Climb to (ft/min-sec)	Ceiling (ft)	Empty weight (lbs)	Loaded weight (lbs)	Wing area (sq ft)	Armament
Gloster Gladiator I	09/1934	840-hp Mercury IX	253/14,000	410 mi.	15,000/5-48	33,000	3,476	4,750	323	4 × mg
Handley Page Harrow	10/10/1936	2 × 950-hp Pegasus XX	198/9,500	1,907 mi.	15,000/24-30	20,200	14,824	23,005	1,090	140 × 14 lb aerial mines
Hawker Tornado	06/10/1939	1,980-hp Vulture V	398/23,000		20,000/7-12	34,900	8,377	10.688	283	12 × mg or 4 × 20 mm cannon
Hawker Demon	1931	580-hp Kestrel IIS	181/15,000	3.3 hrs	10,000/7-24	24,500	3,067	4,464	347	3 × mg
Hawker Hurricane	06/11/1935	1,030-hp Merlin C	315/16,500	425 mi.	20,000/8-21	34,500	4,743	5,672	258	8 × mg
Messerschmitt Bf 109B	29/05/1935	680-hp Jumo 210D	289/13,120	430 mi.	19,685/9-48	26,900	3,318	4,740	174	2 × mg
Messerschmitt Bf 109E	Summer 1938	1,100-hp Daimler Benz DB 601A	354/12,300	412 mi.	16,500/6-12	36,000	4,421	5,523	174	2 × mg 2 × 20-mm cannon
Messerschmitt Bf 110C	12/05/1936	2 × 1,100-hp Daimler-Benz 601A	349/22,965	565 mi.	18,000/8-30	32,000	11,466	14,884	413	5 × mg 2 × 20-mm cannon
Morane Saulnier MS 406	08/08/1935	860-hp Hispano-Suiza 12Y31	302/16,000	497 mi.	16,400/6-0	30,840	4,189	5,364	172	2 × mg 1 × 20-mm cannon
Supermarine Spitfire	05/03/1936	1,030-hp Merlin II	360/20,000	575 mi.	15,000/6-30	31,900	4,482	5,819	242	8 × mg
Westland Whirlwind	11/10/1938	2 × 885-hp Peregrine	360/15,000		15,000/5-48	30,000	7,840	10,270	250	4 × 20-mm cannon

BOMBERS

	Prototype first flight	Engine	Speed (mph) at altitude (ft)	Range (miles)/ Endurance (hours)	Ceiling (ft)	Empty weight (lbs)	Loaded weight (lbs)	Wing area (sq ft)	Bomb load (lbs) Armament
Armstrong-Whitworth Whitley I	16/03/1936	2 × 795-hp Tiger IX	192/7,000	1,250 mi.	19,200	14,275	21,600	1,138	3,365 2 × mg
Bristol Blenheim I	25/06/1936	2 × 840-hp Mercury VIII	279/15,000	1,000 mi.	31,400	8,483	11,776	469	1,000 2 × mg
Bristol Blenheim IV	24/9/1937	2 × 920-hp Mercury XV	266	1,460 mi.	22,000	8,700	13,400	469	1,000 4 × mg
Dornier Do 17 Z-2	1934	2 × 940-hp Bramo Fafnir 323 P	255/13,120	720 mi.	22,965	11,484	18,931	592	2,205 6 × mg
Douglas DB-7 (Boston I)	26/10/1938	2 × 1,050-hp Pratt & Whitney R-1830-SC3G	305	462 mi.	31,650	11,400	15,150	465	1,000 6 × mg (four fixed)
Handley Page Hampden	21/06/1936	2 × 950-hp Pegasus XVIII	254/10,000	1460 mi.	24,300	11,761	18,750	718	2,100 3 × mg
Heinkel He 111P-4	24/02/1935	2 × 1,015-hp Daimler Benz DB 601	247/16,400	1,224 mi.	26,250	14,936	29,762	943	4,400 6/7 × mg
Junkers Ju 88 A-1	21/12/1936	2 × 1,210-hp Jumo 211B/1	280/18,050	1,055 mi.	26,250	16,975	22,840	565	3,960 4 × mg
Martin 167 (Maryland)	14/03/1939	2 × 1,050-hp Pratt & Whitney R-1830-SC3G	294/13,000	1,870 mi.	27,200	11,000	17,890	452	1,800 6 × mg (four fixed)
Vickers Wellington Ia	15/06/1936	2 × 1,000-hp Pegasus XVIII	245/15,000	1,600 mi.	18,500	18,213	26,641	840	4,500 6 × mg

ARMY CO-OPERATION/GROUND ATTACK

	Prototype First flight	Engine	Speed (mph) at altitude (ft)	Range (miles)/ Endurance (hours)	Ceiling (ft)	Empty Weight (lbs)	Loaded Weight (lbs)	Wing area (sq ft)	Bomb load (lbs) Armament
Breguet 693	23/03/1938	2 × 680-hp Gnome Rhone 14M	304/16,000	790 mi.	27,900	6,403	10,614	313	880 1 × 20-mm cannon 3 × mg (2 fixed)
Cierva (Avro) C.30 autogyro	04/1933	140-hp Genet Major	110	285 mi.	7,500	1,220	1,800	N/A	none
Fairey Battle I	10/03/1936	1,030-hp Merlin III	241/13,000	1,050 mi.	23,500	6,647	10,792	422	1,000 2 × mg (1 fixed)
Fokker C V	05/1924	650-hp Rolls Royce Kestrel	155	500 mi.	21,330	4,233		423	440 3 × mg (two fixed)
Hawker Audax	1931	580-hp Kestrel IB	169/5,000	3.5 hrs	21,500	2,938	4,386	347	160 2 × mg
Hawker Hart	06/1928	580-hp Kestrel IB	184/5,000	500 mi.	20,600	2,780	4,592	347	500 2 × mg
Hawker Hector	1933	805-hp Napier Dagger IIIMS	187/6,500	2.4 hrs	24,000	3,389	4,910	346	224 2 × mg (1 fixed)
Hawker Henley	10/03/1937	955-hp Merlin I	292/17,100	600 mi.	27,000	6,434	9,400	342	500 2 × mg
Henschel HS 123	08/05/1935	870-hp BMW 132Dc	212/3,940	534 mi.	29,525	3,316	4,888	267	440 2 × mg (fixed)
Henschel HS 126	Autumn 1936	830-hp BMW Bramo Fafnir 323 A-1	221/9,840	360 mi.	27,000	4,480	7,209	340	330 2 × mg (one fixed)
Junkers Ju 87 B-2	Spring 1935	1,200-hp Jumo D	237/13,120	370 mi.	5,071	9,321	26,248	343	1,102 3 × mg (2 fixed)
Northrop Nomad	1933	750-hp Pratt & Whitney Twin Wasp	225	800 mi.	20,700	5,106	7,440	362	400 5 × mg fixed (4 fixed)
Taylorcraft Plus	1939	55-hp Lycoming	110	275 mi.	15,000	700	1,200	155	None

ARMY CO-OPERATION/GROUND ATTACK (*Continued*)

	Prototype First flight	Engine	Speed (mph) at altitude (ft)	Range (miles)/ Endurance (hours)	Ceiling (ft)	Empty Weight (lbs)	Loaded Weight (lbs)	Wing area (sq ft)	Bomb load (lbs) Armament
Tiger Moth	26/10/1931	130-hp de Havilland Gipsy Major	109/1,000	300 mi.	13,600	1,115	1,770	239	160 / 1 × mg
Vickers Virginia	1922	2 × 570-hp Lion V	108/4,920	985 mi.	15,530	9,650	17,600	2,178	1 × 37-mm COW cannon (proposed)
Westland Lysander	16/06/1936	890-hp Mercury XII	229/10,000	600 mi.	26,000	4,065	5,920	260	500 / 3 × mg

NAVAL PLANES

	Prototype First flight	Engine	Speed (mph) at altitude (ft)	Range (miles)/ Endurance (hours)	Ceiling (ft)	Empty Weight (lbs)	Loaded Weight (lbs)	Wing area (sq ft)	Bomb load (lbs) Armament
Avro Anson	24/03/1935	2 × 335-hp Cheetah IX	188/7,000	660 mi.	19,000	5,140	7,342	680	360 / 2 × mg
Blackburn Skua	09/02/1937	730-hp Perseus XII	224/6,500	610 mi.	19,100	5,859	8,228	319	500 / 5 × mg
Bristol Beaufort 1	28/12/1938	2 × 1,130-hp Taurus VI	265/6,000	1,035 mi.	26,000	13,107	21,228	503	1,600 / 4 × mg
Fairey Swordfish	17/04/1934	690-hp Pegasus IIIM	139/4,750	546 mi.	10,700	5,200	9,250	607	1,500 / 2 × mg
Short Sunderland	16/10/1937	4 × 1,010-hp Pegasus XXII	213/5,000	2,750 mi.	17,900	28,290	58,000	1,487	2,000 / 8 × mg

Appendix II:
Aircraft Deliveries 1938–40

Numbers in brackets are those planes in the total that were exported
Hampden and Hurricane figures include planes built in Canada
* Built as trainers
† Number of packs arriving

1938

FIGHTERS

	J	F	M	A	M	J	J	A	S	O	N	D
Gladiator	24(15)	6(6)	26(26)	2(2)	7(7)	0	6(6)	24(15)	15	4	0	14
Hurricane	4	9	9	1	17	11	15	21	23	26	36	23
Spitfire							3	2	2	13	13	13

BOMBERS

	J	F	M	A	M	J	J	A	S	O	N	D
Battle	23	20(3)	20 (7)	26(5)	32	25	36	25	42	40	54	37
Blenheim	21	22(4)	35 (4)	32(2)	39(4)	37(4)	42(5)	36	51	51	61(6)	49(3)
Hampden									7(1)	12	11	8
Henley										2	3	5
Hind	6	6	7	2	4	4(3)			20(20)	15(15)		
Wellesley	17	21	13	9	2							
Wellington										8	11	10
Whitley	10	9	10	7	7	3	0	2	11	6	8	20

ARMY/ NAVY CO-OPERATION PLANES

	J	F	M	A	M	J	J	A	S	O	N	D
Anson			2	2	9	12	22	19	22	19	25	37
Lysander					4	7	12	9	19	22 (9)	10(8)	7 (1)
Skua										1	2	11
Sunderland					3	3	3	2	3	3	2	1
Swordfish	17	14	20	15	17	8	14	10	15	10	4	0

1939

Fighters

	J	F	M	A	M	J	J	A	S	O	N	D
Gladiator	24	22	46	33	51	48	39	27 (12)	12 (6)	4	7 (6)	0
Hurricane	34 (7)	56	42 (11)	47 (13)	48 (3)	36	49 (13)	37 (5)	44 (20)	49 (4)	65 (7)	79
Spitfire	20	29	35	37	41	44 (1)	36	22	32	49	50	40
Defiant									5	4	4	3

BOMBERS

	J	F	M	A	M	J	J	A	S	O	N	D
Battle	56	78	82	91	99	92	94	100	116	85	100	44
Blenheim	59 (5)	74 (4)	107	81	101	74	108	81	112	100	102 (4)	80 (3)
Whitley	15	12	5	1	9	15	7	15	17	19	23	19
Wellington	18	17	23	19	20 (2)	24 (3)	19	14	25	33	29	32
Hampden/Hereford	21	25	27	21	28	35	17	22	32	41	41	32
Henley	5	13	17	16	17	17	18	18	21	14	8	7

ARMY AND NAVY CO-OPERATION PLANES

	J	F	M	A	M	J	J	A	S	O	N	D
Anson	28	50	58	48	59	57 (9)	70 (5)	41	78	65 (3)	73	64
Hudson			2	5	9	17	19	29	37	20	0	6
Beaufort										1 (1)	8	17
Sunderland	1	4	2	2	3	2	3	2	3	2	2	2
Lysander	18	19	22	21	24	27 (6)	34 (1)	26	36	33	32	33
Skua	8	14	25	16	23	20	20	14	14	13	5	3
Swordfish	0	19	22	18	20	20	20	19	20	23	15	3
Roc	0	1	3	2	2	7	6	10	13	15	12	9

1940

FIGHTERS

	J	F	M	A	M	J	J	A	S	O	N	D
Beaufighter				1		2	5	23	15	21	25	19
Buffalo							19 (21†)	0 (11†)	1 (1†)	11		
Defiant	5	5	12	19	22	30	56	38	41	48	53	37
Gladiator	7	4	2		3							
Hurricane	108	83	123	178	233	313	288)	275	253	251	236	244
Martlet								2 (6†)	3 (38†)	36 (6†)	14 (15†)	14 (6†)
Mohawk							5 (32†)	49 (37†)	10 (117†)	48 (18†)	29	43
Spitfire	37	51	40	60	77	103	160	163	156	149	139	117
Tomahawk								(1*)	1	0 (69†)	26 (50†)	43 (161†)
Whirlwind						2	3	1	3	1	8	5

BOMBERS

	J	F	M	A	M	J	J	A	S	O	N	D
Battle	70	62+14*	87+39*	13+74*	83*	82*	45*	53*	48*	23*	4*	1*
Blenheim	86	65	75	91	124	167	173	177	112	154	163	134
Boston I, II						0(16†)	8 (0†)	22 (44†)	49 (87†)	49 (7†)	6 (0†)	8 (12†)
Halifax										1	2	3
Hampden/Hereford	36	31	35	44	63	81	56	41	40	38	40	37
Henley	9*	4*	2*	2*				2*				
Manchester									2	3	11	6
Maryland						0 (26†)	2 (12†)	11 (10†)	10 (39†)	14	1	1
Nomad							23 (61†)	30	5			
Stirling					1	1	4	1	1	0	1	4
Wellington	38	17	35	56	80	108	141	134	84	97	102	105
Whitley	22	18	21	30	40	50	45	39	39	32	27	24

ARMY /NAVY CO-OPERATION PLANES

	J	F	M	A	M	J	J	A	S	O	N	D
Albacore	0	4	9	13	15	21	23	26	20	25	27	19
Anson	60	66	72	71	50	94						
Beaufort	23	25	30	35	50	62	33	36	21	14	15	15
Fulmar				1	6	12	20	25	20	27	29	19
Hudson	14	26	21	44	13	30	18	24	19	8	7	23
Lysander	26	43	35	29	46	56	78	66	58	51	77	54
Roc	11	8	7	11	7	7						
Skua	1											
Sunderland	1	3	0	2			1	3	1	3	2	2
Swordfish	2	1										1

Bibliography

Air of Authority (http://www.rafweb.org)

Alanbrooke, *War Diaries 1939–1945* (London: Orion, 2001)

Astier de la Vigerie, F., d', *Le Ciel n'etait pas Vide* (Paris: 1952)

Baumbach, W., *Broken Swastika* (London: Robert Hale, 1986)

Bekker, C., *The Luftwaffe War Diaries* (London: Macdonald, 1966)

Bingham, V., *Blitzed* (New Malden: Air Research, 1990)

Bond, B., *Chief of Staff Vol. 1* (London: Leo Cooper, 1972)

Bowen, E. G., *Radar Days* (Bristol: Adam Hilger, 1987)

Bowyer, M., *Aircraft of the Few* (Yeovil: Patrick Stephens, 1991); *No. 2 Group RAF* (London: Faber and Faber, 1974)

Boyle, A., *Trenchard* (London: Collins, 1962)

Brown, A., *Airmen in Exile* (Stroud: Sutton Publishing, 2000)

Buttler, T., *British Secret Projects, Fighters and Bombers 1935–1950* (Hinckley: Midland, 2004)

Calder, A. *The People's War* (London: Jonathan Cape, 1969)

Chapman, G., *Why France Collapsed* (London: Cassell, 1968)

Chisholm, R., *Cover of Darkness* (Morley: The Elmfield Press, 1975)

Churchill, W., *Their Finest Hour* (London: Reprint Society, 1952)

Clarke, R., *British Aircraft Armament Vol. 2* (Sparkford: Patrick Stephens, 1994)

Collier, B., *The Defence of the United Kingdom* (London: Imperial War Museum, 1995)

Cull, B., Lander, B., Weiss, H., *Twelve Days in May* (London: Grub Street, 1995)

Cuny, J., Danel, R., *L'Aviation de Chasse Francaise 1918–1940* (Paris: Lariviere, 1973); *L'Aviation Francaise de Bombardment et de Renseignement, 1918–1940* (Paris: Lariviere, 1978)

Derry, T., *The Campaign in Norway* (London: HMSO, 1952)

Divine, D., *The Broken Wing* (London: Hutchinson, 1966)

Douglas, W., and Wright, R., *Sholto Douglas* (London: Collins, 1966)

Ellis, L., *The War in France in Flanders* (London: HMSO, 1954)

Fleming, P., *Operation Sea Lion* (London: Pan, 1957)

Flint, P., *Dowding and Headquarters Fighter Command* (Shrewsbury: Airlife Publishing, 1996)

Foot, M., *Holland at War Against Hitler: Anglo-Dutch Relations, 1940–1945* (London: Frank Cass, 1990)

Franks, N., *Air Battle for Dunkirk* (London: Grub Street, 2006)

Furse, A., *Wilfred Freeman* (Staplehurst: Spellmount, 1999)

Galland, A., *The First and the Last* (London: Fontana, 1970)

Gibson, G., *Enemy Coast Ahead* (London: Pan, 1955)

Goulding, J., *Interceptor* (Shepperton: Ian Allan, 1986)

Green, W., *Warplanes of the Second World War Fighters Vol. 4* (London: MacDonald, 1966)

Guderian, H., *Panzer Leader* (Aylesbury: Futura, 1976)

Gunston, B., *Night Fighters* (Cambridge: Patrick Stephens, 1976)

Gunston, B., *Rolls Royce Aero Engines* (Frome: PSL, 1989)

Hanbury Brown, R. *Boffin* (Bristol: IOP, 1991)

Harris, A., *Bomber Offensive* (London: Greenhill, 1990)

Hooton, E., *Phoenix Triumphant* (London: Arms and Armour Press, 1994); *Eagle in Flames* (London: Arms and Armour Press, 1997)

Horne, A., *To Lose a Battle* (Harmondsworth: Penguin, 1982)

Irving, D., *The Rise and Fall of the Luftwaffe* (London: Futura, 1976)

Jackson, B., Bramall, D., *The Chiefs* (London: Brassey's, 1992)

James, T., *The Growth of Fighter Command 1936–1940* (London: Frank Cass, 2012)

Johnson, J., *Full Circle* (London: Pan, 1969)

Jones, R., *Most Secret War* (London: Coronet 1981)

Larson, R., *The British Army and the Theory of Armoured Warfare 1918–1940* (London: Associated University Presses, 1984)

Lasserre, J., *La Bataille de France Vol. 9: L'Aviation Neerlandaise; La Bataille de France Vol. 10: L'Aviation d'Assaut; La Bataille de France Vol. 8: L'Aeronautique Militaire Belge; La Bataille de France Vol. 3: Le Bombardment, La Reconnaissance*

Latham, L., and Stobbs, A., *Radar: A Wartime Miracle* (Stroud: Sutton Publishing, 1996)

MacBean, J., and Hogben, A., *Bombs Gone* (Wellingborough: PSL, 1990)

Mason, F. K., *Battle Over Britain* (London: McWhirter Twins, 1969)

McVickar Haight, J., *American Aid to France 1938–1940* (New York: Atheneum, 1970)

Mead, P., *The Eye in the Sky* (London: HMSO, 1983)

Meekcoms, K., and Morgan, E., *The British Aircraft Specifications File* (Tonbridge: Air Britain Publication, 1994)

Middlebrook, M., and Everitt, C., *The Bomber Command War Diaries* (London: Penguin, 1990)

Newton Dunn, B., *Big Wing* (Shrewsbury: Airlife Publishing, 1992)

Offenberg, J., *Lonely Warrior* (St Albans: Mayflower Publishing, 1974)

Omissi, D., *Air Power and Colonial Control: The Royal Air Force, 1919–1939* (Manchester: MUP, 1990)

Paquier, P., *Aviation de Bombardment Francaise* (Paris: Berger-Levrault, 1948)

Parham, H., Belfield, E., *Unarmed into Battle* (Chippenham: Picton Publishing, 1986)

Peden, G., *British Rearmament and the Treasury* (Edinburgh: Scottish Academic Press, 1979)

Postan, M., *British War Production* (London: HMSO 1952)

Price, A., *Blitz on London 1939–1945* (London: Ian Allan, 1976); *The Hardest Day* (London: Macdonald and Jane's, 1979); *The Spitfire Story* (London: Jane's, 1982); *World War II Fighter Conflict* (London: MacDonald and Jane's, 1975)

Probert, H., *High Commanders of The Royal Air Force* (London: HMSO, 1991)

Rawnsley, C., *Night Fighter* (London: Corgi, 1975)

Ray, J., *The Battle of Britain: New Perspectives* (London: Arms and Armour, 1994)

Richards, D., *Portal of Hungerford* (London: Heinemann, 1977); *The Fight at Odds Vol. I* (London: HMSO, 1974)

Richey, P., *Fighter Pilot* (London: Hutchinson, 1956)

Ritchie, S., *Industry and Air Power* (London: Frank Cass, 1997)

Schenck, P., *Invasion of England 1940* (London: Conway Maritime Press, 1990)

Sharp, M., and Bowyer, J., *Mosquito* (London: Faber and Faber, 1971)

Shirer, W., *The Collapse of the Third Republic* (London: Heinemann, 1970)

Shores C., *Fledgling Eagles* (London: Grub Street, 1991)

Simpson, W., *One of Our Pilots is Safe* (London: Hamish Hamilton, 1942)

Sinnot, C., *The Royal Air Force and Aircraft Design 1923–1939* (London: Frank Cass, 2001)

Slessor, J., *The Central Blue* (London: Cassell, 1956); *Air Power and Armies* (London: OUP 1936)

Speidel, W., *The German Air Force in France and the Low Countries* (unpublished)

Terraine, J., *The Right of the Line* (London: Sceptre, 1988)

Trevor-Roper, H., *Hitler's War Directives 1939–1945* (London: Pan, 1973)

Webster, C., and Frankland, N., *The Strategic Air Offensive Against Germany 1939–1945* Vols 1 and 4 (London: HMSO, 1961)

White, I., *The History of Air Intercept Radar and the British Nightfighter*, (Barnsley: Pen and Sword, 2007)

Whitford, R., *The Fundamentals of Fighter Design* (Marlborough: Crowood Press, 2004)

Wood, D., and Dempster, D., *The Narrow Margin* (London: Arrow, 1967)

Wright, R., *Dowding and the Battle of Britain* (London: Corgi, 1970)

Index